239 GREAT PLACES TO
ESCAPE TO NATURE
WITHOUT ROUGHING IT

FROM RUSTIC CABINS TO LUXURY RESORTS

EDITED BY CONSTANCE JONES

FODOR'S TRAVEL PUBLICATIONS New York Toronto London Sydney Auckland

Fodor's 239 Great Places to Escape to Nature Without Roughing It

Editor: Constance Jones

Editorial Production: Aviva Muse-Orlinoff

Editorial Contributors: Rosemary Allerston, Shelley Arenas, Michele Bardsley, Andrew Collins, Kristi Delovitch, Lisa Dunford, Amy Eckert, Joyce Eisenberg, Amy Pugsley Fraser, Jennifer Garrett, Tim Gihring, Hollis Gillespie, Tom Griffith, Marilyn Haddrill, Pat Hansen, Cynthia Hirschfeld, Sue Kernaghan, Cheryl Krett, Mary Sue Lawrence, Janet Lowe, Diane Mehta, Diana Lambdin Meyer, Carrie Miner, Cynthia Mines, Candy Moulton, Hilary Nangle, Jacinta O'Halloran, Debbie Olsen, Tom Reale, Susan Reigler, Sophia Schweitzer, Catherine Senecal, Amanda Theunissen, Lori Tobias, John Vlahides, Chelle Koster Walton, Julie & Paul Waters, Ana Watts, CiCi Williamson, Maggie Wunsch, Bobbi Zane, Jane Zarem

Design: Fabrizio La Rocca, *creative director*; Guido Caroti, *art director*; Melanie Marin, *senior picture editor*

Production/Manufacturing: Robert B. Shields

Cover Photos: Ken Redding/Corbis (top), Dunton Hot Springs (bottom)

Copyright

Second Edition

ISBN: 1–4000–1670–3

ISBN-13: 978–1–4000–1670–9

ISSN: 1559–078X

Special Sales

Contents

ESCAPE TO NATURE IN CANADA

DIRECTORIES

About This Book
Special Vacations with Nature

When you dream of vacation, do you dream of rest, relaxation, peace, and solitude in beautiful natural surroundings? If you are like a lot of 21st-century people, you crave a connection with nature and even a little outdoor adventure on your time off. You know just what it takes to shed the tensions of your workaday life and you find solace and renewal at the beach, in the mountains, by the lake, or in the desert. At the same time, you don't want to sacrifice hot showers or cold mineral water when you're on vacation. You don't want to struggle with packing bulky gear, fixing the RV's leaky toilet seal, or setting up a campsite. *Escape to Nature Without Roughing It* has good news for you: you don't have to give up your comforts to escape to nature.

Escape to Nature Without Roughing It presents 239 resorts, inns, lodges, and ranches where you can temporarily leave civilization behind . . . but not too far behind. Whether you are looking for soft adventure or sybaritic bliss, for a budget-friendly family resort or an extravagant romantic hideaway, for great hiking and fishing or the best in bird-watching and skiing, you'll find plenty to choose from here. You can read about getaways all over North America, from Arizona to Nova Scotia and from Alaska to Georgia. All the lodgings listed in these pages offer gorgeous natural settings and tranquility-oriented amenities.

Because everyone has a different vision of the perfect vacation spot, *Escape to Nature Without Roughing It* presents a wide range of options, from the most private housekeeping cabins to the most sophisticated resorts and from the most rugged mountain lodge to the laziest seaside inn. Some of these places nourish the soul with utmost simplicity: morning walks in the woods, afternoon naps on the porch, and evenings of reading by the fireplace, with nothing but the scents and sounds of the forest for company. Others cosset you with spa treatments, exquisite organic meals, and the freshest cotton bedding, all against a backdrop of manicured grounds and breathtaking coastal views.

Accommodations selected for inclusion in *Escape to Nature Without Roughing It* have been hand-picked according to four primary criteria: wilderness setting, serenity, seclusion, and environmental awareness. A fifth criterion applies to properties that serve food: they should offer delicious, healthful meals.

Wilderness setting: Nature is central to each property's identity, providing ample opportunity for outdoor activity, inspiration, and reflection.

Serenity: Each lodging offers the peace and quiet, the slow and unstructured pace, essential to physical and mental rejuvenation.

Seclusion: Located as they are in out-of-the-way—yet readily accessible—spots, the properties remove you far from the worries and obligations of your life. All are at least several miles from the nearest sizable towns, and all are on enough land to be buffered from neighbors and traffic.

Environmental awareness: As much as possible, the accommodations operate in harmony with the ecology around them and with a sensitivity to global environmental issues. Many strive to reduce their impact on nature through recycling, energy and water conservation, the use of eco-friendly products, and other efforts. The design and architecture of many of the properties complement the surrounding landscape and enhance your experience of the natural setting.

Meals: Many of the lodgings serve one or more meals a day, and most use fresh, local, and often organic and free-range produce. Vegetarian and other healthwise selections are ample and appealing at many properties.

GETAWAY CATEGORIES

To help you choose the nature vacation that's right for you, the listings have been divided into several categories. The category designations, which are indicated below each property's name, describe the type of experience you might have there. Some accommodations fall into more than one category because they appeal to a variety of people.

Family Hideout: These are full-service resorts and guest ranches that allow families to discover the pleasures of nature together. Kid-friendly activities such as nature walks, horseback riding, swimming, treasure hunts, gold-panning, and arts-and-crafts sessions are available. Organized children's programs are typically offered. You might stay in your own cabin or in the main lodge, where delicious, wholesome meals are served. These may not be the quietest places, but Mom and Dad can escape onto a forest trail or take a canoe excursion on their own. Indeed, the aroma of pine needles and wood smoke and the fun of spying on rabbits or lizards might make grown-ups think they're back in camp.

Laid-Back Adventure: If you're not keen on camping out but you enjoy a trail ride or fishing trip, you might want to stay at a property that operates extensive outdoor activity programs or works closely with local outfitters. You can spend your days mountain biking, kayaking, rock climbing, or cross-country skiing but come home to a refreshing bath and, often, a well-prepared meal. Your accommodations might be a log lodge or a modern lakefront hotel, where activity staff can recommend the best day hikes or river-rafting sites in the area.

Luxurious Resort: In this category are lavish lodgings with abundant amenities, such as sports and fitness facilities, spas, and one or more top-flight restaurants. Rooms are cushy, and you can feel pampered even though you are miles away from civilization in the desert or mountains. These are no ordinary high-end resorts, though: here you are inspired to get out of the gym and take a hike into the canyon, or to leave your poolside lounge chair to swim in the bracing waters of the bay. You won't run into too many fellow guests along the way, because these resorts do what it takes to ensure that your stay is peaceful and restorative.

Romantic Retreat: These adult-oriented accommodations include bed-and-breakfasts and country inns that do not accept younger children as guests. They are comfy and sometimes luxurious, and they might or might not have televisions or telephones in the rooms. Some have a restaurant, but if not, you'll still wake up to homemade granola or whole-grain waffles each morning and perhaps come home to herbal tea or local wine each afternoon. Explore the nearby nature preserve or take a snooze in the garden where the flowers for your room are grown. Town is a few miles away down the winding back road, but you might prefer to take the path to the beach and do some tide-pooling.

Rustic Escape: These lodgings offer simple comfort and wilderness surroundings but no swimming pools or jetted tubs or other similar extras. You can be thoroughly immersed in nature at these properties, which include humble inns with plain rooms and clusters of basic housekeeping cabins. You may be able to do your own cooking here, make your coffee the way you like it, and perhaps fire some farm-stand vegetables on the grill outside. Your cottage might or might not be cleaned during your stay, and you might have to drive some distance to the general store, but a crystalline creek or a wildflower meadow lies just beyond your doorstep.

Tranquil Outpost: Isolated establishments with plentiful amenities, many with a restaurant on site, fall into this category. Cozy inns, old-fashioned and out-of-the-way resorts, and national park lodges are among your choices. Here you can fuel up on a breakfast of fresh fruit and buckwheat flapjacks before heading out for a day of hiking or bird-watching. When you return you might browse in the library, soak in the hot tub, or take in an ecology talk, since your room might not have a phone or TV. But you won't even miss them: your focus is outdoors, where you can enjoy relative solitude amid scenic beauty. Children are permitted, but there might not be any special services for them.

WHAT'S IN A LISTING?

The USA and Canada chapters present states and provinces in alphabetical order. Within each state or province section, accommodations are listed in alphabetical order. Following the lodging name and getaway category designation, each listing contains all the information you need to decide if the property is a likely vacation spot.

Tip: Supplementing every hostelry's description is an insider's tip that will help you get the most out of your stay. Suggestions range from when *not* to come, to what to bring, to special things to do, to which room to choose.

Recreation: Here you'll find a roster of the recreational activities that you can pursue on or near the property, seasonally or year-round. Whether it's wildlife viewing or scuba diving, dogsledding or golf, if it's available there, you'll find it here.

Services: Look here for a summary of lodging- and recreation-oriented services available on-property, such as sports equipment rental, sauna, laundry service, and Internet access.

Classes and programs: The nature, outdoors, and self-improvement programs offered on-property, such as fly-fishing lessons, photo safaris, and children's programs, are detailed here.

SYMBOLS

A breakdown of the number of rooms, suites, cabins, chalets, and other accommodations.

This is an enumeration of meal plans available, restaurants and bars on the property, and guest cooking facilities.

Room amenities, such as fireplaces, VCRs, and jetted tubs.

A small ticket indicates the price of accommodations. Unless otherwise indicated, the price is per room, per night, double occupancy, not including service and tax.

Major credit cards accepted: AE = American Express; D = Discover; DC = Diners Club; MC = MasterCard; V = Visa.

Mailing address.

Phone number.

Fax number.

Web address.

If applicable, dates the property is closed.

DIRECTORIES

At the back of the book is an excellent planning tool: three directories that can help you find exactly the kind of nature getaway you're looking for.

Type of Escape: A breakdown of lodgings by Getaway Category.
Activities Available: A breakdown of properties by major recreational options offered. For reasons of space, the list includes only selected activities. Widely available activities (such as hiking) are not included.
Alphabetical List: A list of all 250 properties, in alphabetical order.

BE A FODOR'S CORRESPONDENT

Your opinion matters. It matters to us. It matters to your fellow Fodor's travelers, too. And we'd like to hear it. In fact, we *need* to hear it.

When you share your experiences and opinions, you become an active member of the Fodor's community. That means we'll not only use your feedback to make our books better, but we'll publish your names and comments whenever possible.

Here's how you can help improve Fodor's for all of us.

Tell us when we're right. We rely on local writers to give you an insider's perspective. But our writers and staff editors—who are the best in the business—depend on you. Your positive feedback is a vote to renew our recommendations for the next edition.

Tell us when we're wrong. We're proud that we update most of our guides every year. But we're not perfect. Things change. Hotels cut services. Museums change hours. Charming cafés lose their charm. If our writer didn't quite capture the essence of a place, tell us how you'd do it differently. If any of our descriptions are inaccurate or inadequate, we'll incorporate your changes in the next edition and will correct factual errors at fodors.com *immediately*.

Tell us what to include. You probably have had fantastic travel experiences that aren't yet in Fodor's. Why not share them with a community of like-minded travelers? Maybe you chanced upon a beach or bistro or B&B that you don't want to keep to yourself. Tell us why we should include it. And share your discoveries and experiences with everyone directly at fodors.com. Your input may lead us to add a new listing or highlight a place we cover with a "Highly Recommended" star or with our highest rating, "Fodor's Choice."

Give us your opinion instantly at our feedback center at www.fodors.com/feedback. You may also e-mail editors@fodors.com with the subject line "Escape to Nature Editor." Or send your nominations, comments, and complaints by mail to Escape to Nature Editor, Fodor's, 1745 Broadway, New York, NY 10019.

You and travelers like you are the heart of the Fodor's community. Make our community richer by sharing your experiences. Be a Fodor's correspondent.

Happy traveling!

Tim Jarrell, Publisher

Escape to Nature in the United States

Alabama

JOE WHEELER STATE PARK RESORT
Family Hideout

On a wide stretch of the Tennessee River, one hour from Huntsville and two from Birmingham and Nashville, these 2,550 wooded acres make up one of several wonderful state-park resorts in Alabama. But Joe Wheeler differs from many of its siblings, which tend to suffer from tightly spaced recreational facilities and intense summer crowds. Most facilities here, including the 75-room lodge and restaurant and the golf course, occupy a bluff overlooking a tributary of the Tennessee River, known as First Creek. On the south side of the river lies a more secluded patch of parkland, a peaceful and pine-shaded nature retreat with about two dozen brick or wood-frame cabins. The north and south shores of Wheeler Park are connected by Wheeler Dam, which divides two very broad swaths of the Tennessee River, known as Wilson Lake on the western side and Wheeler Lake on the east.

Made of wood with expansive glass windows, the lodge fits in with its environment. Inside, rooms look like those in a mid-price chain hotel; some have kitchenettes. Attached is a restaurant with a high-pitched timber ceiling and huge windows that give you unimpeded river and pine-forest views. Behind the lodge is a marina that rents pontoon boats, pedal boats, and motorized fishing boats. This is a family-oriented place, and the area around the pool can get a little noisy with the sounds of kids playing, family sing-alongs, and playful socializing.

Nonetheless, you're never far from quiet nature trails that skirt the river and creeks, where it's not uncommon to spot bald eagles in winter and deer and migrating waterfowl throughout the year. The golf course is one of the top courses in northern Alabama—with nicely kept greens and fairways seeded with Bermuda grass (an especially lush type of grass, used at better courses). Rolling but not steep, the course has tight fairways lined mostly with towering evergreens.

To reach the south-side cabins from the main lodge area, you have to drive out of and back into the park, a total distance of about 12 mi. The cabins are surrounded by hardwoods, conifers, and shrubs, and from most windows you see nothing but greenery and the river. Inside, they have dark-pine paneling and functional but graceful wooden furniture and cabinets, but no TVs or phones. The brick cabins have fireplaces, and all have easy access to a multi-use trail along the waterfront, popular among mountain bikers, hikers, and joggers.

Tip *Joe Wheeler makes a great destination for groups. The largest cabins sleep up to eight, and the park has several group picnic pavilions.*

72 rooms, 3 suites, 26 cabins ¡©¡ Restaurant, grocery store, grills, picnic area, some kitchens, some kitchenettes, refrigerators. **Recreation:** biking, bird-watching, fishing, hiking, mountain biking, running, wildlife viewing, beach, pool, river swimming, tubing, water-skiing, windsurfing, boating, canoeing, kayaking, rowing, sailing, driving range, 18-hole golf course, putting green, 9 tennis courts, basketball, horseshoes, playground. **Services:** boat and golf rentals, boat launch, marina, golf pro shop, laundry facilities, Internet access, meeting rooms. **Classes and programs:** bass fishing competitions. ♿ Some in-room data ports, some in-room fireplaces, some jetted tubs, private balconies or decks, some pets allowed, no-smoking rooms; no phones in some rooms, no TV in some rooms ⚏ $65–$145 ⊟ AE, D, MC, V.

🏠 *4401 McLean Dr., Rogersville, AL 35652* ☎ *256/247–5461 or 800/ 544–5639* 📠 *256/247–1449* ⊕ *www.joewheelerstatepark.com.*

MOUNTAIN LAUREL INN
Tranquil Outpost

In the DeKalb Highlands, an hour from Chattanooga and two hours from Birmingham and Atlanta, high elevation and dense woodlands generally keep temperatures 5°F to 15°F cooler than in the rest of the region. Here, Lookout Mountain extends along an unbroken ridge for 82 mi southwest from Chattanooga. On the mountain in the sleepy small town of Mentone, the Mountain Laurel Inn perches on a bluff high above the Little River.

Mountain laurel fills the grounds, accented by extensive stands of rhododendron, dogwood and redbud trees, and wild azalea. Along some of the trails leading through the property you can pick wild raspberries and blackberries. Innkeeper Sarah Wilcox is a font of knowledge about the area's flora and fauna. Inside her home, you check in and dine family-style on a complimentary full breakfast—perhaps huevos rancheros or French toast (coffee is delivered to your room by 7 AM). You can also stop in to pick up a board game, borrow a book, or enjoy a fresh oatmeal cookie.

Your room is about 200 feet away, in a modest but pretty guesthouse. On the ground floor there are two guest rooms in front and two in back, each with direct access to a broad veranda with rockers. The rooms in back look entirely out at the woods, while the front rooms face both woods and the dirt lane leading back to the main house. All have private entrances. The Wildflower Room has white wicker furniture; the endearing Bridal Room has pink floral-and-twig-print fabrics. Double beds are standard in all the rooms, but you can add a cot for an additional $10–$15 per night. On the upper floor of the guesthouse, there's a loft with two rooms, one containing a king bed, the other a trundle bed and a kitchenette; pitched roofs and skylights make it even cozier. Relax or mingle with other guests in a small gathering room that has a TV (no cable) and VCR as well as a deck overlooking the woods. There's a microwave and a common refrigerator stocked with fruit drinks and water, and you can also borrow one of the portable CD players to take back to your room.

The tiny town of Mentone (population 500) is a gateway for DeSoto State Park, a stunning preserve with miles of hiking and boardwalk trails, picnic groves, and swimming areas. In the park you can take a guided hike along the Little River. From the inn, you can easily stroll the ¼ mi to the park's DeSoto Falls or hike along the ledge high above the Little River. Next door to the inn, the Shady Grove Dude Ranch runs horseback-riding tours through the park to DeSoto Falls. Cloudmont Ski Resort, the southernmost ski resort in the East, is just a 10-minute drive from the inn.

Tip *DeSoto State Park has programs on rare animals and plants, parasites that thrive in the park, DeSoto's role in the Cherokee Trail of Tears, the geological history of the river and Lookout Mountain, and Native American tools and weapons.*

🛏 4 rooms, 1 loft 🍽 Full breakfast, grills, some kitchenettes. **Recreation:** bird-watching, hiking, rock climbing, running, wildlife viewing. Nearby: horseback riding, river swimming, cross-country skiing, downhill skiing, board games, library, videocassette library. **Services:** meeting room. ♿ In-room VCRs; no room phones, no smoking 💳$92–$160 (2-night minimum on May, Oct., and Nov. weekends) 🗖 D, MC, V.

🏠 *Box 443, Mentone, AL 35984* ☎ *256/634–4673 or 800/889–4244* 🌐 *www.mountain-laurel-inn.com.*

Alaska

CHENA HOT SPRINGS RESORT
Family Hideout ~ Laid-Back Adventure

Rare among Alaska resort properties, Chena Hot Springs Resort is road accessible, stays open all year, and considers winter its peak season. It's only 60 mi northeast of Fairbanks, but the resort's 440 acres of boreal forest lie deep in the state's interior. Discovered in the early 1900s, the mineral-rich waters of the hot springs soothed the aches and pains of gold prospectors. The site soon sprouted cabins, stables, and a bathhouse, and it has been in constant use ever since. Today you can stay in a Mongolian-style yurt or a log trapper's cabin or, for a more indulgent stay, you can book a room in the Moose Lodge. It's a contemporary hotel complete with an excellent restaurant, a bar, a friendly multi-national staff, and all the modern amenities.

If you've always wanted to visit Alaska in the winter but hesitated because of the extreme climate, this is the place for you. The resort even rents out warm winter clothing. Viewing the aurora borealis is one of the signature attractions of the resort between mid-August and April. From the hilltop "aurorarium," a glassed-in and heated cabin, you can view this phenomenon of nature for as long as you can stay awake. Curtains of shimmering light, in shades of blue, green, and red, paint the sky and dazzle even the most jaded observers. Other winter pastimes include cross-country skiing, snowmobile rides (if you don't want to be labeled a *cheechako,* or newcomer, call them snow machines), sleigh rides behind a pair of draft horses, and dog-mushing rides and lessons. Mushing dogs is Alaska's official state sport, and there are few adventures more exhilarating than speeding through the woods behind a team of trained Alaskan huskies.

From May to mid-August, the long hours of daylight more than compensate for the absence of snow sports and the aurora borealis. Hike the trails through the woods and over the hills (with a guide or by yourself), go fishing or canoeing, or sign up for a flightseeing trip by small plane. Summer and winter, all of the facilities and activities here are kid-friendly. There are even mini-snowmobiles for youngsters—who ride under supervision of adult guides, of course.

And what about those hot springs? Year-round, you can choose from several locations for soaking your weary bones. There's an indoor pool, a rock-lined outdoor mineral hot-springs pool, an outdoor hot tub, and two indoor whirlpool tubs. The hot springs are also the foundation of the resort's clean energy efforts. All of the buildings are heated by the hot-spring water; a new geothermal well is expected to provide all of the necessary electricity; and experiments with solar, wind, and hydro power are also under way.

Tip *For a no-holds-barred north country night, book a stay in the ice museum, a Gothic-style structure complete with gargoyles and a turret. Its six guest rooms have ice beds topped with reindeer hides; ice chandeliers and an ice pipe organ are only some of its other attractions. The museum is open year-round. If you're not up to sleeping in frozen splendor, just have a drink at the ice bar.*

🔄 70 rooms, 8 suites, 8 cabins, 1 yurt ❖ Café, restaurant, bar, grills, picnic area. **Recreation:** biking, bird-watching, fishing, hiking, horseback riding, mountain biking, running, wildlife viewing, 2 pools, indoor pool, canoeing, rafting (nearby), cross-country skiing, dogsledding, ice-skating, sleigh rides, snowmobiling, snowshoeing, volleyball, library. **Services:** cross-country ski, fishing, mountain-bike, and winter clothing rentals; hot tub; massage; mineral springs; airstrip; laundry facilities; airport shuttle. **Classes and programs:** guided hikes, guided nature walks, flightseeing tours. ♿ Satellite TV, some private balconies and decks, some pets allowed; no a/c in some rooms, no smoking 💳 $65–$200 ▭ AE, D, DC, MC, V.

📍 *Mile Marker 56.6, Chena Hot Springs Rd. (Box 58740), Fairbanks, AK 99711* ☎ *907/451–8104 or 800/478–4681* 🖷 *907/451–8151* 🌐 *www. chenahotsprings.com.*

DENALI BACKCOUNTRY LODGE
Romantic Retreat ~ Tranquil Outpost

Denali National Park is the most heavily visited national park in Alaska, but there's a big difference between merely visiting the park and getting to know it. To protect Denali's animal residents from tourist traffic, access to the single, 95-mi-long road into the park is restricted. Private vehicles are banned from most of the road, and visitors are largely confined to shuttle buses and vehicles operated by a few concessionaires. There's only so much wilderness you can see this way. Most of the best wildlife habitat is well beyond the busy entrance to the park, and from the road it is rare to catch a good view of Mt. McKinley, which most Alaskans refer to as Denali (the Athabascan word meaning "the high one").

At the end of the park road, however, is the community of Kantishna. Here, a four- to five-hour drive from Anchorage or a two-hour drive from Fairbanks, stands Denali Backcountry Lodge, a blip of civilization in the midst of backcountry. The ride into Kantishna takes you through spruce forests near the park entrance, then across open tundra after you emerge above the tree line. As you roll through the hills you see mountain ranges in all directions. At closer range you may spot such wildlife as caribou, moose, Dall sheep, grizzly bears, foxes, wolves, lynx, black bears, and numerous bird species. The trip to the lodge is one of the best opportunities for wildlife sightings anywhere in the state.

At the lodge, on the bank of Moose Creek, your cedar cabin has running water, private bath, and heat—all rarities in such a remote location. Activities are coordinated from the main lodge, where you also take your meals. Breakfast is served buffet-style, and lunch is either soup and sandwiches in the lodge or a boxed meal packed for eating out in the wilderness. Dinners of hearty and fresh American entrées are served family-style. Hang out with friends in the two gazebos on the grounds or over a drink in the lounge.

Based at the lodge, you can see Denali as few do. It is estimated that less than a third of park visitors actually get to see Mt. McKinley. The mountain is often shrouded in clouds for much of the day, but staying in the heart of the park, you will be around in early morning and late evening, when the peak usually sheds its cloudy layers. The rest of the day is filled with fishing, mountain biking, gold panning, and flightseeing. A suspension bridge across Moose Creek gives access to trails where the lodge staff leads hikes of varying skill levels every day. Well versed in Denali's natural history, flora, and fauna, your guides will introduce you to Alaska's wilderness.

Tip *Bring plenty of film and a good pair of binoculars for each member of your party: a family of grizzlies may just show up 100 yards away.*

38 cabins American plan, dining room, lounge. **Recreation:** birdwatching, fishing, hiking, mountain biking, running, wildlife viewing, library. **Services:** mountain bikes provided, airstrip. **Classes and programs:** guided hikes, guided nature walks, natural history programs, Alaska natural history talks. No a/c, no room phones, no room TVs, no kids under 4, no smoking $340 MC, V.

410 Denali St., Suite C, Anchorage, AK 99501 907/644–9980 or 800/841–0692 907/644–9981 www.denalilodge.com Closed mid-Sept.–mid-May.

KACHEMAK BAY WILDERNESS LODGE
Laid-Back Adventure

It's hard to imagine a more placid location than the shores of China Poot Bay, an isolated inlet off south-central Alaska's Kachemak Bay. The inlet is a rich estuarine environment, ringed by spruce forests that climb the flanks of the Kenai Mountains. Visible between the mountain peaks are glaciers flowing downhill, destined to melt into white-water streams on their way to the sea. Kachemak Bay is considered one of the finest halibut fisheries in the world and is also home to all five species of Pacific salmon as well as an abundance of shellfish and crabs.

For more than 30 years, Michael and Diane McBride have been welcoming nature lovers to the bay and working to preserve this amazing ecological resource. They are also dedicated to the history of their land. When the resort was being developed, numerous Eskimo artifacts turned up on the property. Some of these—from relatively recent metal tools to ancient seal-oil lamps and from stone tools to weapons—now decorate the lodge and cabins. A staff archaeologist is on hand to explain these items and to put the history of the place and its previous inhabitants into perspective.

Arranged around a small cove off China Poot Bay, the main lodge, guest cabins, and outbuildings of Kachemak Bay Wilderness Lodge are carefully positioned for sweeping views and maximum privacy. The cabins are furnished in an old-fashioned style, with nostalgic chairs and bedspreads. Local artwork and antiques adorn the immaculate rooms. Each cabin is a little different from the next. Stroll footpaths through the woods, always within sight of the water, to reach the lodge for meals. The food you'll eat is either grown on-site, harvested from Kachemak Bay, or purchased locally. Accommodating vegetarian and other special diets is no problem for the kitchen staff.

No more than 12 guests are registered at Kachemak Bay at any time. Stays at the resort are structured on a five-day, four-night, Monday-through-Friday schedule. On Monday morning you are transported to the lodge, checked in, and introduced to the staff and your fellow guests at a meeting in the solarium. Once you are familiarized with the activities and facilities, your week begins. You can scale nearby mountain peaks or fish for fresh- or saltwater fish. Go beachcombing or kick back and watch the tide flow in and out. You won't be on your own when exploring the area, unless you really want to be. Staff can lead you on hiking or tidal-pool trips, show you where to catch the best fish, and help you to understand the flora and fauna you'll see.

Tip *Transportation to Kachemak Bay from Homer—a boat trip of 20 to 30 minutes—is provided. Homer is a five-hour drive or a 50-minute flight from Anchorage. If you want to extend your stay past Friday, the McBrides will fly you to an isolated lakeside lodge that accommodates two to four.*

 5 cabins American plan, dining room. **Recreation:** bird-watching, fishing, hiking, wildlife viewing, boating, sea kayaking, library, videocassette library. **Services:** boats and sea kayaks provided, outdoor hot tub, sauna, dock, guided fishing trips, Internet access. **Classes and programs:** guided hikes, guided nature walks, natural history pro-

grams. ♿ No a/c, no room phones, no room TVs, no smoking 🍽 $2,800 per week ▱ No credit cards.

📫 *Box 956, Homer, AK 99603* ☎ *907/235–8910* 🖷 *907/235–8911* ⊕ *www.alaskawildernesslodge.com* ☾ *Closed late Sept.–mid-May.*

ULTIMA THULE LODGE
Laid-Back Adventure

If your idea of a vacation involves mountains, rivers, forests, glaciers, and a hideaway where you and a few other guests are separated from the world by thousands of square miles of wilderness, then Ultima Thule Lodge might be the place for you. The lodge is in the heart of the 13-million-acre Wrangell–St. Elias National Park, the largest national park in the country. John Claus had the foresight and good fortune to establish a small homestead in the area in the late 1960s, long before the park was even a gleam in the government's eye. When the park was established it surrounded the property, but Claus's inholding status was guaranteed. Now, noisy neighbors will never be a problem.

John's son Paul (who claims close familial ties with Santa) operates the lodge with his wife, Donna. Paul flies you in to the property, and the flight alone could be one of the highlights of your adventuring life. If the weather gods smile on you, the flight will reveal a stunning up-close view of the jagged peaks and knife-edge ridges of the Twaharpies Mountains and the huge, icy sweeps of Twaharpies Glacier. Paul, who has been flying these mountains for all of his adult (and much of his juvenile) life, knows how to show off the dramatic terrain. Mountain flying is a very specialized form of the bush pilot's art, and there are few more adept than Paul Claus. He has spent thousands of hours in cockpits perfecting his craft. Paul and his pilots fly a small fleet of assorted aircraft that'll get you into, and back out of, any terrain.

After your flight, you'll begin to understand that remote doesn't begin to describe the setting of the lodge. On the bank of the Chitina River, way out in the middle of nowhere, this place offers you an impressive array of opportunities for serious, Alaska-style adventure, year-round. Care to land on a glacier and make a first ascent of an untrammeled peak? No problem. How about a white-water rafting trip down the Chitina? Easily accomplished. Or you can go skiing, snowboarding, ice climbing, rock climbing, beachcombing, dog mushing, wildlife viewing, fishing—the list goes on and on. All of your trips are fully guided, no experience is required, and everything is included in your room rate.

The wood-fired sauna, shared by all the cabins, will likely be a welcome sight at the end of the day. The log cabins vary in size and style, but all are modern and are decorated with Alaskan artwork and artifacts. Much of the interior woodwork and furniture is made from trees felled and processed on the property. In the main lodge, meals are served family-style and often include local fish and game dishes, supplemented by herbs and vegetables grown on-site. Three generations of the Claus family are on hand to make sure that your stay is enjoyable and that your adventures are safe and memorable.

Tip *Air transport is provided from the Valdez or Cordova airport, or from the airstrip in Chitina if you choose to drive there.*

🛏 5 cabins ⏐◎⏐ American plan, dining room. **Recreation:** bird-watching, fishing, hiking, rock climbing, wildlife viewing, kayaking, rafting, cross-country skiing, dogsledding, downhill skiing, ice climbing, snowshoeing, telemark skiing, board games, library, piano, videocassette library. **Services:** sports equipment provided, sauna, airstrip, guided fishing trips, babysitting, laundry facilities, laundry service, Internet access, travel services. **Classes and programs:** guided hikes, guided nature walks, natural history programs. ♿ Private decks; no a/c, no room phones, no room TVs, no smoking 🛏 $990 (4-day minimum) ⊟ No credit cards.

🖅 *Box 109, Chitina, AK 99566* ☎ *907/688–1200 or 206/529–4241* 📠 *206/688–8805* ⊕ *www.ultimathulelodge.com.*

Arizona

ACROSS THE CREEK AT ARAVAIPA FARMS
Tranquil Outpost

As you travel the 100 mi southeast from Phoenix and venture down the dirt road that takes you deep into the Aravaipa Canyon Wilderness, crossing Aravaipa Creek and then winding back over it again, you realize that you are truly leaving behind the trappings of civilization. Only 40 families hold homesteads in the protected 19,410-acre wilderness area in southeastern Arizona, and only 50 people per day receive permits to hike in the preserve. The Aravaipa Canyon Wilderness contains habitat ranging from desert grasslands to the deciduous riparian forest. Seven species of native fish live in Aravaipa Creek. White-tailed and mule deer, javelina, coyotes, and mountain lions prowl through the forest. Troops of coatimundi wander the canyon bottom, and desert bighorn sheep clamber up cliffs. More than 150 documented bird species, including the bald eagle, cactus ferruginous pygmy-owl, and southwestern willow flycatcher, swoop through the skies.

At 300-acre Aravaipa Farms, innkeeper Carol Steele will show you to your private casita. Steele's joie de vivre shines through in the details: The patios combine southwestern styling with creative kitsch in a profusion of geranium-filled terra-cotta pots, brightly painted doors, hammock swings, Mexican ceramics, and chairs made from tree trimmings from the orchard. Inside, little nooks overflow with vibrant folk art, hand-painted tile from Carol's studio, Mexican rugs, and oversize beds.

The grounds, much like the casitas, are a study in color. In spring the farm's blossoming peach, pear, and apricot trees contrast with delicate wildflowers and the tangled willow-sycamore-cottonwood forest. In fall the trees burst in a riot of red, yellow, and orange foliage against black limbs and rough canyon walls. Hiking, bird-watching, and wildlife viewing reign supreme in this Sonoran Desert canyon. Nine major side canyons, plus caves and outcrops, invite exploration. About 1½ mi south of the east trailhead is a cliff dwelling that was inhabited by Salado Indians until they mysteriously disappeared from the region in 1450. Another unusual treat is Aravaipa Creek, which unlike many desert streams flows year-round. You'll be getting your feet wet if you hike the creek bed.

Steele calls Aravaipa Farms a reverse bed-and-breakfast. You serve yourself breakfast from your refrigerator, stocked with homemade granola, orchard fruit, imported cheeses, fresh baked breads, and homemade jams and jellies. A picnic-style lunch includes fresh sandwiches, homemade chocolate-chip cookies, fresh orchard fruit, assorted cheeses, trail mix, and fresh garden vegetables. Between 6 and 7 PM, Steele serves a creative dinner. Decadent delights such as green salad, Moroccan chicken, and fresh green beans are followed by dessert, which might be an apple-berry crumble. Outdoor adventure never tasted so good.

Tip *Spaces on the Aravaipa Canyon Wilderness hiking roster fill up fast, so make your reservation well in advance. Phone the Safford Field Office of the Bureau of Land Management at 928/348–4400. The fee is $5 per person daily. Mountain bikes and dogs are not allowed in the wilderness area, but a limited number of horses are permitted.*

🛏 5 casitas 🍽 American plan, dining room, refrigerators. **Recreation:** bird-watching, hiking, wildlife viewing, library. **Classes and programs:** cooking classes. ♿ In-room fireplaces, private patios; no room phones, no room TVs, no smoking 💲$325 ▭ No credit cards.

🏠 *89395 E. Aravaipa Rd., Winkelman, AZ 85292* ☎ *520/357–6901* ⊕ *www.aravaipafarms.com.*

THE ARIZONA SLED DOG INN
Laid-Back Adventure

You might not expect to find sled dogs in north-central Arizona, but these energetic bundles of fur not only survive in Arizona's high country, they thrive. Innkeepers Jaime Ballesteros and Wendy White met their first husky in 1989, when they went out looking for a black Labrador and instead came home with a frisky Siberian named Rutger. They now have an entire kennel of sled dogs. If you are lucky enough to be staying at this inn near Flagstaff when Mother Nature lays down a thick coat of fresh snow, ask to tag along and watch the dogs work out with the sled. You might even get a ride.

Backed up against the largest contiguous ponderosa pine forest in the world, the Sled Dog Inn caters to active explorers. Elks often amble across the property and have been known to walk right up to the porch to nibble on the shrubbery. Guest rooms decorated in mountain and wildlife themes are basic but roomy, with private bath. Two capacious living rooms—one upstairs and one downstairs—provide all of the amenities of home: couches, soft rugs, and tables filled with magazines and board games.

A few miles north of the inn lie the San Francisco Peaks, part of the active San Francisco Volcanic Field around the mountain town of Flagstaff. A multitude of trails lead through the mountains and up 12,633-foot Humphreys Peak, the tallest mountain in Arizona. You can get an up-close look at a bizarre landscape of volcanic squeeze-ups and hornitos on the trails through nearby Sunset Crater Volcano National Monument. Less taxing trails start at the Sled Dog Inn, and some of the lesser-known trails in the area lead to prehistoric ruins and petroglyphs. Jaime and Wendy will point you in the right direction and will also provide information on mountain-biking and rock-climbing sites.

It's not all forest and woodland in the rolling high country—lakes and prairies punctuate the landscape, and opportunities for water sports and wildlife-watching abound. You might come across mule deer, black bears, coyotes, and smaller animals. In winter, downhill skiers from all over the state converge on the Arizona Snowbowl. With 2,300 feet of vertical drop, the Snowbowl has 32 trails suitable for skiers of all levels. The Flagstaff Nordic Center maintains more than 25 mi of groomed cross-country ski trails, or you can take to the forest on your own.

After a full day of action, head back to the inn to soak away some stiffness in the hot tub under the stars. Don't worry about setting an alarm clock—the dawn chorus of the dogs will get you up and moving in the morning. The haunting howls of their Siberian serenade promise another beautiful day in Arizona's ponderosa paradise.

🛏 8 rooms, 2 suites ⍾ Full breakfast, dining room. **Recreation:** bird-watching, hiking, mountain biking, wildlife viewing, sledding, snowmobiling, snowshoeing, tobogganing. Nearby: fishing, horseback riding, rock climbing, cross-country skiing, downhill skiing. **Services:** outdoor hot tub, sauna. ♿ No pets allowed; no room phones, no room TVs, no kids under 5, no smoking ⌨ $105–$225 ▭ AE, D, MC, V.

⌂ *10155 Mountainaire Rd., Flagstaff, AZ 86001* ☎ *928/525–6212 or 800/ 754–0664* 📠 *928/525–1855* ⊕ *www.sleddoginn.com.*

THE BOULDERS RESORT AND GOLDEN DOOR SPA
Luxurious Resort

Before designing the Boulders, architect Bob Bacon pitched a tent near the mammoth rock formations on the property. He camped out there for a few weeks, wandering the desert to discover its secrets. The result of his obsessive study is a resort that blends seamlessly into the Sonoran Desert foothills north of Phoenix. Pathways detour around existing trees and cacti, and casitas and villas reflect the shapes and hues of the 12-million-year-old granite monoliths nearby. Even the fairways are environmentally correct: nontoxic chemicals (including a jalapeño-pepper insect deterrent) keep the local grasses golf-friendly. Indigenous plants thrive, and native wildlife roams the grounds. Especially at dawn and dusk, you might see mule deer, javelina, coyotes, Gambel's quail, rock squirrels, jackrabbits, and Gila monsters. Art galleries, boutiques, and nightclubs are only a few minutes away, but the sounds and lights of the city do not reach these enchanted 1,300 acres.

In the main lodge, stunning examples of Native American weavings, carvings, pottery, and painting set a tone of relaxed southwestern elegance. The casitas are equally handsome, with hand-hewn wood-beamed ceilings, leather recliners, private patios or decks, beehive fireplaces, deep-set tubs, and Native American art. The Palo Verde, in the main lodge, is open for breakfast and lunch only and offers a casual southwestern-style setting and dishes such as duck and wild mushroom quesadilla. The Latilla delivers the finest in intimate dining paired with gorgeous views of the resort's namesake boulders. The cuisine stays true to the region with offerings such as rack of lamb. But if you choose to be good, you can order signature spa cuisine made with fresh, organic produce. The Golden Door Spa Café promotes a balanced diet and lifestyle with a chef-dietician who prepares unique breakfast, lunch, and early dinner dishes.

The resort's Golden Door Spa is modeled after the original Golden Door in Escondido, California, but the spa here combines a Zen-like approach inspired by Japan's ancient Honjin inns with Native American–influenced spa treatments. Wraps of turquoise, adobe clay, or aloe; raindrop therapy; and native grain exfoliation are among your choices, or you can take sports and fitness classes ranging from tai chi to yoga. Outdoors, get even more active by mountain biking, hiking, and rock climbing. Using the granite boulders for practice, rock-climbing experts teach different types of climbs, climbing etiquette, belaying techniques, and knot tying. Other guides lead nature hikes by day. At dusk, take a walk to witness the subtle nuances of the Sonoran Desert. While the last gleam of sun strikes up a chorus of color in the boulders, admire a golden cascade of delicate palo verde blossoms and glimpse the flick of a chuckwalla's tail.

Tip *If you want to be pampered in the spa, reservations are recommended.*

160 casitas, 55 villas 7 restaurants, room service, bar, lobby lounge, some kitchens, minibars. **Recreation:** biking, bird-watching, hiking, mountain biking, rock climbing, running, wildlife viewing, 4 pools, driving range, two 18-hole golf courses, putting green, 8 tennis courts. Nearby: horseback riding, ballooning. **Services:** golf-gear, mountain-bike, and tennis-racket rentals; gym; outdoor hot tub; salon; spa; pro shop; dry-cleaning service; laundry service; business services, Internet access; concierge; travel services. **Classes and programs:** guided hikes, guided nature walks, rock-climbing lessons, fitness and yoga classes. Cable TV, in-room data ports, in-room fireplaces, in-room safes, in-room VCRs, private decks or patios $149–$1,350 AE, D, DC, MC, V.

📠 *34631 N. Tom Darlington Dr. (Box 2090), Carefree, AZ 85377* ☎ *480/ 488–9009* 🖨 *480/488–4118* ⊕ *www.wyndhamboulders.com.*

LAKE POWELL RESORTS & MARINAS
Family Hideout ~ Rustic Escape

The blue-green waters of Lake Powell and the red sandstone cliffs of Glen Canyon National Recreation Area meet along almost 2,000 mi of contorted shoreline. Backed up behind Glen Canyon Dam, the lake is actually a wide spot on the Colorado River and fills what was once Glen Canyon. It looks otherworldly and intense, with a riot of geology— swirling, cross-bedded rock and petrified sand-dune domes—almost pulsing with color beneath the most brilliant of blue desert skies. Fluctuating water levels and bare stone prevent plants from rooting along the shore, so there is no foliage to soften the austere line where lake and desert collide. The soft, easily eroded sandstone twists into inlets and coves off the lake. Sinuous and smooth, the walls of these watery canyons often narrow quickly to 60-foot-deep, shoulder-width slots. By spending a few days on a houseboat, you can find complete seclusion here. There is no better way to witness the many moods of the lake.

Sprawling across the northern border of Arizona, through the desert into Utah, the second-largest artificial lake in the country is a fantastic place to explore by boat. With a houseboat rented from Lake Powell Resorts & Marinas near the town of Page, you can be your own captain, setting your own course to explore. The lake is immense—185 mi from end to end—with branches reaching in all directions, so it is easy to leave behind the crowds that congregate here in warm weather. The farther you go toward the middle stretch of the lake, the less populated the waters. Summer is the busiest season for Lake Powell water sports, but the slightly cooler spring and fall months are better for hiking. Boat rentals are discounted from November through March, and even though it's too cold to swim, the lighter traffic makes the off-season a great time to visit.

Tow a powerboat, fishing boat, or kayak with you to explore the narrower sections of the many-fingered side canyons. Fish for largemouth and striped bass, crappie, and walleye, most abundant from March to November. A hike through the canyon lands surrounding the lake may take you past prehistoric cliff dwellings (inhabited by Ancestral Puebloan Basketmakers from 1050 to 1250) and petroglyphs left behind by nomadic Indians. In the Utah portion of the Navajo Indian Reservation, Rainbow Bridge is the world's largest natural bridge, a sandstone formation 275 feet long and 290 feet high. Steer your boat to Rainbow Bridge National Monument Marina, 50 mi up-lake from Wahweap, to visit this site, which is sacred to the Navajo.

Your houseboating excursion starts at Wahweap, the major marina at the south end of Lake Powell. Here you can choose from five classes of houseboats, all of which have a blue-green-mauve interior palette and equipment such as a CD/tape player, grill, ice chests, and kitchen with utensils and tableware. Your boat comes with biodegradable cleaning supplies, soap, shampoo, and paper products. The *Commander,* the smallest boat, sleeps six to eight. The largest of the houseboats, the *Admiral,* sleeps 10 to 12 and has extra creature comforts such as air-conditioning and a waterslide from the upper deck to the lake's cool aquamarine water. The *Admiral* is also the only houseboat that comes with linen; for others, you need to bring your own sheets and towels or rent them from the marina. All houseboats come equipped with a marine radio for use in case of emergency. You supply all your food and drink.

Before you set out to explore the lake, marina personnel will instruct you on the operation of the houseboat and will provide an orientation to the lake. Then off you chug, at a top speed of 12 mph. When you weigh anchor for the night, you're in for the treat of a lifetime: a sunset that ignites the crimson rocks of this surreal place in the desert.

Tip *Be sure to bring storage containers for leftovers, measuring cups, a first aid kit, paper towels, firewood, a fishing license and tackle, a shovel, a tent or canopy to set up for shade on the beach, kerosene lamps or flashlights, binoculars, and barbecue utensils. To hike around Rainbow Bridge, you must obtain a permit from the Navajo Nation Parks and Recreation Department (928/871–6647).*

🛥 Five boat classes: 36' *Commander,* 46' and 54' *Sport,* 52' *Captain,* 59' *Admiral* 🍽 Grills, kitchens. **Recreation:** fishing, hiking, wildlife viewing, beach, lake swimming, tubing (water), water-skiing, boating, jet skiing, kayaking. **Services:** water-ski, kneeboard, wakeboard, kayak, jet-ski, and water-toy rentals; boat launch; marina; tackle shop. ♿ In-room VCRs, some pets allowed (deposit required); no a/c in some rooms, no room phones 🛏 $520 for 2 days (*Commander*)–$6,262 for 7 days (*Admiral*) 🖃 AE, D, MC, V.

🏠 *100 Lakeshore Dr. (Box 56909) Phoenix, AZ 85079* ☎ *602/278–8888 or 800/528–6154* 🖷 *602/331–5258* 🌐 *www.lakepowell.com.*

RED SETTER INN & COTTAGES
Romantic Retreat

In 1540, when Spanish conquistador Francisco Vasquez de Coronado passed through the lushly forested White Mountains along the Mogollon Rim, he wrote about the "huge, trackless wilderness." Settlers arrived in the Greer Valley, at the eastern edge of the White Mountains near the Little Colorado River, in 1870, but 50 years later western writer Zane Grey proclaimed that this laid-back patch of east-central

Arizona was still "God's Country." Sitting pretty at 8,500 feet, the valley remains sparsely populated by humans—only 1,000 people live in the mountain hamlet of Greer—and wildlife continues to thrive. It's only natural that when you visit, you do as the locals do: just sit back and relax.

Route 373 leads directly to the Red Setter Inn & Cottages, then deadends in a lazy loop. Located 198 mi east of Flagstaff and 228 mi northeast of Phoenix, the inn sits on 10 acres of land that's hugged by the Apache-Sitgreaves National Forest. Thirty-four lakes and reservoirs and more than 680 mi of rivers and streams water the more than 2-million-acre preserve, making it one of Arizona's premier fishing destinations. Nearby Big Lake Recreation Area is stocked with 30,000 trout each fall and spring. The Little Colorado River rushes through the inn's property, so you can cast a line without leaving the grounds. You might net rainbow, German brown, brook, Apache, or cutthroat trout or arctic grayling.

Out of respect for the forest, innkeepers Jim Sankey and Ken Conant designed the inn to have as little environmental impact as possible. The Adirondack-style log building resembles a vintage hunting lodge constructed from hand-peeled logs, with dormer windows on the roof. The interior is pure West, with fireplaces warming the common rooms and plenty of chairs and couches for lounging. On the main floor, the living room is stocked with a wide selection of books; on the lower level, a game room is a laid-back place for watching videos. The bedrooms have eclectic furnishings, including everything from delicate antique tables to leather easy chairs. Three red-roofed cabins are also built of hand-peeled logs. The two smaller cottages, built for two, feature a king-size bed, a snug living room with a fireplace, a full kitchen, and a jetted tub for two. The larger cabin can accommodate eight with its four bedrooms, three bathrooms, three fireplaces, living room, and kitchen.

More than 400 species of wildlife live along this stretch of the Mogollon Rim, the escarpment that defines the southern edge of the Colorado Plateau. As you hike along one of the three trails leading from the inn grounds, you might see elks, antelope, deer, black bears, and mountain lion. You can hike up the East Baldy Trail or along the West or East Fork of the Little Colorado River. Birding is another favorite pastime here: bring your binoculars and your bird checklist and see how many feathered creatures you can identify. If you're lucky you'll spot a bald eagle or wild turkey.

On Friday be sure to reserve your spot at the inn's Saturday-night dinner ($25). The home-style cooking is designed to stick to your ribs: cream of mushroom soup; roasted beef sirloin with garlic mashed potatoes, glazed carrots, and spinach ricotta pie; and apple strudel with ice cream might be the menu. The meal is served in a large dining room furnished with antique tables and chairs, beneath an 18-foot ceiling. On any given evening, as the sun sets behind the White Mountains, you can relax on the porch or settle into the family room for a bit of quiet competition over one of the many board games. The inn is a perfect place to put your feet up after a long day of exploring roads less traveled.

Tip *For some of the best lunches and dinners in the area, take a 5-mi drive to Greer. Cattle Kate's (928/735–7744) serves dishes with a western flair, including western fried tomatoes, barbecued ribs, and the hearty City Slicker—fried shrimp and filet mignon. The spacious dining room celebrates the American cowgirl, including the restaurant's namesake, 19th-century cowgirl Ellen Liddy Watson, a.k.a. Cattle Kate.*

🛏 10 rooms, 1 suite, 1 penthouse, 3 cottages 🍽 Full breakfast, dining room, grills, some kitchens. **Recreation:** bird-watching, fishing, hiking, wildlife viewing, sledding, tobogganing, tubing (snow), library, recreation room, videocassette library. Nearby: horseback riding, mountain biking, cross-country skiing, downhill skiing, sleigh rides. ♿ Some cable TVs, some in-room fireplaces, some in-room VCRs, some jetted tubs, private balconies and decks; no kids under 16, no smoking 💳 $150–$600 ▭ AE, D, MC, V.

🗺 *8 Main St. (Box 133), Greer, AZ 85927* ☎ *928/735–7441 or 888/ 994–7337* 🖷 *928/735–7425* ⊕ *www.redsetterinn.com.*

SAN PEDRO RIVER INN
Rustic Escape

In southernmost Arizona, the San Pedro River meanders for miles, watering one of the last remaining stands of Fremont cottonwood–Goodding willow habitat in the Southwest. Almost all of the nation's desert riparian areas were destroyed in the 20th century by dam-building and water diversion, but the San Pedro has never been tamed.

Designated one of the "last great places" by The Nature Conservancy, the river is a linear oasis in the midst of a harsh desert. Although today the San Pedro is more stream than river, it nevertheless sustains a food-rich ecological highway for resident desert creatures and for birds migrating between the winter-friendly tropics and the summer-bountiful sprawl of North America. The San Pedro Riparian National Conservation Area (RNCA) protects a 35-mi stretch of the river and 58,000 surrounding acres that are a marvel for bird-watchers and other nature lovers. Watered by the river, the lush San Pedro Valley stretches out in grassy meadows. Long-limbed trees reach over the shallow river, and birds flit through the canopy in flashes of color and trilling birdsong.

About 70 mi from Tucson in Hereford, at the southern end of the San Pedro RNCA, the San Pedro River Inn is base camp for people interested in exploring the river. The inn was once a dairy farm that provided milk products to the miners in nearby Bisbee. Its adobe houses, each accommodating up to six, are scattered around the inn's 20 acres. Furnished very simply, the houses have outdoor grills and kitchens with dishes, pots and pans, silverware, staples, and cleaning supplies—there is no daily maid service. The cheery innkeepers, Donna Knox and Michael Marsden, encourage children to climb in the property's tree houses and to whirl about on tire swings hanging from towering cottonwoods. Two ponds soften the sharp edges of the desert, but best of all, you can watch and listen to the San Pedro River gurgling along.

Since most desert creatures depend on riparian areas for survival, it's no surprise that wildlife viewing is a favorite activity in the San Pedro RNCA. Bobcats, foxes, and white-tailed deer are drawn to the river. Biologists have recently reintroduced beavers, which were hunted out by the first white trappers to wander into the Southwest. Now the beavers have begun to restore the chain of ponds and marshes that once typified desert riparian areas. Most spectacular, though, is the San Pedro's avian population. Some 400 species of breeding, migrant, and wintering birds flutter through the multi-storied canopy above the river. The waterway lies along a major migratory corridor, so countless birds pass this way. You might see orioles, vermilion flycatchers, Gila woodpeckers, red-shafted flickers, kingbirds, kinglets, scrub jays, creepers, gnatcatchers, black hawks, hummingbirds, and a host of other species.

Tip *The San Pedro River and the surrounding area present a few hazards hikers should be wary of, including rattlesnakes, quicksand, and flash floods. For more information, call the Bureau of Land Management, Tucson Field Office (520/258–7200).*

4 houses Continental breakfast, dining room for special events, grills, picnic area, kitchens. **Recreation:** bird-watching, fishing, hiking, horseback riding, mountain biking, wildlife viewing, croquet, recreation room, playground. **Services:** horse boarding, laundry facilities, Internet access, meeting rooms, 5 RV hookups. **Classes and programs:** guided nature walks, birding tours. In-room VCRs, some pets allowed; no room phones, no smoking $95–$230 No credit cards.

8326 S. Hereford Rd., Hereford, AZ 85615 520/366–5532 or 877/ 366–5532 www.sanpedroriverinn.com.

SUNGLOW RANCH
Tranquil Outpost

Sunglow Ranch bundles solitude, history, and scenery into one restorative package. Surrounded by the 1,780,000 acres of Coronado National Forest, the ranch sits on 400 acres near Turkey Creek, 100 mi from Tucson. Here, on the west flank of the 150-mi-long, 9,700-foot-high Chiricahua Mountain range, you'll see grasslands spreading out between rocky hills dotted with oaks, mesquite, juniper, and pine. A small lake reflects the landscape, offering a place for quiet contemplation.

Each casita—the Butterfly Room, the Gecko Room, the Mountain Lion Room, etc.—is decorated in its own nature motif. Hardwood, concrete, and tile floors are scattered with colorful rugs. Hand-painted murals brighten up the rooms, and down comforters add to the homey atmosphere. In the main building the dining room is modeled after that in the original 1800s ranch house, which was torn down. The large hand-painted buffet, painted concrete floors, throw rugs, and high-backed wooded chairs painted hot pink, orange, and teal give the room vivid southwestern style.

The area around the ranch is one of the Sky Islands for which southern Arizona is famous. The dark, jagged terrain of lava, ash, and limestone surrounded by desert grasslands is a refuge for a profusion of plants and animals, many of which are found nowhere else in the United States. More than 360 identified avian species and animals such as deer, bears, and mountain lions thrive in Coronado National Forest. Blue heron and snowy egrets frequent the ranch's small lake. If you are especially lucky, you'll catch a glimpse of the elusive, exotic Elegant Trogan.

Penetrated by a handful of good dirt roads, a scattering of hair-raising jeep trails, and a wealth of scenic hiking trails, the Chiricahuas offer a wealth of recreational opportunities for those willing to wander off the beaten path. Not far from the ranch, hiking trails through Chiricahua National Monument lead through a geologically fascinating landscape of fused-ash spires, hoodoos, volcanic castles, balanced rocks, shaded streams, and deep canyons. Bicycle trails, which you can ride on the ranch's dual-suspension mountain bikes, wind through ranch property and the adjoining Coronado National Forest.

Before a day of mountain exploration, enjoy a hearty breakfast. Pack lunches are also available. A few steps away, back at your casita, you can spend the evening stargazing or reading about local history. This is where Cochise waged his fierce and futile war, Geronimo exacted his revenge, Ike Clanton bought his stolen cattle, and Wyatt Earp hunted his brother's killer. Legions of oddballs, lunatics, and hard cases have pitted themselves against the Chiricahua Mountains and each other, but now it is a place of profound serenity.

Tip *Bring binoculars to help you spot deer, black bears, and mountain lions.*

 9 casitas Microwaves, refrigerators. **Recreation:** bird-watching, fishing, hiking, mountain biking, rock climbing, wildlife viewing, horseshoes, board games, library. **Services:** mountain bikes provided. **Classes and programs:** cooking and writing classes. Some in-room fireplaces, private patios, some pets allowed (fee); no room phones, no room TVs, no smoking $100–$225 D, DC, MC, V.

 14066 S. Sunglow Rd., Pearce, AZ 85625 *520/824–3334 or 866/ 786–4569* *520/824–3176* *www.sunglowranch.com.*

Arkansas

AZALEA FALLS
Laid-Back Adventure ~ Tranquil Outpost

Frank Lloyd Wright believed architecture should reflect the natural world, and Alf Carter and Kathy Trimble created Azalea Falls with that same philosophy in mind. Deep in the forest, 50 mi southeast of Eureka Springs, Alf built a redwood-and-stone lodge with large expanses of glass. Kathy created an outdoor meditation nook, with gardens and a stone bench in a small clearing. Elsewhere, an octagonal picnic table stands on an octagonal platform—an island in the woods.

On these 137 undulating acres of mixed forest and canyon land in the Ozarks, outcroppings of sandstone are stained with rust and covered with green moss. They stand next to trickling green creeks or on hilltops, offering views over a valley. American goldfinches, white-breasted nuthatches, yellow-bellied cuckoos, wild turkeys, red-tail hawks, and many other birds visit the property. Elks, bobcats, deer, foxes, and flying squirrels all live around here, too. You can look for wildlife along Azalea Falls' marked 1-mi trail, which loops along a canyon rim, down and up through woodland, and past the eponymous 85-foot and 40-foot waterfalls, which flow strongest in spring or after a good rain.

Alf leads hikes ($50 per person for an eight-hour day) to the many area waterfalls, rivers, and bluffs, tailoring the trips to your skills and preferences. His favorite day hike is to the waterfall at the end of Bowers Hollow in the little-visited Upper Buffalo Wilderness area. Alf also gives rock-climbing lessons for beginners and leads guided rock-climbing trips for the more experienced ($100 per person for an eight-hour day). Transportation to sights is included, but you need to pack a lunch. You can book a package that combines lodging and hiking or climbing at reduced rates. On your own you might explore the nearby Buffalo River Trail, or ask your hosts to help you schedule a canoe trip or horseback-riding trip with an off-property outfitter.

Or you might choose not to venture off the property at all. Azalea Falls is awash in flowers. In April, at the start of wildflower season, redbud and dogwood trees bloom. Wild azaleas and fragrant umbrella magnolias deck the month of May. Equally colorful June brings the delicate pink blossoms of the climbing prairie roses. Appearing from July until first frost are hardier flowers, such as Queen Anne's lace and wild bergamot (bee balm). Kathy and Alf have also planted Japanese maple, hydrangea, and irises.

Accommodation at Azalea Falls is in two three-bedroom houses, each with a large kitchen, queen beds, and three couches that fold out into additional queen beds. The 3,000-square-foot lodge has three bathrooms and two stone fireplaces, including one in the master bedroom's sitting area. Wood floors and stonework columns and walls lend the house a rustic elegance, and modern fabrics update the classic furniture. Part of the enormous deck overlooks a waterfall. The 1,700-square-foot, 2½-bath cabin is a hewn pine-log home with vaulted ceilings. Carved-wood chairs; beige, cocoa, and ivory upholstery; and tapestry carpets fill the combination living-dining room, while the master bedroom loft is done in muted florals. Local restaurants will cater guests' meals—barbecue and Italian are favorites—and, for a fee, even clean up after dinner. Now that's not-roughing-it in style.

Tip *The best time to see the area's distinctive rock formations is when tree limbs are bare; lodging prices drop $15 per night in January and February. In any season, bring your food (Boxley has only a small grocery), or send a list ahead; for 25% of the cost ($25 minimum) your hosts will stock the cupboards.*

🛏 1 cabin, 1 lodge ⍾⦿⍾ Grills, kitchens, microwaves. **Recreation:** birdwatching, hiking, rock climbing, wildlife viewing, library, videocassette library. Nearby: horseback riding, tubing (water), canoeing. **Services:** grocery shopping. **Classes and programs:** guided hikes, rock-climbing lessons. ♿ Cable TV, in-room data ports, in-room fireplaces, in-room VCRs, jetted tubs, private decks; no smoking ▭ $160–$200 for 2 people, $20 for each additional person ▭ AE, D, MC, V.

🏠 *HC 30 (Box 140), Kingston, AR 72742* ☎ *870/420–3941* 🖶 *870/420–3942* ⊕ *www.azaleafalls.com.*

CINNAMON VALLEY RESORT
Romantic Retreat

Only half a mile from the hubbub of Eureka Springs, Cinnamon Valley Resort is a peaceful hideaway designed specifically for couples. The town is a huge destination for newlyweds, and T-shirts bearing the slogan "I got married in Eureka Springs" sell briskly. But Cinnamon Valley eschews over-the-top romance. Centered on a small man-made lake surrounded by lawn, the 170-acre property sits in a valley. Hardwood forest covers the hillsides, hiding the resort's cabins and two spring-fed lakes. In fall, the leaves of the many oaks turn deep ambers and oranges, while the dogwood leaves turn red. The glory of the Ozarks is amorous inspiration enough.

Each of the cushy log cabins has a fireplace (supplied with Duralogs from November through April), a CD stereo, queen or king beds, and a full kitchen. Choosing a cabin might be your biggest challenge, as each is unique. One of the newest, Fannie's Barn, is among the best: dark and light grains alternate in the polished wood floors, russet and straw colors predominate in the upholstery and wall treatments, and the furniture shows a Craftsman-era influence. You can relax in your glass-enclosed hot tub safe from the bugs but still surrounded by woods on the edge of the small lake. Uphill, north of the large lake, a road leads into the forest to the six original cabins. Country Dream, all patchwork quilts and gingham curtains, has a good view of the woods, two bedrooms, and an outdoor hot tub. Southwestern furnishings and accents decorate the Mountaineer (but avoid this one if you don't like hunting: a trophy deer stands in an alcove above the Jacuzzi). On a separate road, away from the other cabins, Elk Lodge also has a southwestern theme. Deep reds and blues blanket the pine-log bed, and there's an outdoor hot tub under a gazebo.

Sway in your porch swing and think pleasant thoughts, or explore the grounds. You can hike on trails that crisscross the woods and maybe catch a glimpse of deer, rabbits, turkeys, or raccoons. Off a road that winds past a split-rail fence into the woods is a small clearing with a lake. For fishing, the resort's 1-acre artificial lake is stocked with bass, and you can also go catch-and-release fishing on the larger of the two spring-fed lakes. If you don't catch anything, rest assured that you won't go hungry. Alternatives to cooking—burger shacks, diners, cafés, upscale restaurants, and grocery stores—are just minutes away in Eureka Springs.

Tip *Reserve at least a month in advance for weekends in mid- to late October—peak fall foliage time. The Country French and Mountaineer cabins have the best views of the changing leaves across the valley and of the large lake below, which reflects the autumn colors above.*

🛏 9 cabins ⏐◎⏐ Grills, kitchens, microwaves. **Recreation:** fishing, hiking, wildlife viewing, canoeing. ⛄ Cable TV, in-room VCRs, in-room fireplaces, jetted tubs, private decks; no room phones, no kids, no smoking ⚑ $170–$225 ⊟ D, MC, V.

⌂ *Box 717, Eureka Springs, AR 72632* ☎ *479/253–5354 or 800/424–3344* ⎙ *479/253–7100* ⊕ *www.cinnamonvalley.com.*

DEVIL'S DEN STATE PARK CABINS
Family Hideout ~ Rustic Escape

Built in 1933 by the Civilian Conservation Corps (CCC), Devil's Den State Park is cradled in a densely wooded valley in northwestern

Arkansas's Ozark Mountains, 50 mi north of Fort Smith. Lee Creek runs through the 2,500-acre park, cascading slowly over a native stone dam at the end of a small lake. The Devil's Den that gives the park its name is a cave that lies along a 1½-mi loop trail. On your way to the cave you pass a spring and waterfalls, and you can cool off in the Devil's Ice Box, a deep fissure where the temperature is 52°F year-round. In the leafy green glades of the park, it is easy to shed the cares of your workaday life.

The CCC built the park under the mandate that "none of the necessary man-made things spoil the natural scenery." Constructed of stone and wood gathered on-site, the park's cabins fulfill that mandate handsomely. Some of them have a stonework base capped with dark wood construction, while others are completely of stone or of wood. Inside, the studio and one-, two-, and three-bedroom cabins are summer house mix-and-match, with wood floors. Some of the original handmade wood beds, kitchen tables, and chairs are still there, along with low-slung 1980s-style furnishings. However, the cabins are in good condition, and all the basic kitchens and bathrooms have been updated. All cabins have fireplaces that you can use Labor Day to Memorial Day; you are provided with a bundle of firewood a day and can buy more at the visitor center. Make sure to load up on supplies before you get to the park, as culinary options are limited. The small store is more gift shop than grocery, but you can get ice, charcoal, soda, hot dogs, and a few types of soup. Open 8 to 3 in the summer, a nine-table café near the store serves breakfast and lunch: eggs, pancakes, hamburgers, and sandwiches.

On summer weekends Devil's Den Trail is well traveled, so to avoid the crowds, head up to Yellow Rock Trail, a 3-mi route to sweeping vistas over a valley of treetops. Along the Woody Plant Trail, wildflowers such as bird's foot violet and the showy evening primrose are numbered and identified in a corresponding booklet. A series of instructional panels along the CCC Interpretive Trail show old photos and descriptions of CCC programs and buildings. The steep 15-mi backpackers' trail is for experienced hikers only—you have to pack all your supplies and water in and out. Daily in summer, and weekends the rest of the year, rangers lead hikes along various trails and present natural history talks—bats are a favorite subject, as well as the CCC. On the 8-acre lake, you can rent pedal boats and water bikes as well as kayaks, but no swimming is allowed. For that, go to the large pool about 25 yards away. Surrounded by a rock wall, the curvy pool overlooks the lake.

Tip *Cabin 16 is an especially attractive stone-and-log studio above the road. If you are looking for quiet, this is a good choice because it's at the end of a row of cabins, surrounded on three sides by woods.*

16 cabins ⏐◎⏐ Café, grocery store, picnic area, kitchens. **Recreation:** hiking, mountain biking, pool, kayaking, softball, playground. **Services:** dock, laundry facilities. **Classes and programs:** guided hikes, guided nature walks, natural history programs and lectures. In-room fireplace; $75–$140 AE, D, MC, V.

11333 W. Arkansas Hwy. 74, West Fork, AR 72774 ☎ *479/761–3325* *www.arkansasstateparks.com.*

California

DRAKESBAD GUEST RANCH
Tranquil Outpost

Where California's Sierra Nevada and the Pacific Northwest's Cascade Range converge, 17 mi northwest of Chester, the historic lodge and cabins of Drakesbad Guest Ranch lie at 5,784 feet above sea level. Clustered together in the shadow of towering volcanic-rock formations at the edge of a broad wildflower meadow, the ranch is in Lassen Volcanic National Park. The 106,000-acre park, one of California's least-visited national parks, is lorded over by giant Mount Lassen, a volcano that exploded from 1914 to 1916. Drakesbad sits well off the beaten path, accessible only by a rough, winding 3½-mi dirt road that dead-ends at the ranch. Once you park your car, if you want to see the sights you'll have to don your hiking boots or saddle up a horse.

If you've never ridden horseback, Drakesbad is the place to give it a whirl: the ranch operates saddle trips as short as 45 minutes and as long as eight hours. Hikers can trek across the giant meadow into coniferous forest and connect to a network of 150 mi of trails that crisscross the national park. Birders love to watch the many migratory birds that stop to rest among the tall grasses of the boggy meadow surrounding the ranch. In Hot Creek you can fish for brook, brown, and rainbow trout; the ranch rents waders, fly rods, and tackle. To see the major sights of the national park, hop in the car. Spend a half day climbing Mount Lassen, exploring steam vents and lava beds, and hiking the forests and alpine tundra.

At Drakesbad you'll stay in one of several cabins or in the 1937 lodge. All the accommodations are comfortable if spartan and have hand-carved lodgepole beds, with double or twin mattresses and full or half baths. Guest rooms have no electricity. Instead, a kerosene lamp lights your room at night, adding to the old-fashioned wilderness charm. If you want privacy, opt for one of the cabin rooms, since the lodge is the evening gathering place: outside there's a campfire where everyone comes to roast marshmallows and stargaze; inside you can play cards or backgammon in the large downstairs common area. Day and night, a hot spring on the property feeds the swimming pool with 50 gallons per minute of running 105°F water. It's a bit hot for lap swimming, but it's deliciously warm for an early-morning or evening dip. You can follow your swim with a massage in the bathhouse at the edge of the pool deck.

Your room rate includes three meals per day, which are announced by the pealing of a brass bell. Well balanced and delicious, the menu is creative without being overly ambitious, perfect for hungry hikers and families with kids. Once seated at your own table in the knotty-pine dining room, you choose either a meat or vegetarian meal; the menu changes daily. There's also a respectable beer and wine list. If you're planning an expedition for the next day, sign up the night before for a sack lunch to take with you on the trail.

Tip *If you can't book a year or more in advance, it's hard to snag a prime-season reservation at Drakesbad. But after Labor Day, rooms are often available on short notice.*

6 rooms, 8 bungalows, 4 cabins, 1 duplex ❯❮ American plan, restaurant, picnic area. **Recreation:** bird-watching, fishing, hiking, horseback riding, wildlife viewing, pool, canoeing (nearby), badminton, croquet, horseshoes, Ping-Pong, volleyball, recreation room. **Services:** massage, mineral springs, guided fishing trips, tackle shop, shop. **Classes and programs:** natural history programs. No a/c, no room phones, no room TVs, no smoking $134–$185 D, MC, V Closed mid-Oct.–May.

c/o California Guest Services, 2150 N. Main St., No. 5, Red Bluff, CA 96080
530/529–1512 Ext. 120 530/529–4511 www.drakesbad.com.

EL CAPITAN CANYON
Family Hideout ~ Rustic Escape

If you love camping but hate sleeping without luxury linens and a good mattress, book a stay at El Capitan, some 18 mi north of Santa Barbara, and discover how to camp without getting dirt under your fingernails. The resort occupies 200 acres abutting a state beach, a huge land conservancy, and the Los Padres National Forest, and its cedar cabins and safari-style canvas tents are scattered along the oak-shaded banks of a creek that runs out of the Santa Ynez Mountains to the Pacific Ocean.

By day you can beachcomb or ride one of the resort bicycles on a 6½-mi loop at adjacent El Capitan State Beach. If you want to play in the ocean, ask about renting a Boogie board, a snorkel kit, or a kickboard. You can hike or horseback ride up the canyon into the mountains, take a guided botanical walk or yoga class, lie by the heated pool, get a massage in your room, or sit by the brook. On Saturday evenings from April through October, you can kick back at the resort's outdoor barbecue and concert series, with notable jazz, blues, and bluegrass performers.

The cabins and tents here are temporary structures, built to have the least possible impact on the land, and they're well spaced from each other—you won't see many of your neighbors. All accommodations have stylish chenille rugs and Chumash Indian–inspired prints or the like. Cabins have kitchenettes, private baths, and king- or queen-size beds; some also have sleeping lofts or bunk beds. A few cabins are split into suites. Tents have electric lights and queen-size beds with dramatic willow-branch headboards and down comforters, but if you stay in a tent, you have no kitchenette and you share central bathing facilities.

You can eat in the little tin-roof café–cum–general store at the front of the resort, where they make breakfast burritos, organic salads, and delicious sandwiches. Otherwise, you cook over an open fire—each of the tents and cabins has its own picnic table and fire pit and grill. The store sells complete barbecue kits and basic provisions like wine, wood, ice cream, fire starter, condiments, eggs, and milk, but if you can, bring a cooler stocked with lunches and snacks, as well as anything you might want to throw on the grill. If you forget anything, don't worry. You may feel a world away from civilization, but Santa Barbara and its superb restaurants and shopping lie a half hour down the highway.

Tip *For the best stargazing, avoid the cabins next to the lighted parking area. If you're looking to avoid kids, come in spring, fall, or winter, when you can enjoy relative solitude and quiet. Finally, if you plan to cook, bring kitchen supplies: there's not so much as a fork in any of the cabins.*

🛏 26 safari tents, 23 suites, 82 cabins ⑩ Café, grocery store, grills, picnic area, some microwaves, some refrigerators. **Recreation:** biking, bird-watching, hiking, running, wildlife viewing, pool, golf privileges, badminton, horseshoes, volleyball, playground. Nearby: horseback riding, mountain biking, beach, scuba diving, surfing, snorkeling, windsurfing, sea kayaking, soaring. **Services:** bicycles provided; Boogie boards, kickboards, and snorkeling-gear rentals; massage; babysitting; shop; meeting rooms. **Classes and programs:** guided hikes; guided nature walks; fitness and yoga classes; stargazing, food, and wine talks; concerts; storytelling. ⚘ Some in-room data ports, some in-room fireplaces, some jetted tubs, some private decks; no a/c, no phones in some rooms, no room TVs, no smoking ▣ $135–$305 ▤ AE, D, MC, V.

🏠 *11560 Calle Real, Santa Barbara, CA 93117* ☎ *805/685–3887 or 866/ 352–2729* 🖷 *805/968–6772* ⊕ *www.elcapitancanyon.com.*

LA CASA DEL ZORRO
Luxurious Resort

Two hours northeast of San Diego and three hours southeast of Los Angeles, a manicured desert oasis straddles the boundary between a sleepy little town and the largest and least-developed state park in the United States. La Casa del Zorro is in Borrego Springs, which is entirely surrounded by the scrub and mountains of the 600,000-acre Anza Borrego Desert State Park. Proof that you can find comfort in the wilderness, the resort gives you the choice of indulging in a deep radiance facial or a hike into a canyon to spot bighorn sheep, between a set of tennis and a horseback ride along a lonely trail.

La Casa del Zorro started out as a single adobe lodge built in 1937. You can still see original beams and adobe walls in some rooms of the main building. Hanging in the dining room, lobby, lounge, and other public areas, paintings by Marjorie Reed chronicle the history of the Butterfield Stage, which carried mail from St. Louis to California in the 1870s along a route that passed through the Anza-Borrego Desert. Beyond the main lodge, one- and two-story buildings contain oversize southwestern-theme guest rooms, some with views of the putting green and a water course. All have patios or balconies, fireplaces, dining areas, minibars, and fine linens—including bathrobes.

The casitas scattered over the resort's 40 acres were once privately owned. Averaging 1,300 square feet, they each have their own personality. Bathrooms are finished in marble or glazed Mexican tiles, furnishings are custom upholstered, and lighting fixtures are forged-iron. The larger casitas have dining rooms, spacious patios, and desert gardens. Private pools and/or hot tubs make several of the casitas a supremely agreeable place to chill out all day, with room service at your beck and call. After sunset, you can take a dip in your pool and watch Orion swagger across the dark black sky.

Come prepared to dress for dinner in the Butterfield Dining Room, where fireside tables are set with white linen, fine china, crystal, and silver. The dinner menu offers huge portions of New York strip steak, Gulf prawns with saffron risotto, and free-range chicken. European-trained servers help you pair your choice with a selection from the resort's wine cellar. If you prefer a less formal setting you can go for soup, salad, and sandwiches in the Fox Den Lounge.

You might start or end your day with a swim in one of the sparkling swimming pools, among them a regulation lap pool and a huge, shallow exercise pool. When you're ready to chill out, hit one of the teak chairs scattered around the sandstone pool deck.

When the desert beckons, you can go out on your own or take one of the guided tours available through the resort. Escorted half- and full-day tours in four-wheel-drive vehicles take you into slot canyons, along the route of the Southern Emigrant Trail, or out to the Salton Sea to view migratory birds. Head into the state park on your own and take a hike from the park visitor center to Palm Canyon, a cool, green spot even on the hottest day. Explore the prehistoric oyster beds at Split Mountain or watch the sun play on the peaks and valleys of the Western Borrego badlands. Each March and April, when nature puts on one of the most awesome wildflower displays anywhere, carpets of white, pink, red, and yellow flowers stretch as far as the eye can see. The tips of spiny ocotillo bushes turn crimson following rainstorms any time of year.

Tip *Peak season in the desert runs mid-January to mid-May. The rest of the year this is a quiet resort where you can stay at greatly reduced prices. Summer (which in the desert lasts all the way from mid-May through October) can be blistering hot, but other seasons are quite pleasant.*

⌨ 48 rooms, 12 suites, 19 casitas ⦿ Café, restaurant, room service, bar/lounge, minibars, microwaves. **Recreation:** biking, bird-watching, running, 5 pools, putting green, 6 tennis courts, archery, boccie, croquet, Ping-Pong, shuffleboard. Nearby: hiking, horseback riding, mountain biking, rock climbing, wildlife viewing, golf privileges, entertainment. **Services:** local bicycle rentals, health club, outdoor hot tubs, salon, spa, shop, airport shuttle, business services, concierge, Internet access, meeting rooms. **Classes and programs:** guided nature tours, tennis lessons, fitness classes, astronomy talks. ♿ Cable TV, private balconies and patios, no-smoking rooms. ▦ $265–$1,500 ▭ AE, D, DC, MC, V.

3845 Yaqui Pass Rd., Borrego Springs, CA 92004 ☎ 760/767–5323 or 800/824–1884 ᐩ 760/767–5963 ⊕ www.lacasadelzorro.com.

MAR VISTA COTTAGES
Tranquil Outpost

Three hours north of San Francisco on the southern Mendocino coast, it's easy to forget whatever is bothering you when you rent one of the little vacation cottages at Mar Vista, a 9-acre property across the road from a dramatic, rocky cove of a beach. Built in the 1930s, each of the 12 cottages has been lovingly restored, but not to excess: you'll find only the things you need, and nothing you don't. Uncluttered and uncomplicated, it's a place to relax and unwind, where after reading in a hammock all day you can soak in an outdoor redwood tub and contemplate what to barbecue.

Owners Tom and Renata Dorn, whose background is in luxury hotels, have put the fundamentals of a typical high-end lodging into a low-key property. Every bed has a top-quality mattress, high-thread-count cotton sheets, a down comforter, and a fresh duvet cover; bathrooms have thick terry towels; and every room is spotless right down to the windows, a rarity in coastal California. But this is not a fancy resort, with too many pillows on the bed and packets of bath salts by the tub. Instead it's a dressed-down, do-it-yourself vacation spot for people who prefer quiet conversation to television, badminton to tennis, and hiking boots to high heels. Neither the furniture in your living room nor the dishes in your kitchen match, but like a second home that's been in the family for generations, the place exudes happiness and calm. Indeed, many adults who return year after year spent every summer of their childhood here.

Mar Vista is a little Shangri-la. It is also a small working farm of sorts, with several chickens, two pet goats, and an organic garden that's open to guests. When you check in, you'll receive a list of what's ready to pick. In the morning, you'll find freshly laid eggs at your door in a basket; step outside to the garden and snip some herbs to make an omelet. If you like to sleep late, request black-out curtains in your cottage. But if you can't bring yourself to lollygag all day, you can venture out to some of northern California's best beaches (think Hitchcock, not *Baywatch*), as well as to the 10-story-tall Point Arena Lighthouse, the only one in California that you can climb. Within an hour's drive you can be at the great wineries of the Anderson Valley or in Mendocino, where you can poke around in the shops before sitting down to a white-tablecloth dinner.

There's no restaurant at Mar Vista, but there are several nearby, and in the town of Anchor Bay is a terrific grocery store with organic meats and produce as well as local fish in season. Bring home your goodies and cook them outside on the fieldstone barbecue, or steam up the kitchen in your cottage.

Tip *Mar Vista makes special accommodations for dogs, including towels to dry Rex off after a day at the beach. Non-canine lovers, take heart: if the previous tenant brought a dog, you won't see—or smell—any trace of the beast.*

↪ 12 cottages ⏍ Grills, picnic area, kitchens, some microwaves. **Recreation:** bird-watching, hiking, running, golf privileges, badminton, boccie, croquet, horseshoes, volleyball. Nearby: fishing, horseback riding, beach, surfing, kayaking, sea kayaking. **Services:** softball equipment and soccer balls provided, outdoor hot tub, massage, babysitting, grocery shopping, Internet access. ♿ Some private decks, some pets allowed; no a/c, no room phones, no room TVs, no smoking ▭ $140–$230 ▭ AE, MC, V.

35101 S. Hwy. 1, Gualala, CA 95445 ☎ *707/884–3522 or 877/855–3522* ⊕ *www.marvistamendocino.com.*

POST RANCH INN
Luxurious Resort ~ Romantic Retreat

High above the Pacific Ocean, atop a narrow ridge on the jagged coastline of Big Sur, 28 mi south of Carmel, sits the Post Ranch Inn, one of the world's finest small resorts. As soon as you check in, grab the carved wooden walking stick and the fold-up bird-watching chart from your room, and head out for a hike through the breathtaking mountains and hills. You might spot a fox, a wild turkey, or a bobcat. All around the ranch, great respect is paid to nature: only one tree was cut down to build the inn.

Each of the inn's distinctive buildings is an architectural gem, constructed of slate, wood, and other natural materials to blend into the landscape. Lots of glass brings the outdoors in. You can stay in a tree house—yes, in a tree—or in an ocean house built into the cliff, with a roof covered in wildflowers and a spectacular view of the sea. Or choose a butterfly house, mountain house, or coast house. Whichever room is yours, you'll find luscious privacy and seclusion. Televisions are nowhere to be found, and bedside alarm clocks are available only upon request. Each ultra-restful room has a wood-burning fireplace, stereo, massage table, binoculars, books on poetry and art, and wet bar. In the bathrooms are oversize slate-lined spa tubs, fragrant hand-milled soaps, and even a remedy for poison oak.

Spa services are available throughout the day and evening in redwood-and-glass studios that look out to the forest or mountains. There's no better place for a wildflower facial, therapeutic massage, or body wrap. Depending on the weather, classes in tai chi and yoga are held outdoors or in a yurt. You can take a swim in the 60-foot lap pool, which is surrounded by a meadow, and then head to the giant, stone-tiled 102°F warming pool, perched on a cliff 1,100 feet above the ocean.

The inn's Sierra Mar restaurant takes in dramatic views of the Pacific and offers contemporary cuisine made from local, organic ingredients. Lunchtime choices range from smoked salmon to sandwiches, or you can request a fancy picnic, packed in a knapsack, to take on a hike around the ranch. The flexible prix-fixe dinner menu changes nightly. The next morning, don't rush to breakfast if the weather is foggy and cool. Instead, get up and light a fire, and ask for a tray to be delivered. You may never want to leave your room.

Tip *At dinner, if you're a wine lover, ask for the reserve list of outstanding and rare vintages. Five days a week you can take a guided nature walk through the magical Big Sur landscape with Billy Post, a descendant of the original owners of the ranch. Inquire about the inn's occasional cooking classes, whale-watching presentations, and architecture talks.*

➤ 30 units ﺍ◎ﺍ Continental breakfast, restaurant, bar, minibars. **Recreation**: bird-watching, hiking, running, wildlife viewing, pool, board games, library. Nearby: horseback riding, mountain biking, beach. **Services:** gym, outdoor warming pool, spa, shop, Internet access. **Classes and programs:** guided hikes, guided nature walks, yoga classes, shamanic sessions. ⚛ In-room fireplaces; in-room safes; jetted tubs; private balconies, decks, patios, and terraces; no room TVs, no kids under 18, no smoking 📭 $485–$935 ⊟ AE, MC, V.

🖃 *Box 219, Big Sur, CA 93920* ☎ *831/667–2200 or 800/527–2200* 🖷 *831/667–2512* ⊕ *www.postranchinn.com.*

REQUA INN
Laid-Back Adventure

Way up north on the craggy California coast, 60 mi north of Eureka and 1 mi inland from where the Klamath River meets the Pacific, stands a 1914 country inn surrounded by Redwood National Park.

There's nothing particularly noteworthy about the homey whitewashed exterior, but once you step inside you'll know that you have arrived somewhere special. The common room's books, board games, and fireplace, and the river and forest views through giant picture windows are the first things you'll notice. Your thoughts easily turn to days spent in a rocking chair, staring out at the estuary while assembling a jigsaw puzzle. The Requa Inn is lovely but unpretentious, a place that could easily fall into the category of romantic B&B. But the affable innkeepers prefer to think of it as a home base for outdoors explorers rather than as a honeymoon hideaway. After all, nature is so abundant here that it would be a shame to stay holed up indoors. You're within walking distance of some of the tallest trees in the world, and once you've seen the sun peeking through the canopy 300 feet overhead, dappling the lush, green mosses and ferns lining the forest floor, you may have a hard time heading home for the evening.

When eventually you do, you'll find a good dinner in a convivial atmosphere. Generally, only guests eat in the dining room, but sometimes on weekends the innkeeper invites locals as well. The menu is straightforward: steak, pasta, local seafood, or chicken, depending on what's in season and available at market. It's all very straightforward and casual. Your accommodations follow suit. Rooms are pleasant and homey, with king-size beds in several and superb river views from those in front. The inn delivers all the warmth and welcome of Grandma's house, with none of the frills or fuss—and it's almost as good a value. Despite its desirable location and outstanding views, few people venture this far north in California, so rates remain quite low.

Tip *Because of the inn's age, rooms aren't soundproof. If quiet matters to you, do let the innkeeper know when you book, and she'll do whatever she can to put you away from the action.*

🛏 10 rooms ◎ Full breakfast, dining room. **Recreation:** bird-watching, fishing, hiking, running, wildlife viewing, river swimming, kayaking, golf privileges, board games, library, piano. Nearby: beach, swimming hole, boating, rafting, sea kayaking. **Services:** dock, guided fishing trips. **Classes and programs:** guided hikes, guided nature walks. ♿ No a/c, no room phones, no room TVs, no kids under 8, no smoking 💳 $79–$135 ➡ AE, D, MC, V.

📫 *451 Requa Rd. Klamath, CA 95548* 📞 *707/482–1425 or 866/800–8777* 📠 *707/482–0457* ⊕ *www.requainn.com.*

SORENSEN'S RESORT
Family Hideout ~ Laid-Back Adventure

The eclectic assemblage of cottages surrounded by mature aspen trees lies at the edge of one of the largest undeveloped alpine meadows in the Sierra Nevada mountain range, less than a half hour south of Lake Tahoe. But it's a world away from the lake's crowds and traffic. The housekeeping cabins are surrounded by snowcapped peaks, cobalt-blue lakes, and backcountry wilderness.

Although you could always while away the day sitting on the porch, Sorensen's is better suited to people who like to explore outdoors. In summer there's spectacular hiking, from easy hour-long treks through grassy meadows to full-day ascents of 10,000-foot peaks yielding 360-degree views across 50 mi of wilderness. If you want help exploring, book a guided nature trek, bird-watching tour, fly-fishing class, wildflower walk, or kayak paddle, all near the property. In winter, cross-country skiers tackle the miles of tracks right outside their cabin doors, while downhill skiers drive a short distance to Kirkwood, one of California's best ski resorts. Kids can fish for trout in the tiny pond or play along the little creek through the property. There's a campfire ring where moms and dads can roast marshmallows with their little ones.

If you wanted to, you could eat three meals a day in the knotty-pine-paneled café with fireplace. The food is good, particularly at breakfast; at dinner, stick to the grilled meats and other simple fare. The café is fine for your first and last nights, but since your cabin will most likely have a kitchen and outdoor barbecue grill, there's no need to spend your money on restaurant fare.

Among the many accommodations choices are an A-frame duplex log cabin with peaked knotty-pine ceiling, several tin-roof cottages made of rough-hewn timbers, a dormitory-style bunkhouse, and a Norwegian-style farmhouse with a hand-carved facade. Many have woodstoves or gas fireplaces, and there are kitchens in all but three (whose nightly tab includes breakfast). Each of the rooms is decorated with country pieces like lodgepole bed frames. Some rooms have pull-out sofas and futons. Daily housekeeping service is available on request, but you're likely to spend so little time indoors that you might not need someone to clean up after you.

Tip *Unlike other High Sierra resorts, which get buried in deep snow from October through April, Sorensen's can stay open all year because it lies fairly close to the road and consequently gets plowed out after snowstorms. For the quietest rooms, book a cabin in the back of the property. When you come, remember that Sorensen's is 20 minutes from the nearest market, so be sure you've stocked up on food and drink before you settle in.*

↪ 2 rooms, 27 cabins, 4 houses ⊧◎⊧ Restaurant, grills, picnic area, some kitchens. **Recreation:** bird-watching, hiking, running, wildlife viewing, cross-country skiing, dogsledding, sledding, snowshoeing, telemark skiing, board games, playground. Nearby: fishing, horseback riding, mountain biking, river swimming, kayaking, rafting, downhill skiing. **Services:** mountain-bike, cross-country and telemark-ski, snowshoe, and snowboard rentals; massage; sauna; guided fishing trips; ski shop; babysitting; concierge; meeting rooms, wireless Internet. **Classes and programs:** guided hikes, guided nature walks, natural history programs, cross-country skiing and fly-fishing lessons, art and photography classes, nature and stargazing talks, storytelling. ♿ Some in-room fireplaces, some jetted tubs, some private decks, some pets allowed; no a/c, no room phones, no room TVs, no smoking ▤ $95–$350 ▭ AE, D, DC, MC, V.

⌂ *14255 Hwy. 88, Hope Valley, CA 96120* ☎ *530/694–2203 or 800/ 423–9949* ⊕ *www.sorensensresort.com.*

TAMARACK LODGE
Laid-Back Adventure ~ Romantic Retreat

The Tamarack Lodge epitomizes mountain charm. Surrounded by towering pine trees, the lodge sits at 8,600 feet on the edge of a high-alpine lake just east of the Sierra-Nevada Crest, on the back side of Yosemite and the Ansel Adams Wilderness, 2½ mi west of the town of Mammoth Lakes. It's a place of almost daunting splendor, where giant sawtooth mountains drop into the deserts of the Great Basin. Everything is so big that it's hard to judge distance or height. But at the lodge, all is snug and perfectly scaled to humans.

In summer you might come to fish for trout in Mammoth Lakes Basin. Opposite the lodge you can launch a rowboat or canoe in Twin Lakes and spend the afternoon casting a line in the shadow of a 500-foot basalt canyon wall. If you prefer to scale high peaks, climb 11,000-foot Mammoth Mountain; from the top, on a clear day, you can see well over 100 mi. Hate to hike but want the view? Drive to the mountain's gondola and be whisked 3,000 vertical feet to the summit. You can ride back down, too, but if you're feeling more adventurous you can hike the distance. Or you can rent a mountain bike at the base of the gondola and take it with you to the top, then ride down. If the altitude gives you vertigo, head 15 minutes southeast to Hot Creek, in the Great Basin, and soak in hot springs among sagebrush and tumbleweeds.

In winter the lodge gets an average 400 inches of snowfall and sparkles like a miniature Christmas village. Nordic and alpine skiers come to the area for some of the West's best skiing. The Tamarack has its own cross-country center and 45 km of trails. Downhill skiers take a shuttle from the lodge to Mammoth Mountain, which has 3,500 acres of terrain and one of the country's most advanced high-speed lift networks. If you prefer to be alone, rent snowshoes and head for the woods.

The focus of activity at the resort is the lobby of the original 1924 lodge. Guests gather here to play backgammon and cards beneath exposed, bark-covered timber beams and in front of a stone fireplace. Upstairs you can stay in an old-fashioned knotty-pine bedroom (with or without a bath) or in a top-floor two-bedroom suite with kitchen. Surrounding the lodge are cabins that range from 50-year-old studio cottages with basic furnishings to two-bedroom cabins with stylishly mismatched decor. Many of the cabins have fireplaces, and all have kitchens.

You can shop for groceries in town, a 10-minute drive away, or eat out there in the Tamarack's restaurant, one of the region's best. As you look out to the woods and lake during a relaxed summer lunch or a candlelit dinner, the intimate knotty-pine dining room is idyllic. The talented chef prepares hearty French-California cuisine, with an emphasis on game; quail or venison here paired with a top-notch California wine make for the best meal of your vacation.

Tip *For the best rates and package deals, come in the spring or fall, between skiing and fishing seasons. Each unit is different, so be sure to call the front desk, rather than the toll-free reservations number, if you have specific questions about amenities. But note that lodge rooms have little soundproofing; if hearing footsteps in the hall bothers you, book a cabin.*

↩ 10 rooms, 1 suite, 33 cabins ⍾ Restaurant, lobby lounge, grills, some kitchens, some kitchenettes, some microwaves. **Recreation:** bird-watching, fishing, hiking, running, wildlife viewing, lake swimming, canoeing, rowing, golf privileges, cross-country skiing, snowboarding, snowshoeing, telemark skiing, board games. Nearby: horseback riding, mountain biking, rock climbing, swimming hole, ballooning, dogsledding, downhill skiing, ice climbing, ice-skating, sleigh rides, sledding, snowmobiling, snow tubing, skate park. **Services:** cross-country-ski, telemark-ski, and snowshoe rentals; boat launch; tackle shop; ski shop; ski storage; shop; meeting rooms. **Classes and programs:** guided hikes, guided nature walks, cross-country skiing competitions, cross-country skiing and snowshoeing lessons, fishing classes and guided fishing trips. ♿ In-room data ports, some in-room fireplaces, some private decks; no a/c, no room TVs, no kids under 12 in some rooms, no smoking ▱ $84–$390 ▭ AE, MC, V.

✉ *Box 69, Mammoth Lakes, CA 93546* ☎ *760/934–2442 or 800/626–6684* 📠 *760/934–2281* ⊕ *www.tamaracklodge.com.*

Colorado

DEVIL'S THUMB RANCH
Family Hideout ~ Laid-Back Adventure

Though just 1½ hours west of Denver, Devil's Thumb guest ranch feels much father away on its 3,700 acres of wildflower-dusted meadows and in deep forests of lodgepole pine. The resort lies at an elevation of 8,700 feet, at the base of the Continental Divide's western face, and takes its name from a rock formation that juts up from one of the peaks above. Ute and Arapahoe Indians used to come here in summer for the cool weather, and now outdoor enthusiasts come for the same reason.

An activities center, in a restored 1850 barn, serves as the ranch's nerve center, with equipment rentals, a pool, and spa treatment rooms. In summer you can go horseback riding, fly-fishing, or hiking or take a naturalist-led bird walk. The ranch will take you white-water rafting on the Colorado River or on a float trip if you're looking for something a little calmer. Within a 20-minute drive of the ranch, an extensive network of biking trails laces the west side of the Fraser Valley. Rocky Mountain National Park, with 350 mi of hiking trails, is about 45 minutes north. Three golf courses are 15 minutes from the ranch.

Winter activities focus on the ranch's 125 km of cross-country ski and snowshoe trails, recognized as one of the top Nordic trail systems in the country. While you work up a sweat, your kids can spend some time with resort staff, who will teach them basic cross-country techniques, lead them through obstacle courses, show them some games, and give them lunch. On your own or with the kids, you can view the quiet, snow-draped ranch on a Sno-Cat or sleigh ride, or on horseback. Not far away are Winter Park's downhill ski trails, as well as those of the smaller, family-oriented Sol Vista ski area. Winter Park also has lift-served mountain biking in summer.

The ranch's original hand-hewn log homestead (1937) and lodge (1941) now house the Ranch House Restaurant and Saloon. Continental breakfast is served daily for overnight guests, and the general public is welcome for dinner daily and lunch on weekends. Chef Trish Cyman has created a seasonally changing menu that emphasizes organic vegetables and meats, as well as fresh seafood flown in regularly from Cape Cod. On weekend nights you can usually catch a set of live acoustic or bluegrass music in the Saloon.

The most private and cushy of the ranch's accommodations are the eight log cabins on a ridge ¾ mi from the main lodge. With giant stone-sur-round fireplaces, vaulted ceilings, hardwood floors, and lofts or sitting areas, they're a 21st-century evocation of frontier living. Closer to the lodge are older, refurbished cabins set among the trees, and in the lodge are no-fuss guest rooms with log-beamed ceilings. Throughout the ranch, furnishings include lodgepole-pine beds, oversize leather arm-chairs, and a carefully selected eclectic mix of antiques.

Tip *The ranch is popular for weddings on weekends from late June through mid-September; consider staying during the week for a quieter time.*

16 cabins ⦿ Continental breakfast, restaurant, bar, kitchenettes and kitchens. **Recreation:** bird-watching, fishing, hiking, horseback riding, running, wildlife viewing, indoor-outdoor pool, cross-coun-try skiing, ice-skating, sleigh rides, sledding, snowshoeing, badminton, croquet, horseshoes, videocassette library. Nearby: biking, mountain biking, kayaking, rafting, 27-hole golf course, dogsledding, downhill skiing, telemark skiing, snowmobiling. **Services:** cross-country ski, ice-skate, fly-fishing equipment, and snowshoe rentals; hot tub; mas-sage; sauna; guided fishing trips; tackle shop; ski shop; ski storage; business services; Internet access; shop; meeting rooms. **Classes and programs:** guided hikes; guided nature walks; cross-country skiing, fly-fishing, and horseback-riding lessons. ⟁ In-room data ports, some in-room fireplaces, in-room VCRs; no a/c, no smoking ▢ $275–$750 ▭ MC, V.

☐ 3530 Cty. Rd. 83 (Box 750), Tabernash, CO 80478 ☎ 970/726–5632 or 800/933–4339 ⊟ 970/726–9038 ⊕ www.devilsthumbranch.com.

DUNTON HOT SPRINGS
Luxurious Resort ~ Tranquil Outpost

In the mid-1880s, weary gold miners retreated at day's end to a rough camp called Dunton, where they soothed their muscles, heavy from gru-eling labor, in the geothermal springs. Today the former ghost town is a high-end resort where you can soak in those same springs and, per-haps, achieve an almost ethereal state of relaxation. The miners would hardly recognize the place.

When German-born Christoph Henkel and Austrian Bernt Kuhlmann purchased the town of Dunton in 1994, they saw beyond the dilapi-dated remains to envision a sanctuary among the San Juan Mountains of southwestern Colorado. By refurbishing existing buildings and im-porting and restoring log structures from elsewhere in the state, they succeeded in creating a singular interpretation of the old West. The first thing to do when you arrive here is take a deep breath and let your cares float far, far away, to the top of 14,000-plus-foot Mount Wilson and El Diente. Then settle into your cabin, which is deceptively unassuming outside and casually upscale within, furnished with a mix of western antiques, animal-hide rugs and throws, Turkish kilims, Indian and African *objets,* and slate-tiled showers or tubs.

Meals are served at the long, communal table in Dunton's main lodge, originally the town's saloon and dance hall. But the Wild West nostalgia ends there. The four-course dinner is nouveau western, prepared with local organic produce and meats. Your meal might include delicate onion tartlets and mixed greens as a starter, followed by almond-crusted fish with a warm vegetable salad. Toast your day, and your good fortune to be at Dunton, with the signature West Fork mojito, made with Dickel whiskey instead of rum.

Dunton has three sites for soaking: the source, sheltered within a tepee; a small, rock-lined outdoor pool; and the original bathhouse, updated with radiant-heat slate floors, a steam room, and floor-to-ceiling windows that frame views of the craggy San Juans. You can even take a few strokes in the large bathhouse pool. A onetime Pony Express station now houses a massage room (therapists are on call) and yoga studio (with videos for guidance). The two-story library, in a restored barn, is the place to sink into a leather chair by the fire with a title from its extensive collection.

When you need a respite from relaxing, head out on foot or mountain bike to one of the trails in the surrounding San Juan National Forest, or fly fish on the West Fork of the Dolores River, which runs through the resort. In winter, you can cross-country ski, snowshoe, or book a trip with the heli-skiing operation out of Telluride, which will land right outside the lodge and whisk you to backcountry slopes.

Tip *Ask for the Well House cabin, which has its own hot spring. The sandstone tub gets filled directly from the spring, and a large copper tub serves as a cold-water plunge pool. On request, there's shuttle service to the Cortez, Telluride, and Durango airports.*

11 cabins American plan, bar. **Recreation:** fishing, hiking, horseback riding, wildlife viewing, cross-country skiing, snowshoeing, heli-skiing, ice skating, library, DVD library. Nearby: mountain biking. **Services:** fly-fishing equipment and mountain-bike rentals, massage, mineral springs, steam room, guided fishing trips, dry-cleaning service, laundry service, airport shuttle, business services, Internet access, meeting rooms. Some in-room fireplaces, some in-room DVD players, some pets allowed (fee); no a/c, no room TVs, no smoking $250–$400 AE, D, MC, V.

✏ *52068 West Fork Rd. (Box 818), Dolores, CO 81323* ☎ *970/882–4800*
🖷 *970/882–7475* ⊕ *www.duntonhotsprings.com.*

THE HOME RANCH
Family Hideout ~ Luxurious Resort

Since 1980, this guest ranch in the Elk River valley of northwestern Colorado—just outside the blink-if-you-miss-it town of Clark and about four hours' drive from Denver International Airport—has drawn a loyal clientele, many of whom form lasting friendships during their stays. The atmosphere is decidedly social, particularly in summer, thanks to the festive communal dinners, schedule of outdoor activities, and evening events such as barn dances and campfires. Yet with a maximum of 50 guests in summer and winter (when children under six aren't allowed), you're apt to feel like you're part of a large family rather than one among a crowd. And there are plenty of opportunities to steal away on your own, whether on the ranch's 1,500 acres, in the adjacent Routt National Forest, or in the exceptionally lovely Mount Zirkel Wilderness nearby. An excellent children's activity program keeps young ones occupied throughout the day and even during dinnertime, ensuring that parents—and nonparents—can have a true vacation. There's also a program for teens.

The ranch specializes in horseback riding, with about 140 horses that are raised and trained on-site. You won't find your typical, plodding, nose-to-tail trail rides here. Daily outings cater to all skill levels and include kids' rides, horsemanship clinics, slow rides, fast rides, and all-day rides. Learn how to communicate with your horse, play tag on horseback, or even cut and pen cows. There's a cow-penning competition for guests on Saturdays, following a Friday-night trip to the Steamboat rodeo for inspiration. Guided activities on or near the ranch range from hiking to rock climbing. Fly-fishers can warm up at the stocked trout pond, then head for 2 mi of private frontage on the Elk River. In winter, cross-country skiers or snowshoers venture out on the ranch's own 20 km of groomed trails; skiers and snowboarders catch a shuttle to the downhill ski area at Steamboat, a half hour away.

Accommodations and food are first-rate, perhaps no surprise given that the ranch is one of only two Relais & Châteaux properties in Colorado. For extra privacy, stay in one of the cabins, each with a woodstove and front porch with outdoor hot tub. Both the cabins and lodge rooms are outfitted with antique or handcrafted furniture, Native American rugs, lodgepole pine or wrought-iron beds, and hardwood floors. Several sitting rooms and nooks in the main lodge have oversize leather chairs and couches, so you can settle in and play backgammon.

Jars of home-baked chocolate-chip cookies and dried fruit in every room may tempt your sweet tooth, but save your appetite for the hearty fare of executive chef Clyde Nelson: four-course dinners with a choice of four entrées and cooked-to-order breakfasts such as raspberry-ricotta pancakes or huevos rancheros. In summer, lunch—a buffet of salads, sandwiches, and grilled items—is served on the poolside patio. Meals are a focal point, allowing families to regroup and guests to compare notes on their trail rides or fishing outings. By the end of a stay, many are more than a little reluctant to leave Home for home.

Tip *The ranch does not offer its children's program in winter, except during the Christmas and New Year holidays. These two holiday periods are one of the few times of year when children under six may stay at the ranch.*

6 rooms, 8 cabins American plan, bar, refrigerators. **Recreation:** fishing, hiking, horseback riding, wildlife viewing, pool, cross-country skiing, sleigh rides, snowshoeing, horseshoes, Ping-Pong, volleyball, piano, recreation room. Nearby: mountain biking, rock climbing, downhill skiing, telemark skiing. **Services:** cross-country ski, fly-fishing equipment, and snowshoe rentals; outdoor hot tub; massage; sauna; guided fishing trips; ski shop; ski storage; babysitting; dry cleaning; laundry service; shop; airport shuttle; business services. **Classes and programs:** guided hikes; guided nature walks; cross-country skiing, fly-fishing, and horseback-riding lessons; children's programs (ages 6–12); teen programs; dances; entertainment, sing-alongs. Some in-room fireplaces; no a/c, no room phones, no room TVs, no kids under 6, no smoking $350–$2,420 AE, MC, V.

54880 Routt County Rd. 129 (Box 822), Clark, CO 80428 970/879–1780 970/879–1795 www.homeranch.com.

SMITH FORK RANCH
Family Hideout

Colorado's southwest quadrant sees far fewer visitors than do areas closer to Denver. Around the ranching community of Crawford, a 1½-hour drive from the Montrose airport and a 5-hour drive from Denver, the climate is milder than in higher-altitude locations like Aspen or Vail. To the east are the Elk Mountains, and to the west lie acre upon acre of rolling ranch- and farmland. This is where you'll find 260-acre Smith Fork Ranch.

Homesteaded in the late 1890s, the spread has undergone extensive restoration with an eye toward western-style elegance. Many of the furnishings were crafted by local artisans, and the leather used in some furniture and accessories was supplied by Ghurka, Marley Hodgson's high-end leather company. You'll stay in one of five cabins, each with a gas log stove or fireplace, or in one of five guest rooms in the ranch house.

Every part of the ranch, including the dining room, draws on the best of the surrounding area. Head chef Patrick Walley turns out exquisitely flavored five-course dinners that may include smoked game or fresh trout, organic vegetables (the nearby North Fork Valley is one of Colorado's most prolific growers), and desserts made with peaches or cherries from the valley's orchards. The organic meat is from neighboring farms, wines from nearby Paonia are included in the extensive cellar, and even the ranch's drinking water comes from a spring halfway up nearby Saddle Mountain. Lunches and dinners are usually served on the main lodge's log-beamed, open-air dining porch (with fireplace), so you can take in both the restorative mountain breezes and the view out to Mendicant Ridge. There's also a weekly breakfast cookout, and you can arrange for a trailside picnic or dinner on the deck of your cabin.

Almost completely surrounded by Gunnison National Forest, the ranch abuts West Elk Wilderness, so hikers and riders have innumerable trails to choose from. You'll ride the ranch's own horses, who are available for lessons, short trail rides, all-day rides, and breakfast or sunset rides. You can cast for trout (catch and release) in one of six stocked ponds on the property or along 2½ mi of private frontage on the Smith Fork River. Ranch staff customize children's activities according to your kids' ages and interests. Your little ones can learn fishing, horseback riding, and roping and have fun with Frisbee golf and arts-and-crafts classes. One evening they might hear a mountain man tell stories of the Wild West, and another they might sleep over in one of two tepees behind the lodge. While they dream of cowpunchers, you can peek through the ranch's telescope at the clear night sky.

Tip *Book one of the ranch's overnight pack trips to a wilderness camp in the Elk Mountains. You'll "rough it" in style, with platform tents and a camp chef.*

🛏 5 rooms, 5 cabins ⏅ American plan, dining room, bar. **Recreation:** archery, bird-watching, fishing, hiking, horseback riding, hot-air ballooning, wildlife viewing, billiards, horseshoes, team penning cattle. Nearby: mountain biking, rafting, sporting clays. **Services:** fly-fishing equipment provided, gym, outdoor hot tub, massage, guided fishing trips, tackle shop, dry-cleaning service, laundry service, shop, airport shuttle, business services, meeting rooms. **Classes and programs:** guided hikes, guided nature walks, fly-fishing and horseback-riding lessons, children's programs (ages 3–7), concerts, sing-alongs. ⏅ In-room data ports, some in-room fireplaces; no a/c, no room phones, no room TVs, no smoking ⏅ $2,100–$3,000 per wk ⏅ AE, MC, V.

⏅ *45362 Needle Rock Rd. (Box 401), Crawford, CO 81415* ☎ *970/921–3454* 📠 *970/921–3475* 🌐 *www.smithforkranch.com* ☯ *Closed Dec.–late May.*

TALL TIMBER
Luxurious Resort

Tall Timber is no ordinary resort. Located on 180 privately owned acres of riverfront meadow within the San Juan National Forest, it is accessible only by a two-hour ride aboard the historic Durango & Silverton narrow-gauge steam train or a 15-minute helicopter ride from Durango. There are no phones in the rooms because there is no phone service (communication is by radio phone and cell phone), and the nearest road is some 6 mi away. The resort accommodates only 30 guests, and there are usually far fewer. The sense of being on a private "island" in the wilderness somehow makes the stars seem brighter, the silence quieter, the pine trees more fragrant.

On arrival at the resort, you'll find the attentive staff lined up to greet you with homey, country club–like hospitality. You'll then get a personal tour of the resort's facilities—the four-story atrium where seedlings for the numerous flowers that dot the grounds are started, the vintage 1950s-style soda fountain/ice-cream parlor from Durango, the small golf course—while your bags are golf-carted to your suite. The two-story suites are furnished in the style of traditional hotel rooms; set among groves of aspen and ponderosa pine, they have large living areas with sunken fireplace pits and wet bars. Each day a treat, such as a bowl of fruit and cheese or a small tin of cookies, is placed in your suite. And you get to take home the plush, monogrammed velour bathrobes.

You set your own pace at Tall Timber; about the only thing you'd need to schedule in advance is the optional helicopter ride to privately owned Emerald Lake, near the base of the Continental Divide. Otherwise, you can spend the day hiking to one of the nearby waterfalls, taking a guided canopy tour through the forest, casting for trout in the Animas River, playing nine holes of high-altitude golf, or just lounging by the pool. For lunch you can request a picnic to eat on the small deck by the hot tubs, overlooking the river. Sack lunches are also available if you plan to spend the day hiking or fishing. At dinner in the main lodge, you'll always have a great view of the dusky-violet mountain sunset— each table is by a bay window. The preset meals tend toward classics such as beef Wellington or grilled salmon; as much as possible, produce comes from Tall Timber's own vegetable and herb gardens. With your stomach full, you might spend some time in the carpeted hush of the library. An hour amid the leather couches, big stone fireplace, and 12,000 titles will get you ready for bed.

Several times a day, the steam train rolls through the resort, punctuating the silence with a brief reminder of the outside world; as you wave to the passengers, you may smile to yourself, realizing that you're likely the first sign of human life they've seen for miles.

Tip *Most guests arrive by helicopter, but the train is an enjoyable way to ease into the resort's isolation and take in the canyon scenery.*

📟 10 suites ▯◎▯ American plan, dining room, ice-cream parlor, bar, refrigerators. **Recreation:** fishing, hiking, horseback riding (nearby), running, wildlife viewing, soaring treetop adventures, indoor-outdoor pool, driving range, 9-hole golf course, putting green, basketball, board games, library. **Services:** golf equipment provided, 2 outdoor hot tubs, indoor hot tub, massage, sauna, helipad, tackle shop, laundry service, shop. **Classes and programs:** guided hikes, fly-fishing lessons. ♿ In-room fireplaces, some jetted tubs, private balconies; no a/c, no room phones, no room TVs, no smoking 📺 $440–$900 ▭ AE, D, MC, V.

🏠 *1 Silverton Star, Durango, CO 81301* 📞 *970/259–4813* ⊕ *www. talltimberresort.com.*

UTE MEADOWS INN BED & BREAKFAST
Laid-Back Adventure ~ Tranquil Outpost

With the peaks of the Elk Mountains as its backdrop, this gracious B&B stands on 300 acres of land that has been in Larry Darien's family since the 1930s. Based here, a 60-minute drive from the Aspen airport and a four-hour drive from Denver, you can spend your days hiking up to Lily Lake or along Raspberry Ridge or mountain biking along a jeep road to the ghost town of Crystal. Horseback riding, fly-fishing trips, and guided nature hikes take off from Outwest Guides, adjacent to the inn. You don't have to leave the grounds in winter, when the inn operates its Nordic center—15 km of trails groomed for classic and skate skiing. Snowshoers are allowed, too, as well as dogs, on all of the trails. The Dariens also maintain a couple of backcountry snowshoe trails. Climb up the one that ascends the flanks of Chair Mountain, and you'll be able to glimpse the tops of the Maroon Bells, a famous pair of peaks near Aspen.

Cap off your daily expeditions with a soak in the hot tub on a deck overlooking the Crystal River, or take a pre-dinner nap in your room. The Ute Meadows Inn's seven generously sized guest rooms are furnished in a combination of Mission-style and southwestern furniture, with small decorative details like horseshoes turned into curtain holders. All rooms and baths have radiant-heat floors. If you've brought your pooch, a basket of treats and cleanup aids is also provided. You'll wake up to a breakfast that's cooked to order from a small menu of dishes like omelets, French toast, and breakfast burritos. Early risers can scarf down a Continental breakfast before heading out. You can buy lunch next door at Elk Mountain Sandwich Shop, also run by the Dariens, where the specialties are barbecue beef and turkey sandwiches.

Just down the road from the inn is Marble, a hamlet with a one-room schoolhouse, quintessential Rocky Mountain scenery, and a marble quarry that provided the stone for the Lincoln Memorial and the Tomb of the Unknown Soldier in Washington, D.C. A 10-minute drive north brings you to Redstone, which has several restaurants and crafts galleries, and a castle built by the town founder in 1902. For more options, venture farther up the Crystal River valley to Carbondale or Glenwood Springs. Wine and dine to your heart's content, and then return to the comfort of the inn. Nightlife here might be a game of Scrabble in front of the river-rock fireplace in the living room. If that's too exciting for you, just enjoy the silence, punctuated only by the murmur of the river, from the balcony off your room.

Tip *The scenery around Marble shines in all seasons, but fall, when the aspens shimmer in hues of gold and sometimes orange, is the prettiest.*

↶ 7 rooms ⁑⃝ Full breakfast, restaurant. **Recreation:** fishing, hiking, horseback riding, wildlife viewing, cross-country skiing, snowshoeing, board games. Nearby: mountain biking, kayaking, rafting, telemark skiing. **Services:** cross-country ski and snowshoe rentals, outdoor hot tub, guided fishing trips, ski shop, horse boarding, kennel, laundry facilities, shop. **Classes and programs:** guided hikes, fly-fishing lessons. ⌂ Satellite TV, in-room data ports, some private balconies, some pets allowed (fee); no a/c, no room phones, no smoking ⌨ $119–$159 ▭ AE, D, MC, V.

⌂ *2880 County Rd. 3, Marble, CO 81623* ☎ *970/963–7088 or 888/883–6323* ▤ *970/963–0951* ⊕ *www.utemeadows.com.*

Connecticut

THE BOULDERS INN
Luxurious Resort ~ Romantic Retreat

The Boulders Inn is one of the most impressive inns in Connecticut—an 1890 Dutch colonial stone-and-shingle mansion built into Pinnacle Mountain and overlooking boomerang-shape Lake Waramaug in the blink-and-you'll-miss-it village of New Preston, 85 mi from New York and 45 mi from Hartford. A stately carriage house adjoins the inn, and eight sweet cottages are tucked into the woods behind. A refined air keeps company with a pleasant informality—the key to the inn's appeal.

The Boulders closed for several months in 2003 to completely refurbish the property, including the addition of a fitness room and spa suite. Reflecting the sophisticated touch of the designers commissioned to do the restoration, the inn again exudes an atmosphere of country elegance.

The main building contains three guest rooms and two suites, as well as a woodsy lounge and the inn's regionally renowned restaurant. In the carriage house are five rooms and two luxury suites, and there are eight guest cottages. Most units offer gratifying lake (and sunset) views. Outdoor decks or patios and stone fireplaces or freestanding woodstoves (plenty of firewood is piled outside each door) add appeal to all rooms but those in the main inn. All rooms and suites are decorated similarly in a palette of earth tones, with sepia prints on the walls, club chairs on either side of the fireplace, ceiling fans, and Berber carpet. Topped with damask-covered down duvets, beds are piled with pillows, a Pashmina shawl casually folded at the foot. All accommodations have a private bath with a deep tub (some jetted) and robes; each room also has a CD/DVD player.

The restaurant is wildly popular among locals and New York foodies, so advance bookings are required, even for guests. It's difficult to say which is more tantalizing: the view from the dining room or the selection of breakfast goodies. For dinner, Chef Paul Bernal highlights local and organic ingredients, which can be paired with more than 400 different wines from California and France.

For a brisk early-morning hike, hit the mile-long trail up Pinnacle Mountain, which begins right on the Boulders' property. It's an easy uphill climb, with the view from the top a worthwhile reward. Lake Waramaug, the second-largest natural lake in Connecticut (after nearby Bantam Lake), is steps from the inn. An 8-mi scenic drive around the shoreline is perfect for walking or biking. Canoeing and kayaking on the lake are three-season activities but are particularly nice in autumn when the leaves turn. Add swimming in summer and, if the temperature dips low enough for long enough, ice-skating in winter.

About 10 mi northwest of the inn, on U.S. 202 between Bantam and Litchfield, is White Memorial Foundation, a 4,000-acre wildlife sanctuary crisscrossed with 35 mi of old carriage roads and trails. There's no charge for hiking, biking, cross-country skiing, snowshoeing, or birding here, but the nature museum charges a small fee.

New Preston is right in the middle of the Litchfield Hills. Whether you want to fish for trout in the Housatonic, picnic at the base of Kent Falls, bird-watch at the Audubon Center in Sharon, ride the rapids near Cornwall Bridge, go to the Goshen Agricultural Fair, leaf-peep in Lakeville, or ski Mohawk Mountain, you're never more than a half-hour drive away.

Tip *Gardeners make the pilgrimage to White Flower Farm, a nursery 3 mi south of Litchfield on Route 63. A self-guided walking tour takes in the grounds, greenhouses, and display gardens. It will give you some good ideas to use in your yard at home.*

🛏 16 rooms, 4 suites ▯◯▮ Full breakfast, restaurant. **Recreation:** Nearby: biking, hiking, lake swimming, canoeing, kayaking, cross-country skiing, downhill skiing, ice-skating, snowshoeing. **Services:** bikes, canoes, and kayaks provided; gym; spa; meeting room. ⚓ In-room data ports, some in-room fireplaces, some jetted tubs, some private decks; no kids under 12, no smoking 💳 $350–$595 ▭ AE, MC, V.

📫 *P.O. Box 2575, New Preston, CT 06777* ☎ *860/868–0541 or 800/ 455–1565* 📠 *860/868–1925* ⊕ *www.bouldersinn.com.*

Delaware

INN AT MONTCHANIN VILLAGE
Tranquil Outpost

One of the nation's last intact examples of a 19th-century village is also one of the loveliest getaways in Delaware, about 5 mi from Wilmington. This small village began as a crossroads. Most of the original inhabitants were laborers who worked at the Du Pont powder mills along the nearby Brandywine River. Years later the settlement became a part of Winterthur, the showcase residence of the du Pont family, and to this day it remains part of the family's huge portfolio of real estate. Most of the current guesthouses were once living quarters for the workers; the old blacksmith shop is now the inn's restaurant; and the former dairy barn is where you check in.

Bits of Du Pont history can be found under just about any stone in the Brandywine Valley, and the inn is no exception. A fine example is the whimsical engravings of the trademark cow and crow hidden in each bathroom. Most rooms are completely restored and decorated with traditional, period antiques. The rooms are filled with paintings that range from traditional images of the surrounding landscape to colorful, fanciful paintings of animals. All rooms are spacious, but the suites are mammoth and have separate parlors. A great deal of attention was put into designing the bathrooms, each with Frette linens, large soaking tubs, marble-and-tile floors and walls, and European towel warmers. The majority of the rooms also have small porches with rocking chairs overlooking the rest of the hamlet.

Krazy Kat's restaurant presents a creative menu amid tiger-print chairs and vivid paintings of feisty felines. Fresh, organic ingredients dominate the tasty and sometimes indulgent menu. The jumbo lump crab bisque is topped with red pepper crème fraîche; the handmade potato gnocchi is infused with tomato and basil and completed with large slivers of shaved Parmesan. Hoisin-grilled organic chicken and grilled lamb satay are typical offerings on the menu.

Idyllic spots abound in and around the property. A full-time horticulturist tends to 4,000 square feet of gardens between the buildings. Take a stroll down Privy Lane, a cobblestone carriageway lighted by lanterns each evening. Aside from lanterns, the narrow walkway is lined with ivy-covered outhouses (no longer in use). Take time also to explore the expansive countryside that surrounds the inn. By bike, car, or foot, the relatively flat terrain is easy to navigate.

An authentic, though more expensive, way to see the valley is by horse: you can ride amazing public trails here. This is horse country, and fox hunting remains a pastime of the well-heeled locals. Bellevue State Park, about 15 minutes from the inn, has an equestrian center, and Brandywine Creek State Park, a two-minute drive from the inn, has trails that trace the shores of the Brandywine River (you'll need to rent a mount from a nearby stable). A few of the state parks also organize astronomy nights with seminars.

World-class greenhouses and gardens, housing rare and splendid flora, are a short drive from the inn. Winterthur, the du Pont estate turned into a museum in 1951 by H. F. du Pont, has a spectacular 60-acre garden that blooms almost year-round. Save plenty of time to explore the French-style gardens that stretch a third of a mile along Nemours, the 300-acre estate of Alfred du Pont. Longwood Gardens, also a du Pont estate, is a must-see, with more than 1,000 acres of gardens, greenhouses, meadows, and woodlands. If you have a fetish for orchids, you can spend hours collecting memories of many rare varieties.

Tip *Six miles from the inn in a 19th-century grist mill, the Brandywine River Museum displays paintings by N. C. Wyeth and his five children, among them Andrew Wyeth, as well as illustrations, still lifes, and landscapes by other American artists.*

➥ 28 rooms ⏸ Restaurant, room service, microwaves, refrigerators. **Recreation:** Nearby: biking, bird-watching, hiking, running, canoeing, golf privileges, tennis courts. **Services:** workout room, massage, laundry service, concierge, Internet access, meeting rooms. ♿ In-room data ports, in-room safes, in-room VCRs, some private porches; no smoking ⏀ $169–$375 ⊟ AE, D, DC, MC, V.

⌂ *Rte. 100 (Montchanin Rd.) and Kirk Rd., Montchanin, DE 19710* ☎ *302/888–2133 or 800/269–2473* 🖷 *302/888–0389* 🌐 *www.montchanin.com.*

LITTLE CREEK INN
Romantic Retreat ~ Tranquil Outpost

Even nature's freest creatures can't resist a stop at this three-story Italianate farmhouse at the end of a long and narrow tree-lined drive. Two miles east of Dover, Little Creek Inn sits in the migratory path of many different birds, especially waterfowl, and the surrounding property seems to be a favorite place for them to rest. In the eaves of the barn, swallows return each spring to their mud-packed nest. Mature bald eagles that make their home just a few miles down the road often fly overhead. And each autumn, thousands of geese land on the surrounding farmland. Other yearly visitors include mockingbirds, red-winged blackbirds, yellow and purple finches, and purple martins.

Miles of potato, corn, and soybean farms, as well as coastal inlets of Delaware Bay, surround this bed-and-breakfast. A large, red dairy barn peeks out from behind the circa-1860 farmhouse. Each guest room has a private bath and is filled with antiques and reproductions. The beds are tastefully covered in imported all-cotton linens, Amish quilts, and soft down pillows. The lounge is decked out in an eclectic mix of leather, cotton, and velvet.

An intense, power-packed jolt of nature awaits at Bombay Hook Wildlife Refuge. Car is the most popular method of exploring the large loop roads that traverse the Delaware Bay inlets, including saltwater ponds, marshland, and forest, but you can also hike one of the many marked trails or bike on the flat terrain. On a short visit to the refuge you can see dozens of silver and white heron and colorful characters like the oriole, depending on the time of year. If you visit in summer you may want to stick to driving—the bugs can be horrendous.

A smaller version of Bombay Hook, Little Creek Wildlife Refuge is managed primarily for waterfowl. This refuge has numerous viewing platforms that offer excellent perspectives on the wetlands and ponds. You can also go fishing and crabbing. If you're in the area at the end of May or beginning of June, you may want to visit Delaware Bay, a few miles from the inn, for the annual spawning of a strangely archaic arachnid: the horseshoe crab. The event draws thousands of spectators to Pickering and Bower's Beach, as well as hundreds of unusual shorebirds who come to dine on the eggs.

Tip *A popular event in the Delaware lowlands is the Amish bike tour. Each September thousands of people ride from 10 to 50 mi, stopping along the way at Amish stands that offer water and snacks.*

🛏️ 4 rooms, 1 suite 🍽️ Full breakfast. **Recreation:** biking, bird-watching, boccie, fishing, hiking, running, wildlife viewing, pool. Nearby: canoeing, driving range, 18-hole golf course, tennis court. **Services:** bikes provided, gym, laundry facilities. **Classes and programs:** cooking classes. ♿ Direct TV, in-room data ports, jetted tubs, dogs allowed; no kids under 12, no-smoking rooms, 💰 $100–$195 💳 AE, MC, V.

🏠 *2623 N. Little Creek Rd., Dover, DE 19901* 📞 *302/730–1300 or 888/ 804–1300* 📠 *302/730–4070* 🌐 *www.littlecreekinn.com.*

Florida

LITTLE PALM ISLAND
Luxurious Resort ~ Romantic Retreat

Close enough to Key West for a day trip or an evening out, but far enough from ordinary to seem like it's a world away, 5½-acre Little Palm Island perches on the southernmost brink of the United States. A tiny island off another tiny island (Little Torch Key), 75 mi down the Keys from mainland Florida, about 120 mi from Miami, it couldn't feel more removed. Thatch-roof villas, wind-tossed coconut palms, and luxuriant flowering plants give Little Palm Island a castaway, tropical-island look. This is the South Pacific, transplanted to Florida.

Much of what is special about the resort lies in what it doesn't have: cars, alarm clocks, room phones, and TVs. Fashioned for couples, the one-bedroom suites are furnished in Colonial plantation-style, each with a whirlpool tub for two, a bamboo-fuzzed hot-cold outdoor shower, and a porch with an ocean view. White mosquito netting drapes over your king-size four-poster bed beneath a dramatically pitched ceiling. Thoughtful touches make all the difference: candles, waffle-weave bathrobes, portable clip-on reading lights, personalized stationery, a beach bag packed with towels. Your room comes equipped with binoculars and a field guide for spying on the birds that hang out amid the orchids at the island's bird sanctuary. In the morning and evening you might spot a deer or two.

By day, you can retire to the thickly padded wooden chaises on the small sand beach. Or get out on the water in a sailboat or pontoon boat from the marina or book a scuba or deep-sea fishing excursion. The resort also runs bike tours of the National Key Deer Refuge on nearby Big Pine Key, which protects about 800 Key Deer—an endangered species of small, subtropical white-tailed deer. The tours continue at neighboring Little Heron National Refuge.

Whether you spend the day sea kayaking or swaying in your bungalow's hammock, end it with a visit to the small but complete Thai-inspired spa. A couples massage provides side-by-side pampering, with privacy curtains the only barrier between you and the clear blue, reef-rich Keys waters. Post-massage, a sunset cruise may be in order, or take a seat at the Palapa Bar and try a Piptini, a fresh citrus juice–and-rum libation that tastes deceptively like pink lemonade. The indoor-outdoor dining room serves top-notch Florida fusion fare made with local seafood and mangoes, avocados, coconuts, or key limes. Ask for a table right on the beach.

Tip *The resort offers a choice of meal plans. You may want to opt for the modified American plan and take your lunches at some of the colorful eateries on Key West and Big Pine Key.*

⇗ 30 suites ❘◎❘ Modified American plan, restaurant, room service, bar, lounge, minibars. **Recreation:** biking (nearby), bird-watching, fishing, wildlife viewing, beach, pool, scuba diving, snorkeling, boating, canoeing, kayaking, sailing, sea kayaking, library. **Services:** Windsurfers, sailboats, kayaks, canoes, fishing gear, and snorkeling equipment provided; boat and scuba-gear rentals; health club; hot tub; spa; dive shop; dock; guided fishing trips; marina; shop. **Classes and programs:** sightseeing tours. ♿ Jetted tubs, private porches; no room phones, no room TVs, no kids under 16, no smoking ▭ $745–$2,395 ▭ AE, D, DC, MC, V.

⌂ *28500 Overseas Hwy., Little Torch Key, FL 33042* ☎ *305/872–2524 or 800/343–8567* 🖷 *305/872–4843* ⊕ *www.littlepalmisland.com.*

OLD SALTWORKS CABINS
Family Hideout ~ Rustic Escape

From the Florida Panhandle, Cape San Blas juts into the Gulf of Mexico like the prong of a sprung safety pin. The long and lanky peninsula has such a tenuous grasp on the mainland that it might as well be an island, and it is so skinny that not much has ever been built here. Tall pines and magnolias line the lonely road that leads to this little-known strip of land. On Cape San Blas, the sandy soil supports whatever scrubby pines, reindeer moss, and oaks manage to survive salt assaults. From the road you can see practically everything there is to see, including St. Joseph Bay on one side and the Gulf of Mexico on the other.

Confederate troops once pumped seawater to make salt here, but Union forces destroyed the Old Saltworks in 1862. Today, a low-key resort with a minimuseum and a replica fort where children play recalls this history. Along 600 feet of bayfront across the road from the Gulf beach, Old Saltworks Cabins offers plain cabins, quaint cottages, and rental homes in the woods. At one end of the spectrum are motel cabin units with microwaves, and at the other, two-bedroom homes that sleep up to six with full kitchens. All the units are homey and functional, but the decor and furnishings vary from one to the next. Instead of maid service, you'll find profound peace and quiet.

Fishing, canoeing, and critter watching are the favorite pastimes at Old Saltworks. Ghost crabs, some bigger than a man's hand, mark the beach with their holes and scuff marks. In summer, loggerhead turtles nest while shorebirds and gulls patrol the dunes. In winter, you can help the resort owners keep an eye out for the green sea turtles that feed here. Throughout the year, you can see crabs, eagles, and ospreys along a 2-mi paddle run that passes the resort and state property.

The beach often feels desolate in its isolation, especially at St. Joseph Peninsula State Park, only 6 mi away. The park is a good place for swimming, snorkeling, fishing, hiking, and paddling. Farther afield, scalloping and scuba diving are the water sports of choice. You can sign up for either of these activities with local charters in nearby Port St. Joe. Take a scalloping charter to gather the blue-eyed sea scallop, an easy prize that can be collected only in a small area in summer. For the ultimate in beach seclusion, charter a boat to unbridged St. Vincent Island National Wildlife Refuge. Its native wildlife—white-tailed deer and reintroduced red wolves—coexists with exotic species such as Asian sambar deer and black bucks, imported when the island was a private hunting preserve.

Tip *Other than the blue-eyed sea scallops, the local culinary specialty is the Apalachicola oysters. You can get them raw, steamed, or baked at waterfront Indian Pass Raw Bar, east on Route C-30A in Indian Pass.*

⇨ 7 cabins, 7 houses ❑ Grills, some kitchens, microwaves, refrigerators. **Recreation:** biking, bird-watching, fishing, wildlife viewing, boating, canoeing, kayaking. Nearby: beach, scuba diving, snorkeling, playground. **Services:** canoe and kayak rentals, laundry facilities. **Classes and programs:** sightseeing tours. ⟁ Cable TV, some pets allowed (fee), private decks and porches; no TV in some rooms ▤ $89–$139 ▭ AE, D, MC, V.

🖃 *Box 526, Port St. Joe, FL 32457* ☎ *850/229–6097* ⊕ *www.oldsaltworks. com.*

WAKULLA SPRINGS LODGE
Tranquil Outpost

During the cotton-shipping era of the early 1930s, railroad magnate and entrepreneur Edward Ball built a railroad that steamed between Tallahassee and St. Marks. He so loved the eastern Florida Panhandle that in 1937 he erected a magnificent lodge with marble floors, handmade imported ceramic tile, and hand-painted cypress beams. The

Wakulla Springs Lodge is now the centerpiece of a 6,000-acre state park with nature trails, a playground, boat tours, and, of course, crystalline springs.

Edward Ball Wakulla Springs State Park lies in a part of Florida that was one of the first to be settled, yet it remains pristine. The park, along with St. Marks National Wildlife Refuge, preserves the woodsy landscape and the springs much as they were in the 16th century. Monarch butterflies, alligators, deer, herons, anhingas, ruby-throated hummingbirds, and cooter turtles dwell among the springs, river, and forest. In fall, migrating monarchs stop in St. Marks en route to Mexico, congregating at its historic lighthouse and setting the trees colorfully aflutter. Birding is good year-round but particularly during winter migrations.

Wakulla Springs Lodge stands at the edge of the park's 3-acre spring bowl. One of the world's largest freshwater springs and one of its deepest (at up to 185 feet), Wakulla pumps 400,000 gallons of 70°F water per minute into the Wakulla River. Kids love to leap off the dive tower into the deep, chilly waters. You can keep an eye on the young ones from the gently sloping sand beach or take a swim yourself. Many rooms and the suites (a bit more plush) have a view of the cypress-edged springs. On your way to the dining room, stop in the lobby to visit Old Joe, a 12-foot alligator mounted in a glass showcase. Then take a seat in the lodge's southern-style restaurant and order local seafood, fried chicken, or steak. Treat yourself at the ice-cream parlor afterward.

From the lodge, nature trails thread along high-ground hammocks and into a dreamy cypress dome. You can learn about the area's ecology at the state park's Waterfront Building, whose educational exhibits include a freshwater aquarium. A glass-bottom boat tour is a must, as Wakulla is one of the clearest springs among Florida's many. You'll easily spot fish, and you might catch a glimpse of the bones of a mastodon, lying at the mouth of an underwater limestone cave.

Within the park, the Historic Big Bend Saltwater Paddling Trail begins on the Wakulla River. The trail then runs out to the Gulf of Mexico past small fishing communities and up into the legendary Suwannee River, all the way to Georgia. (Look for outfitters in Tallahassee.) The Tallahassee–St. Marks Historic Railroad State Trail, the converted rail bed of Edward Ball's line, passes within 5 mi of the state park. Running 20 mi through town and country, the trail is used by cyclists, runners, skaters, and horseback riders. At its end lie the remains of a circa-1600 Spanish fort and a connection to the Florida National Scenic Trail, a great route for hikers.

Tip *Summer is high season in northern Florida. To avoid crowds, come after spring break and before summer vacation or, even better, in fall.*

27 rooms ⓘⒺ Restaurant, ice-cream parlor, grills, picnic area. **Recreation:** biking, bird-watching, fishing, beach, lake swimming, boating, canoeing, playground. **Services:** gift shop, meeting rooms. **Classes and programs:** guided nature walks, sightseeing tours. ⚐ No room TVs ⊠ $85–$105 ☰ AE, D, MC, V.

550 Wakulla Park Dr., Wakulla Springs, FL 32327 ☎ *850/224–5950* *850/561–7251* ⊕ *www.floridastateparks.org/wakullasprings.*

Georgia

BARNSLEY GARDENS
Luxurious Resort

Among the wonderfully preserved ruins of an antebellum mansion, this otherworldly resort is just 60 mi north of Atlanta. It's hard to believe the distance is so short—the journey to Barnsley Gardens doesn't just transport you from the city, it effectively transports you to another era.

Gardens and vine-draped antebellum ruins are the centerpiece and inspiration for this sumptuous retreat in the foothills of Georgia's Appalachian Mountains. A stroll through the gardens and past the brick-and-wood skeleton of the former mansion gives you a full sense of the pride and the sorrow this place held for its inhabitants so long ago. "Straight from the pages of a classic novel" is a phrase you read in many a brochure, but in the case of the mansion at Barnsley Gardens, it's true.

The mansion was built in the early 1840s by Godfrey Barnsley, a British expatriate, for his new Southern bride, who died before the mansion was completed. Heartbroken, Barnsley left the estate unfinished until, legend says, the spirit of his wife appeared to him in the fountain of the formal garden and instructed him to finish the estate for their children and future generations. Barnsley later lost his fortune in the Civil War, but it was a tornado in 1906 that ultimately rendered the main mansion uninhabitable, though Barnsley descendants continued to live on the property until 1942, when the estate was finally auctioned.

Consider this: Almost every remaining antebellum structure of the South—rare as it is after the marauding torches of Union troops during the Civil War—has been restored to its former glory. Staircases have been rebuilt, window-seat cushions have been sewn with attention to detail of the period, and occasionally matrons wander the grounds in period garb offering lessons in turn-of-the-20th-century candle making. The mansion at Barnsley Gardens, on the other hand, is preserved rather than restored, as a glorious ruin. As you walk within the moss-covered brick walls, along the remaining mottled pine floor planks, and look out at the gardens through the archways where giant windows once stood, the history of this house seems right at hand.

But the ruins are only one facet of this resort. In all, the 1,300-acre Barnsley Gardens has fishing, horseback riding, and other outdoor sports—and one of the most sophisticated spas in the region. The garden is always flourishing, with honeysuckle and magnolias in early summer and Carolina yellow jessamine and Christmas roses in late winter. The garden itself is so large that a walk through it qualifies as an easy hike. An additional 12½ mi of trails run along double-track fire roads and more strenuous single-track trails through forest, meadows, and mountains. The trails take you past a 10-acre lake perfect for fly-fishing and a lazy pasture that is home to a small herd of bison.

The 33 cottages on the property are more like micro-mansions, the kind you might find decorating the miniature golf course of a very wealthy, very pampered population of giants. The cottages house 70 individually decorated suites, each with a front and back porch. In the suites are stone fireplaces, king-size sleigh or poster beds, deep claw-foot bathtubs, and 12-foot ceilings. The three superb restaurants (one open Friday and Saturday evenings only) offer a successful mix of southern and Continental cuisines, with entrées like wild mushroom–and–goat cheese strudel and Vidalia onion–crusted Alaskan halibut. The wine lists deserve attention, as well.

Tip *Barnsley Gardens is immensely pet-friendly and even offers a turndown service specifically suited to four-legged critters, with gourmet kibble and Evian water as an evening treat.*

🛏 70 suites ❙○❙ 3 restaurants, lounge, grocery store, picnic area, kitchenettes. **Recreation:** biking, hiking, horseback riding, wildlife viewing, pool, 18-hole golf course, putting green, 3 tennis courts. **Services:** gym, health club, hot tub, spa, steam room, babysitting, dry-cleaning service, laundry service, meeting rooms. **Classes and programs:** guided hikes, guided nature walks, history tours. ♿ Satellite TV, in-room fireplaces, private porches, some pets allowed, no-smoking rooms 💳 $289–$390 🖃 AE, D, MC, V.

🗐 *597 Barnsley Gardens Rd., Adairsville, GA 30103* 📞 *770/773–7480 or 877/773–2447* 📠 *770/773–1779* 🌐 *www.barnsleyresort.com.*

GLEN-ELLA SPRINGS
Tranquil Outpost

Once an Indian trail, a 5-mi gravel road leads to this restored hotel. Built in 1875, the inn has served as a hotel on and off over the decades. In the reception area hang old photographs of tired travelers, saddles in their hands and dust in their hair. The hotel retains much of the flavor that has made it such an appealing resting spot all those years ago.

It's a wonder that this marvelous place is still a relative secret, but the bigger wonder is that the proprietors, Barrie and Bobby Aycock, have managed to preserve the property without pasteurizing it.

The rooms are fine examples of bucolic grace and comfort. There are no in-room TVs, but no worry: there is plenty to see once you open the French doors onto the veranda with rocking chairs. The scenery is a panorama of meadows, complete with deer. Depending on the season, the pastures are lush with wild blackberries, muscadines, honeysuckle, or mountain laurel. The beds are big and comfortable, with hand-stitched quilts and bed frames that look as if they were built by pioneers. The floors are the original heart of pine, smoothed to a handsome polish by time and care, and splendidly uneven. The bathrooms are contrastingly modern, though, with jetted tubs and toiletries.

The inn proper is the same size it was at the turn of the 20th century, but modern structures have been added around it. A recreation building stands close by, at the other end of the inn's extensive, immaculate garden. Here you can mingle with other guests or watch satellite TV. The Glen-Ella Springs restaurant draws a loyal crowd with a dinner menu that is as sophisticated as the surroundings are rustic. Entrées range from macadamia nut–encrusted chicken to Low Country shrimp on stone-ground grits. Breakfasts are just as mouthwatering with their blueberry pancakes and vegetable and meat frittatas.

All but enveloped by 750,000-acre Chattahoochee National Forest, the inn puts you close to hundreds of miles of trails. Hire a local outfitter to show you the forest's best fishing spots; the lakes are stocked with rainbow trout. Tallulah Gorge, Black Rock Mountain, and Moccasin Creek state parks offer more fishing and hiking. There is some world-class white-water rafting in the area as well as flat-water paddling. Horseback riding is available at local stables.

Tip *Habersham County is dry, so bring your own spirits.*

⇨ 12 rooms, 4 suites ⦿ Restaurant, picnic area. **Recreation:** biking, bird-watching, fishing, hiking, horseback riding, running, wildlife viewing, swimming, library, recreation room. **Services:** pool, meeting room. ⬙ Some in-room jacuzzis; no room TVs ⊠ $140–$265 ▤ AE, D, MC, V.

⌂ *1789 Bear Gap Rd., Clarkesville, GA 30523* ☏ *706/754–7295* ⎙ *706/ 754–1560* ⊕ *www.glenella.com.*

GREYFIELD INN
Laid-Back Adventure ~ Romantic Retreat

Cumberland Island National Seashore lies along Georgia's southern coast, accessible only via a single ferry, and only to a limited number of visitors daily. The island is a sanctuary of marshes, lakes, ponds, estuar-

ies, and inlets. Its waterways are home to alligators, crocodiles, sea turtles, otters, snowy egrets, great blue herons, ibises, wood storks, and
hundreds of other bird species. Its oak forests thrive with wildlife as
well—armadillos, deer, mink, raccoons, and snakes. Tree frogs sing from
the tangle of gnarled, moss-festooned tree limbs. Perhaps the most magical attraction on Cumberland Island is its nearly untouched beach.
Rolling dunes expand a shoreline that is nearly 1,000 feet wide at low
tide, and fiddler, hermit, and ghost crabs and wild horses are your only
companions.

Cumberland Island's only accommodations are in Greyfield Inn, a
stately, shaded mansion built in 1900 by the family of Thomas Carnegie
(brother of industrialist Andrew). Their several splendid homes fell to
ruin over time and the island remained essentially as nature created it.
You can explore the mansions as you discover them during hikes, bike
rides, and naturalist-led jeep outings. The remains of Thomas Carnegie's
great estate, Dungeness, have a special tumble-down beauty.

Today the Greyfield Inn remains the sole habitable structure on the island, but what a magnificent relic it is. It was opened to the public in
1962 by Thomas Carnegie's granddaughter, and it retains its original
furnishings from the turn of the 20th century. The inn's public areas
are filled with Carnegie family mementos, accoutrements, and portraits.
It is a wonderfully isolated and atmospheric place, with no TVs, phones,
or newspapers.

There's no place else to eat on the island; all of your meals, as well as
hors d'oeuvres, are included in your room rate. Breakfast is a lavish affair, with fresh-squeezed juices, eggs, an assortment of bread, and such
chef's specialties as lemon-cottage cheese pancakes. Lunch is provided
as a picnic that you can take on your daily outings. The evening cocktail
hour is a gracious segue to such a comfortably elegant dinner as roast
tenderloin of beef, shrimp mashed potatoes, and homemade seasonal
berry pies.

Tip *January and February are the best months for beachcombing. Winter
storms blow through from the northeast, leaving the beaches littered with
seashells.*

🛏 12 rooms, 4 suites 🍴 Dining room, bar. **Recreation:** biking, bird-
watching, fishing, hiking, kayaking, wildlife viewing, beach, library.
Services: massage. **Classes and programs:** guided hikes, guided nature walks, off-road tours. ⚒ No room TVs, no kids under 5
💳 $350–$575 🖃 AE, D, MC, V.

🏠 *8 N. 2nd St. (Box 900), Fernandina Beach, FL 32035* 📞 *904/261–6408*
📠 *904/321–0666* 🌐 *www.greyfieldinn.com.*

LAKE RABUN HOTEL
Tranquil Outpost

A cross between a country inn, a mountain lodge, and a prairie boardinghouse, Lake Rabun Hotel stands against an embankment across the road from the peaceful 835-acre lake after which it is named. Lake Rabun, near the little town of Tallulah Falls in far northeastern Georgia, is straight from the pages of a Mark Twain masterpiece. Bordered by the Blue Ridge Mountains and surrounded by Chattahoochee National Forest, the lake is in waterfall territory, near the Southeast's most magnificent waterfall. In Tallulah Falls Gorge State Park, hiking trails range in difficulty from challenging to downright daredevil, and the endangered peregrine falcon soars overhead.

Dating as far back as the 1920s, some of the summer homes along the shores of Lake Rabun are contemporaries of the Lake Rabun Hotel, which remains almost exactly as it was constructed in 1922. With the exception of some mended patches here and there, the hotel is completely paneled—walls, ceilings, and floors—with the original wood. The structure itself is in amazing shape, considering it hasn't seen much modernization in the last century, but what improvements there are make a stay here more than restful.

Evidence abounds that this place is treasured by its present owner, Mark Harrison. A builder who grew up nearby, he has taken care to preserve the hotel's character. The rooms at the Lake Rabun Hotel are somewhat small and not all have private baths, but the price and the place more than make up for it. Much of the furniture was fashioned of mountain laurel and rhododendron birch by early-20th-century craftsmen. The rugged fireplace in the Great Room serves as a focal point, embodying the hotel's convivial style.

The Boars Head Saloon—part roadhouse and part fish camp—has been a favorite local watering hole for ages. In the morning it doubles as the breakfast room. And what a breakfast! It's a wonderful way to spend each morning—sitting on the saloon's deck under a canopy of trees, overlooking the lake, coffee in hand. In the evening, after a drink in the saloon, you can take a seat in the restaurant for hearty entrées like prime rib and pub fare like fried chicken wings. Harrison's mother runs the kitchen, and it's worth waiting for her to emerge from behind the stove for some conversation steeped in sweet, genuine southern charm.

Tip *Ask the hotel staff for detailed directions to some of the area's numerous unmapped waterfalls.*

🛏 11 rooms ⑩ Restaurant, bar. **Recreation:** biking, bird-watching, fishing, hiking, horseback riding, wildlife viewing, lake and river swimming, swimming hole, boating, canoeing, jet skiing, kayaking, rafting, rowing. ⚠ No a/c in some rooms, no room phones, no room TVs, no smoking 💳 $59–$79 ☰ AE, D, MC, V.

⌕ *Lake Rabun Rd. (Box 10), Lakemont, GA 30552-0010* ☎ *706/782–4946* ⊕ *www.lakerabunhotel.com.*

LODGE ON LITTLE ST. SIMON'S
Laid-Back Adventure

Accessible only by boat, the Lodge on Little St. Simons Island is set amid 7 mi of beaches teeming with red-tailed hawks, pelicans, armadillos, and other wildlife. This former hunting lodge, built in 1917, was once popular among presidents and dignitaries. Sepia-tinged photographs from the past line the walls in the lodge's main building.

Aside from a few unpretentious private cabins occupied by the staff, the lodge stands by itself on the island. The main building, referred to simply as the Hunting Lodge, looks much as it always has. The hefty, sprawling cabin, with mounted animal-head trophies in the Game Room, looks like the sort of place Hemingway would have liked. The living room, which houses the bar (drinks are complimentary), serves as a gathering place. It has a large brick fireplace, pine-bough and antique wicker furnishings, hunting paraphernalia, and other memorabilia faded to an aged patina. Off the living room are two guest rooms, each filled with period furniture and framed photographs. The newer cabins are fresh and minimalist, many with sprawling verandas where you can watch sunsets over the virgin marshland. Each cabin houses two or more guest rooms around a great room with an elegant fireplace.

Little St. Simon's Island is alive with wildlife, including fallow deer, river otters, and blue herons. The American alligator is at home in the island's briny Myrtle Pond. Many birders consider the island, with its more than 280 species of birds, one of the best birding locations on the eastern seaboard. The lodge proprietors have long been devotees of wildlife conservation, and they offer educational tours daily as part of the room package. Their interpretive programs are a matchless opportunity to observe and learn about the natural history of a pristine barrier island. Any activity related to the water—fishing, canoeing, beachcombing, swimming—is popular.

Low Country cooking prevails in the kitchen. This is, after all, where Low Country cuisine originated. The menu draws amply on seafood and shellfish from the waters surrounding the island. Breakfast specialties include peach-pecan pancakes, coarsely ground grits with tasso gravy, and homemade buttermilk biscuits. Meals are served in the main lodge, at long oak tables braced by big cedar tree trunks.

Tip *On the Atlantic flyway, Little St. Simon's attracts nonresident birds during spring and fall migrations. Look for bird-lover specials and lectures by bird experts.*

⤴ 15 rooms ⏹ Dining room, lounge. **Recreation:** biking, bird-watching, fishing, hiking, horseback riding, running, wildlife viewing, beach, boating, canoeing, kayaking, library, recreation room. **Services:** Internet access. **Classes and programs:** guided hikes, guided nature walks, natural history programs. ⏺ No room TVs 🖭 $450–$675 ▭ AE, D, MC, V.

✉ *Box 21078, Little St. Simons Island, GA 31522-0578* ☎ *888/733-5774* 🖨 *912/634–1811* ⊕ *www.littlestsimonsisland.com.*

THE OVERLOOK INN
Romantic Retreat

Perched 3,000 feet on Fort Mountain, near the towns of Chatsworth and Ellijay in northeastern Georgia, the Overlook commands a panoramic view of Chattahoochee National Forest and the Blue Ridge Mountains. The vista is especially brilliant in fall, when the trees surrounding the Lake at Fort Mountain erupt into color. Based at the inn, you can explore Fort Mountain State Park to your heart's content.

At the inn's heart is the Council Room, a clubby space of hardwood floors, seasoned leather furnishings, ornately woven rugs, and a wood-burning fireplace. Here you take your breakfast, play cards and board games in the afternoon, or relax with wine and cheese in the evening. Guest rooms are abundantly furnished, and each has its own character, but there are certain unifying features, such as private porches, hot tubs, gas fireplaces, and that spectacular mountain view. Most rooms have 12-foot-high ceilings and beds plush with quilting, lace, and pillows. Some have double-pedestal sinks in the vanity, and one has a wall constructed of local stone.

A wooded trail makes the mountain accessible practically from your door. As you hike the Fort Mountain trails you can easily uncover arrowheads and other Indian artifacts with your hand or a garden trowel. A nearby excavation site, the Etowah Indian Mounds, is a relic of the Mississippian Period. A city populated by thousands of people stood on this site 500 years ago, protected by a ditch that is still 100 feet deep in some places. On the earthen mounds within stood the city's temples and a ceremonial plaza. Cherokee once lived here as well, and Fort Mountain is named for several stone forts surrounded by mystery. The Cherokee said they were built by a race of "Moon Eyes," whose blue or light eyes were said to pierce the darkness. Another account tells of a mysterious Welsh prince who came up from the South and constructed the forts as protection against the Cherokee. A third account attributes the stone forts to a Spanish conquistador.

Tip *Nearby Ellijay is the heart of Georgia apple country. Several u-pick orchards operate late August through December, and roadside stands sell* *apples galore. The town hosts the Georgia Apple Festival the second and third weekends of October, when you can taste all kinds of apples and everything that can be made with apples.*

🛏 5 rooms, 9 cabins ⏐◎⏐ Dining room, lounge, picnic area. **Recreation:** library. Nearby: biking, bird-watching, fishing, hiking, horseback riding, mountain biking, running, wildlife viewing, lake and river swimming, boating, canoeing, kayaking, rafting. **Services:** yoga classes, Internet access, meeting rooms. ⚷ In-room fireplaces, some jetted tubs, private porches; no room phones, no kids under 16, no smoking 💳 $159–$229 ▭ AE, D, MC, V.

🏠 *864 Wilderness View, Chatsworth, GA 30705* ☎ *706/517–8810* 📠 *706/517–9418* ⊕ *www.theoverlookinn.com.*

PURA VIDA USA SPA & YOGA RETREAT
Tranquil Outpost

This country retreat is so cheerfully dedicated to your relaxation and mental rejuvenation that it gives any major-league spa a run for its money. Eighty miles north of Atlanta, it stands at the base of the Blue Ridge Mountains minutes from the former gold-mining settlement of Dahlonega.

The retreat's main building is a reproduction 1920s-style farmhouse with a sprawling porch to take advantage of the phenomenal view of the mountains and forest. In the 12 guest rooms, memorabilia, antiques, and collectibles establish a country style. In addition to the rooms in the main guesthouse and the Barn, a number of cabins, called Bear Dens, dot the woods. The Barn, which serves as a communal gathering area, is attached to the main guesthouse via a breezeway overlooking the wildflower gardens.

You can spend your days strolling the gardens, feeding the fish in the pond, or exploring the nature trails through the property's stands of mountain laurel, great oaks, pines, and dogwoods. Not far away is the southern terminus of the Appalachian Trail, along with Amicalola Falls, Talullah Gorge, and several state parks. Head for the hills or stay home and try the yoga classes for which the retreat is known. A sophisticated menu of spa treatments is also available, and the outdoor Jacuzzi is heaven-sent.

Tip *Dahlonega is chock-full of shops, restaurants, and historic attractions from gold-mining days. It seems there's always a festival or special event going on.*

🛏 12 rooms, 8 cabins ⏐◎⏐ Restaurant, lounge. **Recreation:** biking, bird-watching, fishing, hiking, horseback riding, running, wildlife viewing, boating, canoeing, kayaking, rafting, wine tasting, recreation room. **Services:** outdoor hot tub, spa, shop, meeting rooms. **Classes and programs:** fitness and yoga classes. ⟨ No-smoking rooms; no room phones, no room TVs ⟨ $100–$160 ⟨ AE, MC, V.

⟨ *400 Blueberry Hill, Dahlonega, GA 30533* ⟨ *866/345–4900* ⟨ *706/ 865–7442* ⟨ *www.puravidausa.com.*

Hawai'i

FOUR SEASONS RESORT HUALALAI
Family Hideout ~ Luxurious Resort

On the west coast of the Big Island, 7 mi north of Kona International Airport, endangered green sea turtles forage the reefs, and tide pools warmed by the sun provide shelter to hundreds of black crabs. "Kona nightingales," the shy, feral offspring of the donkeys that lugged Kona coffee around in earlier days, wander the land. And on a $\frac{1}{2}$-mi stretch of beach at historic Ka'upulehu, the Four Seasons Resort Hualalai is a fantasyland of ponds and swimming pools, lush with laua'e fern and heliconia flowers.

Arranged in groups, low-rise bungalows contain spacious Hawaiian vintage-style guest rooms decorated with Hawaiian artwork. Floors of copper-gray slate, details in local wood, and rattan furnishings in soothing whites and earth tones create a cool tranquillity indoors, and a private garden or lanai allows you to savor the soft, subtropical breeze. Some rooms have an outdoor shower surrounded by orchids and ferns and shaded by a bamboo roof.

When you leave your room, you walk on meandering pathways through meticulously landscaped grounds. For a little exercise, hike or jog a $4\frac{1}{3}$-mi loop around the property, part of it on ancient foot trails along the shoreline. The resort is surrounded by lava flows where you can glimpse Hawai'i's volcanic essence, but the three-hour drive to Hawai'i Volcanoes National Park is worth your time. Within the park is 13,677-foot Mauna Loa, the world's biggest volcano, and Kilauea, the world's most active. A network of trails crisscrosses the eerie lava landscape, where unfamiliar native plants grow and exotic native birds trill against a backdrop of volcanic steam plumes.

Ka'upulehu was once an important fishing center, a fact reflected in the anchialine fishponds (brackish ponds subject to the ebb and flow of the tide) scattered around the resort. Filled with fish and surrounded by native grasses and plants, the ponds attract wildlife. At dawn or dusk, walk over to Waiakauhi Pond, on the southern end of the property, and you might glimpse a *koloa* (Hawaiian duck) or a *ae'o* (Hawaiian stilt), native birds that are returning to the area after an absence of many years. To see the fish, go snorkeling at King's Pond, carved from an 18th-century *pahoehoe* lava flow and fed by natural springs. Three spotted eagle rays hold court in its waters, among 4,000-plus fishes of 40 species. Learn about the history of the ponds and the culture of the people who once fished them by visiting the resort's Cultural Center. Interpretative *koa*-wood–framed paintings by Herb Kawainui Kane depict the people's arts and endeavors, and a Hawaiian star compass reveals how they navigated the ocean according to the skies.

When you don't feel like exploring the area, go to the spa for some pampering. Spa treatments, such as the vanilla- and honey-scented South Seas sugar scrub, followed by a Vichy shower, will leave you thoroughly relaxed. The pampering continues when night falls and the aroma of grilled fresh fish fills the air. The resort's restaurants base their menus on local ingredients and offer many wellness-oriented and vegetarian dishes. While you dine, the sinking sun sets the sandy beach aglow before the stars come out.

Tip *Bungalows are clustered around the resort's swimming pools. The quietest grouping surrounds the secluded adult pool, near Waiakauhi Pond. For families, the Sea Shell Pool bungalows are a favorite.*

243 rooms, 31 suites ❙◎❙ Coffee shop, 3 restaurants, 2 bars, refrigerators. **Recreation:** bird-watching, running, beach, 5 pools, snorkeling, 18-hole golf course, 8 tennis courts, basketball, volleyball, recreation room. **Services:** health club, 4 outdoor hot tubs, spa, pro shop, babysitting, dry cleaning service, laundry service, shop, business services, Internet access, concierge, meeting rooms. **Classes and programs:** fitness classes, children's programs (ages 5–12), teen activities. In-room data ports, in-room safes, private patios and porches. $560–$7,320 AE, DC, MC, V.

100 Ka'upulehu Dr. (Box 1269), Kailua-Kona, HI 96745 ☎ *808/325-8000 or 800/332-3442* 🖷 *808/325-8100* ⊕ *www.fourseasons.com.*

HOTEL HĀNA-MAUI AND HONUA SPA
Luxurious Resort

It doesn't matter how you get here, by commuter air or the famous Hāna Highway: Hāna will impress you even if you've been everywhere and done everything. If you drive, your journey along cliff-hugging Hāna Highway will be an introductory immersion course in the splendor of this part of Maui. The road's 600 curves and 54 one-lane bridges take you past magnificent bays, pristine beaches, towering waterfalls, and pastureland so green that you might envy the cattle who graze here. Along the way, linger over the scent of banks of wild ginger, or pluck a fresh guava from a tree. In fruit season, signs in residents' yards invite you to pick your own mangoes.

The abundance of Hāna begets a generosity that is at the heart of the Hotel Hāna-Maui. From the moment the staff greets you with a fresh flower lei, a cold towel, and a glass of freshly squeezed island juice, the hotel is at your service, ready to help you have the vacation of your dreams. If that means never leaving your lanai for the duration of your stay, so be it. There are no clocks here, no in-room televisions. Cell-phone service is pretty much nonexistent. Your body clock will be reset by the sound of the surf, the call of the birds, and the path of the sun as it makes its lazy way west over a somnolent ocean.

On 67 acres that slope to the sea, Hotel Hāna-Maui offers plantation-style cottages with ocean views and garden suites. Interiors, in sea-foam greens and terra-cotta yellows, are accented with patterns taken from ancient Hawaiian Kapa prints. Feather-top beds are made up with Coyuchi-brand organic cotton sheets. Large bathrooms have a soaking tub and separate walk-in shower; many of the Sea Ranch cottages also have a hot tub on their private outdoor deck. You reach your room via pathways that cross manicured lawns planted with blossoming trees, ginger plants, wild orchids, and coconut palms whispering in the breeze.

You can learn about the foliage on a plant walk or learn a little bit about the local culture at hula, ukulele, and lei-making lessons. Let your body unwind at yoga classes. A full-service spa features massage suites and a Watsu pool. A three-hole pitch-and-putt golf course overlooking the bay invites casual practice. A few minutes away via complimentary shuttle is a beach called Hamoa, a perfect crescent strand of black and silver sand. The hotel will deliver a picnic lunch to you at the beach at a predetermined time. If you're feeling energetic, you can explore Hāna on foot or horseback, or by ocean kayak or jeep. Guided excursions will take you to 472-acre Kahanu Gardens and its *Pi'ilanihale Heiau* (temple), Ka'eleku Caverns, Waimoko Falls, Ohe'o Gulch, and Waianapanapa State Park.

It's easy to nourish your body as well as your soul at Hotel Hāna-Maui. Begin your day with mango sausage or an heirloom spinach omelet, and at lunch move on to a pohole fern salad and kalua pig melt. Lunch or dinner, vegetarian choices include a crispy tofu roll or edamame ravioli. For heartier appetites, there is Angus beef and the fresh bounty of the sea, such as fennel-crusted mahimahi. And if the regular delivery of fish doesn't arrive, no worry: there's always someone in town willing to share the catch of the day.

Tip *For the utmost in privacy, request Sea Ranch Cottage 217 or 218, which are closest to the ocean. Both have a private hot tub with a cliffside view of the surf and the starlit sky.*

23 suites, 46 cottages, 1 house ❯ 2 restaurants, room service, bar, lounge, mini-refrigerators. **Recreation:** biking, croquet, hiking,

horseback riding, 2 pools, 2 whirlpools, snorkeling, 3-hole golf course, 2 tennis courts, library. Nearby: beach, basketball, softball. **Services:** bicycles, Boogie boards, golf clubs, snorkeling gear, and tennis rackets provided; fitness room; salon; spa; babysitting; laundry service; shops; airport shuttle; car rental; concierge; Internet access. **Classes and programs:** guided hikes and nature walks; ukulele, hula, and lei-making lessons; fitness and yoga classes. ☖ Private patios and decks; no a/c, no room TVs, no smoking ▱ $425–$1,625 ▭ AE, D, DC, MC, V.

⌂ *Hāna Hwy. (Box 9), Hāna, HI 96713* ☎ *808/248–8211 or 800/ 321–4262* 🖷 *808/248–7202* ⊕ *www.hotelhanamaui.com.*

KALANI OCEANSIDE RETREAT
Tranquil Outpost

On the Big Island's peaceful southeastern coast lies a retreat on 19 acres of cleared jungle. As remote as can be, Kalani, which means "heavenly" in Hawaiian, delivers on its name. Here you can stroll amid banana and papaya trees and ginger, plumeria, and heliconia plants. Close by, on the other side of a narrow, winding road, you can look for sea turtles and whales from grassy outcrops above the turquoise ocean while the surf pounds at steep cliffs and black-sand coves below. Maybe you'd prefer to hike across a lava flow that has wiped out a spectacular beach, or take a walk under the oceanfront ironwood trees in 13-acre Mackenzie State Park.

This isolated retreat set in rural Hawaiian wilderness attracts those who seek genuine friendliness, a healthful lifestyle, and artistic inspiration. In spacious hexagonal lodges or smaller cottages, the basic guest rooms are decorated with Hawaiian prints. Most rooms share baths. The focus is clearly on nature and its benefits for human nature. About 40 resident volunteers and guest teachers offer a smorgasbord of activities that range from Watsu treatments, massage, and music jams to yoga, tai chi, and dance sessions held in light-filled studios and a big tent with a suspended wood floor.

You can take part in as many or as few retreat activities as you wish; you can even be quite alone. Off-property, incredible landscape awaits exploration. Close to steaming inland thermal springs, the burned tree molds of Lava Tree State Park provide a powerful introduction to Hawai'i's unsettled, volcanic nature. Not far away, at an elevation of 4,000 feet and up, is Hawai'i Volcanoes National Park, where the Pu'u O'o vent of Kilauea has been erupting since 1983. Hundreds of hiking trails lead across lava and through rain forest. As you hike, the trill of native honeycreeper birds may draw your attention to the yellow and red blossoms of 'ohia trees and to tree ferns that are taller than you.

After a day spent looking outward or inward, you can replenish yourself with a meal made with locally grown organic produce and served on a lanai. Most of the dishes at Kalani's restaurant are vegetarian, but fresh fish appears on the menu almost daily. When dinner's through, head for the pool and take a clothing-optional dip beneath the stars, or put yourself in the hands of a water therapy practitioner in an aquatic bodywork pond. Take a hula lesson or hang out in the retreat's funky no-smoking café and sip a mug of local coffee. Or just spend your night gazing at the thousands of stars above.

Tip *Kalani hosts family weeks, African drumming workshops, retreats for naturalists, gay and lesbian gatherings, and other programs that you might enjoy or that might intrude on your time off. Check the schedule of events on the retreat's Web site, or telephone before you book.*

⤎ 37 rooms, 3 with private bath; 13 cottages ⑩ Café, restaurant, some refrigerators. **Recreation:** biking, hiking, clothing-optional beach (nearby), pool, tennis court, volleyball, weight room. **Services:** outdoor hot tub, massage, sauna, yoga studio, laundry service, shop, wireless Internet access. **Classes and programs:** guided hikes; off-road tours; meditation, stress management, and tai chi lessons; yoga classes; sightseeing tours. ♿ Some a/c, no room phones, no room TVs, no smoking ▱ $110–$240 ▭ AE, MC, V.

🏠 *R.R. 2, (Box 4500), Pahoa Beach Rd., Pahoa, HI 96778* ☎ *808/965–7828 or 800/800–6886* 📠 *808/965–0527* ⊕ *www.kalani.com.*

LODGE & BEACH VILLAGE AT MOLOKA'I RANCH
Family Hideout ~ Laid-Back Adventure

As you exit Moloka'i (Hoolehua) Airport, you drive past a hand-painted sign that reads, "Aloha. Slow down, this is Moloka'i. Thank you." It's good advice, and it's easy to follow on this island, where there are no stoplights and no buildings taller than a mature coconut tree. In the blink of an eye, the rain can color the valleys a deep velvet green or the sun can parch the ranch lands into a soft, creamy yellow for as far as the eye can see. The world's tallest sea cliffs reside on Moloka'i, and the ancient art of hula was born here. Hawai'i's history, spirit, and beauty are revered throughout the islands, but here they seem most protected.

The Sheraton Moloka'i Lodge & Beach Village, on the western end of the island, embodies Moloka'i's contrasts. Sitting grandly at an elevation of 1,200 feet, above the western slopes of Moloka'i Ranch, is the luxurious Hawaiian Lodge. Eight miles below via coral and dirt road, on Kuapoa Beach, is the ranch's Beach Village, a collection of canvas bungalows. Whichever accommodation you choose, you will have access to 54,000 acres of extravagantly forested glens, open pastureland,

and white-sand beaches backed by cliffs. You'll also be treated to some of the island's most glorious sunsets.

The beach bungalows, which might be described as permanent tents on platforms, are likely to appeal to your inner Robinson Crusoe. The bungalows have no phones, no electricity, and no place to plug in your hair dryer or phone charger. Solar power provides lighting, as well as hot water for the pull-string shower (complete with sunroof), and your private bath is equipped with a compost toilet. Instead of an alarm clock or an automated wake-up call, you can ask to be awakened by Beach Village staff, who will rouse you gently into consciousness from outside your canvas door. From your bungalow you step right out onto your own deck, and you have a private picnic table.

If you prefer a few more creature comforts, such as cable television, a king-size bed, and a claw-foot soaking tub, the Hawaiian Lodge might be more to your liking. Designed in traditional plantation style, the lodge centers on a great room with a two-story fireplace and oversize sofas and chairs. Guest rooms, with a residential look, are decorated with Hawaiian artwork and classic Hawaiian quilt-pattern bedspreads.

Whether you stay in the Beach Village or the Hawaiian Lodge (you might spend a few nights at each), you will have access to all of the ranch's facilities. The lodge even has showers and changing rooms with lockers for Beach Villagers who want to tidy up when they come to the lodge for meals. Children can participate in organized shoreline walks, tide-pool explorations, or lessons in how to catch fish the way the ancient Hawaiians did—by casting nets into the sea. You can take guided hikes to ancient temple sites, go on ocean adventures like sea kayaking and spear-fishing, and take beachside or cliff-top horseback rides led by *paniolo* (cowboys). Try your hand at archery, clay-shooting, and paintball, or sign up for a workout or a treatment in the spa. If you're here during one of the annual festivals honoring the taro plant or the Hawaiian performing arts, be sure to attend: events are held at the beach park, in the town of Kaunakakai, and on the ranch grounds. Festival or not, evenings bring storytelling, stargazing, and marshmallow roasting on the beach.

In the lodge's casual bar, you can play billiards, or watch sports on big-screen TVs. Open-air seating on the veranda lets you enjoy a drink before views of Moloka'i's sweeping ranch lands. Usually cooked on the grill or in a wok over an open fire, three meals a day are served buffet style in an open-air dining pavilion on the beach. The Maunaloa Dining Room offers indoor-outdoor dining from a menu that embraces both land and sea—Moloka'i prawns, sake-glazed salmon, and mai tai mahimahi, along with beef and pasta entrées. It's unlikely your appetite will need any coaxing, but just in case, a hand-painted Hawaiian inscription on the wall reminds you that "the body enjoys health when the stomach is well filled."

At the Sheraton Moloka'i, laid-back adventure might mean swinging in a hammock on the beach or mountain biking the single-track trails of the island that's been called the Moab of the Pacific. The choice is yours. Should you forget why you're here, check out the ranch's stop signs: they don't say "stop" but "whoa!" Slow down—this is Moloka'i.

🛏 22 rooms, 40 bungalows ⭕ Restaurant, room service (lodge), bar/lounge, picnic area, some minibars. **Recreation:** biking, fishing, hiking, horseback riding, mountain biking, running, wildlife viewing, beach, pool, snorkeling, sea kayaking, golf privileges, archery, billiards, horseshoes, sporting clays, library, piano, recreation room, playground. **Services:** kayak, bicycle, snorkeling-gear, Boogie-board, and fishing-equipment rental; gym; spa; guided fishing trips; dry-cleaning service, laundry service, and laundry facilities; shops; meeting rooms; business services; concierge; Internet access. **Classes and programs:** guided hikes and nature walks; natural history programs; mountain-biking lessons; fitness classes; children's programs (ages 5–12); arts and crafts classes; astronomy talks; sightseeing tours. ♿ Cable TV, some in-room safes, some private decks; no a/c in some rooms, no phones in some rooms, no TVs in some rooms, no smoking 🛏 $398–$470 rooms; $268–$358 bungalows 🚪 AE, D, DC, MC, V.

📖 *100 Maunaloa Hwy., Maunaloa, HI 96770* ☎ *808/552–2741 or 888/ 627–8082* 📠 *808/660–2724* 🌐 *www.molokairanch.com/hawaii.*

RESORT QUEST WAIMEA PLANTATION COTTAGES
Tranquil Outpost

If you are looking for a place of endless summer and splendid isolation, the west end of Kaua'i could be your spot. Tucked away here is a resort that keeps alive the plantation legacy of this island. Early in the 20th century, waves of immigrants came to work on the sugar plantations, sweetening the island's already rich ethnic mix. The cottages pay tribute to those who lived and worked on Waimea Plantation. Mounted on the front door of each cottage is a plaque that names its original owner and notes the years they lived here. Restored with period furnishings from the 1920s and '30s, each one- to four-bedroom cottage has a sizable living room, fully equipped kitchen, large bath with claw-foot tub, and two showers—one indoor and one outdoor. A screen door opens onto a shaded porch, and windows are placed to best catch the prevailing trade winds.

The cottages are set amid a coconut grove; orchards of avocados, mangoes, and limes; and plantings of other tropical greens and flowers. Manicured lawns are your backyard, the ocean is your picket fence, and the tropical sun makes every day summer. Take a dip in the swimming pool, toss a few balls on the volleyball court, or stroll on the black-sand beach. (Swimming off the beach is less tempting, because the ocean is clouded by waters entering from the mouth of the Waimea River.) Itching with wanderlust? Seek out the services of the resort's knowledgeable concierge, who will point your compass toward eco-adventures, cultural events, and sporting activities from the West End to the North Shore. Minutes away by car is 10-mi-long Waimea Canyon, which Mark Twain called the "Grand Canyon of the Pacific." You can hike into the vividly colored canyon from adjoining Kokee State Park, where many rare species of plants, birds, and other wildlife thrive. That park in turn adjoins Napali Coast State Park, known for its sensational sea cliffs, deep valleys, and high waterfalls.

If you have something a little more horizontal in mind, you need look no further than the plantation's Hart-Felt Massage and Day Spa, where you can submit to several types of massage and spa treatments such as wraps and facials that use the essences of passionflower, mango, and ginger. You can take your massage indoors or oceanside, where the sounds of the surf will lull you. Elsewhere on the grounds, visit the plantation museum for a glimpse of Kaua'i's agricultural history. Also on the grounds is Waimea Brewing Company, where you can fill up on standard American fare and try a beer brewed right here. Another pleasure is to barbecue your own dinner on an outdoor grill and enjoy it alfresco, at a picnic table.

One of the plantation's sweet traditions is its unconventional guest book. Before you check out, find a perfect piece of driftwood on the beach and sign it. Thread the driftwood into the fishing net hung along the breezeway and leave a tiny bit of yourself on Kaua'i.

Tip *The sounds of the ocean partially mask the crowing of the area's feral roosters, but if you are a light sleeper you may want to bring earplugs.*

📡 66 cottages ⦿ Restaurant, bar, grills, picnic area, kitchens. **Recreation:** hiking (nearby), beach, pool, volleyball court, horseshoes, library. **Services:** spa, grocery shopping, laundry facilities, laundry service, shops, Internet access, meeting rooms. ⬧ Cable TV, private porches; no a/c 🖾 $140–$735 ⊟ AE, D, DC, MC, V.

🏠 *9400 Kaumualii Hwy. (Box 367), Waimea, HI 96796* ☎ *808/338–1625 or 866/774–2924* 🖷 *808/338–2338* ⊕ *www.ResortQuestHawaii.com.*

Idaho

ELKINS RESORT
Family Hideout

Since the 1930s summer vacationers have been loading up their cars with kids, dogs, gear, and groceries and driving to Elkins Resort on Priest Lake for a week at "the lake." These days SUVs have taken the place of Studebakers and the cabins have indoor plumbing and electricity, but a vacation at Elkins, 95 mi (2½ hours) northeast of Spokane, Washington, is nevertheless a flashback to a simpler time. People still come here to shift gears and spend time with the family. Togetherness takes the form of exploring the forest, cooking out, playing on the beach, or just lazing the days away in the sun or under the shade of towering trees.

Priest Lake lies in the heart of the Selkirk Mountains in Idaho's northern panhandle, near the Canadian border and adjacent to half a million acres of public land. Surrounded by the pure mountain air, you can gaze at the lake's clear, glistening water; listen to the birds; and watch for elk, deer, and bears. In summer you can swim, fish, boat, water ski, jet ski, and play beach volleyball. Venture away from the shore and you'll find trails for hiking, jogging, horseback riding, mountain biking, and huckleberry and mushroom picking. Spring is best for seeing meadows in bloom and waterfalls at their thundering peak. In fall, the forest takes on a palette of brilliant autumn colors—you'll see red huckleberry leaves, golden aspens, and tamaracks, the only coniferous trees with needles that change from green to gold. Winter brings snowshoeing, cross-country skiing, sledding, and snowmobiling on more than 400 mi of groomed trails that surround the lake.

Your log cabin at Elkins isn't plush, but it is pleasant and spacious, decorated with country antiques and log furniture. On hot summer days, open the windows to let the breeze in; by evening, nature's own air-conditioning will have cooled your room for restful slumbering. In winter, gather before your fireplace to read, tell stories, play games, or just talk. There are no TVs or phones to distract you.

Though you could cook all your meals in your cabin's well-equipped kitchen or on the grill outside, don't miss the resort's very good restaurant. Fresh organic vegetables and herbs go into creative presentations of steak and seafood. Local huckleberries are a highlight, too—the resort buys about 700 gallons annually to make such specialties as huckleberry breakfast crepes and the lounge's signature item: the frozen huckleberry daiquiri.

Tip *Take a ¾-mi walk down Reeder Bay Road to visit the area's noted fine arts gallery. Entrée Gallery shows works by more than 100 national and regional artists.*

🛏 27 cabins 🍽 Restaurant, lounge, grocery store, grills, picnic area, kitchens, microwaves. **Recreation:** biking, bird-watching, fishing, hiking, mountain biking, running, wildlife viewing, beach, lake swimming, tubing (water), waterskiing, windsurfing, boating, canoeing, kayaking, sailing, cross-country skiing, snowshoeing, volleyball, board games, playground. Nearby: horseback riding, 18-hole golf course, sledding, snowmobiling, tobogganing. **Services:** canoe, kayak, mountain-bike, water-tube, fishing-boat, water-ski, and pontoon boat rentals; boathouse; boat launch; dock; marina; shop; meeting rooms. **Classes and programs:** children's programs (ages 6–12), concerts. ♿ Some in-room fireplaces, some private balconies and decks, some pets allowed; no a/c, no room phones, no room TVs 💳 $75–$440 ⊟ MC, V.

🏠 *404 Elkins Rd., Nordman, ID 83848* ☎ *208/443–2432* 📠 *208/ 443–2527* ⊕ *www.elkinsresort.com.*

HIDDEN CREEK GUEST RANCH
Family Hideout

Hidden Creek's slogan, "Calm your soul," is one hint that this place, 70 mi from Spokane, Washington, is not your ordinary dude ranch. Sure, you can ride horses, participate in a rodeo, and learn to round up calves, but there's much more than wrangling in store here. The ranch seeks to teach personal harmony with nature and holistic living that integrates body, mind, and spirit.

The Adventure Challenge Course includes a ropes course, climbing tower, and zip line. There's also archery, fishing, nature walks, and miles of trails for hiking. (Take a companion with you when you hit the mountain trails: the ranch is surrounded by more than 350 square mi of national forest, and anyone could get lost or encounter bears.) You can arrange off-site activities, such as white-water rafting and golfing in the summer and downhill skiing in the winter, but you're likely to find more than enough to occupy yourself without ever leaving the ranch. In the fitness center, you can take a yoga class, work out on the equipment, or have a treatment with the on-site massage therapist. Take part in the pipe and sweat-lodge ceremonies to delve into indigenous peoples' teachings and nature awareness. Around the campfire in the evening, join a sing-along or listen to the visiting cowboy poet. In the saloon you can learn western dancing. Do some stargazing as you soak your tired muscles in one of two outdoor hot tubs before heading to your log cabin for a blissful sleep under down comforters.

In the big log lodge at the heart of the ranch, meals are served before the rock fireplace in the dining room, and books and videos are available in the library. Duplex and four-plex log cabins house the guest rooms on hillsides above the lodge, offering fine views of the valley below. Log furniture, down comforters, and western and Native American art make the rooms snug and colorful. Decks are furnished with rocking chairs ideal for whiling away an afternoon.

Hidden Creek is a place where you can get away with your kids but get away *from* them at the same time. A full summer children's program keeps the younger set busy learning about nature and animal care, doing arts and crafts, and listening to Native American stories. One night each week, kids get to camp overnight in tepees. They have their own riding program and learn to be "one" with their horse through Centered Riding® techniques. Kids can ride horses with their parents, too, but they often choose to stay with the energetic counselors, joining the grown-ups for meals and evening programs. At the end of the week they can show off their newfound skills in the kids' rodeo.

Owners Iris Behr and John Muir play an active role in creating a memorable and enriching stay. Join Iris on her early-morning, heart-thumping fitness walks and John in the weekly rodeos. You meet the owners early in the week, at a cocktail get-together in their home, and at the end of the week you celebrate with them at a seven-course candlelight dinner. While the wine flows freely, chef Rose Ludwig's creations remind you of the excellent and hearty food you've enjoyed all week, and new friends recount their experiences.

Tip *Adults-only weeks are offered in May, early June, September, and October. Some of these weeks have themes, such as outdoor photography, hands-on horsemanship, and Centered Riding clinics. The winter program includes snowshoeing, cross-country skiing, sleigh rides, and snowmobile tours.*

◁ 6 cabins ⑩ American plan, dining room, bar, lobby lounge, picnic area. **Recreation:** bird-watching, fishing, hiking, horseback riding, running, wildlife viewing, swimming hole, cross-country skiing, sledding, snowmobiling, snowshoeing, tobogganing, archery, horseshoes, volleyball, library, playground. Nearby: biking, boating, mountain biking, lake swimming, canoeing, kayaking, sailing, 18-hole golf course, downhill skiing. **Services:** gym, 2 outdoor hot tubs, heated swimming pool, massage, babysitting, concierge, laundry facilities, shop, airport shuttle, business services, meeting rooms. **Classes and programs:** guided hikes; guided nature walks; natural history programs; off-road tours; fly-fishing, horseback-riding, roping, and trapshooting lessons;

children's programs (ages 3–11); teen programs (12–19); photography and yoga classes; holistic living and environmental awareness talks; concerts; dances; sightseeing tours; sing-alongs. ♿ Private balconies and patios; no a/c, no room phones, no room TVs, no smoking ▨ $330–$402 ▭ AE, MC, V.

▱ 11077 E. Blue Lake Rd., Harrison, ID 83833 ☎ 208/689–3209 or 800/446–3833 ☒ 208/689–9115 ⊕ www.hiddencreek.com.

PARADISE VALLEY INN
Laid-Back Adventure ~ Tranquil Outpost

In the Kootenai Valley, seemingly endless stretches of fields and farmland are punctuated by a few homes and barns, a verdant green golf course, and the small town of Bonners Ferry. Spokane is 120 mi southwest; Canada is less than 40 mi away. Driving through the area to Paradise Valley Inn—the final few miles on unpaved roads—you'll be cut loose in wide-open space.

Set atop a hill, the contemporary Northwest-style inn commands a magnificent prospect of the valley and the Selkirk, Cabinet, and Purcell mountain ranges. You don't have to sacrifice the view when you step inside, for walls of windows in the Great Room frame the expansive vista. Soaring cathedral ceilings and wood-and-log architecture create a woodsy mood, and couches are positioned to take advantage of the panorama. Throughout the common areas, suites, and cabins, the expansive landscape is always in sight.

The inn's suites include the 600-square-foot L'amour Suite, which as the largest suite sleeps five. A private deck, fireplace, and two-person vintage-style claw-foot bathtub make this suite especially appealing. All of the suites are illuminated by ample windows. If you stay in the main building, you'll be served a full breakfast in the dining room. Adjacent to the lodge, the Garden Cabin has vaulted pine ceilings and a kitchenette. It sleeps only two and overlooks the valley.

At the inn, you can roam 18 acres of cedar forest, meadows, and areas landscaped with native, drought-resistant plants. You may encounter wild turkeys and other birds, but for real wildlife viewing or bird-watching, drive 20 minutes to 2,800-acre Kootenai National Wildlife Refuge. There, more than 200 species of birds and 45 species of mammals make their home. In the surrounding area, hike, ride horses, or mountain bike on more than 300 mi of national forest trails; go river-rafting or kayaking on the Upper Moyie or Kootenai River; and go boating on Lake Pend Oreille, Idaho's largest lake. In winter, there's excellent downhill skiing at Schweitzer Mountain Ski Resort, 45 minutes away.

Tip *The innkeepers also cater meals for special events. To find restaurants, drive 30 minutes south to Sandpoint.*

5 suites, 1 cabin Full breakfast, dining room, picnic area. **Recreation:** biking, bird-watching, hiking, running, wildlife viewing, cross country skiing, sledding, snowshoeing, tobogganing, tubing (snow), board games, library, videocassette library. Nearby: fishing, horseback riding, mountain biking, rock climbing, lake swimming, river swimming, swimming hole, parasailing, snorkeling, tubing (water), canoeing, jet skiing, kayaking, rafting, rowing, sailing, driving range, two 18-hole golf courses, putting green, tennis court, downhill skiing, ice climbing, ice-skating, sleigh rides, snowmobiling, basketball, bowling, in-line skating, playground. **Services:** outdoor hot tub, massage, airport shuttle, business services, concierge, meeting rooms. Some in-room fireplaces; some in-room VCRs; some private balconies, decks, and patios; no a/c in some rooms, no phones in some rooms, no TV in some rooms, no kids under 9, no smoking $99–$150 AE, MC, V.

300 Eagle Way, P.O. Box 878, Bonners Ferry, ID 83805 208/267–4180 or 888/447–4180 *www.paradisevalleyinn.com.*

PINNACLE PEAKS SAWTOOTH LODGE
Laid-Back Adventure

The valley surrounding Atlanta, Idaho, is known as the Green Valley, and for good reason: its lush landscape of evergreen trees and wildflowers is fed by the middle fork of the Boise River, known for icy clear waters and trout fishing. Atlanta, an old mining town, and its environs remain largely untouched by tourism and development. Here, below the cliffs and peaks of Greylock Mountain, 80 mi (three hours) northeast of Boise, Pinnacle Peaks Sawtooth Lodge sits on 500 acres of land next to the Sawtooth National Recreation and Wilderness Area. Creatures from beavers, chipmunks, foxes, and squirrels to mule deer, coyotes, black bears, and elks live here. Birds include Clark's nutcrackers, juncos, chickadees, sandhill cranes, and golden eagles. The number of waterfowl in the region has grown significantly in recent years, thanks in part to the environmental stewardship of Pinnacle Peaks Lodge. The lodge established wetlands and two small man-made lakes, thereby attracting the birds. From its choice of cleaning products to its methods of waste disposal, the lodge is committed to protecting nature.

The living room in the contemporary log-and-rock lodge harks back to the great wilderness lodges rooms of the Teddy Roosevelt era. A stone fireplace is the grand centerpiece, and a circular cove serves as a conversation area. Furnishings throughout the lodge are unpretentious and broken-in. Guest rooms are simply decorated (no designer paint or themes here), without phones or alarm clocks. Two television lounges have satellite reception. All of your meals are included in the price of a room, and the food is good. Relying on fresh, locally grown produce and meats, the chef prepares imaginative dishes that satisfy, whether you are hungry for rich Idaho beef or are a dedicated vegetarian. Meals are served in the dining area, on the veranda, or on the front patio.

But Pinnacle Peaks is not about hanging around the lodge. Lakes on the property are stocked with brookies and rainbow trout. From shore or pedal boat, your chances of a catch are good—just watch the ospreys flying overhead as they look for a meal and throw your line that direction. Not into fishing? There are enough other activities here, from horseback riding to boccie, to fill your nights and days. If you want some quiet time, you can easily find a place to be alone. Go ahead and relax under a 100-year-old ponderosa, or take a soak in the non-sulfuric hotspring pool and natural spring spa—neither is chemically treated. At night, take a seat in a Sky Chair, which has a seat specially angled up toward the stars.

From this peaceful, rambling retreat, 756,000-acre Sawtooth National Recreation and Wilderness Area (NRA) is about a half-hour drive, an hour's horseback ride, or half a day's hike away. Its four mountain ranges—the Sawtooths, Boulders, White Clouds, and Smokies—have more than 50 peaks over 10,000 feet. More than 1,000 high mountain lakes are protected here, as well as the headwaters of four of Idaho's major rivers: the Salmon, the South Fork of the Payette, the Boise, and the Big Wood. Most of the 250 mi of trails (wilderness trails excluded) within the Sawtooth NRA are open to mountain-bike users.

Tip *Children of all ages are welcome here, but it's not a great place for kids under eight. Bigger kids who are into wildlife and hiking, and who are fairly responsible and able to follow directions well, are more likely to enjoy a vacation at the lodge.*

⇥ 16 rooms, 2 suites ⵏⵓⵏ American plan, snack bar, grills, picnic area. **Recreation:** biking, bird-watching, fishing, hiking, horseback riding, mountain biking, rock climbing, running, wildlife viewing, pool, lake swimming, river swimming, swimming hole, snorkeling, canoeing, 5-hole golf course, putting green, tennis court, cross-country skiing, ice climbing, snowmobiling, snowshoeing, telemark skiing, archery, badminton, basketball, boccie, carriage rides, croquet, horseshoes, Ping-Pong, soccer, sporting clays, pedal boats, volleyball, piano, recreation room, video-game room, videocassette/DVD library. **Services:** gym, outdoor hot tub, mineral springs, airstrip, helipad, horse boarding, laundry facilities, laundry service, shop, airport shuttle, business services, meeting rooms. **Classes and programs:** off-road tours, concerts, movies, sightseeing tours, sing-alongs. ♿ Some pets allowed (fee); no room phones, no smoking ⊞ $125–$300 ⊟ AE, D, DC, MC, V.

📪 *Box 39, Atlanta, ID 83601* ☎ *208/864–2168* 📠 *208/864–2167*
🌐 *www.pinnaclepeaks.com.*

SALMON RAPIDS LODGE
Laid-Back Adventure

As the mighty Salmon River snakes its way through central Idaho, dropping 1,200 feet over a course of 89 mi, it attracts an avid following of anglers, rafters, and wildlife watchers. Its power has earned the Salmon the moniker River of No Return, and its waters are especially furious around Riggins. Tiny Riggins (population 410) itself has a wild side. Early white settlers called it Gouge-Eye, for a saloon brawl that took place here. Before that, the site at the confluence of the Salmon and Little Salmon rivers was a Nez Perce fishing camp. Now it's a whitewater rafting center, where the river surges as high as 9 feet. Between June and August the rafting around Riggins is rafting at its best.

Riggins lies in the Salmon River Canyon between Hells Canyon National Recreation Area and the Seven Devils Mountains to the west and Gospel Hump Wilderness and Frank Church River of No Return Wilderness to the east. It's no surprise that the town has some of the deepest canyon views and best hiking in North America. Salmon River basin trails travel along scenic ridges, past mountain lakes, and through lush meadows. River and lake fishing is excellent in the area, and your chances of spotting moose, elk, deer, mountain goats, and bears are good, depending on the season.

Salmon Rapids Lodge—about three hours north of Boise, 47 mi north of McCall, and 116 mi south of Lewiston—puts you right in the middle of all this, making the quiet and unpretentious Best Western a great nature retreat. In the main lobby and small mezzanine library of the wood-and-stone lodge, cathedral ceilings, 32-foot timber columns, and log furnishings stand before giant windows with a view of the hills. Wilderness photographs by local artist Frank Mignerey decorate the walls, and another local bakes the breakfast treats for the complimentary Continental breakfast. The guest rooms (which vary in size) are standard motel issue, but it's the location and the staff that count. Friendly and knowledgeable about the area, employees are as happy to direct you to nearby restaurants, hiking routes, or adventure outfitters as they are to sit down and chat about the region's history and lore. An integral part of the community, the lodge extends a warm welcome.

Your days might be filled with horseback riding up the canyon, whitewater rafting down the Salmon, collecting garnets at Ruby Rapids, or lounging on the river's many soft white-sand bars. When you return to the lodge, sip a complimentary coffee, tea, or hot chocolate on the patio; then head to the outdoor hot tub to watch the sun as it sets in hues of purple, orange, and azure.

Tips *Request a riverside room and take in stunning views of hills and rivers from your small balcony. In spring, you'll have a bird's-eye view of salmon leaping upstream on their return to the local hatchery.*

◄⊃ 40 rooms, 15 suites ¶◎¶ Continental breakfast, picnic area, some microwaves, refrigerators. **Recreation:** fishing, wildlife viewing, indoor pool, croquet. Nearby: biking, bird-watching, hiking, horseback riding, mountain biking, rock climbing, running, beach, lake swimming, river swimming, boating, kayaking, rafting, driving range, 18-hole golf course, putting green, cross-country skiing, snowmobiling, snowshoeing, telemark skiing, board games, library, playground. **Services:** exercise equipment, outdoor hot tub, laundry facilities, shop, meeting rooms, wireless Internet. **Classes and programs:** guided hikes, sightseeing tours. ♧ Cable TV with movies, in-room data ports, some jetted tubs, some private balconies, some pets allowed (fee); no smoking ▭ $74–$184 ▭ AE, D, MC, V.

⌂ *1010 S. Main St., Riggins, ID 83549* ☎ *208/628–2743 or 877/957–2743* 🖷 *208/628–3834* ⊕ *www.salmonrapids.com.*

Illinois

GIANT CITY STATE PARK LODGE
Family Hideout

About as far south as you can go in Illinois where the Mississippi and Ohio rivers converge, a blacktop road leads from the tiny community of Makanda, south of Carbondale, to Giant City State Park. The cliffs and ravines here seem a world away from the farmland and fruit orchards of this sparsely settled region. Native American legend says that in the distant past giants visited the area and laid out streets in the form of sandstone bluffs and boulders. According to science, the Earth's faulting and folding produced the unusual formations around 12,000 years ago. Today they are covered with ferns, moss, wildflowers, and dozens of varieties of trees.

In the 4,100-acre state park stands Giant City Lodge, constructed of native oak and sandstone by the Civilian Conservation Corps in the 1930s. The oversize stone fireplace and the powerful exposed timbers of the lodge's lobby leave no doubt that you are in the care of Mother Nature here. More likely than not, you'll want to grab a book or a glass of wine and settle into the lobby's leather lounge chairs. Within the lodge is the Bald Knob dining room, a favorite place for locals to gather for Sunday dinner or on special occasions. The main draw is the regionally famous fried chicken dinner, served family-style with mashed potatoes and gravy—the ultimate in comfort food. Country-style ham, biscuits and gravy, and local eggs draw just as big a crowd for breakfast.

One- and two-room log-frame cabins, tucked away around the lodge along pine-needle paths, are equipped with televisions but no cooking facilities. Each cabin has an ample sitting area and beds with rough pine frames and warm woolen blankets. If you want maximum privacy, request one of the four cabins on the bluff; from them you'll have a view of the sunset and the entire Mississippi River valley.

One of the best ways to appreciate Giant City State Park is to climb the 82-foot water tower, where an observation deck provides an unobstructed view of the canyons and cliffs as well as of Bald Knob Cross, one of the world's largest man-made crosses, on a hilltop west of the park. From the observation deck you can also see the confluence of the two mighty rivers. Hike the 23 mi of nature trails and ride horseback on the 12 mi of equestrian trails to get a closer look at the park's flora, fauna, and geology. Among the less cuddly creatures you might see are turkey vultures, who are honored during a small festival held in Makanda each October.

Tip *The lodge books six months ahead for the dogwood bloom in late March and early April, and for foliage season in October.*

⊃ 34 cabins �’◯❘ Full breakfast, restaurant, lobby lounge, grills, picnic area, some refrigerators. **Recreation:** biking, bird-watching, fishing, hiking, horseback riding, rock climbing, running, wildlife viewing, pool, horseshoes, softball, playground. **Services:** shop, meeting rooms. 🖐 Some in-room fireplaces, some private decks ⊟ $65–$115 ⊟ AE, DC, MC, V.

⌂ *460 Giant City Lodge Rd., Makanda, IL 62958* ☎ *618/457–4921 lodge, 618/457–4836 park* 🖨 *618/457–0228* ⊕ *www.giantcitylodge.com* ☯ *Closed mid-Dec.–mid-Feb.*

PINE HOLLOW INN
Romantic Retreat

In a way, it's Christmas all year long at Pine Hollow Inn—the 120 acres in an out-of-the-way valley are a Christmas tree farm. A heavily timbered forest covers one side of the valley, a rocky prairie-grass field covers the other, and Hughlett's Branch Creek flows through. The variety of habitats and the many bird feeders placed around the inn attract more than 80 species of birds, including blue and green herons, ducks, and other waterfowl. In this enclave, deer graze peacefully and wild turkeys parade grandly.

Larry and Sally Priske lived here for 15 years, enjoying their private nature preserve, before they opened Pine Hollow Inn in 1989 as a way to share the land with others. Their home stands a few hundred yards from the inn, and Sally's black-and-white photographs of the landscape accent the inn's outdoorsy decor. Lots of wooden accent pieces, plaid fabrics, and a woodland motif create a relaxed, casual mood. A wraparound porch is an excellent place to use the binoculars that come with your room. Each guest room is a suite with a sitting area, fireplace, jetted tubs, and puffy down comforter. There are no televisions, telephones, or computers.

The tree farm is a wonderful place for hiking or bird-watching. In this part of northern Illinois every season has its charms. The hollow is protected from harsh winter winds. Snowshoeing and cross-country skiing are favorite activities, and you can perform the old-fashioned ritual of cutting down a Christmas tree. Choose from the white or Scotch pine, spruce, and Frazier pine that are raised on the farm; the Pine Hollow staff will prepare the tree for the trip to your own living room. When you're finished playing lumberjack, have a hot cocoa or cider. For dinner, head 1 mi down the country road to the village of Galena, whose winding streets are lined with buildings dating from the mid-1800s.

Tip *Bring along a bag of marshmallows or s'mores fixings. The Priskes often light a campfire down by the creek after the sun sets.*

🛏 5 suites ❢◯❢ Full breakfast, snack bar. **Recreation:** bird-watching, hiking, running, wildlife viewing, cross-country skiing, snowshoeing. Nearby: fishing, canoeing, kayaking, 9- and 18-hole golf courses, tennis, ballooning, downhill skiing, ice-skating, biking, sleigh rides, skate park. **Services:** binoculars provided, meeting rooms. **Classes and programs:** Christmas-tree pruning classes. ♿ In-room fireplaces, jetted tubs; no room phones, no rooms TVs, no kids under 12, no smoking 💳 $95–$145 ▭ D, MC, V.

🖃 *4700 N. Council Hill Rd., Galena, IL 61036* ☎ *815/777–1071* ⊕ *www. pinehollowinn.com.*

STARVED ROCK STATE PARK LODGE
Tranquil Outpost

It's hard to say what the most popular activity is at this, Illinois's most popular state park. Hiking the 18 mi of trails is energizing in any season. In summer, water sports are the focus on the Illinois River, which bounds the park on the south. Ice climbing, skating, and cross-country skiing are a way to enjoy the landscape in winter. Whatever you do in Starved Rock State Park, you'll be surrounded by fabulous river views and 18 canyons that slice dramatically through tree-covered sandstone bluffs. On the floor of the red oak, hickory, and red-cedar forest is an abundance of plant life—American witch hazel, black huckleberry, bracken fern. Nuthatches and chickadees feed on nuts, seeds, and insects found in tree bark. Raccoons and flying squirrels search the forest for berries and nuts.

About three hours south of Chicago in north-central Illinois, Starved Rock is named for a conflict between the Ottawa and Illiniwek tribes around 1760. During one of many battles, a band of Illiniwek hid atop a 125-foot sandstone butte. The Ottawa and their allies, the Potawatomi, surrounded the bluff and held their ground until the trapped Illiniwek died of starvation. The best way to become familiar with the park and its history is on an hour-long trolley ride that leaves hourly every day from the visitor center. The tour covers much of the 2,630 acres of Starved Rock State Park and visits nearby Buffalo and Matthieson state parks. The trolley is also used for bald eagle–watching tours, wildflower tours, and other activities. In early January, the bald eagle festival is one of the most spectacular shows in the park.

Starved Rock State Park Lodge is a laid-back place where you and your family can participate in as many or as few activities as you like. An evening in the rec room is just as likely to include performances by magicians and clowns as an interpretive program on Native American art or geology. Day or night, you can hide away and read a book in your cabin, whose heavy log interior is brightened by decorative rugs on the floor and walls. Fireplaces made from stone gathered in the park bring warmth to the cabins. Motel-style rooms in a wing added to the lodge in 1993 are a good value if you plan to stay busy exploring this remarkable state park.

Tip *Poison ivy grows throughout the park. Watch for its distinctive trilobed leaves.*

🛏 72 rooms, 22 cabins 🍴 Café, restaurant, snack bar, lounge. **Recreation:** biking, bird-watching, fishing, hiking, horseback riding, running, wildlife viewing, indoor pool, waterskiing, boating, canoeing, jet skiing, kayaking, golf privileges, cross-country skiing, ice climbing, ice-skating, snowshoeing, tobogganing, boccie, piano, recreation room, playground. **Services:** horse, canoe, and cross-country-ski rental; hot tub; massage; dock; 3 shops; Internet access; meeting rooms. **Classes and programs:** guided hikes, Native American culture and history talks, entertainment, sing-alongs. ⛄ Cable TV, some in-room fireplaces, in-room DVD players, no-smoking rooms 💳 $80–$110 ⊟ AE, D, DC, MC, V.

📪 *Box 509, Utica, IL 61373* ☎ *815/667–4726 or 800/868–7625* 📠 *815/667–4455* 🌐 *www.starvedrocklodge.com*

TARA POINT INN & COTTAGES
Romantic Retreat

The front porch of Tara Point Inn affords a truly magnificent view: the confluence of the brawny Mississippi River with the smaller, yet powerful, Illinois River. Along this stretch the Mississippi flows west to east, an unusual phenomenon along the river's 1,100-mi path from Minnesota to the Gulf of Mexico. Outlined by bluffs and teeming with wildlife and waterfowl, the area is a kaleidoscope of color, the waters changing from deep green in the morning to a coppery red as the sun sets.

It was this view that Marge and Larry Wright discovered one day in the 1980s as they were out driving around and found the small home for sale on this property. The Wrights named their place Tara Point, which comes from the Gaelic word meaning "house on the hill." At first they used Tara Point for themselves, but in 1990 they built their dream home with a guest wing near the original house and began inviting others to share their view. One of Marge's favorite activities is to watch the river barges and watercraft along the Mississippi River at dusk. Here the river is so wide and smooth that riverboat captains named the spot Alton Pool.

Guests have their choice of staying in the main house, where a modern suite adjoins the game room and two standard rooms share a deck, or the cottages, which afford more privacy and have spacious porches with rocking chairs. All accommodations have river views and get lots of sun. Breakfast for guests in the main house is served in a dining alcove, whose floor-to-ceiling windows make the most of the fabulous view. Fresh fruit and homemade pastries are served on fine china, and fresh flowers adorn the table.

If you can tear yourself away from the view, take in some more scenery along the Meeting of the Great Rivers National Scenic Byway, which passes right by the inn. You can occupy yourself on or along the river, at the Melvin Price Locks and Dam in nearby Alton. At the dam you can fish for crappie, bluegill, catfish, and other prizes or watch the swooping waterfowl as they search for a meal. More than 230 species of birds are found in the area, and guided hikes and nature programs in the local state parks can teach you more about them. Bring your newfound knowledge back to the front porch of your cottage or the inn and see how it enhances one of the finest views in Illinois.

Tip *American bald eagles return to this area in late November and remain for much of the winter. Bring your binoculars and camera, for you are sure to see these great birds from the dining room at Tara Point.*

⮑ 2 rooms, 1 suite, 3 cottages ⦿ Continental breakfast, snack bar, some kitchenettes. **Recreation:** biking, bird-watching, hiking, running, wildlife viewing, billiards, shuffleboard, library, recreation room. Nearby: horseback riding, boating, 9-hole golf course, putting green, tennis courts, miniature golf. ♿ In-room VCRs, some private porches; no room phones in some rooms, no kids under 9, no smoking 📺 $140–$180 ▭ No credit cards.

▭ *Box 1, Grafton, IL 62037* ☎ *618/786–3555* 🖷 *618/786–3255* ⊕ *www.tarapoint.com.*

Indiana

SPRING MILL INN
Tranquil Outpost

In southern Indiana's 1,300-acre Spring Mill State Park, about 85 mi from Indianapolis, a 2-mi loop trail passes through an oak forest that shelters patches of colorful fungi, then enters Donaldson Woods Nature Preserve, home to giant 300- and 400-year-old oaks, tulip poplars, and beeches. Red-bellied woodpeckers, Acadian flycatchers, red-eyed vireos, bluebirds, summer and scarlet tanagers, and Kentucky, worm-eating, and yellow-throated warblers live here, along with a large stand of delicate ferns. It's green and wonderfully quiet.

On the south shore of the park's lake, the three-story, limestone-faced Spring Mill Inn was built in the 1930s. To match the park's 1814 pioneer village, the inn was originally to have been constructed of logs, but limestone proved more practical. Surrounded by tall oak trees, the inn looks as though it has always been here. Guest rooms have large windows that look out over the woods and make the rooms sunny and cheerful by day. In winter, a fire warms the lobby. There's another fireplace at one end of the high-ceilinged dining room, whose tall windows fill the room with views of nature. After a dinner of home-style cooking, it's pleasant to take a stroll on the shady grounds.

The centerpiece of the park is Pioneer Village, a short walk from the inn. At its working gristmill you can buy stone-ground cornmeal. There's also a sawmill, post office, hat shop, boot shop, and a pharmacy complete with early-19th-century apothecary instruments.

A 2-mi loop trail leads from the inn through the village and past a pioneer cemetery. It then meanders through an old-growth forest of stately beeches and maples past the ruins of an old lime kiln and the remains of the quarry where the limestone for the mill and other buildings was taken. If you've packed a picnic lunch (available at the inn), you can eat it at sheltered tables along the trail. The trail continues to Donaldson Cave, one of several that lie along the park's network of underground streams. These streams are inhabited by many species of blind fish and invertebrates, and on a boat tour of the cave you may encounter the northern blind cave fish, first discovered here in 1896.

When you emerge back into the sunlight, follow the trail along the lakeshore. Waterfowl, including geese and ducks, is abundant here. Even if you don't see them, you are likely to hear large black-and-white pileated woodpeckers drumming on hollow tree trunks in search of juicy insects.

Tip *Bring a flashlight for spelunking in the park's other caves.*

74 rooms Restaurant, grills, picnic area. **Recreation:** bird-watching, fishing, mountain biking, wildlife viewing, indoor/outdoor pool, boating, Ping-Pong, volleyball, playground, recreation room. **Services:** shops, meeting rooms. **Classes and programs:** guided nature walks. Satellite TV, no-smoking rooms. $49–$89 AE, D, MC, V.

Box 68, Mitchell, IN 47446 812/849–4081 or 877/9SPRING 812/849–4647 www.in.gov/dnr/parklake/properties/inn_springmill. html.

STORY INN
Tranquil Outpost

In south-central Indiana's Brown County, once devoted to farming and timbering, much of the landscape is again as the pioneers found it—densely wooded two-lane roads meander through the hills, often following covered bridges over streams and rivers. Nowadays the occasional small farm crops up in the bottomland. Brown County State Park and a portion of Hoosier National Forest now protect large areas of the reforested landscape, and hikers, equestrians, and casual paddlers enjoy themselves in the tranquil woods most of the year.

In the Great Depression, family farmers and small-time timber cutters left the countryside in search of work. They never returned, and the land has been sparsely populated ever since. The town of Story, about 60 mi south of Indianapolis, was almost completely abandoned and lay frozen in time until the mid-1970s, when an enterprising Hoosier couple opened a restaurant in a vintage gas station and general store. It thrived, rooms were added, and Story was once again on the map. Still tucked away at the end of a country road and hemmed in on three sides by wooded hills, the village is as sleepy as it must have been in the 19th century. Clapboard and tin-sided buildings dating from the turn of the 20th century stand around a small common. Horses at the hitching posts next to the general store often outnumber cars in the lot across the street.

Almost all the village buildings, from the general store to the one- and two-bedroom cottages, are now accommodations for visitors. There are no televisions, radios, or phones in any of the lodgings, and the hilly topography means that even cell phones don't work. From the common you can look out over fields to the distant barn and silo of a working farm. The common is a good spot for stargazing.

From the outside, the Story Inn looks pretty ramshackle, with its tin siding, pair of old gas pumps, and sagging front porch. But inside, all is welcoming. Narrow, crooked stairs lead up to four guest rooms furnished with country antiques. The rooms, like the stairs, are decidedly off-kilter. Floor plans are irregular, and the ceiling of your room may slope, depending upon what side of the building you're in. Mismatched flower patterns predominate in the upholstery and window treatments. The Blue Lady Room is said to be haunted by a mirthful, cheeky spirit in flowing white robes. For more privacy and space, you can take a suite in one of the cottages shaded by the trees around the common. Some have kitchens, and some have private hot tubs.

The spacious dining room on the main floor is dimly lighted almost exclusively by candles and has a high tin ceiling and a bar on one side. Country-style wooden tables are dressed up for evening meals with linens and small vases of flowers. On the lively menu, rack of lamb, grilled duck breast, and seafood linguini are typical offerings, though the menu varies with the seasons. The chef usually includes one or two meatless options, and there's a short but well-chosen wine list. By day, the dining room sheds its white tablecloths and sunlight illuminates shelves stocked with antique farm implements, toys, and other goods. You can have a hearty home-style breakfast or a casual lunch here.

In one corner of the dining room stands the reception desk and a table stacked with area maps and guides. An 8½-mi multi-use trail, open to hikers, horseback riders, and mountain bikers, starts at the end of the village road and goes straight into the woods. The trail intersects with trails in Hoosier National Forest (to the west) and Brown County State Park (to the north). If you'd rather paddle than hike, you can put in at Salt Creek in Story. It's part of a 100-mi system of navigable streams that lace Brown County. If you're looking for a little civilization, drive 13 mi north to touristy but still charming Nashville, an 1870s artists' colony whose galleries and shops still attract collectors.

Tip *There's no place nearby to rent a bike or canoe, so you'll have to bring your own. But you can rent a mount at the Brown County State Park horse camp, 2 mi north of the village.*

↘ 4 rooms, 18 suites ⑧ Restaurant (wine and beer only), pub, some kitchens, some kitchenettes. **Recreation:** Nearby: biking, bird-watching, hiking, horseback riding, mountain biking, canoeing, golf privileges. **Services:** meeting rooms. ♿ Some jetted tubs, some private porches, some pets allowed (fee); no room phones, no room TVs, no smoking ▭ $107–$210 ▭ MC, V.

⌂ *6404 S. State Rd. 135, Nashville, IN 47448* ☎ *812/988–2273 or 800/ 881–1183* 🖷 *812/988–6516* ⊕ *www.storyinn.com.*

Iowa

COUNTRY HOMESTEAD BED & BREAKFAST
Tranquil Outpost

At the foot of the Loess Hills of western Iowa, on land that once was covered by tallgrass prairie, Country Homestead Bed & Breakfast overlooks the Missouri River valley. From the front porch you can gaze upon seemingly endless rows of corn and soybeans growing on some of the world's most productive farmland. From the back porch you get an up-close view of the lush Loess Hills jutting up. The farmhouse was built by R. T. Reese and his family, who homesteaded here starting in 1855. Descendants of the Reeses enlarged the white frame house, and David and Lin Zahrt opened it to guests in 1992.

Photographs of David's ancestors are found through the house, along with numerous occasional chairs and tables built by family members. A 1911 Steinway player piano in the living area often draws guests who like to sing along. If you are celebrating an anniversary, David will sing love songs from the era of your wedding. Breakfast is also an encounter with David's ancestors. Grandmother Reese's waffle iron still works, producing the whole-wheat and banana waffles that show up on the breakfast table accompanied by fresh strawberries from a neighbor's patch or baked apples from the trees out back. Floor-to-ceiling windows make the guest rooms bright and sunny and show off the striped wallpaper, wood-plank floors, and handwoven rugs to good advantage.

Peace and quiet prevails. The only noise at sunrise is the singing of hundreds of birds going about their morning business, and all you'll hear of a summer evening are the cicadas. The creatures inhabit the B&B's 160 acres of Loess Hills prairie and the adjoining 320-acre Turin Nature Preserve. You can learn all about the surrounding landscape by browsing in the library in the living room or by chatting with David and Lin, who are active in the effort to restore the tallgrass prairie and preserve the Loess Hills.

Five miles to the north is the 2,500-acre Loess Hills Wildlife Area, where you can spot everything from wild turkeys, deer, and beavers to foxes and antelope. A black bear or two also live in the reserve.

Tip *Dozens of varieties of wildflowers bloom in the Loess Hills. Check the Country Homestead Web site for the estimated bloom dates and time your visit accordingly.*

⌘ 3 rooms ⏛ Full breakfast. **Recreation:** biking, bird-watching, hiking, running, wildlife viewing, cross-country skiing, ice-skating, sledding, piano. **Services:** binoculars provided, Internet access. **Classes and programs:** guided hikes, natural history programs. ⌂ TV, no-smoking rooms ▦ $65–$85 ▭ No credit cards.

⌂ *22133 Larpenteur Rd., Turin, IA 51040-8747* ☎ *712/353–6772* ⊕ *www.country-homestead.com/*

ELMHURST COTTAGE
Family Hideout

As a little girl growing up on her family's farm, Bobbi Underbakke didn't particularly enjoy doing her chores. So as an adult running a bed-and-breakfast while maintaining the farm, she marvels at the delight children and adults take in feeding the chickens and gathering eggs. It's a task she gladly shares with her guests. She'll let you milk the goat in the morning and, in spring, feed and care for the newborn lambs.

Delicate roses and wildflowers attract butterflies and songbirds to the Elmhurst Cottage gardens, where you can relax on scattered benches and lawn chairs. A red-tailed hawk lives in the orchard, and a heron or bald eagle occasionally stop by. Indoors, Bobbi's Norwegian heritage shows up everywhere. The guest rooms are filled with family antiques and mementos, and common areas display Norwegian knickknacks that the Underbakkes are pleased to explain to you. The morning meal includes not only bacon and eggs, pancakes, fried potatoes, and muffins but Norwegian specialties, such as *kringle* (sweet buns), *lefse* (soft, flat potato bread), and fruit soup.

In a part of northeast Iowa characterized by spring-fed creeks, low hills, a few limestone bluffs, and farmland, Bobbi's 120-acre spread has been in her family for four generations. Iowa farm families have a deep commitment to the land, a commitment that inspires local enterprises like the Seed Savers Exchange and Heritage Farm. Dedicated to preserving heirloom produce—fruit and vegetable varieties that have been forgotten by commercial farmers—the organization cultivates such crops at its farm. A quiet stroll through the gardens and orchard is a trip back into America's agrarian past. The past also lives on in nearby towns that were settled by Scandinavian immigrants and that still follow many of the old traditions. A number of Amish families also live here, and Bobbi can take you to visit the homes of some of her Amish friends.

Tip *For a look at life as it was when Iowa was still a little wild, visit the Laura Ingalls Wilder Museum in Burr Oak. The famous author was nine years old when her father operated a hotel here in the late 1870s.*

🛏 6 rooms, 1 suite ¶◎¶ Full breakfast. **Recreation:** biking, bird-watching, fishing, hiking, wildlife viewing, cross-country skiing, badminton, basketball, croquet, horseshoes, volleyball, piano. Nearby: kayaking, canoeing, 9-hole golf course, downhill skiing, sleigh rides. **Services:** Internet access. ♿ No room phones, no room TVs, no smoking ▨ $55–$275 ▭ D, MC, V.

🖰 *3616 258th Ave., Decorah, IA 52101* ☎ *563/735–5310 or 888/413–5600.*

GARST FARM RESORT
Tranquil Outpost

The Garst family has owned this land, 4,300 acres straddling an 8-mi stretch of the Middle Raccoon River, since the 1880s. Beyond the pastures and fields of crops you'd expect to find on a farm, the property also encompasses woodlands, wetlands, wildflower meadows, and prairies. Using advanced land management practices, the Garst family strives to maintain the ecosystem of the property. As a result, you'll see different bits of wilderness around every bend, birds such as quail and pheasant, and bison roaming restored prairie.

Innkeeper Liz Garst has stocked the common areas of the main house with board games, darts, CDs, videos, and video games. The decor of guest accommodations ranges from knickknacks and fluffy curtains to trophy mounts to basic farmhouse furnishings. Breakfast also offers a little bit of everything. You can tuck into country ham, biscuits and gravy, pancakes and waffles, and homemade applesauce or go for fresh fruit, granola, and oatmeal. Everything is served on fine china. Other meals are available by request.

Garst Farm is a working farm, so you may watch or participate in farm activities. A favorite diversion is horseback riding that Liz calls "a real riding experience," which allows you to walk, trot, or canter at your own pace. Trails often cross the shallow river, or you can ride in the river itself if the weather's warm. The farm's stable includes Arabians, Morgans, quarter horses, and a Belgian thoroughbred that can carry the heaviest of riders. If you are uncertain about climbing into the saddle, ask for Lawrence. According to Liz, this old nag hasn't gotten excited about anything in 20 years. Other ways to enjoy the outdoors on the farm are volleyball or croquet games or bird-watching. In winter you may take a bobsled ride, go ice-skating, or just take a hike.

A point of pride for the farm is that Soviet premier Nikita Khrushchev visited in 1959, to learn about the high level of productivity that had been attained by midwestern farmers. You can learn about Khrushchev's visit and the evolution of the region's agriculture in the extensive library of books and videos and at the nightly history lecture given by a member of the Garst family. Agriculture tours give you an even closer look at Iowa's farming heritage. From Liz, you can can take classes in arranging flowers, as well as growing, drying, and pressing them. A matted and framed pressed flower, or a live African violet descended from flowers grown by Liz's grandmother, makes a great souvenir.

Tip *The guided late-night astronomy tour is one of the most memorable experiences you can have at the farm. Take an afternoon nap so you're ready for some incredible stargazing.*

🛏 5 rooms, 2 cottages, 1 house, 1 cabin 🍽 Full breakfast, grills, picnic area, some kitchens. **Recreation:** biking, bird-watching, fishing, hiking, horseback riding, mountain biking, running, wildlife viewing, river swimming, canoeing, basketball, croquet, horseshoes, volleyball, library, piano, recreation room. Nearby: 9-hole golf course, tennis courts. **Services:** canoe, mountain bike, and telescope rentals; guided fishing trips; babysitting; horse boarding; kennel; shop; meeting rooms. **Classes and programs:** guided nature hikes; flower-arranging classes; astronomy, falconry, and raptor talks. ♿ Some jetted tubs, some satellite TVs, some pets allowed; no room phones 💲 $60–$300 ▭ AE, MC, V.

🏠 *1390 Hwy. 141, Coon Rapids, IA 50058* ☎ *712/684–2964* 📠 *712/ 684–2887* 🌐 *www.farmresort.com.*

Kansas

1874 STONEHOUSE
Romantic Retreat

As you drive along two-lane Highway 177, a state-designated Scenic Byway in the heart of Kansas, you can see the Flint Hills for miles in every direction, your view broken only occasionally by hand-hewn limestone fences and farmhouses. This is the country William Least Heat-Moon chronicled in *PrairyErth*, an epic history of the tallgrass prairie that has been called a "modern-day Walden Pond." Two-story 1874 Stonehouse, a limestone house in east-central Kansas, 80 mi northeast of Wichita, is where the author stayed when he came for a book signing. The home was built by the same mason who constructed the historic courthouse in nearby Cottonwood Falls. Built from stone quarried nearby, the first stone house to be built in Chase County has walls 22 inches thick. Like many early structures in the region, it was built of stone because native timber was scarce in the area.

The exterior of the house has remained virtually unchanged over the years, but the interior received extensive renovation before it opened as a bed-and-breakfast in 1995. Three large guest rooms upstairs are furnished with antiques, such as the sleigh bed in the Rose Room. On the first floor, the spacious Prairie Flower Suite has a fireplace, a two-person jetted tub, and a two-person shower. Robes, a homemade quilt, and a four-poster bed make the suite even more enticing.

Half of the 120-acre property is open for you to explore via 1½ mi of maintained hiking trails. Along the Cottonwood River, sycamore and cottonwood trees provide shade while you wander. On your walks you are likely to see many kinds of birds as well as an occasional deer, turkey, quail, bobcat, or coyote. Many locals don't even know about the property's pond, hidden down a trail behind the house. Forty acres of former farmland around the stocked pond (you can go catch-and-release fishing here) have been restored to native tallgrass prairie grasses and wildflowers. Around the pond are some chairs and picnic tables, a porch swing hanging from a tree, and lots of quiet.

The personality of 1874 Stonehouse changes with the seasons: the most peaceful time is winter, when you can have breakfast in front of the stone fireplace and poke around the library filled with more than 300 books about Kansas. Outdoors, the only other footprints you'll find in the snow are those of birds or animals. In spring, the inn is a favorite of artists, who attend a special event to create paintings for auction at a local benefit. No matter when you stay, you'll start your day with a hearty breakfast of home-baked muffins, fruit, and maybe waffles or French toast. Innkeepers Billie and Joe Altenhofen keep a small fridge off the parlor stocked with snacks and bottled water; coffee, hot chocolate, and popcorn are always available. Billie will visit with you at breakfast, but she then makes a point to stay out of the way unless you need assistance.

Six miles away is Tallgrass Prairie National Preserve, one of the country's newest federally protected sites and the only one dedicated to the preservation of the tallgrass prairie. You can take a ranger-led tour of the grassland and its 1881 limestone mansion, carriage house, and limestone barn (which houses the visitor center). In Cottonwood Falls, 1½ mi away, check out the 1873 courthouse and art galleries.

Tip *Have an espresso or lunch at the Prairie Coffee Co. in Cottonwood Falls, and make reservations for dinner at Grand Central Hotel and Grill. The sophisticated menu here is a pleasant surprise, especially in a town with fewer than 1,000 residents.*

📭 3 rooms, 1 suite ⏺ Full breakfast, picnic area. **Recreation:** birdwatching, fishing, hiking, horseback riding (nearby), wildlife viewing. ⛄ Some in-room fireplaces, some jetted tubs; no room phones, no room TVs, no kids, no smoking. 🎫 $95–$150 ▭ AE, D, MC, V.

🏠 *R.R. 1 (Box 67A), Cottonwood Falls, KS 66845* ☎ *620/273–8481 or 866/464–3214* ⊕ *www.stonehousebandb.com.*

CIRCLE S RANCH & COUNTRY INN
Tranquil Outpost

Your cares melt away as you walk through the meadows and hills of northeast Kansas. By day you can see a panorama of unspoiled woodlands and by night a canopy of stars. You can have it almost to yourself on 1,200-acre Circle S Ranch, although it's only an hour from Kansas City International Airport.

Though from the outside the inn resembles a Kansas barn, it was purpose-built as an inn in 1998. That's when fifth-generation ranch owner Mary Cronemeyer decided to open the property, which has been in her family since the 1860s, to the public. Oil paintings, many depicting Kansas and midwestern themes, hang throughout the inn's hallways, and above the door to some guest rooms is a stained-glass transom. The eight rooms and four suites are individually decorated; each has a name, such as the Polo Room, the Trail Room, and the Cowboy Room. Outfitted with plush towels and robes, the baths have everything you need for a good, long soak in your claw-foot or the tub for two. Each room has its own special view, and some rooms have a two-way fireplace that you can watch from the sitting area or the tub. A CD player comes with music by local musicians.

On each floor is a sitting room and parlor with a fridge stocked with complimentary drinks and snacks. Downstairs in the great room–dining room, a large stone fireplace and wood floors evoke a mountain lodge, but the silo that houses an eight-person hot tub confirms you're still in Kansas. When you look outside, you're reminded again. Large windows afford impressive views of the surrounding Kaw River Hills.

Watch the visitors to bird feeders placed around the property, or try your hand at fishing in the ranch's catch-and-release ponds. Hiking trails allow you to explore, but if that seems like too much effort, you can sink into a high-backed rocking chair on the broad wraparound porch and wait for the animals to come to you. The sight of deer grazing is common, and horses, buffalo, longhorn cattle, and peacocks may wander into view. The porch is also the perfect place for sunset watching. Need to get even more relaxed? Pay a visit to the spa, which offers tempting treatments ranging from scalp massages to foot rubs. It's a difficult choice between the Prairie Flower Aroma Massage and the Kansas Native Grains Exfoliation.

When you check into the inn, you'll be offered fruit, cheese and crackers, or homemade chips and salsa. Breakfast is country-style, with eggs, meat, potatoes, and fruit. On Saturday nights the inn serves a dinner with a choice of entrées: beef tenderloin, salmon, or chicken breast. For $50, the staff will pack a picnic basket with a roasted chicken, salad, dessert, and fresh bread for two. The food and the setting have made the ranch popular for weddings. But don't worry about being caught in the midst of the festivities, since the entire ranch is usually booked for these occasions.

Tip *A romance package adds bubble bath, champagne, bath oil, rose petals, chocolates, and fruit and cheese to your room for $50.*

🛏 8 rooms, 4 suites ⑩ Full breakfast, dining room, picnic area. **Recreation:** bird-watching, fishing, hiking, wildlife viewing. **Services:** hot tub, spa, business services, Internet access, meeting rooms. ♿ Some in-room fireplaces, some jetted tubs; no room TVs, no smoking 💳 $155–$245 ▭ D, MC, V.

🏠 *3325 Circle S La., Lawrence, KS 66044* ☎ *785/843–4124 or 800/625–2839* 🖨 *785/843–4474* ⊕ *www.circlesranch.com.*

Kentucky

NATURAL BRIDGE STATE RESORT PARK
Family Hideout ~ Laid-Back Adventure

Surrounded by Daniel Boone National Forest in eastern Kentucky, about 35 mi from Lexington, 2,200-acre Natural Bridge State Resort Park takes its name from the largest of its 150 or so sandstone bridges. The park, riddled with ravines shaded by evergreen and hardwood forest, is alive with such rare and endangered species as the Virginia big-eared bat, as well as more common animals, such as raccoons, red foxes, and white-tailed deer. In spring, wildflowers (including such rarities as *Cypripedium parviflorum*—small, yellow lady slippers) and rhododendron bushes that grow on rocky outcroppings bloom. In fall, poplar, maple, and hickory produce a rainbow of leaf colors amid the pine and hemlock on the mountainsides.

All the park's trails lead to Natural Bridge, a 65-foot-tall and 78-foot-long span. You can hike across the 20-foot-wide bridge to take in the view of the surrounding landscape or you can take it easy on a chair-lift that brings you within 600 feet of the bridge and provides an equally panoramic perspective. Whether you climb or ride, you'll see steep cliff walls and a seemingly endless blanket of treetops spreading out in all directions. Before you set out on your hike, stop by the visitor center and pick up checklists of the plants and animals you're likely to see.

A favorite destination for rafters and canoeists, the Red River also flows through 26,000-acre Red River Gorge Geological Area, northeast of the park. One of the most scenic drives in Kentucky winds from the park through the gorge. You can also have a hands-on encounter with the gorge: several outfitters offer canoe rentals, rock-climbing instruction and trips, and hiking and caving excursions in Red River gorge. While you're out on expedition, your kids can participate in a junior naturalist program conducted by Natural Bridge park rangers. A swimming pool and a miniature golf course are other favorites with youngsters.

Once you arrive in Natural Bridge State Resort Park, you don't have to leave until you're good and ready. Book a room in the handsome stone-and-log Hemlock Lodge or a cabin nearby. You'll register in a lobby where armchairs and sofas are ranged before a copper-hooded fireplace. It's a fine place to meet friends or put your feet up after a day of hiking. The spacious lodge rooms are furnished with modern hotel furniture, have wildlife prints on the walls, and have balconies. For more privacy and less bustle, stay in one of the cottages nestled in the woods near the lodge. All the cottages have kitchens, and fresh linens are supplied.

If you're staying in the lodge or if you don't feel like cooking, stop by the lodge dining room. A balcony hung with bird feeders wraps around windows, which overlook the woods. At lunchtime in summer, it's not uncommon for hundreds of bright yellow goldfinches to descend on the seed feast. Meanwhile, you can dine on fare ranging from fried fish to country ham and grits. After dinner on weekend evenings, kick up your heels at the square dances held on Hoe Down Island in the small lake below the lodge.

Tip *The trails to Natural Bridge are popular, but if you take Balanced Rock Trail you can avoid the press of other hikers. Its series of limestone steps makes it more challenging than other trails, and it leads past a boulder that seems to be standing on end, before winding along a ridge top to Natural Bridge.*

🛏 35 rooms, 11 cabins 🍽 Restaurant, snack bar, grills, picnic area, some kitchens. **Recreation:** biking, bird-watching, fishing, hiking, wildlife viewing, pool, boating, canoeing, miniature golf. **Services:** pedal boat and hydrobike rentals, shops, meeting rooms. **Classes and programs:** guided hikes, guided nature walks, natural history programs, children's programs (ages 6–14), concerts, dances. ♿ Some private balconies, no-smoking rooms 💳 $43–$180 ⊟ AE, D, MC, V.

⌂ *2135 Natural Bridge Rd., Slade, KY 40376* ☎ *800/325–1710* 📠 *606/663–5037* ⊕ *www.kystateparks.com.*

PENNYRILE FOREST STATE RESORT PARK
Tranquil Outpost

A member of the mint family, American pennyroyal has slender, foot-high stems with lancet-shaped leaves. In fall, blue flowers bloom along the stems, so tiny they are barely visible amid any surrounding greenery. This aromatic plant is so common in west-central Kentucky that geographers dubbed the entire region the Pennyroyal. But the name rolls off local tongues as "pennyrile," so that's how the state christened this densely wooded park, which lies 167 mi southwest of Louisville and 75 mi northwest of Nashville, Tennessee. After driving through the strip coal-mining fields of western Kentucky to reach the park, you will feel like you've found a secret hideaway.

The state park is small—only 863 acres, with a 56-acre lake—but it is surrounded by 15,000-acre Pennyrile State Forest. Several trails lace the park's woods, including the 2⅔-mi Lake Trail along the shoreline of Pennyrile Lake. The trail passes through old hardwood forest, along a sandy beach, and near a sandstone ridge overhung with ferns and wildflowers. You'll go by a boggy inlet where patches of native cane, most of which was long ago cleared by settlers, still grows. Leave the Lake Trail for the ¾-mi loop of Pennyroyal Trail, and wander through oak-hickory woods and along a ridge topped by evergreen forest. On the loop in August and September you can spot the park's namesake wildflower.

Lake Trail starts and ends near the pretty stone Pennyrile Lodge, which looks more like a large cottage than a state park lodge. On a cliff overlooking the lake, the building is surrounded by lawn furniture and plantings of native species, such as purple coneflowers and brown-eyed Susans. The small lobby has both a fireplace and a big-screen television, each surrounded by sofas and chairs. Sizable guest rooms have modern furniture and overlook the forest or lake. Wood-and-stone cottages are tucked into the woods around the lodge or perched on the shore of the lake. Screened porches, fireplaces, and loft bedrooms reached via spiral wooden stairs make a cottage stay fun; some of the lakeside cottages even have their own small dock. All have kitchens. Note that access to the lake cottages is via stone stairs and a narrow walkway over a dam. The lodge restaurant serves traditional southern fare—ham and grits at breakfast, fried fish at lunch, and fried chicken at dinner.

The lake is the center of activity in the park. You might spend a lazy day floating in a boat—be prepared to row, since no gasoline motors are allowed on the lake. The lake is stocked with bass, crappie, and channel catfish. Geese, ducks, and other waterfowl are attracted to the lake, especially during spring and fall migration. The park lies along a major north–south flyway in a region known for its birdlife (Audubon lived in and explored the area), so bring your binoculars.

Tip *If you are accustomed to the finer things in life, rent one of the lake cottages and bring your own provisions. The lodge dining room serves no alcohol, and its country cooking is passable but not memorable.*

🛏 24 rooms, 12 cottages 🍽 Restaurant, grills, picnic area, some kitchens. **Recreation:** bird-watching, fishing, hiking, lake swimming, canoeing, rowing, 9-hole golf course, 2 tennis courts, recreation room. **Services:** rowboat, pedal boat, golf club, and golf-cart rentals; shop; dock. **Classes and programs:** guided hikes, guided nature walks, photography classes, concerts. ♿ Some in-room fireplaces, some private porches, some pets allowed, no-smoking rooms 💳 $43–$120 💳 AE, D, MC, V.

20781 Pennyrile Lodge Rd., Dawson Springs, KY 42408 ☎ 800/325–1711 🖷 270/797–4887 ⊕ www.parks.ky.gov/resortparks/pf/index.htm.

SHAKER VILLAGE OF PLEASANT HILL
Tranquil Outpost

History comes to life at Pleasant Hill, which occupies 2,900 rolling acres of pastures and woods 25 mi south of Lexington. This restored Shaker village of early-19th-century buildings is a living history museum. Here you can witness a re-creation of life as it was lived by a religious sect that revered work and forbade marriage. In the village, the graceful Georgian architecture has a soothing symmetry. Self-guided tours show off artisans in period costume engaged in weaving, barrel-making, woodworking, gardening, and other activities that once occupied the Shakers. Stone fences enclose sheep pastures, and draft horses plow croplands or rake freshly cut fields of hay. This National Historic Landmark may seem an unlikely place for a close encounter with nature, but when you stay here, you find that you are largely undisturbed by day visitors. Beyond the village, the acreage encompasses meadows, ponds, creeks, woods, and the palisades of the Kentucky River.

There is something about stepping back in time that puts you in closer touch with the rhythms of the earth. Fifteen of the historic buildings contain guest rooms, each furnished with the characteristic Shaker simplicity that calms the mind. Handcrafted reproductions of wooden Shaker beds, chairs, and chests contrast with the white-painted walls, which in turn are striped with the peg rails on which the Shakers hung everything from ladder-back chairs to coats. There are some concessions to modernity, notably air-conditioning, private baths, and televisions, but you won't forget where you are. Rooms range from basic quarters in the East Family Dwelling to suites in the Farm Deacon's Shop. There are even rooms in the old washhouse—you reach them via stairs suspended over the machinery. You can eat in the Shaker Village Trustee's Office Inn, which serves three meals a day. Many of the dishes, including a marvelously tart lemon pie, are made according to Shaker recipes, and the restaurant staff wears period clothing.

Hiking and equestrian trails, many leading to the banks of the Kentucky River, wind through Pleasant Hill's woods and prairie. In winter, whenever there's enough snow, you can ride in a sleigh pulled by draft horses. In warm weather, board the village's open-top sternwheeler, the *Dixie Belle,* for a pleasure trip on the river. The soaring limestone cliffs on either shore are overhung with plants and punctuated with waterfalls. It's not unusual to spot belted kingfishers and great blue herons on the water. More than 440 species of plants grow on the protected land, including spring wildflowers such as toad trillium, bloodroot, and trout lily. Wild turkey, white-tailed deer, and coyotes are at home here. Crack your window open at night to hear the hooting of owls and the howl of coyotes; in the morning a symphony of birdsong will wake you.

Tip *If you visit in autumn or winter, request one of the lodgings with a fireplace. Firewood is supplied daily.*

81 rooms Restaurant, some microwaves, some refrigerators. **Recreation:** biking, bird-watching, hiking, horseback riding, wildlife viewing. **Services:** horse boarding, shops, meeting rooms. **Classes and programs:** Shaker crafts demonstrations, concerts, sightseeing tours. Some in-room fireplaces, no-smoking rooms $78–$94 MC, V.

3501 Lexington Rd., Harrodsburg, KY 40330 800/734-5611 *859/734-7278* www.shakervillageky.org.

Louisiana

BUTLER GREENWOOD PLANTATION
BED & BREAKFAST
Tranquil Outpost

Butler Greenwood Plantation is in the heart of Audubon country. John James Audubon drew 32 of his *Birds of America* while in nearby West Feliciana Parish. So don't forget to bring your binoculars when you walk around the gardens by this raised English plantation house, or sit on your deck in the evening to watch white-tailed deer graze, or roam the grounds among the big old live oaks, keeping an eye out for foxes, chipmunks, and the occasional bobcat. The plantation's woodlands and the surrounding hundreds of acres of undeveloped forest still attract such songbirds as the Carolina wren and the rare red-breasted nuthatch. Ducks and such waterbirds as egrets and herons flock to the pond and creeks, and hawks to the open pastures.

The house you first see when you arrive has been in Anne Butler's family since it was built in the 1790s, and it's filled with Victorian furnishings, antique dresses, and heirloom artwork. You can tour it as part of your visit, but you'll stay in one of the cottages loosely set around a pond. The Old Kitchen, a two-bedroom, two-bath house with exposed brick and beams and fireplace, was built in 1796. Cook's Cottage, from the 1800s, has wood-paneled walls, a fireplace, and one bedroom with a queen four-poster. The rest of the eclectic cottages are of more modern vintage, from the six-sided Gazebo, which has 9-foot-tall antique stained-glass windows, to the former windmill called the Dovecote to the Treehouse, a studio with a wall of windows and back stairs that lead straight into the woods. The kitchens or kitchenettes in each cottage are stocked with breakfast fixings: coffee, tea, hot cocoa, milk, orange juice, croissants, jam, butter, fruit, and cereal. St. Francisville (population 1,800), almost 3 mi away, has a café, a roadhouse, and a few other restaurants. But you may prefer to grill out on your deck so you can scan for a rare pied-billed grebe at sunset.

The plantation manager's cousin, wildlife artist Murrell Butler, leads bird walks by appointment. No footpaths have been cut through the thick, dense, prickly underbrush of the surrounding forest, so host Anne Butler provides hiking maps of and directions to nearby trails. Entrances to Audubon State Commemorative Area, Cat Island Wildlife Refuge, and Tunica Hills State Wildlife Area are all within 10 to 15 mi.

Tip *This territory is along a migratory flyway. When the bird population peaks the first weekend in April, the local nature society hosts a bird fest and distributes a three-plus-page bird list. Book early if you intend to come at this time of year.*

⤵ 8 cottages ⦿ Continental breakfast, grills, some kitchens, some kitchenettes. **Recreation:** bird-watching, hiking (nearby), horseback riding (nearby), wildlife viewing, pool. **Classes and programs:** guided nature walks. ⬧ Cable TV, some in-room fireplaces, jetted double tubs, private decks; no smoking ▦ $135–$185 ▭ AE, MC, V.

⌂ *8345 U.S. 61, St. Francisville, LA 70775* ☎ *225/635–6312* ⊟ *225/635–6370* ⊕ *www.butlergreenwood.com.*

WILDLIFE GARDENS B&B
Tranquil Outpost

In the swamp, past cypress trees hung with Spanish moss and cypress knees sticking up through green water, Helen and Troy wait to meet you at this B&B modeled on trappers' camps like those their grandfathers lived in during the 1930s. These two alligators (11 and 14 feet long) are parents to the many young ones you can see nearby and to some of those living in the swamp. At 30-acre Wildlife Gardens in the Louisiana bayou, 14 mi southwest of Houma and 80 mi west of New Orleans, you can meet baby alligators, yearlings-plus, and three- and four-year-olds. An alligator snapping turtle and smaller turtles live in other pens, and wood ducks, mallards, and other waterfowl occupy an aviary. Injured creatures, such as a jumpy red fox and two bobcats (who produced a third), find sanctuary here as well. From the walkways, paths, and bridges, watch for free-roaming bayou inhabitants, including alligators, white-tailed deer, and egrets.

Owner Betty Provost leads guided nature walks through Wildlife Gardens, or you can explore on your own. Betty raises the hundreds of alligators in the gardens for educational purposes. During the school year many classes come to see the swamp animals that live here. The "wildlife" part of Wildlife Gardens is fenced off from the rest of the 30-acre property. Elsewhere, none-too-shy peacocks, including all-white ones, roam loose. Two miles of trails are set aside for overnight guests.

Cabins are built over or next to the water in a separate area reserved for overnight guests. Early Cajun swamp residents didn't have many comforts, and the small cabins are rough around the edges, with plywood walls, bare lightbulbs, and tight bathrooms. But the beds (one or two queens or doubles) are comfortable, and the most necessary amenities—mosquito spray, window air-conditioners, and a flashlight—are supplied. When you check in, you receive a complimentary bucket of dry alligator food so you can feed the resident gators from your chicken wire–shielded porch.

The gift shop in the main yard, decorated with trophy animals caught long before hunting them was outlawed, stands next to the yellow breakfast building, where you can down a generous, hearty morning meal of homemade biscuits, eggs with sausage, and hash browns with onions (or anything else your diet requires, on request). The nearest restaurant is 8 mi up Highway 20 toward Houma. If you continue into town, you'll come to the Jolly Inn dance hall and restaurant. Friday and Sunday nights there's live music by a Cajun band. The fried catfish, crawfish étouffée, and gumbo are as authentic as the music. Don't be surprised if people ask where you're from; all the locals know each other. And someone's bound to ask you to dance the two-step.

Tip *Damp ground, lots of mosquitoes and other insects, and persistent humidity are all part of swamp life. Especially in July and August, some people find the heat and humidity unbearable. March to May and October to November are more comfortable, but it's muggy and buggy pretty much year-round.*

🛏 4 cabins 🍽 Full breakfast, picnic area. **Recreation:** hiking, wildlife viewing. **Services:** shop. **Classes and programs:** guided nature walks. ♿ No room phones, no room TVs ☒ $80 ☰ No credit cards.

📮 *5306 N. Bayou Black Dr., Gibson, LA 70356* ☎ *985/575–3676* ⊕ *www.wildlifegardens.com.*

Maine

BLAIR HILL INN
Tranquil Outpost

At the three-story-plus Blair Hill Inn you can follow in Thoreau's footsteps in the North Woods, without sacrificing your comforts. Commanding a hillside about 2 mi from Greenville, the place is an island of gentility on the edge of the wilderness. Elegant yet not at all stuffy, the inn embraces you when you enter, sweeping you up with its expansive view. From most rooms as well as from the wraparound porch, you gaze out over the treetops to Moosehead Lake (the state's largest), a blue Rorschach blot on a green backdrop.

The inn was built in 1891 by Lyman Blair, a Chicago businessman, who established a breeding farm for cattle, sheep, and goats, as well as a nursery where he sold rare species of bulbs, perennials, and cactus. Innkeepers Dan and Ruth McLaughlin have meticulously restored the inn and are now restoring the gardens, so you can experience Blair Hill much as Blair did, albeit with modern amenities. Classical music plays in the public spaces, and original artwork by Maine artists such as Carl Sprinchorn hangs on the walls. Fresh flowers perfume the air and magnificent woodwork gleams with the patina of age. Fires blaze in the fireplaces in the living room and half of the guest rooms. Down comforters and featherbeds cover the beds, and rooms have CD players and all-natural toiletries.

It's tempting to settle into one of the easy chairs in the living room, a wicker chair on the porch, or an Adirondack chair on the lawn to while away the afternoon gazing at the lake, but there's plenty to do: hiking, boating, white-water rafting, fishing, and wildlife safaris in summer; magnificent foliage in fall; and in winter, alpine and cross-country skiing, snowshoeing, and dogsledding. Greenville is home base for a number of flight-seeing operators as well as the *Katahdin,* a historic diesel-retrofitted steamboat that cruises Moosehead Lake. Or take a walk up Blair Hill, making sure to turn around every now and then to admire the view.

Or just wander through the inn's gardens and greenhouses, which from late June to mid-October supply much of the produce and herbs and some of the fruit served at breakfast. The morning meal might begin with a peach, pear, and blueberry crisp, followed by almond-cheese pastry stars, and then a lobster-and-fresh-tarragon omelet accompanied by a scrumptious potato pancake. Some of the gardens' bounty also appears in the five-course prix-fixe dinners offered on weekends. Another periodic treat are outdoor concerts, varying from classical chamber music to zydeco.

Tip *Take one morning off from Dan's breakfasts and go on an early-morning moose safari with a local guide. You'll canoe to a remote pond or two seeking the magnificent beasts, then finish with a hearty breakfast at a sporting camp.*

⤴ 6 rooms, 2 suites ⵀ Full breakfast, restaurant. **Recreation:** birdwatching, hiking, sledding, tobogganing, badminton, boccie, croquet, library, piano, recreation room, videocassette library. Nearby: fishing, horseback riding, wildlife viewing, beach, lake swimming, boating, canoeing, kayaking, rafting, driving range, 9-hole golf course, 2 tennis courts, cross-country skiing, dogsledding, downhill skiing, ice-skating, snowmobiling, snowshoeing, volleyball. **Services:** exercise equipment, massage, Internet access. **Classes and programs:** concerts. ⟁ Some in-room data ports, some in-room fireplaces; no room phones, no smoking ▤ $250–$395 ▭ D, MC, V.

✎ *Lily Bay Rd. (Box 1288), Greenville, ME 04441* ☎ *207/695–0224* ▨ *207/695–4324* ⊕ *www.blairhill.com.*

GOOSE COVE LODGE
Family Hideout ~ Laid-Back Adventure

At the end of a dirt road overlooking Penobscot Bay and abutting Nature Conservancy lands, about 60 mi south of Bangor, Goose Cove Lodge is all about spending time with nature. Twelve-foot tides lap at the sand beach and surrounding pink granite ledges, and the sweet scent of beach rose often floats on the breeze. It's a peaceful, restorative spot with few signs of development, and life is simple but with contemporary amenities and excellent food.

You might go sea kayaking or sailing, mountain biking or hiking, or just grab a seat on the inn's wraparound deck, where you can breathe it all in. A free children's program, offered in July and August and centered at the Rec Hall and playground, keeps kids occupied. Owner Dom Parisi leads weekly nature walks, and the lodge provides maps for trails on its property as well as those on the adjacent 50-acre Barred Island Preserve, where eagles nest. You might try to identify the 16 warblers sighted here or any of the other 100-plus species of songbirds and shorebirds that have been identified. Dom also offers astronomy sessions, using his computerized 10-inch Mead Schmidt

Cassegrain telescope to point out night-sky sights that can't be seen with the naked eye. After a full day, you'll fall asleep listening to the waves washing the nearby shore.

The main lodge, built as a nature camp in the 1940s, is classic Down East, with a large fieldstone fireplace, library, and small bar on one level and a semicircular dining area a few steps down. Big windows frame a bay dotted with lobster buoys and spruce-covered islands. Guest rooms in the lodge share the view, as do most of the cottages, which snuggle amid the firs around the inn's 22 acres. No two rooms or cottages are alike, but all are furnished with country pieces, collectibles, and an antique or two, and all have decks or ledge patios. Fireplaces prepared each day by the inn's staff warm you up on chilly nights.

The inn's dining room serves creative renditions of classic fare, using Maine ingredients, organic produce, and local seafood. Breakfast is leisurely with eggs, blueberry or raspberry pancakes, French toast, and a sumptuous poached-egg dish on puff pastry with spinach, smoked salmon, and chive hollandaise sauce. Dinner is served from mid-June through mid-October, when fresh local lobster is always on the menu. Teenagers sometimes sit together at a table in the main dining room, but most children younger than 12 eat dinner separately, munching on kid-friendly foods in Toad Hall while the lodge's staff entertains them from 5:30 until 8 PM.

Tip *Allow time to visit the many artisans' shops and galleries in the area. Most display works by faculty members or former students of the internationally renowned Haystack Mountain School of Crafts, which is nearby. You can also take in an evening lecture at the school.*

◁ 3 rooms, 6 suites, 11 cabins, 2 cottages ⦿ Full breakfast, restaurant, room service, lobby lounge, grills, picnic area, some kitchens, some kitchenettes, some microwaves. **Recreation:** biking, bird-watching, hiking, mountain biking, running, wildlife viewing, beach, sailing, sea kayaking, badminton, Ping-Pong, volleyball, library, piano, recreation room, playground. Nearby: swimming hole, driving range, 9-hole golf course, 2 tennis courts, miniature golf. **Services:** mountain bikes provided, sea-kayak rentals, massage, babysitting, shop, meeting room, Internet access. **Classes and programs:** guided nature walks, sea-kayak and sailing lessons, yoga classes, children's programs (ages 2–12), artists' talks. ♿ In-room fireplaces, some private decks and patios; no a/c, no room phones, no room TVs, no smoking 🖃$111–$525 ▭ D, MC, V.

⌂ 300 Goose Cove Rd. (Box 40), Sunset, ME 04683 ☎ 207/348–2508 or 800/728–1963 🖷 207/348–2624 ⊕ www.goosecovelodge.com ⊗ Closed mid-Oct.–late May.

ISLAND INN
Tranquil Outpost

Monhegan Island's soaring headlands, crashing surf, towering spruce, and winking lighthouse have inspired generations of painters—icons such as Andrew and Jamie Wyeth, George Bellows, Robert Henri, Edward Hopper, Rockwell Kent, and scores of others. But the working fishing village clustered around the small harbor is the island's heart. Upon seeing the jumble of weather-beaten shingled and clapboard buildings that cling to rocky ledges and perch upon rises above the harbor, it's easy to understand the words of Rockwell Kent: "No one planned Monhegan; it just grew."

Its village frozen in a maritime past and much of the rest of the island undeveloped, Monhegan offers reprieve from the modern world. The only way here and back is by boat from Port Clyde, New Harbor, or Boothbay Harbor, and the only vehicles allowed on the island are those owned by year-round residents, primarily lobstering families and a few artists. You hear birds sing, wind run through the marsh grasses, a bell buoy gong, and a distant foghorn bellow. The briny scent of the sea mixes with the sweet scent of rosa rugosa. Little competes with nature for your attention and walking is the only way to explore. The village takes up less than 20% of the land, and the rest is wild. Seventeen miles of trails ring and crisscross the island, leading to rocky cliffs and a shipwreck, through lofty woods, and along the pristine backside.

The rambling, three-story Island Inn, wrapped with a covered porch and topped with a cupola, is the very essence of a Maine summer hotel. Although the accommodations are the finest on the island, there's nothing fancy about it but the views: from the front, mesmerizing sunsets over the boat-filled harbor and stark Manana Island; from the rear, sunrise views over the village and meadows to the lighthouse.

Antique oak and painted furniture, rattan chairs, marine-theme artwork, painted floors, and area rugs make the interior comfortingly unfussy, and down comforters and quilts provide warmth on chilly nights. Some of the rooms share baths. A full breakfast is included, and you can also get lunch and dinner. As you might expect, the emphasis is on fresh fish and seafood—clam chowder made from fresh-shucked local oysters and halibut. As at the few other eating places on the island, you must bring your own wine (it's available at local stores).

In the village around the inn are dozens of artists' studios, a couple of galleries, and a handful of shops and restaurants. An 1807 lighthouse tops the hill that rises beyond. The adjacent Keeper's House is now a museum chronicling island life, and the Assistant Keeper's House displays an impressive collection of island-related art.

Tips *Fish House Fish is the ultimate restaurant for lobster-in-the-rough. It's no frills—just the freshest lobster imaginable, locally smoked fish, and* *homemade stews and chowders. The "dining room" is unbeatable: a picnic table on the beach. Bring your own drinks, dessert, and other accompaniments. Note that Monhegan Boat Line makes three round-trips daily in summer, two in fall and spring.*

🛏 28 rooms, 4 suites ❧ Full breakfast, café, restaurant. **Recreation:** Nearby: bird-watching, fishing, hiking, beach. ♿ No a/c, no room TVs, no smoking 💳 $110–$325 ▣ MC, V.

🏠 *Box 128, Monhegan Island, ME 04852* ☎ *207/596–0371* 📠 *207/594–5517* 🌐 *www.islandinnmonhegan.com* ☽ *Closed mid-Oct.–late May.*

LIBBY CAMPS
Laid-Back Adventure

It's easy to forget the rest of the world exists when you stay at this lakefront sporting camp deep in Maine's North Woods. Libby Camps dates from the late 19th century, when city folk, whom locals called "sports," would retreat here from the heat to relax and fish, sleep in waterfront cabins, and eat hearty meals. Matt Libby and his wife, Ellen, are the fourth generation of their family to operate the camp. Clustered under hardwoods, evergreens, and birches along undeveloped Millinocket Lake, these log cabins and central lodge have not changed much over the years, except that the place has become somewhat more comfortable and convenient.

Getting here is half the fun. The easiest and fastest way is by floatplane (you can make arrangements through Libby's). Adventurous drivers choose to navigate miles of rough dirt roads, perhaps in the hopes of sighting moose, deer, or bears along the way. No matter how you arrive, the reward is peace, quiet, and endless stars at night. You spend your days hiking, swimming, boating, or just walking in the wilderness. A sliver of beach, lined with driftwood, is perfect for sitting and sunning. The fishing is renowned: Libby's was the first Orvis-endorsed lodge in New England, and most folks still come to fish. Some are quite serious about it, whereas others are content just to cast a line and let it drift. Registered Maine Guides, who are available to accompany you, know where the fish are, and they aren't shy about sharing that information. The guides can also help you with wildlife scouting, moose spotting, and bird-watching.

Matt Libby spends much of his day flying guests to isolated ponds and primitive outpost cabins. Ellen busies herself in the kitchen making three home-style meals, served family-style daily. When the bell is rung, signaling breakfast or dinner, you gather at the main lodge. You can also have lunch either in the dining room or packed to go. In the evenings, gas lanterns illuminate your cabins, and a woodstove takes the chill off the air. Under a handmade quilt, you fall asleep to the cries of loons and wake to the music of songbirds.

Tips *Registered Maine Guides are licensed by the state and possess a wealth of information about the outdoors. Hire one for a day, and go on photo safari for moose or other wildlife, canoeing on some of the hidden ponds in the area, or perhaps hiking on wilderness trails. To fly to Libby's, take a flight to Bangor or Presque Isle and arrange for floatplane transportation.*

⤴ 18 cabins ⦿ Modified American plan, dining room. **Recreation:** bird-watching, fishing, hiking, running, wildlife viewing, beach, lake swimming, boating, canoeing, kayaking, rowing, sailing. **Services:** canoes, motorboats, kayaks, and sailboats provided; fishing-equipment rentals; guided fishing trips; dock; tackle shop; laundry facilities; airport shuttle. **Classes and programs:** guided hikes, guided nature walks, photo safaris, sightseeing tours. ♿ Some pets allowed (fee); no a/c, no room phones, no room TVs ▣ $100–$390 ▭ D, MC, V.

⬡ *Box 810, Ashland, ME 04732* ☎ *207/435–8274 or 207/435–2462* ⊕ *www.libbycamps.com* ☽ *Closed late Nov.–Apr.*

MIGIS LODGE
Family Hideout

Migis, an Abanaki word that means "place to steal away to rest," is an appropriate name for this lodge and cabins spread out under a canopy of 100-plus-year-old white pines along the shores of Sebago Lake. Even though it's only 45 minutes northwest of Portland, the lake is a jewel, so clean and clear it serves as the source of the city's drinking water. With 100 acres, a private island, and 3,500 feet of water frontage, Migis Lodge never feels crowded—even when every room on the property is occupied. Few speedboats or jet skis bother to investigate Migis's protected cove, so the stillness is abiding.

Everything except massage services and motorboat use is included in the daily rate here. Your biggest decisions will be whether to swim, canoe, take a boating excursion, go waterskiing, play tennis, build sand castles, or laze away the day on a lakefront lounge chair. Migis caters to families, with daily activities and an afternoon children's program offered from Monday to Friday. Paths carpeted with pine needles connect cabins to the lodge and to the beaches, docks, sauna, fitness tent, playgrounds, and rec hall.

The main lodge houses the dining room and a large living room with a fieldstone fireplace, plentiful seating grouped for conversation, games tables for backgammon, chess, or checkers, and a small library. Six spacious guest rooms, each with fireplace and deck, are on the second floor. Around the main lodge, cabins range in size from one to six bedrooms. Each is bright, and attractively decorated with plush furniture in earth tones. Contemporary artwork accents the pine walls; braided, woven, or Oriental rugs warm the pine floors. Every cabin has a field-stone fireplace and a porch with lake views.

Meals are scrumptious. Sunday brunch and a Friday-night lobster bake are staged by the lake. Lunch in the dining room with a multi-course menu, or at the lakeside outdoor barbecue, where an assortment of salads as well as hot foods is offered buffet-style. On Wednesday, a more extensive buffet lunch is served on Migis's private island.

Each evening before dinner, on the lodge's front porch and terraces, cocktails and hors d'oeuvres are offered. Dinner is formal and men must wear jackets, but the mood is not stuffy. Families with young children may eat together in the family dining room, or you can enroll your children in the supervised Zoo program, where they eat from a children's menu and are entertained while you dine. Any other refreshment you might wish for, whether it's a midday cup of tea or an evening glass of wine, is readily available from the helpful, smiling staff.

Tip *On Tuesday and Thursday, Migis offers cruises on a 1936 Criscraft motor launch. At least once a week, the cruise heads up the Songo River, where there are an old hand-cranked bridge and hand-operated locks.*

📫 6 rooms, 34 cottages ⎮◎⎮ American plan, dining room, refrigerators. **Recreation:** biking, fishing, beach, lake swimming, tubing (water), waterskiing, boating, canoeing, kayaking, rowing, sailing, sculling, golf privileges, 3 tennis courts, billiards, croquet, horseshoes, Ping-Pong, shuffleboard, softball, playground, library, piano, recreation room. Nearby: running, mountain biking, hiking, horseback riding, driving range, 18-hole golf course, putting green, ballooning, miniature golf. **Services:** bikes, water skis, canoes, kayaks, rowboats, sailboats, sculls, tennis rackets, croquet set, and horseshoes provided; motorboat rentals; wellness center; exercise equipment; massage; sauna; boat launch; dock; guided fishing trips; babysitting; dry-cleaning service; laundry service; shops; Internet access. **Classes and programs:** guided hikes; fitness, tai chi, and yoga classes; children's programs (ages 5 and older); lectures; movies; bingo. ♿ Cable TV, in-room fireplaces, private balconies and porches; no a/c in some rooms, no room phones 💳 $255–$330 ▭ No credit cards.

📪 *Box 40, South Casco, ME 04077* ☎ *207/655-4524* 📠 *207/655-2054* ⊕ *www.migis.com.*

OAKLAND HOUSE SEASIDE RESORT
Tranquil Outpost

Oakland House is a dreamy version of the kind of old-fashioned seaside resort that has mostly disappeared. People return year after year, generation after generation, often with children and grandchildren in tow, to enjoy the oceanfront, the hospitality, and the relaxed pace.

Tranquillity pervades this understated, oh-so-Yankee–New England inn and cottages tucked among towering white pine, spruce, and ancient oaks. Lying about 50 mi south of Bangor along the shores of Eggemoggin Reach, a channel that divides the Blue Hill peninsula from Deer Isle, the land was originally a king's grant, made in 1765. In innkeeper Jim Littlefield's family for eight generations, the property has been an inn for four generations.

Oakland House cottages are ideal for families. Most have living rooms with granite fireplaces, porches, and kitchenettes, and all are furnished for comfort. The 1907 Shore Oaks Seaside Inn provides a quieter refuge for adults. Here, Jim's designer-wife, Sally, has masterfully restored the Arts and Crafts detailing while preserving a drowsy, turn-of-the-20th-century feeling. Most guest rooms are furnished with antiques and have big windows that take in views of Pumpkin Island Light and the Camden Hills.

Breakfast and dinner are included in the rates from mid-June through early September. If you stay in the inn, you breakfast in the cheery dining room at Shore Oaks. If you have a cottage, you take your morning meal in the original homestead building. No matter where at the resort you lay your head, you have dinner in the original building. There, separate dining rooms satisfy the needs of families as well as couples. The five-course dinner menu, which changes daily, makes good use of produce from the inn's gardens. Other ingredients, such as free-range chicken, wild salmon, and rope-grown mussels, come from producers who use environmentally sound practices. On Thursday nights, there's a lobster bake on the beach.

The inn's half mile of waterfront encompasses a pebble ocean beach, ledges that hide tidal pools, and a freshwater pond ideal for swimming. Climb an easy trail to a bluff, and Penobscot Bay unfolds below you. Take a day sail, go beachcombing, or try sea kayaking. Or you might just want to snag a seat in the gazebo on the dock. It's an ideal place to read, glimpse windjammers threading their way through narrow Eggemoggin Reach, or, courtesy of the convoluted Maine coastline, watch the sun set over the Atlantic.

Tip *Pack a picnic and spend a few hours at Holbrook Island Sanctuary. At this magical park, you can wander rough paths along the shorefront, watch seals basking on the rocks, and drink in views to Castine. One trail circles a freshwater pond where you can see beaver lodges, ducks, and eagles.*

 10 rooms, 15 cottages Modified American plan, restaurant, some kitchenettes. **Recreation:** bird-watching, fishing, hiking, running, wildlife viewing, beach, lake swimming, rowing, sailing, badminton, croquet, Ping-Pong, volleyball, library, piano, recreation room, playground. Nearby: boating, canoeing, sea kayaking, 9-hole golf course, tennis courts, miniature golf. **Classes and programs:** arts and crafts

classes, photography classes, movies, sightseeing tours. ⛵ Some in-room fireplaces, some private decks; no a/c, no phones in some rooms, no TV in some rooms, no smoking 💳 $149–$1,785 💳 MC, V.

📱 *435 Herrick Rd., Herricks Landing, Brooksville, ME 04617* 📞 *207/ 359–8521 or 800/359–7352* 📠 *207/359–9865* 🌐 *www.oaklandhouse.com* 🕐 *Inn and all but two cottages closed mid-Oct.–mid-May.*

OCEANSIDE MEADOWS INN
Tranquil Outpost

A half hour north of Ellsworth along the sleepy road to Corea, near where author Louise Dickinson Rich made her home, is a 200-acre environmental retreat on a New England saltwater farm. Taken by the ocean out the front door, the fields, woods, and salt marsh out back, and the moose, eagles, and other wildlife, Sonja Sundaram and her husband, Ben Walter, a marine biologist, have created the Innstitute for Arts and Sciences at Oceanside Meadows Inn. It's not as academic as it sounds. Here you can spend your days building sand castles on the beach, exploring tidal pools in the ledges that border it, or hiking the trails laced through the woods, meadows, and salt marsh. A pamphlet prepared by Ben details ecological sights, flora, and fauna to look for along the way.

Farther afield, Ben will help arrange sea-kayaking, canoeing, or boating expeditions, and bike rentals through a local outfitter. The relatively unknown Schoodic section of Acadia National Park, a finger of land tipped by pink-granite shores, has a nice loop road for biking or driving, and trails for hiking. In nearby Steuben, more than 300 bird species have been sighted on Petit Manan Point, a bird-watching site that's part of 2,166-acre Petit Manan National Wildlife Refuge.

No matter how you fill your days, returning to Oceanside Meadows is a joy. The inn is made up of two adjacent 19th-century white clapboard buildings, one built by a sea captain, the other a former farmhouse. Guest rooms in both are simply furnished with antiques, country pieces, family treasures, and finds from Ben and Sonja's travels. Between the two buildings is a barn that's been renovated as a meeting hall, where lectures, musical performances, art shows, and other events are held weekly. Tea and goodies are always available in the living room, where a fire blazes on cooler evenings.

You'll sleep soundly at night, lulled by the rhythmic splash of waves upon the shore. In the morning, breakfast is an extravagant parade of vegetables, edible flowers, and herbs from the inn's organic gardens. Sonja also uses free-range local eggs and produce from area organic farms. You might begin with vanilla pear soup with sweet cicely, then move on to cranberry bread pudding with chocolate mint or ployes (similar to crepes) accompanied by nasturtiums and a blueberry-rhubarb sauce.

Tips *The trails behind the inn can be wet, so bring waterproof hiking shoes. Don't forget binoculars for spotting moose, bald eagle, great blue heron, and other species. A kosher kitchen is available for your use in the farmhouse.*

🛏 12 rooms, 3 suites ️🍽 Full breakfast, dining room, grills, picnic area, kitchen. **Recreation:** biking, bird-watching, fishing, hiking, mountain biking, running, wildlife viewing, beach, surfing, windsurfing, sea kayaking, badminton, boccie, croquet, horseshoes, horseback riding, rock climbing, lake swimming, scuba diving, tubing (water), boating, canoeing, sailing, 9-hole and 18-hole golf courses, 3 tennis courts, piano, playground. **Services:** massage, babysitting, meeting room. **Classes and programs:** guided hikes, guided nature walks, natural history programs, scientific and environmental talks, concerts, lectures, movies. 🐾 Some pets allowed (fee); no a/c, no room phones, no room TVs, no smoking 💳 $98–$198 💳 AE, D, MC, V.

🏠 *Corea Rd./Rte. 195 (Box 90), Prospect Harbor, ME 04669* ☎ *207/963–5557* 🖨 *207/963–5928* 🌐 *www.oceaninn.com* � *Closed Nov.–Apr.*

Maryland

SAVAGE RIVER LODGE
Laid-Back Adventure

If you're seeking unspoiled woodlands, look no further than the mountains of western Maryland, 5 mi south of I–68. The lodge and cabins at the Savage River Lodge sit on 45 timbered acres in the middle of the Savage River State Forest. Here you can enjoy the delights of the Savage Mountains without ever pitching a tent or starting a campfire.

The winding gravel road to the lodge crosses a river and is then engulfed by towering cedar trees and, in summer, thousands of wild, bright green ferns. The first thing you'll notice once you reach the lodge is the huge wraparound porch filled with giant rocking chairs. Bodhi, a yellow Labrador retriever, greets you at the door. Inside, a massive, two-sided fireplace dominates the great room. The library is complete with board games and wilderness books. A small bar serves wines and microbrews. The 50-seat dining room extends onto the porch in summer.

The cabins are a five-minute walk from the lodge, snuggled closely together in the woods. Don't be surprised if your unit has guests—deer commonly graze close by. Each cabin has a large front porch with rocking chairs. On the first level you'll find a spacious living area with a gas fireplace, pullout sofa, and bathroom. Every cabin has a sleeping loft with a queen-size bed. Blankets on the bed keep you toasty in cool weather and a fan on the 12-foot loft ceiling cools things down in the mild summers.

Along the many marked trails keep an eye peeled for black bears, coyotes, beavers, deer, turtles, snakes, and wild turkeys. You can even take a turkey-calling class with the lodge's co-owner, Mike Dreisbach. The staff also offers fly-fishing lessons, especially popular in spring when the scores of cold mountain streams brim with trout. In winter, it's not uncommon for these forests to average 100 inches of snow, so you can cross-country ski, snowshoe, or go sledding. Afterward, warm up with hot chocolate in your cabin.

Your breakfast of juice and warm muffins is delivered to your door in a small, wooden basket. Testament to how dog-friendly this establishment is, home-baked doggie biscuits are included if you bring a canine companion. The menu at the lodge restaurant is a reflection of the environment. It's heavy on game, including venison, bison, and wild boar. Local trout and catfish are staples. If it's available, try the savory meat loaf. The chef tries to use local produce and, in season, has been known to cook with morels, one of the tastiest mushrooms around, and ramps, a kind of onion picked from the forest surrounding the lodge. The berry cobblers and other desserts also incorporate local ingredients.

Tip *Call ahead in winter to make sure the road leading to the inn is drivable. Sometimes, four-wheel-drive's a must.*

⇦ 18 cabins 🍽 Continental breakfast, restaurant, bar, lobby lounge, refrigerators. **Recreation:** bird-watching, hiking, mountain biking, running, wildlife viewing, cross-country skiing, sledding, snowshoeing, horseshoes, board games, library. Nearby: biking, fishing, horseback riding, lake swimming, river swimming, canoeing, kayaking, rafting, three 18-hole golf courses, downhill skiing, telemark skiing, tubing (snow), sporting clays. **Services:** mountain-bike, cross-country ski, snowshoe, and fishing-equipment rentals; massage; guided fly-fishing trips, gift shop, ski shop, airport shuttle, business services, meeting room. **Classes and programs:** guided hikes and nature walks; cross-country skiing and fly-fishing lessons; yoga and cooking classes. ♿ In-room data ports, in-room fireplaces, private porches, some pets allowed (fee); no a/c, no room TVs, no smoking ▱ $190 ▭ AE, D, MC, V.

🖃 *1600 Mt. Aetna Rd., Frostburg, MD 21532* ☎ *301/689–3200* 🖷 *301/689–2746* ⊕ *www.savageriverlodge.com.*

TILGHMAN ISLAND INN
Tranquil Outpost

Across Knapp's Narrow Bridge from the mainland, life seems to slow down. Far from the bustle of St. Michaels, about 72 mi from Baltimore and 80 mi from Washington, D.C., Tilghman Island is a quiet refuge on Chesapeake Bay. After a conversation with a seventh-generation oyster dredger or a home-style meal at a local restaurant, you'll find this place is magically in tune with its seafaring roots. On the island's shore, just about where the bay meets Knapp's Narrow River, Tilghman Island Inn is an eccentric spot where you can settle into the silence of the bay and take in water views from dozens of angles.

Upon entering the inn, you will be greeted by one of three characters— a sassy little parrot, a gregarious innkeeper, or one of the many canine guests that come with their owners each year. After checking in, grab a drink at the bar and, depending on the season, relax in front of the fireplace in the living area or in a waterfront Adirondack chair. All rooms in the inn are simply but impeccably furnished in neutral tones, with light-colored wood furniture, fresh flowers, and, in most rooms, incredible water views. Specially designated rooms without a water view, but with direct outdoor access, are reserved for pet owners. There are also five cushy waterside suites, each with tasteful yet whimsical decor such as animal-print rugs and oversize mirrors. Suites include hot tubs, fireplaces, and spacious decks.

The staff is eager to help you plan your days. Water activities—sailing, kayaking, canoeing, fishing, lighthouse touring, you name it—abound on the property and in the area, and the inn's staff will make all the arrangements for you. The largest charter company on the bay is a five-minute walk from the inn. On land, the flat terrain may tempt you into a long walk or bike ride. You can walk through the tiny town of Tilghman Island and past its harbors to a peninsula with a view of the meeting point of Chesapeake Bay and the Choptank River. Or you can bike to the bustling town of St. Michaels. There are water views on both sides of the road, and you can stop to admire the gorgeous old farmhouses that have sat on the edge of the water for hundreds of years. Fishing off the rocks at the end of the island is rewarding whether or not you reel in a catch—the view of the bay is a treasure in itself.

A favorite destination is the *Rebecca T. Ruark,* the oldest working Maryland skipjack, captained by probably the most entertaining dredger alive. Captain Wade gives an informative, first-hand narrative of his family's three generations in the oyster industry on Tilghman Island. Be careful—if you show too much interest you'll be hand-pulling the dredge out of the water and back onto the deck.

As the day winds down, a sunset wine cruise is well worth your time for the usually lively company and views of the colorful skies over the bay. At the inn, nightly meals are served alfresco in spring and summer on the sunset deck, which has wonderful views of a nearby marsh. You can also dine in the bay room, with a water-facing wall of windows. The regularly changing menu showcases the freshest local ingredients—if it's sweet pea season, expect to see some on the menu along with other local greens. Local seafood dishes are almost always available along with seasonal game like rabbit.

Tip *Bacchus smiles upon the bay when the inn throws its regularly scheduled wine weekends. These culinary extravaganzas start with a wine tasting on Friday, progress to a multi-course meal on Saturday evening, and end with a champagne brunch on Sunday.*

15 rooms, 5 suites ❘❍❘ Continental breakfast, dining rooms, restaurant, 2 bars, lobby lounge, lounge, some refrigerators. **Recreation:** pool, tennis court. Nearby: biking, bird-watching, fishing, horseback

riding, waterskiing, boating, kayaking, sailing, three 18-hole golf courses, carriage rides, croquet, volleyball, playground. **Classes and programs:** Cooking classes, wine talks. ⟡ Cable TV, in-room data ports, in-room fireplaces, jetted tubs, private balconies, some pets allowed, no-smoking rooms ⟡ $175–$300 ⟡ AE, D, MC, V.

⟡ Coopertown Rd. (Box B), Tilghman Island, MD 21671 ⟡ 410/886–2141 or 800/866–2141 ⟡ 410/886–2216 ⟡ www.tilghmanislandinn.com.

Massachusetts

CUTTYHUNK FISHING CLUB FAMILY B&B INN
Tranquil Outpost

Tiny Cuttyhunk, just 2½ mi long and ¾ mi wide, is the largest and westernmost of the Elizabeth Islands, which stretch southwest from Woods Hole, on Cape Cod, to a point 14 mi south of New Bedford, on the southeast coast of Massachusetts. The only island in that archipelago that's neither privately owned nor uninhabited, Cuttyhunk is a frequent destination for weekend sailors who anchor in its protected harbor and for sport fishermen, who come after stripers and blues. The homes of the few year-round residents (and there are truly only a handful) climb a hill overlooking the harbor, but the rest of the 500-acre landfall is mostly vacant scrub grass, protected conservation land that is strictly for the birds—except for the Cuttyhunk Fishing Club B&B Inn.

Back in the late 1800s and early 1900s, rich and powerful men would get together at the Cuttyhunk Bass Club, as it was then called, for a few days or a week of uninterrupted fishing and camaraderie. Accommodations were humble, but the meals could be extravagant. Among the captains of industry, oil magnates, tycoons, and other well-connected guests during that period were two presidents of the United States: Teddy Roosevelt (who knew a thing or two about wilderness) and William Howard Taft. The folks visiting Cuttyhunk now are considerably more freewheeling and down-to-earth, but little else has changed on the island. Then, as now, the activities of choice were fishing, taking long walks, swimming, and generally kicking back in a gorgeously isolated place, with fireflies the only nightlife.

Still fairly simply furnished, guest rooms at the inn are small but pleasant. Double or twin beds have flowered coverlets, and random chairs, tables, and chests from summers past have been refurbished and rearranged. Only two of the eight guest rooms have a private bath, another two have half baths, and the others have shared facilities. Two of the rooms connect to make a suite suitable for four people. Downstairs there's a sitting room with a large stone fireplace and shelves lined with books.

A full breakfast is served daily, and Thursday through Saturday a home-cooked dinner is available by request only—roast chicken, baked pork chops, grilled steak, fresh local fish, and the like. From Sunday through Wednesday, you are welcome to use the kitchen to make your own dinner—perhaps the fish you caught that morning. Outside the inn, check out the pair of seafood shanties on the town dock, which serve lunch and light dinner (lobster rolls, fried fish, shellfish, sandwiches, snacks, and ice cream), and Soprano's Pizza, a short walk from the town dock. Floating Harbor Raw Bar will deliver clams and oysters on the half shell, lobster, and shore dinners to your boat, or you can pick up your order at the dock. Cuttyhunk is dry, however, so if you want a beer, wine, or a cocktail, plan on bringing your own.

Cuttyhunk is strictly about relaxing and communing with nature. Other than the approximate one-third of the island that's "settled," you'll find gentle hills, bayberry and scrub grasses, and woodlands filled with songbirds. Deer paths are good for hiking, and both rocky and sandy beaches invite long walks or lounging and reading. Shorebirds, ducks, geese, and other waterfowl are denizens of Cuttyhunk Pond, the protected harbor that nearly bisects the island. There are very few cars on-island, and a handful of golf carts and motor scooters travel the ¼ mi of paved road. People generally get around on foot, slowing everything down to a pace that makes sense on an island where children can roam safely and grown-ups can soak up brilliant sea views.

Tips *For those who arrive by private boat, the town of Cuttyhunk rents moorings (first-come, first-served) in the large, protected anchorage that you approach from the east through a long channel. To get here from Fisherman's Wharf (Pier 3) in New Bedford, the M/V Alert makes one or two round-trips daily, depending on the season; the ride is 1 hour one-way to Cuttyhunk. From Menemsha on Martha's Vineyard, the catamaran S/V Arabella (508/645–3511) sails one round-trip daily (1½ hours one-way) in summer. Or take a water taxi via Seahawk water taxi (508/997–6387) or Cuttyhunk water taxi (508/789–3250).*

⇨ 8 rooms ⦿ Full breakfast, dining room, kitchen. **Recreation:** bird-watching, fishing, hiking, beach, boating, library. **Services:** dock, guided fishing trips. ⟡ Some pets allowed; no a/c, no room phones, no room TVs ⬚ $135–$170 ⊟ No credit cards.

⬚ *No. 1, Road to the Landing (Box 57), Cuttyhunk, MA 02713* ☎ *508/992–5585* ⊕ *www.fishcfc.com* ☉ *Closed mid-Oct.–mid-May.*

THE INN AT CLAMBER HILL
Romantic Retreat ~ Tranquil Outpost

When the Quabbin Reservoir was created in the 1930s, four towns in north-central Massachusetts were flooded. Quabbin now covers about

40 square mi and is one of the largest man-made bodies of water in the United States. The reservoir holds 400 billion gallons of water and supports 27 species of fish, including trout, landlocked salmon, bass, pickerel, and perch. The forest around the reservoir is a haven for wildlife. In winter, bald eagles call this area home.

Just minutes from the northern shore of the Quabbin Reservoir, an hour from both Hartford and Boston in the pretty little town of Petersham, the Inn at Clamber Hill sits high on its namesake hill. The French country–style manse was built in 1927 by the then-mayor of Springfield, Massachusetts, as a summer residence for his family. Since 1997, innkeepers Mark and Deni Ellis have welcomed guests looking for peace and quiet.

The inn has a spacious suite, with a separate sitting room and a fireplace, and three double rooms, named and decorated according to themes; the European Suite, for instance, has a queen-size four-poster bed, richly colored tapestries on the wall, an antique writing desk, and a fireplace in its sitting room, not to mention a garden view. In the common rooms on the main floor, the sitting room, formal library, and dining room are furnished with the house's original woodwork as well as antiques, Oriental rugs, and artwork. Eight fireplaces grace the inn, so it's especially cozy on crisp fall afternoons and cold winter evenings. Two outdoor terraces are attractive gathering places, and the perennial gardens are resplendent in spring and summer. Marked trails crisscross the 33 acres of woodland property that surrounds the inn.

Besides enjoying the reservoir, where you can fish, canoe, and kayak, you might visit the Harvard University Forest Research Center, only 3 mi from the inn. One of the most intensively and longest-studied (since 1907) forests in North America, the 3,000-acre Harvard Forest has trails where you can hike, ride horseback, mountain bike, snowshoe, and cross-country ski. In the forest's Fisher Museum dioramas portray the history, conservation, and management of New England forests. Multimedia presentations give an overview of two forest trails ($\frac{1}{2}$ mi and $1\frac{1}{2}$ mi) where you can learn about the center's forestry and ecology research.

The inn does serve dinner if you make arrangements in advance, or the innkeepers can recommend nearby restaurants. Each morning you wake up to a hot breakfast of muffins or cinnamon rolls, pancakes speckled with just-picked blueberries, or bacon and eggs.

Tip *If you want to stay at the Inn at Clamber Hill during autumn foliage season, reserve well ahead. Fall room reservations at inns and B&Bs throughout New England are often scooped up a year in advance.*

3 rooms, 1 suite ¶◎¶ Full breakfast. **Recreation:** library. Nearby: biking, bird-watching, fishing, hiking, mountain biking, lake swimming, canoeing, kayaking, 9-hole golf course, cross-country skiing, downhill skiing, snowshoeing. Dogs allowed; no room phones, no room TVs, no smoking $145–$195 AE, MC, V.

111 N. Main St., Petersham, MA 01366 978/724–8800 or 888/ 374–0007 978/724–8829 www.clamberhill.com.

Michigan

THE INN AT BLACK STAR FARMS
Romantic Retreat

The Leelanau Peninsula is what you might think of as a pinky finger sprouting from the mitten shape of Michigan's Lower Peninsula. Surrounded by Lake Michigan on three sides, Leelanau Peninsula is caressed by lake breezes, cool summer rains, and deep snowfall. The thick stands of oak and maple trees; cherry, peach, and apricot orchards; and vineyards that grow on the peninsula's steep hills also grow around the Inn at Black Star Farms, on the eastern shore.

Black Star is a winery, distillery, and creamery. At the large oak bar in the tasting room, you can sample French oak-aged chardonnay, riesling, or pinot gris, the wines characteristic of this region. In each bottle of the distillery's pear brandy is a whole pear. The creamery produces raclette cheese that you can taste as well. About once a week, when the cheese is made, you can watch the process through the big window at the far end of the tasting room.

The B&B stands next door to the tasting room, in an elaborate Georgian-style manse. The mosaic star that gives the inn its name is centered in the Cygnus Lobby's cream marble floor. Just off the foyer are the library and the Pegasus Lounge, a warm lounge with fireplace. Wine and cheese are served here every evening, but you can cozy up to the fire with a book or a board game any time of day. From the lobby a curving oak staircase leads up to guest rooms furnished with wrought-iron bedsteads, fluffy down duvets, thick bathrobes, and a bottle of house wine. All have a private bath, but each room is unique: one has a huge marble bath with mirrored walls, two come with fireplaces. Down the hall is a large common bath outfitted with a two-person Jacuzzi and a sauna. A hearty breakfast is served each morning in the Mimosa Room, where you can watch the chef at work in the open kitchen. Maple sausages, cinnamon French toast, cherry muffins, and fruit from a local orchard might make their way to your plate. In the afternoon, iced tea, fresh cider, or mulled cherry wine awaits.

Outside, you can hike, bike, ski, or snowshoe on the property's 5 mi of footpaths. The Leelanau Trail crosses the peninsula from Traverse City to Sutton's Bay, right from the Black Star grounds. A ½-mi walk takes you to the west arm of a Lake Michigan inlet called Grand Traverse Bay, where sailboats ply the waters. Drive into Sutton's Bay to check out its boutiques and cafés, or ask for a copy of the Leelanau Wine Trail map and take a tour of neighboring wineries. When you return, settle into a deck chair on the patio, a glass of wine at your side, and savor the shade of the hardwoods and fruit trees.

Tip *When you visit the tasting room, ask about discounts for inn guests.*

🗨 8 rooms �🍽️ Full breakfast, dining room. **Recreation:** hiking, wine tasting, cross-country skiing, snowshoeing, library. Nearby: biking, fishing, lake swimming, boating, sailing, downhill skiing. **Services:** massage, sauna, horse boarding, laundry facilities, Internet access, meeting rooms. **Classes and programs:** winery tours, riding lessons. ♨ Some jetted tubs, satellite TV with movies, in-room VCRs; no kids under 13, no smoking 💳 $150–$375 ▭ AE, D, MC, V.

🏠 *10844 E. Revold Rd., Sutton's Bay, MI 49682* ☎ *231/271–4970* 🖷 *231/271–4883* 🌐 *www.blackstarfarms.com.*

KEWEENAW MOUNTAIN LODGE
Tranquil Outpost

At the base of Michigan's Upper Peninsula, where it emerges from the northeastern corner of Wisconsin (160 mi from Green Bay), the Keweenaw Peninsula (whose name is pronounced *kee*-win-awe) aims north while the rest of the U.P. heads east. The wayward peninsula noses 70 mi out into Lake Superior, one of the world's largest freshwater lakes. As it follows the peninsula north, the road to Keweenaw Mountain Lodge twists and turns through a tunnel of hardwood forest, occasionally illuminated by bursts of bright sunlight breaking through the foliage. Eventually you reach Copper Harbor, at the very tip of the peninsula. Here, on its nearly 170 acres, the lodge feels about as far away from everything as it can be, even though you're only a five-minute drive from town and the Lake Superior shore.

Keweenaw Mountain Lodge has changed very little since its construction by the WPA in the 1930s. Copper mining was once the economic backbone of the Keweenaw region, but the mines were abandoned during the Depression. The WPA hired unemployed miners to build a golf course, and they used the logs gathered from clearing the land to put up a clubhouse and cabins. Today the walls still bear the marks of the original workmen, and these unsmoothed knobs, little bits of unstripped bark, and chisel marks lend character. Cabins resemble old family cottages, with prewar fixtures, Grandma's sofa, and curtains in out-of-date patterns. There's an ample supply of firewood for your stone fireplace, which stands ready to add a little romance to an evening or take the chill off a morning—even in August. Rooms in the lodge's motel building (added about 20 years after the WPA project) are quite small and lack character, their log-cabin exterior notwithstanding.

But you come here not for luxury but for once-upon-a-time charm, absolute tranquillity, and pristine nature. A 3-mi hiking trail that bisects the grounds leads deep into the mountains, past the best of the unspoiled north country: hardwood forests, wildflowers, and views of crystal-clear Lake Manganese. On the golf course naturally hilly fairways are tucked between stands of spruce and maple. Within a short drive you can go fishing, hiking, and kayaking in Copper County State Forest or along the Lake Superior shoreline. Tour companies and outfitters can help you get out and about.

In the old clubhouse are the lodge's restaurant and lounge, constructed entirely of native pine and fieldstone. Supported by huge log pillars and beams, thick 30-foot logs form the peaked dining-room ceiling. You can have every meal by the stone fireplace on cool evenings, or on the screened-in porch in warm weather. The highlights of the menu are lake trout and whitefish fresh from Lake Superior; standard American fare such as steak, chicken, and pasta is also available. Strolling back to your cabin after dinner, take time to look up. Out here, far from city lights, the skies are especially dark and the stars especially bright.

Tip *Don't miss the gilded sunset along Brockway Mountain Drive from Copper Harbor with unforgettable views of the Keweenaw Peninsula and Lake Superior.*

🛏 8 rooms, 34 cottages ¶◎¶ Restaurant, lounge. **Recreation:** hiking, mountain biking, wildlife viewing, 9-hole golf course, putting green, tennis court, shuffleboard. Nearby: fishing, lake swimming, boating, canoeing, jet skiing, kayaking, rowing, sailing, sea kayaking. **Services:** pro shop. ♿ Some in-room fireplaces; no a/c ⚏ $85–$129 ▭ D, MC, V.

🏠 U.S. 41 (Box 90), Copper Harbor, MI 49918 ☎ 906/289–4403 or 888/685–6343 ⊕ www.atthelodge.com � Closed mid-Oct.–mid–May.

ROCK HARBOR LODGE
Laid-Back Adventure

Isle Royale National Park, which occupies an entire island in Lake Superior, is the northernmost place in Michigan, closer to Canada than to the United States. If you've heard of it, you probably think of it as a place where Boy Scouts and hard-core backpackers go to rough it in the forest. But if you stay at Rock Harbor Lodge, you can explore all that the island has to offer and still enjoy the comfort of a roof over your head.

After the long ferry trip across Lake Superior (three to seven hours, depending on where you're coming from), the sight of the lakeside lodge is welcome. As your ship approaches Snug Harbor a cluster of half a dozen lodge buildings comes into view beside the dock. The brown clapboard may remind you of summer camp, except that each building has picture windows with views of Lake Superior. From the outside the dining hall is also plain, but inside things are decidedly upscale, with tablecloths, china, and a menu that offers some of the finest, freshest whitefish anywhere in the Great Lakes, harvested just hours before from the waters around the lodge. At least once during your stay, order the blueberry cobbler made from fresh Michigan blueberries.

Stay in the smallish guest rooms of the lodge's four main buildings, and all meals are included in your room rate. A short walk away, 10 duplex cabins contain housekeeping units with a little more space—they have one double bed and two bunk beds, and kitchens. Meals are not included in cabin rates. Lodge or cabin, accommodations are basic. The furnishings date from the 1960s and 1970s, rooms lack TVs and telephones, and water pressure leaves something to be desired. But for nature lovers, this place is nothing short of a miracle.

From the dock, you have access to some of Isle Royale's best canoeing and kayaking. Rent a boat or bring your own on the ferry (for a small fee). Paddle across Tobin Harbor to Hidden Lake, where a natural salt lick attracts the island's moose population. Or head over to nearby Raspberry Island. Some of Isle Royale's most spectacular scenery borders hiking trails that start a few yards from Rock Harbor Lodge. Along these paths you can explore forests of white spruce, aspen, and birch, or walk out to Scoville Point, a limestone promontory with fabulous lake and island views. Watch loons and cormorants fishing in Tobin Harbor, or visit prehistoric Indian copper mines, all within a mile of the resort. In spring you'll see deep purple wild irises, eastern columbines, and other stunning wildflowers. In summer, look for thick carpets of white Canada dogwood, as well as bright orange wood lilies and the white blossoms of the waist-high thimbleberries.

Tip *If you stay in a cottage and plan to cook your own meals, bring your groceries from the mainland. The island store sells only limited provisions, and prices are high.*

⟿60 rooms, 20 cabins ¶⊚⎮American plan (lodge only), snack bar, restaurant, bar, grocery store, picnic area, some kitchens. **Recreation:** fishing, hiking, wildlife viewing, boating, canoeing, kayaking, rowing, sailing, sea kayaking. **Services:** canoe, kayak, rowboat, and powerboat rentals; guided fishing trips; airstrip; dock; marina; laundry facilities; shop. **Classes and programs:** wildlife and nature talks, sightseeing tours.

♿ No-smoking rooms; no a/c, no room phones, no room TVs
🖃 $165–$319 ▤ AE, D, MC, V.

📬 *May–Sept.: Box 605, Houghton, MI 49931; Oct.–Apr.: Box 27, Mammoth Cave, KY 42259* 🖀 *May–Sept.: 906/337–4993; Oct.–Apr.: 270/773–2191* 📠 *906/337–4993* 🌐 *www.rockharborlodge.com* ✖ *Closed Oct.–Apr.*

THE SHACK BED & BREAKFAST
Romantic Retreat

In the early morning, just after sunrise, a heavy mist rises from the surface of Robinson Lake. As you look out your log-framed window your thoughts might turn to errands or the kids or the office. But probably not. The foggy lake will mesmerize you, and the only thing to do is to sit a little longer and lose yourself in the vision.

The Shack Bed & Breakfast has been a place of respite for nearly a century. Built as a family retreat in the early 1900s, the log lodge is surrounded by 100 wooded acres in the west-central portion of Michigan's Lower Peninsula, about 60 mi from Grand Rapids. Over time, the lodge was thoughtfully expanded and turned into a bed-and-breakfast. Inside and out, walls are bare logs chinked with plaster, and four-poster beds, tables, desks, and chairs are hewn from the same bare logs. Modern amenities make the Shack more comfortable than its name would suggest. Beds are covered with plaid muslin duvets and quilts. Bathrooms are large and spacious, with two-person showers. Many rooms have two-person Jacuzzis and fireplaces. And the lodge's front porch is lined with Adirondack deck chairs and end tables, just the place for a glass of iced tea.

In the style of the rest of the lodge, the dining room is built of colossal logs. Tables are set before floor-to-ceiling windows that look out over the lake. A hot breakfast buffet is laid out each morning, and a hearty dinner buffet awaits on Friday and Saturday evenings (the meal is included in your room rate). The buffet includes old-fashioned Sunday-dinner fare: baked chicken, prime rib, mashed potatoes, vegetables, and hot rolls. A bit later, at 9, the dining room's trademark appears—a banana split bar from which you can fill your sundae dish to overflowing with giant scoops of premium ice cream, in flavors like peanut butter–chocolate and Heath Bar crunch.

Outdoors everywhere you look you see impatiens, geraniums, begonias, and daylilies. Flower beds line drives, walkways, and porches and baskets of blooms hang from every porch roof as well as three large gazebos that overlook the lake or shelter in the shade of sugar maples. Like waterborne blossoms, a fleet of swans float on the lake. Footpaths thread through the Shack's property, one of them along Lake Robinson's shoreline. The paths don't really qualify as hiking trails—exploring the terrain around the inn is a gentle exercise in strolling hand in hand and pausing on park benches by the water. If you'd rather go straight for the lake, you can go pedal boating, swimming, and fishing, or bring along your own canoe, kayak, or rowboat and launch it on the lake.

Tip *The Shack is really a place for adults. There is little for children to do here, and they may feel out of place.*

↪ 44 rooms ⱺ Full breakfast, dining room, some kitchenettes. **Recreation:** biking, fishing, hiking (nearby), wildlife viewing, lake swimming, canoeing, kayaking, rowing, horseshoes, Ping-Pong, shuffleboard, piano, recreation room. **Services:** pedal boats provided, exercise equipment, meeting rooms. ♿ Some jetted tubs, in-room VCRs; no smoking ⌨ $70–$200 ▤ D, MC, V.

🖉 *2263 W. 14th St., White Cloud, MI 49349* ☎ *231/924–6683* 🖷 *231/924–5065* ⊕ *www.theshackbedandbreakfast.com.*

Minnesota

BERWOOD HILL INN
Romantic Retreat

As you drive south from the Twin Cities, life seems to grow simpler with each passing mile. Within a couple of hours, Amish buggies and riders on horseback appear on the side of the road. This is Minnesota's bluff country, where cascades of limestone and stands of dry forest surround the Root River. The river is a favorite of bicyclists and cross-country skiers, who trace its meanderings from town to town on well-established trails. Berwood Hill Inn, on a ridge 4 mi up and away from Lanesboro, and about 120 mi from the Twin Cities, is at the area's geographic and emotional center.

Berwood is a Victorian country home at the end of a long gravel drive, where you can expect to be greeted with a glass of wine and tray of cookies. There are wraparound porches on the first and second floors, plus a gazebo. The four guest rooms are full of antiques, a passion of owner Fran Scibora. She was raised in this farmhouse and renovated it with a stylish approach to country curios. The plush attic suite, known as the Owl's Nest, is crammed with owl-related antiques and is the most requested room.

White oak, spruce, and maple trees shade the house, which is surrounded by more than 7 acres of gardens, some floral, some of a more peculiar sort. The Cupola Garden is a favorite. Scibora has long loved the sometimes ornate, weather-vaned cupolas atop old barns, and when nearby farmers demolish their barns, she hauls off the cupolas and sets them in her garden like monuments. Herb gardens supply chef and innkeeper Arlene Woellert with fresh ingredients for her five-course breakfasts, which may include Swedish waffles, rainbow trout, and pork tenderloin, as well as fresh bread and produce from local farmers. The Garden Cottage, a seasonal one-room A-frame, stands amid flowers about 50 yards from the house and is stuffed with collectibles (cottage guests use a private bathroom in the main house).

The Root River Trail and Harmony-Preston Valley Trail, which take hikers, bikers, and cross-country skiers over 60 mi of bluffs, are the main draws for outdoor enthusiasts. Lanesboro, Harmony, and the other towns on the two intersecting trails were little-visited farming villages before the trails opened in the 1990s. Now Lanesboro is chockablock with outfitters who supply bikes for trail riding. You can also rent canoes and inner tubes to take on the Root River, which courses through town. From Berwood, the closest access to the trails is 3 mi away, at the Old Barn Resort, a campground and restaurant.

Several nearby caves worth exploring are Niagara Cave outside Harmony, with winding passageways and a 60-foot waterfall, as well as Mystery Cave, part of Forestville State Park near Preston. Forestville and Beaver Creek Valley state parks have woodsy hiking trails. Anglers cast for brook, rainbow, and brown trout in local streams.

Tip *Amish families sell their fresh jams, handmade baskets, and quilts from buggies parked along Route 52, as well as in several stores. You can arrange to take a tour of Amish farms with a guide in Lanesboro or Harmony.*

4 rooms, 1 cabin Full breakfast. **Recreation:** Nearby: biking, bird-watching, fishing, hiking, horseback riding, canoeing, 18-hole golf course, cross-country skiing, snowmobiling, in-line skating. **Services:** massage, hot tubs, meeting rooms. No room phones, no room TVs, no kids under 12 $75–$195 MC, V.

Box 22, Lanesboro, MN 55949 800/803–6748 507/765–5291 *www.berwood.com.*

BURNTSIDE LODGE
Laid-Back Adventure

Straddling the Canadian border at Minnesota's northern tip, about five hours from Minneapolis, is the million-acre Boundary Waters Canoe Area Wilderness (BWCAW). Here, the northern lights, best seen in winter, are a showy stand-in for urban glow, and the howl of wolves replaces the cry of sirens. With hundreds of pristine lakes and 1,200 mi of canoe routes, BWCAW is a place where you can lose yourself in nature. Burntside Lodge has been hosting summer guests here for nearly a century.

Built before 1914 and now on the National Register of Historic Places, the lodge is almost as legendary as its surroundings. Forty-four log cabins, many hewn by hand by Finnish immigrants, were built here upon a rocky point of Burntside Lake. Today, 21 remain, spread among the pines on stilts like unobtrusive forest creatures. Glowing in the lodge's trademark red-orange varnish, waterfront Cabin 26 is perhaps the most photographed cabin in the state. Its pine logs still bear the marks of the broadax.

Books inside the cabins include those by Thoreau and the late environmentalist Sigurd Olson, who lived on the lake; the library offers similar fare. All cabins have knotty-pine interiors, but each is unique, with potbelly-style gas stoves and many with kitchens. Cabin 27, sublimely built into a bluff, slopes to the shoreline. Open the original swing-in windows and wake up to the sight of a fog-filled lake, views of Indian Island, and the calls of loons. You may spy bald eagles, deer, blue herons, and black bears from the windows.

Burntside Lake, more than 12 mi long and hundreds of feet deep, is dotted with 125 pine-bristled islands. After coffee at the cappuccino bar in the grand old lodge, rent a canoe or kayak from owners Lonnie and Lou LaMontagne and paddle around the islands. The Dead River is especially entrancing in the morning mist, with moose lying in the shallows. Hike to the waterfall of Bass Lake, a 20-minute drive away, picking blackberries along the way. Canoeing or hiking in BWCAW is easy with a day pass, obtainable at trailheads. Arrange a longer excursion (book in advance) with an outfitter in Ely, 6 mi from the lodge.

Return to the inn for a swim or a soak in the Finnish sauna and a sunset dinner. Lonnie and Lou's daughter Nicole runs the kitchen, and it's unexpectedly fine. The ironies here are lovely: there is an excellent six-page wine list, but still you need a flashlight to return to your cabin. For dinner try the signature walleye à la Burntside, served in a mushroom-walnut wine cream. Sip a local beer or the limited-production wines from the Secret Cellar. On Sunday, storyteller Bob Cary, a local legend, holds court in the lounge. Almost any night of the week, the constellations seen from the dock prompt infinitely more imaginings.

Tips *Visit the International Wolf Center in Ely to spend a couple of hours looking at the exhibits and meeting the resident wolves. Quirky little Ely also has many art galleries, including that of nature photographer Jim Brandenburg.*

21 cabins ‖◎‖ Coffee shop, dining room, lobby lounge, grills, some kitchens, microwaves, refrigerators. **Recreation:** fishing, hiking, wildlife viewing, beach, lake swimming, boating, canoeing, kayaking, volleyball, library. Nearby: biking, mountain biking, 18-hole golf course. **Services:** sauna, boathouse, marina, shop. **Classes and programs:** arts and crafts classes, storytelling. In-room fireplaces; no a/c, no room phones, no room TVs $115–$385 AE, D, V, MC.

2755 Burntside Lodge Rd., Ely, MN 55731 218/365–3894 *www. burntside.com.*

CRY OF THE LOON LODGE
Tranquil Outpost

Northwestern Minnesota, far from major cities, is still a relatively undiscovered part of the state. The lakes and forests are giant-size in this legendary haunt of Paul Bunyan. A majestic place some 200 mi northwest of the Twin Cities, Cry of the Loon Lodge on Lake Kabekona dates back to the 1960s. The area has long been a refuge for writers—poets Robert Bly and William Duffy launched an influential magazine here in the 1950s—and their works line mantels in the three cabins and lodge suite, as well as a special shelf in the thousand-book library. Bill Booth, a former English professor, manages the lodge with his wife, Nancy.

Whether the pines are sun-dappled or snow-laden, Cry of the Loon's carpeted and heated cabins are always cozy. The original lodge, built in 1937, has a rock wall and huge wooden beams. There are games in the library, along with a TV and movies, many with a literary bent.

Kabekona means "peace at the end of the trail" in Ojibwe, the local Indian tongue; the cabins also have Ojibwe names, such as Nibinish (summer). The largest town in the area, Bemidji, is half an hour's drive, and the nearest, Laporte, 3 mi away, has only a few more buildings than the lodge. The most exciting place near the lodge is the source of the Mississippi River: Lake Itasca in popular Itasca State Park, about 22 mi away. Follow the park's easy 1-mi Schoolcraft Trail (named for Henry R. Schoolcraft, who definitively identified Itasca as the river's source in 1832) around the north arm of the lake; halfway around, you'll reach the spot where the Mississippi flows out of the lake just a few inches deep and perhaps 20 feet across.

Summers at the lodge inspire sand castles, hammock hang time, and campfire-building on the beach. For a solitary stroll, take the paths right behind your cabin into the forest. More trails for hiking and biking can be accessed in Walker, 10½ mi away, including the Heartland Trail, a converted rail bed, partly paved, partly gravel, which winds 45 mi from Park Rapids to Cass Lake through woods, over trestles, around lakes, and into small towns. One of these, the village of Dorset, jokingly bills itself as the "restaurant capital of the world," because the 30-person hamlet has four restaurants, ranging from a fine Mexican place to a pizzeria. There's no restaurant at the lodge, but each cabin has a kitchen and grill, so you can take advantage of roadside vegetable stands on surrounding highways. At the Forest-edge Winery, tucked among trees a few miles from the lodge, pick up a bottle of wine made from local fruits and berries, perhaps the rhubarb-blueberry blend.

Tip *In your canoe, kayak, or fishing boat, head east on Lake Kabekona, following the northern shore to narrow Kabekona River. The river leads to* *another, smaller lake. In early morning, fog fills the riverbed, and among the high cattails you'll be alone with bald eagles, herons, ospreys, and loons.*

🛏 3 cabins, suite 🍽 Grills, picnic area, kitchens, microwaves. **Recreation:** bird-watching, fishing, hiking, wildlife viewing, beach, lake swimming, boating, canoeing, kayaking, rowing, board games, library, videocassette library, playground. Nearby: biking, cross-country skiing, in-line skating, golfing. ♿ Private patios, some pets allowed, no-smoking rooms; no a/c, no room phones, no room TVs 💳 $85–$95 💳 D, MC, V.

📮 *28822 Marigold Dr., Laporte, MN 56461* ☎ *218/224–2651 or 800/ 524–1979* 🌐 *www.cryoftheloonlodge.com* 🕓 *Closed Jan.–Apr.*

HISTORIC DOUGLAS LODGE
Family Hideout

When Henry Schoolcraft and his Indian guide portaged through pine forest to find Lake Itasca in 1832, they solved a beguiling mystery: the location of the source of the Mississippi River. Today, enclosed in 32,690-acre Itasca State Park, a spread of virgin forest and nearly 100 lakes, the narrow headwaters are still a place of pilgrimage for curious visitors, who delight in wading across the river at its shallowest point. The park's lodge, on the lake's sandy shores, has become a draw in itself.

Historic Douglas Lodge and its surrounding clubhouse and cabins—the Douglas Lodge Complex—are built in the rustic style, with the heavy log architecture of the grand, turn-of-the-20th-century national park hotels. Completed in 1905, the lodge retains its original character and is on the National Register of Historic Places along with other Itasca buildings. It's a four-hour drive from Minneapolis. Today you can retire to a bentwood rocking chair in the wood-beamed lobby and read the newspaper as logs crackle and pop in the huge stone fireplace or admire the lake views from a huge balcony. Also on the first floor, two dining rooms serve breakfast, lunch, and dinner. Walleye, wild rice, and blueberry pancakes are specialties. If you're headed for a hike, get an inexpensive picnic-basket lunch to go.

Upstairs in the main lodge, suites and guest rooms are furnished in 1920s style. Guest rooms share baths, and suites and other complex facilities have private baths. The nearby log Clubhouse, built around 1910 and distinguished by its fireplace lobby and mansard-style roof, has 10 sleeping rooms, frequently booked together for family gatherings. Itasca Suites, the park's newest accommodations, are up the hill. Outfitted with knotty-pine furniture, each suite has a screened porch, sitting area with TV, phone, data port, and kitchenette, plus a living-room futon. The nearby Fireplace Rooms evoke the era of old-style auto touring, with a warm, 1930s motel feel—no surprise, since they were built by the Depression-era Civilian Conservation Corps (CCC).

Lining the lakeshore are 11 one- to three-bedroom log cabins, some CCC-built. The cabins' screened porches are ideal for napping in the lake breeze. Step through French doors to the living room, which has a big stone fireplace.

More than 25 trails, many linked to the lodge complex, wind through Itasca. The more than 30 mi of trails include short walks and all-day hikes. Deer, porcupines, and pileated woodpeckers can be spotted from the trails. Watch for bald eagles and osprey on the Schoolcraft Trail, wildflowers on the Dr. Roberts Trail, and Minnesota's largest red pine (120 feet tall) on the Big Pine Trail. Bike to the headwaters and back, stopping to wade through the Mississippi, or rent a boat or canoe at the Lake Itasca boat landing, where boat tours also begin. Make your way through old-growth pines to Wilderness Sanctuary National Natural Landmark. In the all-but-undisturbed sanctuary, otters ply the creeks and black bears roam the woods. Bohall Wilderness Trail takes you into the sanctuary past orchid-strewn woods, through meadows, and around bogs.

Tip *For a wide-angle view of the Mississippi headwaters, climb Aiton Heights Fire Tower. Peace Pipe Vista, a favorite spot for watching sunsets, offers a similar perspective on Lake Itasca.*

8 rooms, 12 suites, 15 cabins, 1 clubhouse 2 restaurants, picnic area, some kitchenettes. **Recreation:** biking, bird-watching, fishing, hiking, wildlife viewing, beach, lake swimming, boating, canoeing, cross-country skiing, snowshoeing, volleyball, playground. **Services:** canoe, bicycle, and boat rentals; boat launch; tackle shop; meeting rooms. **Classes and programs:** guided nature walks, natural history programs, children's programs (ages 1–12), campfire talks. Some in-room data ports, some in-room fireplaces, some private terraces; no a/c in some rooms, no phones in some rooms, no TV in some rooms $63–$435 MC, V.

36750 Main Park Dr., Park Rapids, MN 56470 *218/266–2122* *218/266–2130* *www.dnr.state.mn.us/state_parks/itasca* *Closed Oct.–May.*

LOST LAKE LODGE
Family Hideout

On 75 forested acres beside a private lake, these 13 cabins are a quiet family hideaway in one of the state's most popular recreational regions. The numerous, interlacing lakes around Brainerd, 2½ hours north of Minneapolis–St. Paul, have been a retreat for Twin Cities residents since the early 20th century.

Lost Lake Lodge began as a restaurant in 1946. Its fourth owners, Doug and Pat Lewis, who boat into work from their home on the lake, have retained the place's longtime ambience—there are no phones or TVs in the cabins—while adding some modern amenities, such as in-cabin air conditioners. Many guests have been returning for a decade or more and don't want too much to change. The cabins range from one-bedroom suites to three-bedroom layouts for 10 to 12 people. All have decks and fireplaces stocked with wood. There's a library and a stack of movies in the lodge; Doug has a passion for classic films.

The lodge's culinary past shines as well, in meals made as much as possible with produce from local sources, including an herb garden off the kitchen. You might have wild rice pancakes for breakfast, for dinner a risotto made with Minnesota forest mushrooms, and for dessert a cobbler made with local berries and rhubarb from the garden. The lodge's own gristmill grinds out flour, cornmeal, and bran that chef Tim Fischer uses in fresh bread baked daily and corn muffins that occasionally appear on the menu. You can wash it all down with a local microbrew.

There is no shortage of recreation both at the lodge and nearby. You can muse among Indian burial mounds on one of the lodge's hiking trails, listen to the lake's resident loons from the private beach, and sing by a lakeside campfire with the lodge naturalist at night. Wander the nature trail with the naturalist or on your own to learn about the forest flora, watching for deer, hummingbirds, and pileated woodpeckers. Bring your binoculars to spot nesting bald eagles. At this all-inclusive lodge, you're free to grab any fishing rod and slip into any fishing boat, canoe, or kayak to explore the neighboring chain of lakes. Gull Lake Narrows runs along one side of the lodge property, providing a link to a chain of watery playgrounds farther afield. The Lewises can hook you up with horses, too, from a couple of neighboring stables.

Kids' activities with the naturalist include learning about the wildlife of Lost Lake, tracking deer, and becoming a Tree Detective. There's a special menu for kids and playthings at the beach.

Tip *If you catch fish, ask the lodge to clean and cook them for your dinner with special Lost Lake Seasoning.*

🛏 13 cabins 🍴 Modified American plan, dining room, refrigerators. **Recreation:** bird-watching, fishing, hiking, wildlife viewing, beach, boating, canoeing, kayaking, badminton, boccie, volleyball, library, videocassette and DVD library, playground. Nearby: biking, horseback riding, 18-hole golf course, in-line skating. **Services:** badminton, boccie, and volleyball equipment provided; pontoon boat rentals; boathouse; laundry service. **Classes and programs:** guided nature walks, natural history programs, children's programs (all ages), campfire talks. ♿ Private decks; no room phones, no room TVs 💲 $120 and up ▭ AE, MC, V.

📫 *7965 Lost Lake Rd., Lake Shore, MN 56468* ☎ *218/963–2681 or 800/450–2681* 🖷 *218/963–0509* 🌐 *www.lostlake.com* 🌜 *Closed mid-Oct.–mid-May.*

PINCUSHION BED & BREAKFAST
Laid-Back Adventure ~ Romantic Retreat

To get to Pincushion Bed & Breakfast, drive 4½ hours from the Twin Cities or 2½ hours from Duluth. Then pull into the village of Grand Marais, turn onto the Gunflint Trail, and head up and up—and up. From its 1,000-foot-high perch near Pincushion Mountain, Scott and Mary Beattie's 43-acre north-shore estate has eagle-eye views of Lake Superior. One of the world's largest freshwater lakes, far too big to see across, it's the closest thing to an ocean between America's coasts. On a clear day you can see Isle Royale National Park, 42 mi across the lake. Bordered by a national forest, the Little Devil Track River, and extensive bluffs, the inn offers profound peace that you can find only in the wilderness. Bald eagles glide overhead, moose and bears lumber through the woods, and the rare wolf scampers across the birch-lined gravel driveway. Million-acre Boundary Waters Canoe Area Wilderness is 24 mi away.

Silent sports, including cross-country skiing, snowshoeing, mountain biking, and hiking, are a passion for Scott and Mary. They have skis and snowshoes for you to use, or you can bring your own to traverse a snowpack that averages 95 inches every winter. A few steps from the house lie well-groomed trails through the dense forest, including the 250-mi Superior Hiking Trail, great for seeing wildlife. Have the Beatties pack you a lunch and take time to soak in the panoramic views of Lake Superior and Minnesota's deepest gorge (more scenic than deep), 2 mi away.

Long-distance hikers often spend a night at Pincushion during a trail trek. But you might be drawn by the fireworks of autumn, when color cascades down to the lake. The guest rooms, named for the trees on the property (Pine, Maple, Birch, and Aspen), are all about the outdoors, offering lake views instead of antiques. Photographs of local icons, such as the Root Beer Lady (one of the last permanent residents of the Boundary Waters wilderness), line the walls. In the beamed breakfast room, plants fill every corner, almost blocking the views from the picture windows. Breakfast may include Danish tarts and wild rice–vegetable frittata, a local specialty. The morning menu makes the most of seasonal fruits. You can pick your own blueberries and raspberries along the trails, if the bears (which are rarely seen) don't get them first.

Tip *If you want a real taste of the North Woods, ask the Beatties to arrange a dogsled excursion for you.*

🛏 4 rooms 🍴 Full breakfast. **Recreation:** biking, bird-watching, hiking, mountain biking, running, wildlife viewing, cross-country skiing, snowshoeing. Nearby: fishing, kayaking, canoeing, sea kayaking, 18-hole golf course, dogsledding, downhill skiing. **Services:** sauna. ♿ No a/c, no room phones, no room TVs, no kids under 12, no smoking 🚬 $95–$125 💳 MC, V.

🏠 *968 Gunflint Trail, Grand Marais, MN 55604* ☎ *218/387–1276 or 800/ 542–1226* ⊕ *www.pincushionbb.com.*

XANADU ISLAND BED & BREAKFAST
Tranquil Outpost

"No man is an island, entire of itself," wrote John Donne in the 17th century. But he never made it to Xanadu Island Bed & Breakfast. Surrounded by the quiet waters of Elbow Lake, amid 5 acres of oaks and maples, you may feel that all you need in life are sun-dappled trees and lazy waves. And all the things you don't need (for a few days, at least), including humankind, are fabulously far away.

Of course, you are not completely on your own. Access to the island is via a gravel road and a rocky causeway. The outsize rustic-style home and its three surrounding cottages, built around 1919 as a millionaire's summer getaway, are the island's only settlement. But before long, from the porch overlooking the lake, you may notice the area's other inhabitants: deer, black squirrels, red foxes, great blue herons, loons, and white egrets. If you're really lucky, you'll discover what no one else has: the missing diamond ring.

The inn has hosted its share of wealthy guests from the East Coast, supposedly including President Woodrow Wilson. Legend has it that one of these socialites, perhaps looped on the moonshine once hidden in a crawl space (there is still a trapdoor in the master bedroom), wandered off and lost a walnut-size diamond ring. It's never been found, and all that remains of those days is the lodgelike home, with its original wood-covered walls, enormous stone fireplace, and wraparound porch.

On the porch, start your hearty breakfast decadently, with a fresh strawberry dessert. In the afternoon, sip a soda concoction made by owners Bryan and Janet Lonski. Amenities in the antiques-filled lodge rooms, some accessed by a winding, metal staircase, range from basic to deluxe—lake views, wood-burning fireplaces, and Jacuzzis. Throughout, original birch furniture underscores the classic cabin feel. Near the lodge, plain red cottages, once used by servants, now offer summer accommodation for families of up to six; the main house, open year-round, is reserved for adults. You can fire up the grill anytime. A campfire circle awaits the starry evening.

Explore the fairly undeveloped lake by canoe or fishing boat or simply hang in the hammock or take a dip at the beach. This is prime migration flyover territory for ducks and geese in the fall, and bird-watchers have spotted more than 40 species at Xanadu with the binoculars available in the sitting room. A prairie-chicken sanctuary 22 mi away can introduce you to the rare birds' spectacular drumming—called "booming"—in the spring. Two miles into the hilly rural surroundings, a gravel road winds through 1,931-acre Glendalough State Park. Having managed to stay more primitive than most other state parks, it is a woodsy preserve of hiking trails and lakes that is off-limits to motorized traffic. At sunset, from two wildlife blinds, with binoculars loaned out at the park headquarters, you might see white-tailed deer by the dozen or owls swooping through the tangled trees. In August the meadow traversed by the park's Prairie Hill Interpretive Trail becomes a monarch migratory site, harboring hundreds of the butterflies.

Tip *On your way from the Twin Cities, pick up a bottle of wine from Carlos Creek Winery outside the town of Alexandria, off I–94. The winery is one of Minnesota's largest and also maintains the state's largest purebred Arabian horse stables.*

⟿ 5 rooms, 3 cottages 🍽 Full breakfast, grills, picnic area, some kitchenettes, some kitchens. **Recreation:** bird-watching, fishing, wildlife viewing, lake swimming, boating, canoeing, piano. ⟳ Satellite TV, some in-room fireplaces; no room phones, no room TVs ▩ $95–$155 ⊟ D, MC, V.

🖰 *35484 235th St., Battle Lake, MN 56515* ☎ *800/396–9043* ⊕ *www. xanadu.cc.*

Mississippi

THE FOREST RETREAT
Rustic Escape

At the heart of Homochitto National Forest in the southwestern corner of Mississippi, a trio of handsomely furnished cabins is enveloped by nearly 100,000 acres of pine, magnolia, hickory, and oak trees. In summer, when much of the region becomes insufferably hot and humid, the Forest Retreat, nestled in a shady ravine, feels relatively cool. In winter, the ravine feels sheltered and the cabins are warmed by pot-belly woodstoves. It is easy to see why artists and writers are attracted to this place about 40 mi from Natchez and McComb, the nearest major towns (and 2½ hours from Jackson and New Orleans). There's virtually nothing here to distract you but the soothing sounds of nature: a rushing creek and the calls of woodpeckers and songbirds.

You can rent a cabin on a daily basis on weekdays and with a two-night minimum on weekends, though many people book them for a week or more. The tin-roof cabins are partially elevated on stilts above the mossy, fern-carpeted ravine; each has a deck and a wall of huge windows facing out toward the forest and away from the other cabins. Inside are wood-paneled walls, soaring vaulted ceilings, and wood furniture with handles and knobs fashioned out of deer antlers. Most of the chairs, lamps, and tables were constructed in New York's Adirondack Mountains from lodgepole pine and twigs. Wooden stepladders lead up to sleeping lofts with down quilts. The place eschews many trappings of modern life: cabins have no phones, TVs, or clocks. Your small but functional kitchen is amply stocked with dishes and cookware, and each cabin has a bath. One also has an open-air outdoor tub and shower, so that you can enjoy unobstructed forest views.

Three cabins are usually available, and occasionally a fourth. The largest cabin on the property, a converted church, is the hideaway of retreat owner Bess Carrick, a New Orleans–based filmmaker. It is also the most private. The three regular rental cabins are clustered relatively close together, but the former church stands about ½ mi away down its own private lane off the main forest road.

Each cabin comes complete with local hiking information. Trails lead directly from the cabins into the forest. You can go bird-watching if you like; Homochitto National Forest is known for sightings of American kestrel and eastern screech owls. The spring-fed Brushy Creek, a branch of the Homochitto River, courses through the property and is fringed by a white-sand beach where you can take a swim. You can also go fishing in the man-made pond, which is stocked with bass and catfish (the trees cleared to dredge the pond were used to build the cabins).

You'll want to bring ample supplies of food and drink. Nearby Glocester has a basic grocery store, but larger places are about an hour away. Besides, who wants to leave the grounds between check-in and checkout? While you're here, you can be assured that your isolation is sacrosanct. The Forest Retreat takes great care to protect your privacy and maintain its reputation as a secluded spot. You must contact the place directly by phone or e-mail in order to get the mailing address, and detailed driving directions are made available only after you book.

Tip *Try to arrive during daylight hours. The property is hidden down a dark, unmarked, and shadowy dirt forest road, and it's easy to lose your way after dark.*

🛏 3 cabins 🍴 Kitchens. **Recreation:** bird-watching, fishing, hiking, mountain biking, wildlife viewing, beach, river swimming. ⌂ Private balconies, some pets allowed; no room phones, no room TVs 💵 $100–$163 ▭ No credit cards.

📞 *Call or e-mail for mailing address* ☎ *601/639–4591* 🌐 *www.forestretreat.com.*

HICKORY HILL CABINS
Tranquil Outpost

A road with the word "airport" in its name might not seem likely to lead to any place nature-oriented. But in this group of cabins on Camps Airport Road, you won't hear jets rumbling overhead: the airport in question is a small municipal facility a mile up the road, and it never sees much traffic. The cabins, at the end of a long dirt driveway, are far enough from the road that you barely hear the few cars that drive by. What you will hear, as you settle into one of the rocking chairs on your cabin porch, is the neighing of a few contented horses trotting around a paddock a few hundred yards down the driveway. All you'll see are fields and woodland. It's an incredibly tranquil spot, and it's 2½ hours from Jackson and Birmingham and 3 hours from Memphis.

Owners Dan and Reita Jackson created most of the structures on this 62-acre northeastern Mississippi spread from scratch. They built their own house, the barn, and the two rental cabins, dug three ponds, and cleared three large pastures out of what had been a dense thicket of mixed pine and hardwood forest. The Jacksons are more than happy to advise you on local sightseeing, to rent you fishing tackle for use in one of the ponds, or to introduce you to their friendly horses (if you ask in advance). But otherwise, you can expect to be left alone at Hickory Hill. The cabins are separated by about 200 feet, so you have plenty of privacy.

With their corrugated roofs and long front porches with slender posts, the cabins look like Reconstruction-era sharecroppers' cottages. They are, however, surprisingly modern inside, with air-conditioning, shiny hardwood floors, and up-to-date fixtures. The kitchen has high-quality utensils and cookware and a full-size refrigerator stocked with breakfast fixings. There's even TV and a VCR with a small selection of movies, tucked away discreetly behind the doors of an armoire. Decorated cheerfully but informally with plain, modern oak furnishings and country quilts and fabrics, your one-room cabin is laid out in four sections. As you enter, you'll find a king-size bed and a bathroom to your left, a kitchen and a living area (with a queen-size sleeper sofa and gas fireplace) to your right. The cabins are roomy, but they are better suited for couples than for families. In addition to the front porch, which runs the full length of the facade, cabins also have a smaller back porch with a gas grill.

Behind the cabins, a lightly wooded hillside (which is often carpeted with wildflowers) tumbles down to a pond. Deer and the occasional raccoon or rabbit can be seen on the grounds, and there are also butterflies and birdlife, including quail, turkeys, doves, and woodcocks.

Tip *A two-night minimum is required on weekends when Mississippi State University, 7 mi away in Starkville, has home football games. It's one of the few times of year when this part of Mississippi is abuzz with visitors.*

🛏 2 cabins 🍽 Continental breakfast, grills, kitchens. **Recreation:** biking (nearby), bird-watching, fishing, hiking, running, wildlife viewing, board games. **Services:** fishing-equipment rentals. ♿ In-room fireplaces, in-room VCRs, private decks; no room phones, no smoking 💳 $70–$80 🚫 MC, V.

📫 *1309 Camps Airport Rd., Starkville, MS 39759* ☎ *662/324–2695* 🌐 *www.hickoryhill.net.*

Missouri

BIG CEDAR LODGE
Family Hideout ~ Luxurious Resort

About 10 mi from Branson, on the Missouri-Arkansas border in the heart of the Ozarks, Big Cedar Lodge stands on the shores of 43,000-acre Table Rock Lake. It's only a few hundred yards from a four-lane highway, but you'll forget that as soon as you enter this world of hillsides blanketed with ferns and wildflowers, deep ravines littered with boulders, and rushing streams shaded by towering oak trees.

Though Table Rock Lake has been here only since 1958, when the White River was dammed, this spot was a nature retreat for wealthy families starting in the 1920s. They came here to unwind near a large, deep spring that the native Osage called Spirit Pool and that whites named Devil's Pool. Now the lake covers much of the area, though some buildings dating back to the 1920s remain as part of Big Cedar Lodge. Three modern lodges in different woodsy styles house guest rooms, or you can stay in a cushy log cabin or knotty-pine cottage in the woods. Each room has been designed to celebrate the Ozarks, offering views of the hills and the lake. Sixteen miles away, at the lodge's Dogwood Canyon Nature Park, more log cabins are tucked even deeper into the wilderness.

At the lodge, which is owned by sporting retail giant Bass Pro Shops, you can jump into first-hand exploration of the lake and its surroundings or merely sit by the water and feed the fish. On a fishing expedition you can savor the thrill of hooking the masterful trout, crappie, and bluegill that attract anglers to this spot from around the world. Get out on the lake in a canoe, or go waterskiing. No Jet Skis or noisy diesel engines are allowed on the lake, and no ATVs or motorcycles are allowed on the grounds. Hiking and horseback riding are great ways to meander on paths lined with hickory, dogwood, and black oak trees. At Dogwood Canyon Nature Park, 10,000 acres of pristine Ozarks landscape are filled with buffalo, elk, and every manner of wildlife. There you can walk, bike, or take a jeep tour.

Less ambitious pursuits include a round of golf on the lodge's 9-hole course or a stroll through the painstakingly maintained gardens. Horse-drawn carriages carry you on 20-minute rides through the landscaped grounds. In the evening you can take a wagon ride to a campfire sing-along. Memorial Day through Labor Day, a children's program keeps the junior set happy day or evening, in three-hour sessions.

To keep you going, the lodge's restaurants present the bounty of the region in dishes that range from the health-conscious to the decadent. Two sprawling old 1920s vacation "cottages," one in the Adirondack style and one in the Tudor style, house two of the restaurants and a smokehouse. Another restaurant perches high above the lake, commanding panoramic views of the mountains.

Tip *If you're looking for real seclusion, ask for a cabin in the Cedar Trails area. If you opt for a lake-view cabin, neighbors will be close by.*

102 rooms, 12 suites, 28 cabins, 9 cottages; 3 cabins in Dogwood Canyon 4 restaurants, bar, sports bar, some kitchens, some kitchenettes, some minibars, some microwaves. **Recreation:** biking, bird-watching, fishing, hiking, horseback riding, running, wildlife viewing, 2 pools, indoor pool, waterskiing, boating, canoeing, 9-hole golf course, 8 tennis courts, sleigh rides, basketball, croquet, horseshoes, miniature golf, video-game room, playground. **Services:** canoes provided, health club, hot tub, sauna, spa, dock, guided fishing trips, marina, golf pro shop, horse boarding, laundry facilities, 3 shops, airport shuttle, Internet access, meeting rooms. **Classes and programs:** guided hikes, low-impact and water aerobics classes, children's programs (ages 4–12), dances, sightseeing tours, sing-alongs. Cable TV, in-room VCRs or DVD players; no-smoking rooms $69–$1,499 AE, D, MC, V.

612 Devil's Pool Rd., Ridgedale, MO 65739 417/335–2777 417/335–2340 www.big-cedar.com.

ROCK EDDY BLUFF FARM
Rustic Escape ~ Tranquil Outpost

The Gasconade River valley of central Missouri is a place of undulating hills and craggy hollows. Here, on a promontory high above the river, lies Rock Eddy Bluff Farm, which takes its name from the centuries-old fall of huge boulders from the cliffs into an eddy (a deep pool of slow-moving water) of the Gasconade. At the farm you can feel on top of the world. The view in every direction is of the Ozark Mountains and their colorful trees, limestone outcrops, and meandering streams and rivers. Wildlife, such as beaver, river otter, wild turkey, deer, and an occasional bobcat, is abundant in the hills. The bird species are all but innumerable and include nesting bald eagles and turkey vultures, who enjoy circling in the updrafts near the river bluffs.

You can choose how far from the world you want to get at Rocky Eddy Bluff Farm. Stay in the suite on the upper level of the home where the proprietors, Tom and Kathy Corey, live, and indulge in Kathy's fabulous breakfasts of Belgian waffles or eggs Benedict. Or take the cottage out in the woods, whose kitchen is stocked with fixings for a breakfast you can whip up on your own. Out here, there's not another soul in sight, and your family can spread out in three colorful bedrooms filled with an eclectic mix of antiques, many of which are for sale. The plush carpeting, hand-stitched quilts, and black iron heating stove of the cabins keep you toasty even in the chilliest months of the year. But if you want to really forget about your workaday life, go for the Line Camp Cabin, which the Coreys call "home à la 1880." Tom built the primitive structure himself using parts salvaged from a number of abandoned cabins in the area. Stay here if the idea of pumping your own water, reading by kerosene lamp, and using an outdoor privy appeals.

The farm is a great place to do nothing in the front porch swing, but if you're more ambitious you can wade in the river or take a tour of the area with Tom in an Amish wagon. If you want to do a little bird-watching, the binoculars and bird-spotting books in your room will come in handy. Crafty types may want to spend some time with Kathy, who makes floral arrangements, Christmas tree ornaments, and other household knickknacks from things she finds while walking through the forest. Perhaps inspiration will find you in a pinecone, a peculiar twig, or an abandoned bird's nest.

Tip *On one morning of your stay, get up in time to see the sun rise over the Gasconade River and the fog lift from the valley. It may well be the high point of your visit.*

↪ 1 suite, 1 cottage, 2 cabins ⫶⊙⫶ Full breakfast (suite only), grills, picnic area, kitchens. **Recreation:** biking, bird-watching, fishing, hiking, wildlife viewing, river swimming, canoeing, rowing, horseshoes, library. **Services:** binoculars, bicycles, and canoes provided; outdoor hot tub; horse boarding; laundry facilities. ⚘ Some pets allowed; no a/c in some rooms, no phones in some rooms, no TV in some rooms ▨ $100–$155 ▭ D, MC, V.

🏠 *10245 Maries Rd. 511, Dixon, MO 65459* ☎ *573/759–6081 or 800/ 335–5921* ⊕ *www.rockeddy.com.*

Montana

AVERILL'S FLATHEAD LAKE LODGE
Family Hideout ~ Laid-Back Adventure

A short drive through a forest of lodgepole pine and larch in northwest Montana brings you to Flathead Lake Lodge, 20 mi from Kalispell. Beside the largest freshwater lake in the western Lower 48, the lodge stands on a 2,000-acre ranch that has been operated by the Averill family since 1945.

Ranch headquarters, along with the historic log lodge and the cabins, overlooks lush lawns and flower beds that sweep down to the water's edge. Two- and three-bedroom log cabins, duded up with western styling, have a sitting room and a porch where you can sit and watch the sunset over the lake. Lodge rooms, each with two sleeping areas, a sitting area, and private bath, are paneled with knotty pine and have log bedsteads. Exposed log beams, a hefty river-rock fireplace, and buffalo-hide couches make the lodge's great room a nice place to spend chilly mornings or evenings. On the deck, you can eat lunch or relax at the end of the day. For indoor dining, log chairs and tables are set up inside, before large picture windows overlooking the lake.

Designed for family vacations, Flathead Lake Lodge operates an extensive children's program. Throughout the day, kids can sign up with the junior wrangler program, join an arts-and-crafts session, learn how to fish in a pond, take part in scavenger hunts, go on guided nature walks, and more. They can camp out in a tepee for a night and roast marshmallows, show off their horseback riding in a kids' rodeo, and ride an old-fashioned fire truck to the ice-cream store. Other activities, such as a beach bonfire with cowboy sing-along and breakfast or lunch rides to a campground in the mountains, are geared for the whole family.

While your kids are busy, you can do as much or as little as you like, because your stay here is all-inclusive for on-site activities. The lake is a good place to start. Go waterskiing or Boogie boarding in the afternoon; if you've never tried it before, the waterfront staff will show you how. For quieter times, take out a canoe, fishing boat, or sailboat.

When a good breeze livens the lake, the ranch runs thrilling one- to two-hour sails aboard two historic 51-foot Q-class racing sloops, the *Questa* and the *Nor'Easter*. Built in 1928 as prototypes of the Americas Cup boats, the Q-boats have been painstakingly restored. Another way to enjoy the lake is on a sightseeing excursion aboard a motor launch. You'll find a waterfowl preserve where you're likely to see ospreys and bald eagles. In the evening, take a cocktail cruise and watch the sun set.

Of course, this is a ranch, so there's plenty of horseback riding. Scenic trails wind through forests and mountain meadows where wildlife abounds, and you can take in spectacular views of Flathead Lake and the Swan Mountain Range. Geared toward different age and ability groups, trail rides of different lengths and tempos are led by wranglers. There are adults-only rides, teen rides, and children's rides (you can accompany your kids on these). Children under six ride near the barn under the watchful eyes of staff or parents. Rodeo games, steer roping, and penning contests let you pretend you're a cowboy.

At the end of the day, grown-ups gather on the lodge deck to watch the sun set over the lake and swap stories during happy hour in the Saddle Sore Saloon (wine and beer are available; bring your own bottle if you want cocktails). Meals are served family-style in the main lodge, with different seatings for children and adults, but families can dine together if they wish. The day begins with a cereal bar and hot breakfast buffet. Lunches include vegetarian dishes and entrées like country fried chicken, hamburgers, tacos, or shish kebabs, plus salads, breads, and desserts. At dinner, the menu includes vegetarian dishes as well as rainbow trout, pheasant, whole roast pig, beef, and ranch-raised buffalo. Breads, desserts, and snacks are baked fresh daily. After dinner there might be a barn dance or a volleyball match between staff and guests.

Tip *The lodge is only a 45-minute drive from Glacier National Park and a 1-mi walk from Bigfork, where there are shops, a summer theater, and a golf course.*

🛏 17 rooms, 15 cabins 🍽 American plan, dining room. **Recreation:** fishing, hiking, horseback riding, mountain biking, running, wildlife viewing, pool, lake swimming, waterskiing, windsurfing, boating, canoeing, kayaking, sailing, 4 tennis courts, basketball, horseshoes, Ping-Pong, volleyball, library, piano, recreation room. Nearby: tubing (water), jet skiing, rafting, 27-hole golf course. **Services:** guided fishing trips, dock, babysitting, laundry facilities, shop, airport shuttle, business services, meeting rooms. **Classes and programs:** children's programs (ages 3–12), dances, sightseeing tours. ♿ No a/c, no room phones, no room TVs, no smoking 🛏 $2,653 per wk 🖃 AE, MC, V.

🏠 *Box 248, Bigfork, MT 59911* 🕿 *406/837–4391* 📠 *406/837–6977* 🌐 *www.averills.com* � *Closed Oct.–May.*

BOULDER HOT SPRINGS BED & BREAKFAST
Tranquil Outpost

For centuries before white settlers arrived, native people gathered in Peace Valley for spiritual and physical renewal at its steaming mineral springs. The valley was respected as a place of peace, and no battles were fought here. People still leave their battles behind when they come to the springs.

In the foothills of the Elkhorn Mountains, on 274 acres bordering Deerlodge National Forest, Boulder Hot Springs Bed & Breakfast has a history stretching back to 1863. That year, a prospector claimed the springs and turned them into a commercial enterprise. The huge hotel that now stands here was built in 1888 and is listed on the National Register of Historic Places. It resembles a Spanish mission and looks out over panoramic views of the valley. The mineral-laden, geothermally heated water ranges in temperature from 140°F to 175°F. Piped to pools, it is mixed with cold spring water until it reaches the desired temperatures for soaking and swimming. In the men's bathhouse a tiled pool is maintained at 104°F, and in the women's bathhouse there is a 104°F hot pool and a 65°F cool pool. No chemicals are added to the indoor pools, but the outdoor swimming pool, maintained at 96°F, is treated with bromine. Water continually flows through the indoor pools so they are completely refreshed every four hours.

Midway between Butte and Helena in west-central Montana, Boulder Hot Springs cultivates an atmosphere of peace and quiet, where you can relax in the healing waters in an alcohol- and smoke-free environment. The resort also practices environmentally sensitive management and has received the Montana EcoStar Award for its efforts in waste reduction, use of nontoxic cleaners, and geothermal heating. Guest rooms are decorated with antique furniture, lace curtains, and quilted coverlets. Hearty breakfasts and the Sunday all-you-care-to-eat buffet are served in a family-friendly dining room. The regional and international dishes are prepared with organically grown meats, grains, fruits, and vegetables that come from local growers whenever possible.

When you're not eating or soaking, relax on the shady veranda and watch antelope, fox, deer, sandhill cranes, blue herons, ducks, and other wildlife visit the meadow and pond. Hike through the wooded hills and along Fornam Creek in Deerlodge National Forest. Here you are apt to see wildlife, and you will have panoramic views of the valley. In winter, the terrain in nearby Elkhorn is great for cross-country skiing.

Tip *Five "health mines" in the Boulder area are internationally known for their alleged therapeutic qualities. Believers claim that breathing the air in the mines relieves pain where conventional medication has failed.*

◁⊃ 33 rooms ⏻◉⏻ Full breakfast, dining room. **Recreation:** biking, bird-watching, hiking, mountain biking, wildlife viewing, pool, 3 indoor pools, cross-country skiing, library. **Services:** massage, mineral springs, steam room, airport shuttle, meeting rooms. **Classes and programs:** yoga classes, yoga retreats. ♿ No a/c, no room phones, no room TVs, no smoking. 🎫 $75–$129 ▭ MC, V.

◻ *Box 930, Boulder, MT 59632* ☎ *406/225–4339* 🖷 *406/225–4345* ⊕ *www.boulderhotsprings.com.*

CIRCLE BAR RANCH
Family Hideout

With the heavily timbered slopes of the Little Belt Mountains in the background, buffalo and purebred Angus cattle graze in pastures. Riders on horseback canter across wildflower-filled meadows. A handsome log lodge, a big red barn, and a cluster of log cabins stand beside a sparkling river. The scene is classic American West, and the place is the Circle Bar Ranch, about 80 mi southwest of Great Falls, in the foothills of the Rockies, in the heart of Big Sky Country. Spend a week here, and you'll learn how to crack a whip, rope cattle, pan for gold, and hunt for Yogo sapphires. The ranch is bordered by national forest and the state elk refuge, so you can take short hikes or all-day expeditions into untouched wilderness. Runners can challenge themselves at the 5,200-foot elevation. There's fishing and mountain biking—and plenty of riding.

At the start of your stay, experienced wranglers match you up with a horse that's yours for the rest of the week. If you're a new or rusty equestrian, they'll give you some lessons, and if you want to hone the skills you already have, you can take equitation classes. The trail rides at Circle Bar are custom-tailored outings, not nose-to-tail tramps. You can ride for an hour or an entire day, or take an overnight pack trip. Out in the hills you'll see abundant wildlife and magnificent panoramic views, and you might come across limestone caves, old homesteads, gold-mining areas, or Blackfoot Indian tepee rings. Back on the ranch, compete with your fellow dudes in a gymkhana, a riding contest in which team penning, barrel racing, pole bending, and water-relay racing on horseback are some of the events. For a full-blown riding experience, come to the ranch for Cowboy Week, when you work alongside the ranch hands; for Cattle Drive Week, when you help move cattle to and from summer pastures; or for Russell Ride Week, when you ride to the places painted by western artist Charlie Russell.

If you're not in the mood to ride, head for the South Fork or Middle Fork of the Judith River for fine trout fishing. Anglers of any age and ability level can have a good day on the river, and there's always someone available to give you a few fly-fishing pointers. You can do some

catch-and-release fishing or keep your catch and let the ranch chef prepare it for your dinner. Kids can fish in their own spot by a waterfall,
where success is all but guaranteed. The ranch has no special children's
programs because its whole philosophy is family togetherness. (One
week each season is specifically for singles, when children aren't allowed.)
Take a nature walk, play games in the yard or the recreation room, or
find the ranch dog and scratch his ears. Many kids like to collect eggs
from the chickens and spend time with the baby animals in the petting
zoo. In the evening, your family can join in the fun around the campfire or spend some quality time in your cabin.

Placed in a semicircle by the river, the log cabins have two or more bedrooms and a homey feeling, with knotty-pine walls, western art, fireplaces or wood-burning stoves in the sitting rooms (they are also
centrally heated), and western-style furniture. Spacious lodge suites have
sitting rooms and bedrooms similarly furnished. Bring a book back to
your cabin from the lodge's library or hang out with your neighbors
around the heated outdoor swimming pool. The glass-enclosed hot tub
is a favorite spot to soothe sore muscles after a long ride.

All this fresh Montana air is bound to whet your appetite, and the chef
cooks up a storm to satisfy it. Western-style ranch food, served both
family- and buffet-style in the main lodge, includes home-baked rolls
and bread, vegetables and herbs grown in the gardens, and eggs fresh
from the ranch chickens. Grass-fed buffalo and lean, tender ranch beef
are healthful choices for carnivores. Special diets can be accommodated
with advance notice. Weekly tailgates and barbecues add some outdoor
variety to your meals, and the kitchen will pack a saddlebag lunch if you're
planning a full day on the trail.

Tip *The ranch does not have a liquor license, but you may bring your own
libations and chill them in your cabin's mini-refrigerator.*

🔁 10 cabins, 4 suites ⦿ American plan, dining room. **Recreation:**
fishing, hiking, horseback riding, mountain biking, running, wildlife viewing, pool, badminton, basketball, croquet, horseshoes, Ping-Pong, volleyball, library, piano, recreation room. **Services:** mountain bikes and
fishing equipment provided, hot tub, massage, guided fishing trips, helipad, baby-sitting, kennel, laundry facilities, shop, airport shuttle, business services, meeting rooms, travel services. **Classes and programs:**
natural history programs, photo safaris, horseback-riding lessons, sing-
alongs. ⚐ Some pets allowed; no a/c, no room phones, no room TVs,
no smoking 🏷 $2,100 per person/wk (minimum three-day May
15–Sept. 15) ▭ MC, V.

🏠 *HCR 81 (Box 61), Utica, MT 59452* ☏ *406/423–5454 or 888/570–
0227* 🖶 *406/423–5686* ⊕ *www.circlebarranch.com.*

PAPOOSE CREEK LODGE
Laid-Back Adventure ~ Romantic Retreat

Tucked among spruce, fir, cottonwood, and aspen trees at the foot of soaring mountains, Papoose Creek Lodge lies in southern Montana's Upper Madison Valley, 40 mi from Yellowstone National Park. From the deck that wraps around the lodge, you can hear Papoose Creek flowing by and birds singing in the trees. It's a great place to eat breakfast or dinner, to enjoy the mountain scenery, and to glimpse passing wildlife.

An air of understated luxury pervades the property. The 1½-story log lodge has an open plan; large picture windows look out over the lawn and pond, with the Gravelly Mountains beyond. At the heart of the lodge is a living room with a lofty cathedral ceiling, easy chairs, an immense river-rock fireplace, and artwork by local artists, including a gargantuan beam hand-carved with the history of the Madison Valley. Spacious guest rooms in the lodge have a private balcony or porch and are casually furnished with western-style furniture and upholstered chairs; some have jetted spa tubs. Built of logs, or of stone and weathered wood, woodland cabins have sitting areas with large windows and porches that invite stargazing. Radiant floor heating assures toasty toes when you get out of bed; one deluxe cabin also has a stone fireplace. Arrange to have a massage in your room or cabin, and in the evening, sink into the hot tub surrounded by aspens beneath a starlit Montana sky.

Owners Cynthia and Roger Lang are committed to conservation. They call Papoose Creek an ecotourism lodge and practice conservation and progressive land stewardship on their ranch and at the lodge. The lodge has a library filled with information on local flora, fauna, and history, and biologists, artists, and historians are often invited to speak on Rocky Mountain history and culture. Throughout the season, special events and festivals celebrate regional food and wine, history, and the fine arts.

Spend your days horseback riding, canoeing, or hiking through breathtaking landscapes and observing moose, elk, otters, ospreys, and bald and golden eagles. On the front lawn, practice fly-casting into the pond stocked with brown trout; then seek wilder quarry in the pristine waters of the Madison, Gallatin, Yellowstone, or Henry's Fork of the Snake rivers or some of the nearby creeks and lakes. You can combine fishing with riding on a personalized excursion with an expert guide and individual instruction. Trail rides might take you to the Sun Ranch, where you can get a taste of the rugged Lee Metcalf Wilderness area, or to Red Canyon, where the view from Skyline Ridge stretches to the Grand Tetons.

Each morning you'll awaken to a hearty country breakfast of fresh fruit, organic home-baked bread, or buckwheat pancakes. Likely as not, your lunch will be a picnic of sandwiches, fruit, salads, and homemade chips, which you can enjoy on the trail. The sophisticated four-course meal makes use of the freshest, often organic, local produce and meats. Specialties include cured wild king salmon, roasted conservation-beef sirloin, zinfandel-braised duck, and roasted pork loin, all served with fine wines. One night a week is dedicated to a barbecue, which starts with a ride in a horse-drawn wagon to Squaw Creek, where dinner is served.

Tips *Papoose Creek is designed for adults. Children under 12 are invited only when the entire lodge is reserved for private use. Beer and wine are available, but bring your own spirits if you want cocktails.*

5 rooms, 3 cabins ❚O❚ American plan. **Recreation:** bird-watching, fishing, hiking, horseback riding, wildlife viewing, canoeing, library. **Services:** fishing equipment provided, outdoor hot tub, massage, guided fishing trips, laundry service, shop, airport shuttle, business services, meeting room. **Classes and programs:** guided hikes, guided nature walks, natural history programs, fly-fishing lessons, horseback-riding lessons, cooking classes, history talks. ♿ In-room safes, some jetted tubs; no a/c, no room phones, no room TVs, no kids under 12, no smoking 🖵 $2,400–$3,900 per person/wk ▤ AE, D, MC, V.

🖃 *1520 U.S. 287 N, Cameron, MT 59720* ☎ *406/682–3030 or 888/674–3030* 🖷 *406/682–3031* ⊕ *www.papoosecreek.com* ☾ *Closed Oct. 16–Apr.*

STONE SCHOOL INN
Tranquil Outpost

In the small community of Valier, just east of the Continental Divide and 80 mi north of Great Falls, Stone School Inn is an integral part of local history. Constructed of sandstone from a nearby quarry, the Stone School was built in 1911 and served as a elementary school until 1952. Now it is listed on the National Register of Historic Places and has been restored as a B&B. Where the children of north-central Montana farmers and ranchers once worked at their desks, you can shed your cares. Sip coffee or wine on the patio overlooking Lake Frances, a public reservoir ¼ mi from the back deck. Unobstructed views of the Rocky Mountains and Big Sky sunsets are reflected in its waters, where Canada and snow geese come and go.

It took five years to restore the schoolhouse, which opened as an inn in 2001. The original bell still hangs in the tower. From the foyer, the grand old staircase leads to a library filled with towering bookshelves and cushy chairs. Opening off the library, the elegant guest rooms are furnished with antiques and each has a private bath. Downstairs, the hallway is surfaced with clay tile recovered from the Montana State Capitol during the capitol's renovation, and laid in its original pattern.

The sunlit basement houses a dining room and a recreation room with a vintage pool table, and a big-screen surround-sound television with

VCR and DVD. Unchanged in size and with its old trim, the recreation room is the most historically correct room in the house—it even has the original chalkboard. In the dining room prepare for a hearty breakfast: fresh fruits, homemade breads, eggs, sausage, country-fried potatoes, and croissant French toast with vanilla sauce and strawberries. Other meals are also available by arrangement, and special diets are easily accommodated.

At the edge of the manicured lawn, shaded by green ash trees, you can spend some quiet time in the gazebo. Antique toys displayed in the flower beds reflect the inn's history. In summer you can swim, water-ski, sail, and windsurf on Lake Frances; in winter you can go ice-skating. The lake is also a great place to fish for pike and walleye year-round. For a little exercise, hop on one of the tandem bikes and ride along the country roads, past grazing cattle and the farm fields of this high plains area, along the shores of Lake Frances, or to the shops downtown. For a little golf, tee off from the back deck and play the inn's two holes. Farther afield, step back to the days of the dinosaurs at museums in Bynum and Choteau, or participate in a dinosaur dig at Egg Mountain. And only an hour northwest of Valier lie all the wonders of Glacier National Park.

Tip *Rock City, 7 mi north of Valier, is a great place for a picnic and an afternoon of hide-and-seek. An eerie geological oddity, the site bristles with hoodoos—large sandstone pillars—and other interesting formations cut out of the land by wind and rain erosion.*

🛏 4 rooms, 2 suites 🍽 Full breakfast, dining room **Recreation:** biking, bird-watching, fishing, hiking, horseback riding (nearby), running, wildlife viewing, lake swimming, waterskiing, windsurfing, boating, canoeing, sailing, 2-hole golf course, ice-skating, horseshoes, volleyball, library, piano, recreation room. **Services:** fishing poles, ice skates, and tandem bikes provided; babysitting; laundry facilities; airport shuttle; meeting rooms. ♿ In-room VCRs; no smoking 💳 $85–$105 💳 AE, D, MC, V.

🏠 *820 3rd Street (Box 24), Valier, MT 59486* ☎ *406/279–3796* 📠 *406/ 279–3233* 🌐 *www.stoneschoolinn.com.*

TELLER WILDLIFE REFUGE
Rustic Escape ~ Tranquil Outpost

In western Montana's Bitterroot Valley, near the small town of Corvallis and about 50 mi from Missoula, 1,200-acre Teller Wildlife Refuge is dedicated to the preservation and restoration of the region's native riparian habitat. Spread out along 3 mi of the Bitterroot River—one of the finest trout fisheries in the world—the refuge shelters whitetailed deer, red foxes, coyotes, porcupines, marmots, beavers, otters, muskrats, and other animals. Ospreys, Canada geese, pileated wood-peckers, waterfowl, raptors, and songbirds also find a haven here. The area is rich in history as well: the Bitterroot Valley was home to the Salish Indians when it was traversed by the Lewis and Clark expedition in 1805 and 1806.

You'll leave everyday life behind when you come to this place bursting with life. Three farmhouses dating from the 1800s and two rustic riverfront cabins accommodate a maximum of five parties at a time, so there's little to interrupt your enjoyment of nature. The Chaffin and Slack Homestead homes have manicured lawns and flower beds, shaded by ancient poplar and cottonwood trees. A bright and tastefully furnished parlor with overstuffed couches and chairs and walls of books is an inviting retreat. Bedrooms are decorated with 19th-century furniture, lace curtains, and quilted coverlets.

Thirty minutes south of refuge headquarters, Ward's Cove House nestles in a grove of evergreens in a hidden meadow on the west bank of the Bitterroot River. The modern, two-story frame cabin has screened-in porches. Also on the west bank of the river is Otto's Fishing Cabin, with screened porch, knotty-pine paneling, western-style furniture, and modern kitchen and bath.

Lie back in your hammock and lose yourself in the tranquillity of the refuge, or take a stroll through the gardens or along the Bitterroot River. You are bound to see an incredible variety of avian life. Pick some huckleberries in season and take them back to your house for dessert. In the river, you can go fly-fishing, take a float trip, or pan for sapphires. Teller is also an ideal base camp in winter: in the surrounding area you can do just about anything imaginable with snow.

Tip *During your stay, you may be able to attend author readings or lecture series sponsored by the Teller Wildlife Refuge Education Program. The Web site posts a schedule of events.*

🛏 2 cabins, 3 houses 🍴 Catering available, kitchens. **Recreation:** biking, bird-watching, fishing, hiking, running, wildlife viewing. Nearby: horseback riding, mountain biking, canoeing, rafting, 18-hole golf course, cross-country skiing, downhill skiing, ice-skating, sleigh rides, snowmobiling, snowshoeing, sporting clays. **Services:** guided fishing trips, refuge tours, dry-cleaning service, laundry service, airport shuttle. **Classes and programs:** guided hikes, guided nature walks, ecology lectures. ♿ Pets allowed (fee); no TV in some rooms, no a/c, no smoking 💲 $175 daily–$2,500 weekly 💳 MC, V.

📫 *Box 548, Corvallis, MT 59828* ☎ *406/961–3507* 📠 *406/961–4489* 🌐 *www.tellerwildlife.org.*

WHITE TAIL GUEST RANCH
Laid-Back Adventure

Midway between Missoula and Helena, in the Blackfoot Valley and next to Bob Marshall Wilderness, White Tail Guest Ranch is surrounded by evergreen forest. Well-groomed lawns and blooming annuals bring a hint of civilization to this wild place, but the fresh mountain air, clear blue skies, and spectacular views will remind you that you're not in suburbia any more. Experienced wranglers and guides will help you explore the valley, mountains, lakes, and streams, where it is not unusual to cross paths with deer and grouse—you might even spot a black bear in the distance.

If you care to ride, you'll be matched with a horse suitable for your experience. The number of people on each trail ride is kept small to maximize your immersion in the wilderness. You can also hike or mountain bike through the forest. Salmon Creek, which runs through the property, is an important tributary to the Blackfoot River, a prime trout stream made famous in the movie *A River Runs Through It.* You can fly-fish on the Blackfoot or other nearby trout rivers, including the North Fork of the Blackfoot, the Missouri, and the Clark Fork. The Blackfoot is also great for rafting, and nearby Cooper's Lake is ideal for canoeing, swimming, or fishing. In winter you can ride through the snowy fields and forests on a sled pulled by a team of Alaskan huskies—and even learn how to drive them yourself with instruction from the resident musher.

When you've had enough adventure, retire to the front porch of your creekside cabin and listen to the wind whispering through towering pine trees and the burbling of Salmon Creek flowing by. You may see wildlife while you sit. Originally homestead buildings, the cabins were moved to the ranch in the 1930s and 1940s. The refurbished one- and two-bedroom cabins are now equipped with electric heat, private bath, rustic furniture, and homey quilted bedding. The two-story, two-bedroom log bunkhouse sleeps six.

The ringing of the dinner bell summons you to the main lodge for buffet- and family-style meals. Hearty home cooking, fresh-baked breads and desserts, and snacks are made from scratch using the freshest ingredients and fruits purchased at the local farmers' market. Special diets are easily accommodated. After supper, relax around a campfire or in the hot tub under a brilliant starlit sky. In the lodge sitting room, put your feet up in front of the crackling fire, play a table game, watch a video in the TV corner, or try your hand at the piano.

Tip *The ranch runs women-only trips that usually include five nights in Bob Marshall Wilderness. You move camp each day, riding horseback from one location to the next. Awesome surroundings, excellent wildlife viewing and fishing, and spectacular photo ops make these adventures the trip of a lifetime.*

🛏 9 cabins, 1 bunkhouse, 1 house ❙◎❙ American plan. **Recreation:** biking, bird-watching, fishing, hiking, horseback riding, mountain biking, wildlife viewing, swimming hole, tubing, boating, canoeing, rafting, cross-country skiing, dogsledding, sledding, snowmobiling, snowshoeing, volleyball, recreation room. **Services:** mountain bikes and canoes provided, outdoor hot tub, guided fishing trips, airport shuttle, meeting rooms, travel services. **Classes and programs:** guided hikes, guided nature walks, photo safaris. ᗕ Some pets allowed, no-smoking rooms; no a/c, no room phones, no room TVs 🖾 3-night package $390–$780 per person; 7-night package $650–$1,645 per person 🖃 MC, V.

🖰 *897 White Tail Rd., Ovando, MT 59854* ☎ *406/793–5627 or 888/987–2624* 🖷 *406/793–5043* ⊕ *www.whitetailranch.com* ☯ *Closed Dec.*

Nebraska

LIED LODGE AT ARBOR DAY FARM
Family Hideout

The Nebraska prairie changed forever the day J. Sterling Morton and his young bride moved to Nebraska City in 1855. Avid gardeners and landscapers, they began planting their property with trees. The trees not only reminded them of home, but provided shade from the hot southeast Nebraska sun and prevented soil erosion on the windy plains. A newspaper editor, Morton popularized the planting of trees in Nebraska and persuaded the state government to create Arbor Day in recognition of the importance of trees. The first Arbor Day was celebrated in 1872.

Today, the National Arbor Day Foundation operates Arbor Day Farm, 260 acres of hills, riparian woodlands, arboretums, and working orchards in Nebraska City (an hour south of Omaha and an hour east of Lincoln). On the farm stands the Lied Lodge & Conference Center, a modern resort designed to operate in harmony with the environment. Lots of stone and nine types of wood were used in the construction of the immense lodge, and wherever the wood appears in public areas, so does an identifying sign that includes a leaf sample and explanation of the various uses of the wood. Wood serves other purposes as well: the center's heating and cooling systems are powered by the burning of waste wood and wood from trees grown on the property. The lamp shades, featuring a leaf motif, are made from recycled paper, and carpeting is made from recycled plastic bottles. Each guest room is equipped with at least four recycling baskets.

On the farm you can wander hiking trails marked with informative signs. Each trail has a theme, from the types of trees in the area to the many birdcalls you can hear on the farm. Families can spend hours building their ecological knowledge at the Tree Adventure, an educational center that explains J. Sterling Morton's passion for taking care of the environment. Learn more about the growth process of trees and other plant life at the greenhouse, and watch apples being processed at the Apple House.

Close to 30 varieties of apple trees grow on Arbor Day Farm, so cider, apple pie, and many other goodies made with apples are always on the menu. Breakfast in the dining room includes oatmeal cooked in apple cider instead of water, with huge dollops of applesauce in the center. The farm also grows peaches—available in the dining room in season—and you can contact the front desk to order fruit that will be ready upon checkout for you to take home. It is one of the benefits J. Sterling Morton envisioned when he planted the first apple tree seedling here in 1855.

Tip *If you plan on visiting during the fall apple harvest, make your reservations early. This is the most popular time of the year at the lodge.*

⛵ 144 rooms ⏹ 2 restaurants, 1 bar. **Recreation:** biking, bird-watching, hiking, horseback riding, running, indoor pool, 18-hole golf course, 9-hole golf course (nearby), tennis court, sleigh rides, bowling (nearby), horseshoes, volleyball, library. **Services:** health club, dry-cleaning service, laundry service, shop, business services, Internet access, meeting rooms. **Classes and programs:** environmental talks, sightseeing tours. ⛄ Cable TV; no smoking ▭ $99–$134 ▭ AE, D, DC, MC, V.

📫 *2700 Sylvan Rd., Nebraska City, NE 68410* ☎ *402/873–8733* 🖨 *402/ 873–4999* ⊕ *www.liedlodge.org.*

FORT ROBINSON STATE PARK
Family Hideout ~ Rustic Escape

In the northwestern corner of Nebraska, the sweep of the prairie meets stark sandstone buttes. White limestone cliffs are striped with deep layers of red, gray, and purplish volcanic ash from prehistoric eruptions. Ponderosa pines and a few stands of cottonwood and hackberry soften the appearance of the bleak outcroppings where bighorn sheep, wild turkeys, deer, and antelope wander. The hills are vibrant with the colors of the purple coneflower, yucca, and western snowberry. This is Nebraska's Pine Ridge country, south of the South Dakota state line, the Black Hills, and Mount Rushmore.

A state park since 1955, Fort Robinson was established in 1874 as a military post to protect pioneer supply trains from Indian attacks. The military abandoned it in 1948, yet most of the original brick-and-adobe structures remain. Bordering the expansive parade grounds, buildings that were once the quarters of officers and enlisted men are now simply furnished guest rooms and cottages. Old photos of officers who served at Fort Robinson hang on the otherwise austere plaster walls. Much of the woodwork, including doors and moldings, is original, so it's chipped and scratched from years of use. The iron beds and wooden dressers are as plain as they would have been 150 years ago. Wide verandas hold Adirondack chairs and chaise longues.

A seemingly endless choice of activities can fill your days at Fort Robinson. The 22,000-acre park is home to a herd of more than 40 buffalo, which you can see by driving 4½-mi Smiley Canyon Road. Mountain biking and hiking are popular ways to take in the scenery. Naturalists with expertise in the geology, flora, and fauna of the region lead jeep rides and hikes through the mountains and into remote wilderness areas. A natural history museum provides an overview of the park's ecology, and another museum details the military history of the fort.

In the evening, sit down to a supper of buffalo burgers, and steaks in the dining room, or join one of the chuck-wagon cookouts. If you're not ready for bed yet, attend a performance at the Post Playhouse Summer Repertory Theater, one of Nebraska's oldest and best-loved summer theaters. The theater mounts three productions each summer in the former quartermaster's warehouse, built in 1887.

Tip *You are most likely to see the park's wildlife in the early evening. Keep watch in the hills for bighorn sheep, and for deer and elk in meadows and near fresh water. Be patient if the buffalo herd commandeers the middle of the road, which they frequently do: they'll move when they are good and ready. In the meantime, by all means stay in the car—these are wild animals.*

🛏 22 rooms, 9 cabins, 25 houses 🍽 Snack bar, restaurant, grills, picnic area, some kitchens. **Recreation:** biking, bird-watching, fishing, hiking, horseback riding, mountain biking, running, wildlife viewing, indoor pool, 18-hole golf course (nearby), tennis court, basketball, horseshoes, playground. **Services:** bicycle, fishing-equipment, and tennis-equipment rentals; horse boarding; kennel; shop; laundry facilities; meeting rooms. **Classes and programs:** natural history programs, children's programs (ages 2–12), arts and crafts classes, sing-alongs. ♿ Some pets allowed; no room phones, no rooms TVs, no smoking 💳 $35–$600 💳 MC, V.

✉ *Box 392, Crawford, NE 69339* ☎ *308/665–2900* 📠 *308/665–2906* 🌐 *www.outdoornebraska.org.*

HEARTLAND ELK RANCH
Tranquil Outpost

Running through the "top" of Nebraska, the Niobrara River lies in a basin of prairie and pine-laden hills. The sheer cliffs along the riverbank contrast with open plains and support abundant wildlife, earning the river the designation of National Scenic and Recreational River. The "recreational" part of the label refers to the Niobrara's status as one of the best canoe rivers in the country. In summer, outdoors enthusiasts come here from around the world to float lazily in inner tubes and canoes. The river is as clear and pure as it was when Native Americans roamed this land in search of buffalo, elk, and antelope.

Set on the rim of a canyon cut by the Niobrara River, Heartland Elk Ranch is run by Kerry and Lisa Krueger, lifetime residents of the region. Pastures on the ranch's 1,000 acres of open prairie are scattered with cattle and a herd of about 75 elk. In this open countryside overlooking the river are four log cabins, each with a fireplace and elk trophy mounts. Handwoven throw rugs cover the pine floors, and easy chairs and a couch are perfect for lounging. Cabins are separated by several hundred yards, so your only visitor may be a curious doe and her fawn.

Instead of a bed-and-breakfast, the ranch might be called a bed-and-barbecue. The Kruegers decided to offer an evening barbecue rather than breakfast because, as Lisa says, "it's a great time just to sit and chat about the day, and no one is in a hurry to get anywhere." Monday, Wednesday, and Saturday nights from Memorial Day through Labor Day, Lisa lays out salad, baked beans, fresh bread, and blueberry cobbler prepared from her grandmother's recipe. You can taste some low-fat elk meat at the barbecue or prepare some to your own taste on the grill outside your cabin.

Fishing is another relaxing treat at the ranch. Six ponds are stocked with bluegill, which makes a nice dinner when a barbecue is not on the schedule. On your fishing expeditions, or on a quiet walk around the grounds, you may be accompanied by the Kruegers' schnauzer, Walter, who seems to think everyone is his best friend. The ranch will arrange horseback-riding or river-tubing trips for you so you can see more of the area's magical scenery. One spot especially worth your while is Fort Niobrara Wildlife Refuge, a 19,000-acre preserve filled with hiking trails and scenic waterfalls. Elk and buffalo live here, as do more than 200 species of birds. Spring is a particularly fine time to visit with binoculars and birding books in hand.

Tip *The best way to explore the river valley is on horseback, which allows you to access wilderness areas that you could not reach on foot or by car. In the backcountry you can get magnificent views of the valley and you are likely to catch glimpses of wildlife.*

⇌ 4 cabins, 1 house ⚬⚬ Grocery store, grills, picnic area, kitchens. **Recreation:** biking, bird-watching, fishing, hiking, horseback riding, mountain biking (nearby), running, wildlife viewing, river swimming, tubing (water), canoeing, 9-hole golf course (nearby), horseshoes, playground. **Services:** canoe, fishing-equipment, and water-tube rentals; shop; laundry facilities. ♿ No room phones, no room TVs ⌨ $79–$189 ▭ D, MC, V.

✉ *Box HC 13, Valentine, NE 69201* ☎ *402/376–1124* 📠 *402/376–2553* ⊕ *www.heartlandelk.com.*

Nevada

COTTONWOOD GUEST RANCH
Laid-Back Adventure

About 70 mi from the nearest town (Jackpot, on the Idaho border) and 30 mi from a paved road (Highway 93), 45,000-acre Cottonwood Guest Ranch lies in the northeastern corner of Nevada. Cattle rustlers once occupied this land in the O'Neil Basin, where a rolling landscape of sagebrush butts up against the mountains of the Jarbridge Wilderness. Cattle and horses still outnumber people here, but the rustlers are gone. They were replaced by the Smith family five generations ago, when the Smiths started up their ranch.

Cottonwood is not a dude ranch but a working ranch that welcomes you any time of year. You set your own schedule and spend your time as you choose, whether soaking in the hot tub or helping out with ranch chores. It seems that everyone eventually pitches in, on the land or in the kitchen, and you're bound to enjoy the spirit of camaraderie. You can ride horses until you're numb and aching, but if you don't feel like spending the day in a saddle, hike out into the hills for some bird-watching or go mountain biking. Fish in Cottonwood Creek or take a swim in the pond. Stretch out and soak up some sun. If you want some action, try out the wrangler's life on a horse drive, bringing a herd of horses to summer pasture, or at a cow camp, riding herd up in the mountains. For a few days you'll eat from a chuck wagon, warm your toes around a campfire, and bed down in a tent. The ranch also offers overnight pack trips into the wilderness.

Back at the ranch, the guest lodge has seven rooms, all with queen-size beds, private bath, and hookups for TVs, phones, and computer modems (TVs and phones must be requested in advance, but there's no charge). The simple furnishings have a southwestern flair. In the communal dining room or on the deck, meals are served family-style around one large table. What kind of eats you get depends on the guests' preferences and the cook's mood: expect anything from old-fashioned ranch grub to fancy western fare. The lodge's spacious great room has paneled walls, wood-beamed ceilings, comfy couches, and a large stone fireplace. It's all so easy and friendly that you might want to take a piece of the ranch home with you. If so, stop by the Cottonwood Trading Post in the ranch's original log cabin and pick up something—hand-made lamps, rope mirrors, and candles—made by the cowboys during winter breaks.

Tip *The ranch doesn't serve alcohol, but you may bring your own.*

7 rooms American plan, grills, picnic area. **Recreation:** bird-watching, fishing, hiking, horseback riding, mountain biking, swimming hole, cross-country skiing, snowmobiling. **Services:** outdoor hot tub, shop, Internet access. **Classes and programs:** bird-watching and pho-tography classes, astronomy and botany lectures. In-room data ports; no room phones, no room TVs $200 No credit cards.

HC 62 (Box 1300), Wells, NV 89835 775/755–2231 775/752–3604 www.cottonwoodguestranch.com.

DEER RUN RANCH BED & BREAKFAST
Tranquil Outpost

About 10 mi from Carson City, the 200-acre Quarter Circle JP ranch once grew produce to ship to the mining boomtown of Virginia City and brewed moonshine in an illegal distillery. The Quarter Circle JP is no more, but in its place stands a B&B surrounded by alfalfa fields, with spectacular views of Washoe Lake and the Sierra Nevadas. Deer Run Ranch is a supremely peaceful place to recharge.

Pottery artist Muffy Vhay and her husband, architect David Vhay, built the timber-frame ranch house as a passive solar home, designed to be cool in summer and warm in winter. The guest wing, with its own en-trance, has only two bedrooms and a common sitting area. Decorated in a southwestern motif with Navajo rugs and paintings by Nevada artists, both rooms have a queen-size bed, private bath, and window seat. In the homey sitting room are all the necessities for a relaxing weekend: a magazine-and-book library, TV and VCR, woodstove, board games, refrigerator, and coffeemaker. Outside are spacious patios and porches ideal for sipping your coffee and watching the wildlife. Right in front of the house, cottonwood trees shade a pond. It has a deck, but if you feel an urge to swim, use the above-ground swimming pool. In win-ter, you can ice-skate on the pond.

When you arrive at Deer Run expect a fruit basket and bottle of wine to be waiting. Snacks and refreshments are available throughout your stay. Served on pottery plates made by Muffy, breakfast includes omelets, coffee and imported teas, and home-baked breads; the house specialty is raised orange waffles. Vegetables and fruits fresh from the B&B's gar-den often appear on the table as well.

Tip *Along with other local artisans, Muffy sells her pottery in a co-op store in Carson City, a 10-minute drive from Deer Run.*

🛏 2 rooms 🍽 Full breakfast. **Recreation:** bird-watching, hiking, wildlife viewing, pool, horseshoes. ♿ No-smoking rooms; no room phones ⚏ $95–$125 ⊟ AE, D, MC, V.

🏠 *5440 Eastlake Blvd., Carson City, NV 89704* ☎ *800/378–5440 or 775/882–3643* ⊕ *www.bbonline.com/nv/deerrun.*

MOUNT CHARLESTON LODGE
Tranquil Outpost

Mount Charleston, part of the Spring Mountain range, is southern Nevada's best-kept secret. With 52 mi of marked and maintained hiking trails, this part of Toiyabe National Forest draws those who want to get away, but not too far away, from the city. As you follow the highway into the mountains, the desert landscape of sand dunes, junipers, and cactus gives way to tall pines, rocky hillsides, and, in winter, lots of snow. In a mere hour, you can leave behind the clamor of slot machines, the crowds on the Las Vegas Strip, and the burden of civilization.

More than 7,700 feet above sea level, Mount Charleston Lodge stands below Cathedral Rock, a majestic spire of stone jutting from the mountain. The complex overlooks the lush pine forests of Kyle Canyon. Private paths over wooden bridges lead to the small, green-roof cabins. Furnishings are nothing special, but each cabin has a fireplace, a jetted tub, and a roomy back deck with an assortment of chairs and tables. Fix a cup of cocoa or pour a glass of wine and unwind outdoors without taking off your bunny slippers. You'll have an endless view of trees and mountains.

Hiking paths start just steps away from the cabins, so you might as well take a hike around Cathedral Rock. Marked trails offer easy jaunts into the forest, but experienced hikers won't be disappointed with some of the more intense trails. You can also get out into nature's glory on a guided horseback ride or carriage ride right from the lodge. Just 25 minutes west of the lodge, in Lee Canyon, Las Vegas Ski and Snowboard Resort is open Thanksgiving through Easter. Drive in the opposite direction to find Spring Mountain Ranch State Park. At the visitor center there you can learn about the history of the ranch, which was started in 1876. Hike some of the trails and have a picnic.

You won't have to forage for your supper. The lodge's restaurant serves pheasant, venison, and elk, as well as standard American favorites. A wood-beam ceiling, low lighting, and a fireplace make the dining room a snug spot to gaze out at Kyle Canyon. In summer, bring a jacket to enjoy the outdoor patio in the evening, when temperatures can drop to 40°F.

Tip *Las Vegas is about 35 mi away. If you want a taste of the glitter, glam, and glory of Sin City, you can make a day trip of it and then return to the lodge for a quiet evening in the mountains.*

➷ 23 cabins ⵏ◎ⵏ Restaurant, microwaves, refrigerators. **Recreation:** hiking, skiing (nearby). ♿ TV with DVD and VCR, in-room fireplaces, private decks; no a/c ▤ $125–$240 ▭ AE, D, DC, MC, V.

⌂ *HCR 38 (Box 325), Mt. Charleston, NV 89124* ☎ *702/872–5408 or 800/955–1314* ⊕ *www.mtcharlestonlodge.com.*

New Hampshire

THE BALSAMS
Family Hideout ~ Luxurious Resort

Especially in the densely populated Northeast, arriving at the Balsams for the first time is an almost surreal experience. You may have thought you'd found seclusion on entering the White Mountains, but now as you approach this resort in the hinterlands of New Hampshire's North Country, a good 40 mi north of the Presidential Range, 3 hours from Manchester and Montréal and 4½ hours from Boston, you find yourself completely surrounded by nature. As you round a bend along tortuous Route 26, you lay eyes on the red-roof towers and gables of a rambling white clapboard structure shrouded by evergreens—the New England version of Shangri-la. It's hard to comprehend such a magnificent and mammoth building in so isolated a mountain setting. But here it is, the most splendid and remote of New Hampshire's grand Victorian hotels.

The Balsams encompasses some 15,000 wooded acres—an area roughly the size of New York City's most populous borough, Manhattan. Even when the resort is filled to capacity (with about 500 guests and another 400 employees), it's still a remarkably solitary place. The resort is certified as a tree farm by the American Forest Foundation and is dedicated to conserving its tens of thousands of trees. Staff naturalists lead both light rambles and more challenging hikes, placing a strong focus on wildlife viewing (from moose to bald eagles to black bears). You're also encouraged to set out on your own or to stroll through the five vibrant gardens, where signs identify what you're seeing—and sniffing. Guided night walks afford a chance to brush up on your astronomy.

There's golf on a challenging, mountainside course; six tennis courts (three are clay, three are all-weather plex-cushion); 40 mi of well-marked mountain-biking trails; a spring-fed, trout-stocked lake with canoes and rowboats available free of charge; a 59-mi cross-country ski trail network; and 16 alpine ski trails and a snowboard terrain park. Concerts, cooking demonstrations, and children's programs ensure that if you're keen on making your visit culturally and social enriching, you'll find plenty to keep you busy. At the same time, the laid-back staff and ample grounds ensure that if your focus is relaxation and quiet, you'll be left to your own devices.

The Balsams opened as an unassuming summer retreat just after the Civil War. In the tradition of 19th-century vacation retreats, the all-inclusive rates cover the cost of all meals and unlimited use of facilities (including golf, tennis, and skiing). Rooms here are spacious, with large cedar closets and ample dressers—there's lots of room to unpack several days' worth of clothing and gear. Among the layouts are family suites (two bedrooms connecting with one bathroom) and parlor suites (with a bedroom and separate sitting room). Floral-print wallpaper, modern bathrooms, full-length mirrors, and reproduction antiques impart a dignified grace; only a few suites have TVs. Most rooms have views overlooking the lake, gardens, and mountains; still, always inquire about the view when booking, as a handful afford less promising vistas (the parking area, for example).

Although the Balsams is very much a place to unwind, men do have to wear jackets in the dining room after 6 PM, but if you don't feel like being civilized, you can always order room service. The food is memorable; menus change daily and ingredients reflect seasonal availability.

Tip *Looking to spot a moose? Saunter along the hiking trails in early morning or early evening. Moose sightings are also relatively common on Route 26 as well as on the North Country's main highway, U.S. 3 (a.k.a. Moose Alley).*

184 rooms, 20 suites American plan, 2 dining rooms, room service, lounge, picnic area. **Recreation:** bird-watching, fishing, hiking, mountain biking, wildlife viewing, pool, lake swimming, canoeing, rowing, driving range, 9-hole and 18-hole golf courses, putting green, 6 tennis courts, cross-country skiing, downhill skiing, ice-skating, snowmobiling, snowshoeing, telemark skiing, badminton, basketball, billiards, boccie, croquet, Ping-Pong, shuffleboard, volleyball, library, piano, recreation room. **Services:** canoes, rowboats, paddleboats, bicycles, and fly-fishing equipment provided; cross-country ski, downhill ski, golf, ice-skate, and snowshoe and kayaking rentals; gym; massage; hair salon; golf pro shop; tennis pro shop; ski shop; babysitting; laundry service; shops; business services; Internet access; meeting rooms. **Classes and programs:** guided hikes; guided nature walks; natural history programs; golf, tennis, and ski lessons; children's programs (ages 4–13); arts and crafts classes; cooking classes; nature talks; concerts; dances; movies. In-room data ports, some jetted tubs, some private balconies, no-smoking rooms; no TV in some rooms $169–$289 AE, D, MC, V.

Dixville Notch, NH 03576 603/255–3400 or 800/255–0600, 800/255–0800 in NH 603/255–4221 www.thebalsams.com.

FRANCONIA INN
Tranquil Outpost

This 107-acre property, deep in the Easton Valley's patchwork of hard-wood forest and open meadows, adjoins the steep and jagged terrain of Franconia Notch State Park, in the heart of the White Mountains, 1¾ hours from Manchester and 2½ hours from Boston. The region suffers its share of condo sprawl and busloads of camera-toting tourists, but the Franconia Inn lies back from scenic Route 116, beside the rushing Hamm Branch River. With just over 30 rooms and lots of acreage, the inn balances a remarkable offering of outdoor activities with the tranquillity and leisurely pace of a mountain retreat; myriad sports options exist, but there's no pressure to mingle or partake in any of them.

There are plenty of things to do here to get your heart pumping. Maybe cycle a few miles into the village of Franconia, or better yet along the topsy-turvy bike paths of Franconia Notch State Park, which also claims a stretch of the Appalachian Trail and challenging rock-climbing terrain. You can access 39 mi of groomed trails and 24 mi of back-country trails from the inn's cross-country ski center (it's inside a big red barn), which also offers ice-skating on an adjacent pond and sleigh rides. The ski trails, which range from level to quite steep, are single-track, so it's easier to soak up the pristine winter scenery and maybe catch sight of a deer or moose here than it is on the wider, busier trails of the region's several other cross-country facilities. The state park is the site of Cannon Mountain, a 42-trail downhill-ski center.

Riding the aerial tram, which carries you 2,000 feet up the mountain to a trailhead leading to an observation deck, is a favorite summertime activity. The cross-country ski barn converts to a horseback-riding facility in summer. Although you have to pay for horseback trips (both group and private trail rides are offered), use of the cross-country ski trails and ski rink is gratis to those staying at the inn (you can rent skis, skates, and snowshoes). Here's an activity you won't find at any other New Hampshire resort: soaring and biplane excursions are offered from the property's grass glider port—it's a thrilling way to take in the eye-popping mountain scenery, especially during fall foliage season.

The white, three-story inn has unfussy country furnishings—you'll find canopy beds and country quilts in the rooms, most of which have period-style wallpaper or wood paneling; many have working fireplaces. The building looks and feels colonial but was actually built in the 1930s to replace the original structure, lost in a fire, which had welcomed visitors since the mid-1860s. A sunny, plant-filled restaurant serves contemporary Continental fare, such as hazelnut-crusted pork tenderloin with a raspberry demi-glace and grilled yellowfin tuna with wasabi and purple-sticky Thai rice. From the guest rooms to the wicker-laden verandas, just about every window at the Franconia Inn affords grand views of the spectacular Kinsman and Franconia mountain ranges.

Tip *For true peace and quiet, forgo the lovely but sometimes busy heated pool on the lawn behind the inn and sneak away to the less crowded swimming hole on the Hamm Branch River—just be prepared for the bracing chill of the crystal-clear waters.*

⤴ 30 rooms, 3 suites, 2 guesthouses ⦿ Full breakfast (optional), modified American plan (optional), restaurant, bar, some kitchenettes. **Recreation:** bird-watching, fishing (nearby), hiking, horseback riding, mountain biking, rock climbing (nearby), wildlife viewing, pool, river swimming, 4 tennis courts, soaring, cross-country skiing, downhill skiing (nearby), ice-skating, sledding, sleigh rides, snowshoeing, badminton, croquet, board games, library, video-game room, videocassette library. **Services:** bicycles provided; cross-country ski, ice-skate, and snowshoe rentals; outdoor hot tub; ski shop; Internet access. **Classes and programs:** ski and tennis lessons, movies. ♿ Some in-room fireplaces, some jetted tubs, some private balconies, no-smoking rooms; no room TVs ▱ $105–$155 ▭ AE, MC, V.

⌂ *1300 Easton Rd., Franconia, NH 03580* ☎ *603/823–5542 or 800/473–5299* 🖷 *603/823–8078* ⊕ *www.franconiainn.com* ☾ *Closed Apr.–mid-May.*

MANOR ON GOLDEN POND
Romantic Retreat

Back in 1981, when the producers of the poignant Katharine Hepburn–Henry Fonda movie *On Golden Pond* sought a New Hampshire lake for location filming, they zeroed in on Squam Lake, a rippling body of water just north of the considerably more commercial Lake Winnipesaukee. The movie earned Squam Lake and the sleepy colonial villages around it a brief burst of notoriety, but the area continued to shun crowds and excessive building, and to this day it remains the jewel of New Hampshire's Lakes Region, which lies one hour from Manchester and two hours from Boston. The posh yet down-to-earth Manor on Golden Pond stands out as the area's most supremely alluring hideaway.

An easy drive from countless day hikes and peaceful fishing holes, the manor sits on a slight rise overlooking Squam Lake. It's within view of a major road, but this particular stretch of U.S. 3 sees little traffic and for many miles is devoid of significant development. Fifteen gently sloping acres of towering pines, along with a fair share of maple, oak, ash, and birch trees, help to insulate the stately 1903 hip-roof inn from the outside world. You can sit on the lawn in one of the Adirondack chairs, gazing out at the lake in one direction or toward the distant White Mountains in the other. Stroll down to the sandy private beach for a dip in the lake, or paddle a canoe for a bit, keeping an eye out for ever-elusive loons or even the occasional bald eagle.

Rooms in the baronial stucco-and-shingle house reflect the copious funds and considerable efforts the building's original owner, a British real-estate magnate, sank into its construction. More than 100 leading artisans of the day were brought in from points far and near to build the dramatic home. The house was later owned by *LIFE* magazine photo editor Harold Fowler, who turned the estate into a prominent photography colony. Today, a British country theme is carried through the guest rooms, most with wood-burning fireplaces and more than half with double whirlpool tubs. Bathrooms come outfitted with fine toiletries, along with downy bathrobes and soft slippers. Canopy beds, vintage blanket chests, British antiques, and tartan fabrics fill the sumptuous bed chambers, which have such modern comforts as CD players, TVs with VCRs, and individual climate control.

Maintaining a delicate balance between formality and insouciance, the inn hosts a genial afternoon tea promptly at 4 each afternoon, either on a breezy patio with unimpeded lake views or, in winter, before the library fireplace. In the first-rate restaurant, dinners may include roasted breast and confit of Maine duck on a bed of creamy polenta, served with glazed root vegetables and port wine sauce. In a dark-paneled pub with copper-top tables, you can sip a glass of cognac or, on many weekend evenings, listen to piano music.

Tip *Especially on a snowy winter day, it can be great fun to enjoy the lavish breakfast before the crackling fire in the manor's original dining room. But romantics seeking utter seclusion should opt for breakfast in bed, especially if you have one of the many rooms with fireplaces.*

➘ 21 rooms, 2 cottages, 2 suites ⦿ Full breakfast, restaurant, pub. **Recreation:** bird-watching, fishing, hiking (nearby), wildlife viewing, beach, pool, lake swimming, canoeing, tennis court, badminton, croquet, library, piano. **Services:** concierge, boathouse, Internet access. ⬦ In-room data ports, some in-room fireplaces, in-room VCRs, some jetted tubs, some private balconies, no-smoking rooms; no kids under 12 ▭ $190–$450 ▭ AE, MC, V, D.

◔ *U.S. 3, Holderness, NH 03245* ☎ *603/968–3348 or 800/545–2141* 🖷 *603/968–2116* ⊕ *www.manorongoldenpond.com.*

New Jersey

WOOLVERTON INN
Romantic Retreat

Four grazing sheep, two attentive innkeepers, and the two of you: that's the recipe for a romantic weekend in the country at the Woolverton Inn in Stockton. Hidden away in your cottage, you can slip in a CD from the inn's extensive collection, maybe Placido Domingo's *Great Love Scenes* or Chet Baker's *Let's Get Lost*, and slide into the double whirlpool that overlooks the blazing fire in the hearth. Later, you can nap on your featherbed, lulled by the sounds of chirping birds and the softly bleating sheep.

The country comforts in this sleepy region 70 mi from Manhattan and 45 mi from Philadelphia lured the New York literati in the 1930s. Dorothy Parker and Oscar Hammerstein bought country homes along the upper reaches of the Delaware River as refuges from the New York rat race. In 1999, when three Chicagoans searched the countryside for the perfect inn to keep, the region was overrun with tourists; finding a quiet B&B here was as tricky as finding a needle in a haystack. They finally found a 10-acre estate cocooned by 300 acres of preserved farmland, on a hill above the Delaware River. The inn is a five-minute walk from the town of Stockton and a 5-mi drive from the antiques shops, art galleries, and restaurants of New Hope, Pennsylvania, and Lambertville, New Jersey, which face each other on either side of the Delaware.

John Prall Jr. built the three-story stone manor house in 1792. The five rooms and three suites inside are cozy and updated, with Egyptian cotton linens, two-person showers, and air-conditioning. Whereas Amelia's Suite, painted deep red, oozes passion with its canopy bed and a crystal chandelier over the tub, the Balustrade is more discreet with its Colonial-style four-poster bed and balcony, where breakfast can be served in season. In Newell's Library, the bed is surrounded by 700 books and antique mirrors, and in Stockton's Hideaway, a window seat for two looks out on the garden. The 1860s carriage house and two barns at the edge of the pasture hold five deluxe cottages, all with private outdoor sitting areas, refrigerators, jetted tubs, and fireplaces. Each is distinct, from the two-level, travel-theme Sojourn

Loft, with Moroccan lamps, Persian rugs, and hammock for two, to the English-style Cotswold, with Moravian tiles around the fireplace, to the rustic-chic Hunterdon, with a rough-hewn timbered canopy bed under a 20-foot-high cupola.

The innkeepers' creativity extends to their elaborate, multicourse breakfasts, which might include Grand Marnier French toast or an omelet of Brie, tomatoes, and herbs from the garden, either one plated with homemade apple-cranberry turkey sausage and muffins. You can have breakfast in bed, in the dining room, or on the porch. Afternoon refreshments—cider and home-baked cookies, brownies, and lemonade—are served in the parlor.

The Delaware River, which forms the boundary between Pennsylvania and New Jersey, provides miles of recreation. You can rent a canoe, kayak, or SnuggleTube for two and drift down the lazy river, past tree-shrouded shores and river islands. Canal towpaths, linked by six bridges, run parallel for 30 mi on opposite sides of the river. You can hike or bike along the shaded paths where mules once pulled barges. Or take a tour of Bucks County's 11 surviving covered bridges, built between 1832 and 1875. They're often called "kissing" or "wishing" bridges, and standing on one of them you might wish that your weekend never ends.

Tip *At dinnertime, stop at Phillips Fine Wines in Stockton, one of the region's best wine stores. Choose a bottle—California wines are a specialty—and uncork it at the Brazilian-accented Atrio Café a few doors away. Afterward, stroll onto the bridge over the Delaware River to see a lovely sunset.*

↪ 6 rooms, 3 suites, 5 cottages ⦿ Full breakfast, dining room, some refrigerators. **Recreation:** biking, hiking, badminton, horseshoes. Nearby: fishing, horseback riding, tubing (water), canoeing, kayaking, rafting, cross-country skiing, board games. **Services:** bike rentals, massage, Internet access. ⚘ Some in-room fireplaces, some jetted tubs, some private patios; no phones in some rooms, no room TVs, no kids under 12, no smoking ▥ $130–$425 ▭ AE, MC, V, D.

⌂ *6 Woolverton Rd., Stockton, NJ 08559* ☎ *609/397–0802 or 888/264–6648* ⊟ *609/397–0987* ⊕ *www.woolvertoninn.com.*

New Mexico

ALMA DEL MONTE BED & BREAKFAST
Romantic Retreat

In early evening, hacienda-style Alma del Monte glows in soft, pale colors that match the rosy hues cast across the sky by the sinking sun. The distant Sangre de Cristo Mountains, including towering Taos Mountain, encircle the flat tableland from which the B&B commands 360-degree views. Its 4 acres are surrounded by undeveloped private land. You do see houses in the distance, but sprawling empty acreage provides a privacy buffer. Within sight of the lodge, horses graze on carpets of green amid sagebrush and chamisa shrubs.

Alma del Monte (Spirit of the Mountain) stands midway between Taos Ski Valley and the city of Taos, in a region that attracts tens of thousands of visitors annually. But it is removed from highway traffic in a quiet, rural spot. Here Jan and Phyllis Waye have realized their lifelong dream of a creating a gracious guest lodge filled with the antiques and art they've collected over a lifetime. The Wayes try to work in harmony with the environment, via techniques such as passive solar heating and composting.

Lodge rooms, all with stunning views, are in two wings. In the south wing, each room has its own small, fenced garden outside a back door. The Pedernal Room has a king bed with headboard and footboard upholstered in leather, matching two of the room's plump leather chairs, and the Wheeler Room has a king canopy bed with views of Taos Mountain. Popular with honeymooners, the Taos Room lies at the end of the hallway and has a four-poster king bed and Victorian-style furnishings. The carved king bed in the north wing's wheelchair-accessible Truchas Room is covered with a handmade Amish quilt; a back door opens to the inn's courtyard and fountain. With views of the mountains to the east and south, the Sangre de Cristo Room (which does not open to the outdoors) has a carved mahogany king bed and a green leather rocker.

Each winter morning, a hot breakfast is served around a wooden table adjacent to the lobby area and kiva fireplace. Bring an appetite, because you'll be presented with three irresistible courses. First comes the lodge's tasty Mountain Magic morning smoothie of maple banana, apricot orange, or ginger honeydew. It's followed by a fruit dish, then by a main course such as stuffed croissant Florentine with turkey sausage links or organic apple-smoked bacon, or French toast with pecans and raisins.

Outdoor adventure is readily available around Taos. Visit nearby Conchiti Lake (within the boundaries of Pueblo de Cochiti) to cast for rainbow trout or walleyes in the Rio Grande and the Santa Fe River. Private ranches offer horseback riding, and Taos Ski Valley is renowned for world-class lifts and slopes, particularly for steep terrain that offers thrilling challenges. The ski area is so expansive that, even when it's busy, you still feel you've got the mountain to yourself.

At the end of the day, return to your gracious country home and lounge in a hammock slung beneath a gazebo. Or surrender yourself entirely to mountain magic by donning a swimsuit and splashing in the outdoor hot tub. Either way, you'll have tremendous mountain views.

Tip *During mellow hour (5–6 daily), you can have a glass of sangria and swap stories with other guests about the day's exploits. It's tough to be anonymous in this cheery, companionable place.*

5 rooms Full breakfast, dining room, picnic area. **Recreation:** biking, bird-watching, hiking, running, wildlife viewing, horseshoes, board games, library. Nearby: fishing, horseback riding, mountain biking, rock climbing, lake swimming, river swimming, tubing (water), canoeing, kayaking, rafting, 18-hole golf course, tennis courts, ballooning, cross-country skiing, downhill skiing, sleigh rides, sledding, snowmobiling, snowshoeing, tobogganing, tubing (snow). **Services:** exercise equipment, outdoor hot tub, massage, ski storage, kennel, horse boarding, wireless Internet, laundry service, business services. In-room data ports, in-room fireplaces, jetted tubs, some private patios; no room TVs, no kids under 15, no smoking $144–$250 AE, MC, V.

Box 617, 372 Hondo Seco Rd., Taos, NM 87571 505/776–2721 or 800/273–7203 505/776–8888 www.almaspirit.com.

BEAR MOUNTAIN LODGE
Romantic Retreat

On 178 acres in southwestern New Mexico, surrounded by Gila National Forest, 3 mi north of Silver City, Bear Mountain Lodge is an elegant mountain refuge operated by The Nature Conservancy. It's a place where you can kick back and simply let nature refresh you, or where you can keep busy all day learning about local Nature Conservancy preservation projects.

The history of the lodge reaches back to 1928, when it opened as the Rocky Mountain Ranch School for "mentally peculiar" children. The school closed following the stock market crash of 1929 and the ranch passed through various hands, becoming a country club at one point and a dude ranch at another. Myra and Frederick McCormick acquired it in 1959, ranching and offering informal guest quarters until Frederick died almost 20 years later. Myra managed to hang on to the property by devoting herself to the guest ranch, where she often conducted birding workshops. A colorful character, she was known for her rather brusque, frugal ways and was beloved for her devotion to the land. In her will (she died in 1999), Myra donated the ranch to The Nature Conservancy, which transformed it into Bear Mountain Lodge.

When you arrive, the sheen of hardwood floors, the delicate carving of ponderosa-pine furniture, and a bear-shape lamp will catch your eye in the lobby. A magnificently carved pine staircase leads up to four second-story rooms. These are the lodge's pricier accommodations, with jetted tubs, private balconies, and panoramic views of mountains and forest. Two downstairs guest rooms open to a shared covered porch. In a separate building are four more rooms, two with pond views. A separate one-room guesthouse, the Wren's Nest, has a wood ceiling and its own kitchen. Wood floors, hand-carved furnishings, and ornate 1920s ceramic tile in the bathrooms distinguish all guest quarters.

The mood here is casual and friendly, as are the two young staff naturalists, Mike and Carol Fugagli. But they know their stuff, and they'll take you on an all-day visit to two Nature Conservancy preserves. They also conduct shorter programs, such as bird-banding demonstrations. You can stray from the premises to explore on your own; 3.3-million-acre Gila National Forest encompasses wilderness ranging from high desert to forests of spruce and fir. Consider a hike to Gila Cliff Dwellings National Monument, where Mogollon Indians lived about seven centuries ago.

Of course, you are welcome to do nothing at all. At the lodge you can watch the birds at the feeders around a rock-lined pond, which also attracts colorful dragonflies. Mischievous Mexican blue jays, found only in the Southwest, show flashes of color as they flit among the nearby pines. If you're extra quiet, a deer might be brave enough to tiptoe up to take a sip of water. This is not the kind of property you want to check into for just one night. Plan on a stay of at least a few days to let nature do its work and to get to know your host, The Nature Conservancy.

Tip *For expeditions with Mike and Carol, wear good hiking shoes, slather on some sunscreen, and purchase the tasty box lunch (sandwich, chips, cookies, and fruit) assembled by the lodge chef. Transportation, plenty of water, and some sodas are provided.*

10 rooms, 1 house Full breakfast, dining room, some kitchens, some microwaves. **Recreation:** biking, bird-watching, hiking, mountain biking, running, board games, library. Nearby: horseback riding,

rock climbing, driving range, 18-hole golf course, putting green, bowling, playground. **Services:** mountain bikes, binoculars, trekking poles, and spotting scopes provided; horse boarding; Internet access. **Classes and programs:** guided hikes, guided nature walks, natural history programs, off-road tours, photo safaris, nature and history talks, sightseeing tours. ⛄ Some jetted tubs, some private balconies; no a/c in some rooms, no room TVs, no kids under 10, no smoking ⛆ $115–$200 ▤ AE, MC, V.

✉ *Box 1163, Silver City, NM 88062* ☎ *505/538–2538 or 877/620–2327* ⊟ *505/534–1827* ⊕ *www.bearmountainlodge.com.*

CASITAS DE GILA
Tranquil Outpost

These five modern guesthouses, set five hours from Albuquerque and 26 mi north of Silver City, place you beneath the darkest of dark night skies. You can gaze up at the Milky Way, the thick, brilliant band of stars splayed across the horizon, a sight that owners Becky and Michael O'Connor say some city folk have never seen until staying here. The casitas offer this glimpse of the galaxy because they are in sparsely populated southwestern New Mexico, miles from the bright lights of any major settlement. Telescopes and spotting scopes are here to enhance your view of the heavens, both by night and by day.

On these 90 acres you can take a solitary stroll on private hiking trails or pick up a printed guide and set out to identify plants and geological features on a self-guided nature tour. In the bottom of a canyon along winding Bear Creek, you stroll alongside gurgling water. A clatter of stones above might alert you that bighorn mountain sheep or mule deer are picking their way down a steep canyon trail on their way to water. Wild sheep have even been known to wander right up to a casita window to peer curiously inside. Next door to the Casitas, you have even more hiking and wildlife viewing opportunities, in the federally owned Gila National Forest. It contains 1,500 mi of trails through wilderness where javelina, deer, coyotes, fox, roadrunners, quail, hummingbirds, and many other birds live.

After a day of hiking—or simply relaxing—you can soak in the outdoor hot tub beneath the stars and allow your mind to wander into infinity. There will be little to disturb your reflection, for privacy is emphasized at Casitas de Gila: a sign at the entrance drive informs you that you are "Entering Stress-Free Zone." This quiet spot is a place for the imagination to run wild, where painters paint and writers write. Himself a painter, Michael O'Connor displays his work and that of other artisans in the art gallery. You can purchase handcrafted boxes, handcrafted jewelry with semiprecious stones, books, southwestern rugs, and ceramics. The gallery has an outdoor patio and fireplace where friends can gather.

Each of the casitas has a theme (Casita del Sol y la Luna is "Little House of the Sun and Moon"; Casita de las Flores is "Little House of the Flowers"). Traditional adobe architectural features, such as ceiling vigas (round wooden beams) and a portal (small porch), are complemented by southwestern accents, hand-hewn Mexican furnishings, and O'Connors artwork. Each casita also has books, games, bird feeders, and a kiva fireplace stocked with wood. The kitchens are equipped with all the basic equipment and supplies, and on the grounds is a garden from which you can pick organically grown vegetables and herbs. The one-bedroom casitas accommodate up to three adults, or two adults and two youths, and the two-bedroom casita takes up to seven people.

Tip *Keep your casita doors shut at all times to bar entry to unwanted desert creatures such as scorpions. Be extra vigilant on trails, as you might encounter the occasional rattlesnake. It's no big deal if you do, as long as you keep your distance.*

5 houses ❏ Continental breakfast, grills, picnic area, kitchens. **Recreation:** bird-watching, hiking, mountain biking, wildlife viewing, board games. **Services:** spotting scopes provided, outdoor hot tub. **Classes and programs:** astronomy talks. ⬧ In-room fireplaces, private decks; no room TVs ❏ $120–$195 ❏ AE, D, DC, MC, V.

❏ *50 Casita Flats Rd. (Box 385), Gila, NM 88038* ❏ *505/535–4455 or 877/923–4827* ❏ *505/535–4456* ❏ *www.casitasdegila.com.*

HURD RANCH GUEST HOMES
Rustic Escape

On their Sentinel Ranch, the late artists Peter Hurd and Henriette Wyeth Hurd were inspired by the gently flowing Rio Hondo, blossoming apple orchards, and hill-country landscape. The ranch lies in the Hondo Valley of south-central New Mexico, in a transition zone between desert to the east and mountainous tall-pine forest to the west. Here you see only the scant beginnings of juniper and piñon forests. With its typically mild year-round weather, the spot offers refuge from bitter high-country cold in winter and from searing lowland heat in summer.

Once used by ranch hands and guests of Peter Hurd, the houses on the ranch range from rustic to luxurious. A one-bedroom guest wing adjacent to the Hurd art gallery has a sunroom, deck, and fireplace and can sleep four. In the one-bedroom Apple and Orchard houses, interiors are simply yet tastefully furnished with rough-hewn, ranch-style furniture. The two-bedroom Wyeth House has an orchard gazebo and is equipped with a commercial stove for serious cooking. Las Milpas Casita, which can accommodate up to 10 people, offers a spacious veranda and sleeper sofas added to the two large bedrooms. All guesthouses come with complimentary, unlimited bottled water. There are only a few restaurants in the area (Roswell is 45 mi east and Ruidoso is 20 mi west), so you'll need to supply your own food. Nearby San Patricio has a small grocery store.

If you want to chill out, read a book, and enjoy the quiet, this is the place. Privacy is the unspoken motto. You have a place to stay, and the rest is up to you. Occasionally, a match is held on the ranch's polo field, but otherwise there are no organized activities, public spaces, or public dining facilities. You're on your own when exploring the property or scouting for wildlife, and for more active pursuits you'll have to go elsewhere. Miles of hiking trails thread through the surrounding Lincoln National Forest, which covers 1.1 million acres of piñon, juniper, and spruce. Ski Apache near Ruidoso has 750 acres of slopes and rents out snowboards. You can go trout fishing in some of the mountain streams and in lakes such as Bonito, 10 mi north of Ruidoso.

On one of your walks around the ranch, you might meet up with one of the permanent ranch residents—Michael Hurd, the congenial artist son of Peter Hurd. He'll be happy to talk about his famous father, who created an impressive body of paintings. Peter Hurd was most renowned for the portraits of famous people that he painted for the cover of *Time* magazine in the 1950s and '60s, but his specialty was landscapes, many of which depict the subtle lighting and contours of these very hills. He had a knack for capturing nature's fleeting moments, such as the diffused rays of sunlight that briefly peek between clouds following a desert rainstorm. Prints of notable works by Hurd and his wife, Andrew Wyeth's sister Henriette, hang in the guesthouses.

Tip *Spend some time viewing the art exhibits at the Hurd La Rinconada Gallery on the ranch. Original works include paintings by N. C. Wyeth, Andrew Wyeth, Henriette Wyeth, Peter Hurd, and Michael Hurd.*

🛏 1 suite, 4 houses 🍴 Grills, picnic area. **Recreation:** biking, birdwatching, fishing, hiking, running, wildlife viewing, library, piano, videocassette library. Nearby: horseback riding, cross-country skiing, downhill skiing, sledding, snowmobiling, snowshoeing, tobogganing, tubing (snow), bowling, carriage rides. **Services:** saunas, laundry facilities, shop, Internet access, meeting rooms. **Classes and programs:** polo matches. ⛄ Satellite TV, in-room fireplaces, in-room VCRs, some jetted tubs, private decks, some pets allowed (fee); no smoking 💳 $140–$450 🍴 AE, D, MC, V.

📪 *Box 100, San Patricio, NM 88348* ☎ *505/653–4331 or 800/658–6912* 📠 *505/653–4218* ⊕ *www.wyethartists.com.*

THE INN AT SUNRISE SPRINGS
Tranquil Outpost

It's near Santa Fe, but don't look for the typical juniper and piñon forests here. Instead, the 69-acre grounds of the Inn at Sunrise Springs are amply shaded by towering cottonwoods and willows fed by natural springs that flow into two placid ponds. Sprinkled with fluffy seed tufts from the cottonwood trees, the ponds are home to bright-orange spotted koi that rise lazily to the surface. Owner Megan Hill has maintained the land so that it closely resembles the countryside that impressed Spanish colonists centuries ago. Indigenous vegetation and landscaping have been preserved, and wooden decks and marked trails allow you to venture through the grounds without disturbing them. You might encounter artists and art students before their easels, trying to capture an image of the true high desert.

A spring-fed oasis near the town of La Cienega, Sunrise Springs lies alongside a centuries-old Spanish trade route, Camino Real del Tierra Adentro (Royal Highway of the Interior Land), that originated in Mexico. For centuries the springs were a stopover for Spanish explorers and colonists who made the journey through hundreds of miles of stark, waterless terrain to reach Santa Fe. The inn now focuses on wellness and rejuvenation enhanced by nature's own healing powers. There are plenty of classes and programs, but you really don't have to do anything at all to benefit from your stay here. Flowing streams and fountains create a soothing environment, and meditation areas, some with Buddhas, are scattered around the property. In the spa, submit to traditional therapies such as massage and yoga, or explore Native American practices such as spirit journeys (with therapeutic touch and chanting) and the use of medicine wheels, which characterize your life through seven different aspects.

Art programs take full advantage of outdoor inspiration: try mindful painting, a technique of awakening the brain's right side and creativity. Raku pottery classes (a four-day stay is necessary to complete projects) introduce you to a Japanese low-heat firing process. Native materials of clay, pumice, manure, and cedar or pine wood are used in the creation of authentic Santa Clara Pueblo-style pottery. On the premises, the Archetype Gallery and Store exhibits and sells textiles, Native American jewelry, and traditional religious icons.

The healing extends to food and drink at the inn. In the Japanese teahouse, Jo Shin An ("Hut of the Nurturing Heart"), you can participate in the elegant, centuries-old tea ritual. At the Blue Heron restaurant, you can dine on a deck overlooking a pond. A delightful mix of Asian and southwestern influences transforms organically grown produce (some from the inn's own garden) into specialty dishes such as flash-fried calamari, Szechwan pork tenderloin, and coconut mashed sweet potatoes.

Built of adobe, wood, and stone, the inn and its casitas also combine Asian and southwestern aesthetics. The most modest of the accommodations are four somewhat spartan and snug pond-view rooms, each with a double bed and a private balcony or patio overlooking the cottonwood trees and water (these rooms do not have televisions). Garden-view rooms are found in two buildings on opposite sides of the grounds. Each building contains a common lounge area with fireplace. The guest rooms, accented with southwestern flourishes and hand-carved wood, have private balconies or patios. The newest of the lodgings are 20 casitas, each with a gas fireplace and kitchenette along with oversize bathrooms. Native American symbols are the theme of lighting fixtures and bed coverings, and some casitas also have separate Zen-style meditation areas.

Tip *Be sure to ask about special packages that include lodging, food, art classes, and healing therapies.*

🛏 38 rooms, 20 casitas 🍽 Restaurant, bar, picnic area, some kitchenettes, some microwaves, some refrigerators. **Recreation:** bird-watching, hiking, wildlife viewing, pool, library. **Services:** health club, outdoor hot tubs, sauna, spa, steam room, meeting rooms. **Classes and programs:** yoga and cooking classes, arts and crafts classes, meditation programs. ♿ Some in-room DVD players, some pets allowed (fee); no TV in some rooms, no smoking 💳 $90–$275 🚫 AE, D, MC, V.

🏠 *242 Los Pinos Rd., Santa Fe, NM 87505* ☎ *505/471–3600 or 800/ 955–0028* 📠 *505/471–7365* 🌐 *www.sunrisesprings.com.*

RANCHO DE SAN JUAN
Romantic Retreat

Against the backdrop of the nearby Jemez Mountains, with unencumbered views of the Ojo Caliente River valley and the wide, wide sky, this elegant lodge occupies 225 acres in northern New Mexico, about 35 mi north of Santa Fe. Rancho de San Juan is a place where every custom-carved pine column and each lighted nicho (wall niche) has been meticulously planned. You might think that it takes a cadre of designers, innkeepers, and gardeners to run this Relais & Châteaux property, but the credit goes to just two people—John Johnson, an architect and self-taught chef, and David Heath, an interior designer. Hoping to create a gracious, hacienda-style retreat, they built and opened Rancho de San Juan in 1994.

The architecture reflects New Mexico's centuries-old Hispanic heritage, beginning with the tiled courtyard fronting the restaurant. A gently flowing fountain and lush gardens with bright flowers make it a pleasant place for a soothing sip of wine or a rejuvenating glass of iced tea. Inside the restaurant and lobby area are collections of hand-carved katsinas. Guest rooms are eclectic in style, with kiva fireplaces and shaded portals. Standard rooms in the main lodge have views, and some have private gardens. With extra amenities such as jetted tubs and more expansive views, superior suites are larger. Outfitted with hand-carved pine furniture, junior suites and casitas have covered porches, ample kitchens, and kiva fireplaces.

John spends much of his time in the kitchen dreaming up new dishes for the dinner-only, James Beard Award–winning restaurant. The changing four-course dinner menu might include leg of lamb with garlic and rosemary and, for dessert, fig tarts with mascarpone cream from cows fed on fresh herbs and flowers. Beneath a high ceiling with vigas, a kiva fireplace illuminates tables draped with hand-starched cloths. You'll need to make dinner reservations at least two weeks in advance, even if you are a registered guest, and your dinner typically costs about $150 for two people, not including wine.

David tends to the gardens and grounds. Natural landscaping blends in with the surrounding juniper and piñon forest, and lighted pathways are perfect for strolling at night. Lighted sculptures lend a spiritual air to the inn, and towering, softly glowing totems loom along the access road like benevolent guardians. An outdoor shrine, Windows in the Earth, is a cathedral-like chamber carved into a cliff for viewing from the inside out. But nature is still the most compelling sight at Rancho de San Juan.

Tip *This is a good base for visits to Georgia O'Keeffe country.*

5 rooms, 5 suites, 5 casitas Dining room, restaurant, lobby lounge, some kitchens, some kitchenettes, some microwaves, some refrigerators. **Recreation:** bird-watching, hiking, rock climbing, running, wildlife viewing, boccie, board games. **Services:** massage, babysitting, dry-cleaning service, laundry service, concierge, Internet access, meeting rooms, travel services. In-room fireplaces, in-room VCRs, some jetted tubs, private decks; no a/c in some rooms, some room TVs, no kids under 6, no smoking $225–$525 AE, D, MC, V.

Box 4140, Espanola, NM 87533 505/753–6818 *www. ranchodesanjuan.com.*

New York

COVEWOOD LODGE
Family Hideout ~ Rustic Escape

Covewood Lodge is a family-oriented Great Camp in the heart of Adirondack Park. On Big Moose Lake in the west-central Adirondacks, 140 mi northwest of Albany and 100 mi northeast of Syracuse, the resort is surrounded by 1,300 acres of pristine woodlands. The highlight of a vacation at this truly laid-back wilderness outpost might be seeing a dozen deer outside your cottage window, sharing a potluck summer supper with other guests, or waterskiing one last time around the lake before the sun sets.

Covewood's classic Adirondack-style main lodge was built in 1928 by Earl Covey, the son of an Adirondack guide. Covey gathered the posts, beams, and other lumber needed for the building from the adjacent woods, and the native stone for its many fireplaces from the mouth of a nearby river. The resort grew to include cottages yet it remains true to Covey's vision and to the Adirondack tradition: it is simple, congenial, hospitable, and certainly out-of-the-way and woodsy.

The main lodge has birch-panel walls, hardwood floors and ceilings, exposed hand-hewn beams, and a well-used porch that wraps around two sides of the building. A large living room, dining room (used only for special events), and library are on the main floor, with stone fireplaces in each room. Guest rooms and apartments are upstairs. Eighteen cottages dot the property, ranging in size from a tiny studio that was once a child's playhouse to an enormous seven-bedroom building that sleeps 12. Several of the cottages were originally the homes of Covey family members or Covewood workers. The lodge apartments and cottages have fully equipped kitchens, fireplaces, and porches. You cook for yourself here, and you furnish your own sheets, pillowcases, and towels. The rates are weekly.

Many families return to Covewood year after year, and some have vacationed here for 10, 20, even 50 years. Parents and kids alike enjoy swimming, boating, learning to water-ski in the lake, and hiking up a mountain for a panoramic view. On the property are some 30 mi of trails, ranging in difficulty from easy to challenging, that are perfect for long hikes. There's a sandy beach for young children, and two counselors are on hand to entertain kids with age-specific group activities, games, and crafts, as well as special treks and picnics—at no charge—for three to four hours each day. That gives adults a chance to find a quiet spot under a tree to read a book, take a canoe or kayak way out on the lake, or do some serious hiking. In fall and spring you can come for fall foliage weekends, canoeing trips, bird-watching adventures, or photographic expeditions.

4 rooms, 3 apartments, 18 cottages ❙◎❙ Grills, picnic area, kitchens **Recreation:** biking, bird-watching, fishing, hiking, wildlife viewing, lake swimming, waterskiing, boating, canoeing, kayaking, sailing, tennis court, badminton, billiards, horseshoes, Ping-Pong, volleyball, library, recreation room. **Services:** boat, canoe, kayak, and sailboat rentals; dock; babysitting. **Classes and programs:** guided hikes and nature walks; photo safaris; sailing and waterskiing lessons; children's programs (ages 4–14). In-room fireplaces, some private decks; no a/c, no room phones, no room TVs, no smoking ⬚ $110–$345 ⬚ No credit cards.

📖 *120 Covewood Lodge Rd., Eagle Bay, NY 13331* 📞 *315/357–3041 or 800/357–7530* 🖶 *315/357–5902* ⊕ *www.covewoodlodge.com* ⊗ *Closed Nov.–Apr.*

INN AT LAKE JOSEPH
Romantic Retreat ~ Tranquil Outpost

To many New York City residents, "going to the mountains" has always meant going to the Catskills. In the 1940s–1960s heyday of the Borscht Belt, when large resorts served as mountain getaways for city dwellers drawn by glitzy showrooms, leviathan dining rooms, and busy rosters of organized activities, the Catskills gained a reputation for kitsch. Today the area has more cachet, as couples and families (including many celebrities) rediscover the pastoral loveliness of this region only 90 minutes north of the city.

Tucked into the mountains in Forestburgh, the Inn at Lake Joseph occupies a vintage 1860s manor house and carriage house as well as a cottage adjacent to a 250-acre lake and surrounded by 2,000 acres of forest. Built as a private summer estate, the manor house is listed in the National Register of Historic Places. Current owners Ivan and Ru Weinger have operated the year-round country inn since 1982.

Guest rooms are generally huge (many from 400 to 925 square feet), and most have working fireplaces and whirlpool tubs. The six rooms in the Manor House are decorated with Victorian wallpaper, Oriental rugs, four-poster beds, antiques, and ceiling fans; some have sitting alcoves, and one has a private deck. In the Carriage House, each of five rooms and one suite are decorated in turn-of-the-20th-century Adirondack lodge style, incorporating original structural elements such as wainscoting, a headboard made from the stable door, and a whirlpool bath in what was once a horse stall. Each accommodation has its own and interesting architectural attributes: some have cathedral ceilings with original wood beams and rafters, one has a separate sleeping loft, another has a cupola skylight, and several have private sundecks with forest views. In the Adirondack-style Cottage, which was built from lumber logged from the nearby forest, the three accommodations have cathedral ceilings, private decks, and full kitchens. Dogs are welcome in the Carriage House and Cottage rooms.

Breakfast is served on the mansion's screened-in veranda (it's glassed-in during winter) overlooking the big lawn and the lake in the distance. You can help yourself all day long at the snack bar, where appetizers are ready to be microwaved, cold cuts and bread are available for sandwiches, and drinks and other goodies are laid out on the counter or in the fridge. Regardless of the season, you have plenty of recreational choices, both on the property and nearby, and the inn provides most of the gear you'll need. Besides the inn's pool and tennis courts, you can head to Lake Joseph for swimming, boating of all kinds, and fishing in the warmer months, as well as ice fishing in winter. The nearby woodlands have 4 mi of trails for hiking, snowshoeing, or cross-country skiing, and miles of paved roads within the 20-acre estate are perfect for biking. Behind the mansion itself, you can play pickup badminton, volleyball, and other lawn games in summer and go sledding and tobogganing in winter.

Tip *September through March, the nonprofit Eagle Institute sponsors bald eagle observation posts in Forestburgh and at Barryville, along the Delaware River Heritage Trail. The institute hosts guided habitat tours from January through March, when the birds return to the region each year to breed.*

11 rooms, 4 suites Full breakfast, dining room, snack bar, some kitchens, some microwaves, some refrigerators. **Recreation:** biking, bird-watching, fishing, hiking, mountain biking, wildlife viewing, pool, lake swimming, kayaking, rowing, golf privileges, 2 tennis courts, cross-country skiing, sledding, snowshoeing, tobogganing, badminton, billiards, volleyball, library. Nearby: tubing (water), canoeing, rafting, downhill skiing, tubing (snow). **Services:** mountain bikes, cross-country skis and boots, snowshoes, sleds, and toboggans provided; massage; meeting rooms. In-room data ports, some in-room fireplaces, some jetted tubs, some private decks, some pets allowed (fee); no kids under 12 (July–Aug. and weekends Sept.–June), no smoking $170–$385 AE, MC, V.

162 St. Joseph Rd., Forestburgh, NY 12777 845/791–9506 845/794–1948 www.lakejoseph.com.

LAKEHOUSE INN
Tranquil Outpost

There's no sign for Lakehouse Inn, and even the closest neighbors don't realize there's a lovely bed-and-breakfast at the end of the long driveway next to the peaceful lake they call Golden Pond. That's the way the inn's many high-profile guests seem to prefer it. Lakehouse Inn is situated on 22 private acres in the sleepy Hudson River valley countryside, about 8 mi east of Rhinebeck and two hours north of New York City. Attractive but certainly not elaborate or ostentatious, the inn's main building appears on first reckoning to be simply a private, mid-20th-century one-story country home framed by perennial gardens. An expansive redwood deck wraps around three sides of the house. Once you enter the reception room in the main building, you realize that your first impression underestimated this retreat and, indeed, you've arrived at an extraordinary place.

The inn's large, welcoming common room has a natural-wood cathedral ceiling and is furnished with leather chairs, an enormous antique sideboard, and several tables laden with flowers. Two adjacent guest rooms, three on the level below, and two more in the lakefront building are nothing short of first-rate. Each room has a wood-burning fireplace with a constantly replenished supply of logs, and a private bath with either a whirlpool tub for two or a deep soaking tub, along with robes and slippers. Romantic and stylish, if a little frilly, the decorating makes use of colorful Oriental or hooked rugs, whimsical objets d'art, and custom-made four-poster or brass beds with lace side curtains, flowered duvets, and plenty of puffy pillows. French-country cupboards or antique armoires hide the TV, VCR (with a selection of tapes), stereo/CD player, and coffeemaker. From your private deck equipped with lounge chairs and a hammock or swing, you get a view of the lake and surrounding forest.

At 9:30 each morning, a knock on your door signals the arrival of breakfast, which innkeeper Judy Kohler delivers in a basket. Freshly squeezed orange juice and a fruit course accompany berry blintzes or Belgian waffles. Have breakfast in bed or in front of the fireplace, or in summer bring it onto your deck or carry it down to the lake.

Lakehouse Inn is quiet and dedicated to relaxation. By day, you can row around or swim in the lake, sunbathe on a tiny private island, ride bikes on country roads, wander through the woods, and contemplate the birds and wildlife. By night, dine in Rhinebeck or at the Culinary Institute of America in nearby Hyde Park. Later, gaze up at the stars in the clear sky or stretch out in front of a crackling fire.

Tip *At the Rhinebeck Farmers' Market in the village parking lot (Sunday from May through October), pick up a picnic of fresh fruit, artisanal cheeses and breads, and a bottle of Hudson Valley wine. A perfect picnic* *spot is the lawn of Vanderbilt Mansion National Historic Site, on the Hudson River in Hyde Park.*

🛏 6 rooms 🍽 Full breakfast, refrigerators. **Recreation:** biking, bird-watching, fishing, hiking, wildlife viewing, lake swimming, rowing, board games, library, videocassette library. **Services:** rowboats and pedal boats provided, dock, Internet access. ♿ In-room data ports, in-room fireplaces, in-room VCRs, jetted tubs, private decks; no smoking ▭ $350–$675 ▭ MC, V.

✉ *P.O. Box 398, Stanfordville, NY 12581* ☎ *845/266–8093* ⊕ *www. lakehouseinn.com.*

TAUGHANNOCK FARMS INN
Tranquil Outpost

Taughannock Farms Inn sits on 12 pretty acres surrounded by Taughannock Falls State Park, 8 mi north of Ithaca. A country inn since 1945, the Victorian manse on the southwest shore of Cayuga Lake was built in 1873 as a country home for one John Jones of Philadelphia. Innkeepers Susan and Tom Sheridan have owned the property since 1997. They have decorated the five guest rooms in the main building in Victorian style and furnished them with many antiques that were original to the home. Impressive mahogany bedsteads, four-poster beds with lacy canopies, and a sleigh bed all have feather mattresses and lots of puffy pillows. Four cottages hold more guest rooms, some with kitchenettes. If you like, you can book an entire cottage. Cottage rooms have televisions, but inn rooms do not.

From the inn you have easy access to 5 mi of hiking trails in Taughannock Falls State Park, where Taughannock Creek flows through a 400-foot-deep gorge. Cascading precipitously off dark, rocky cliffs within the gorge, the park's namesake waterfall has one of the highest vertical drops in the eastern United States: at 215 feet, it's 33 feet higher than Niagara. The ¾-mi Gorge Trail, which begins next to one of the inn's guest cottages and extends to the pool at the base of the falls, is a fairly easy hike along a flat, wide path. The 3½-mi Rim Loop Trail, which overlooks the gorge and waterfall, is more challenging but particularly scenic, with misty views of the gorge through the dense spray of the waterfall. When you've had enough hiking, you can swim, picnic, or fish in the park. Winters are cold and snowy around here, so the opportunity to go cross-country skiing, sledding, and ice skating in the park—and on the inn's 12 acres—is virtually guaranteed.

Cayuga Lake (the name translates from the Iroquois language as "boat landing") is 40 mi long and 435 feet deep. Formed by glacial activity more than 100 million years ago, it is one of the 11 crystal-clear Finger Lakes that spread across central New York State like the digits of a giant hand. Besides the lakes, which are a four-season playground and a boater's dream, the region is also riddled with spectacular, deep gorges and splashed by more than 1,000 waterfalls. It's a great area for walking and for more active outdoor sports, such as rock climbing, hiking, and biking.

The restaurant at Taughannock Farms Inn serves traditional American fare—hand-carved roast turkey with all the trimmings, rack of lamb rubbed with garlic and rosemary, loin of pork with Cortland apple chutney, prime roast rib of beef with horseradish cream, grilled steaks, lobster tails, and broiled seafood with wild rice. The wine list highlights vintages from some of the dozens of wineries along the shores of the Finger Lakes. Overnight guests are treated to a breakfast of pastries, fruit, cereal, coffee, one hot item, and juice.

Tip *In Watkins Glen State Park, on the southern tip of Seneca Lake (14 mi southwest of Taughannock Farms Inn), a 2-mi-long stream washes through a gorge, dropping 400 vertical feet over its course and creating 19 waterfalls along the way. Rim trails overlook cliffs that rise as high as 200 feet above the stream; a gorge path, with 800 stone steps, passes over and under waterfalls.*

📪 22 rooms ⦿️ Breakfast, restaurant, some kitchenettes. **Recreation:** biking, hiking, lake swimming, boating, canoeing, kayaking (nearby), cross-country skiing, ice-skating, sledding, board games. **Services:** Jacuzzis, meeting rooms. ♿ In-room data ports, some in-room VCRs/DVDs; no TV in some rooms, no smoking 🔲$75–$190 🖵 AE, D, MC, V.

🏠 *2030 Gorge Rd., Trumansburg, NY 14886* ☎ *607/387–7711* 🖷 *607/ 387–7721* ⊕ *www.t-farms.com.*

THE WAWBEEK ON UPPER SARANAC LAKE
Tranquil Outpost

The Wawbeek on Upper Saranac Lake is a classic Adirondack great camp where you can pretend you are a big shot of yesteryear. About a half hour's drive west of Lake Placid in the north-central Adirondacks, the resort lies on 40 acres of forest, fields, and lawns around a lake. Several of its buildings date to the Wawbeek's founding in 1902: the Mountain House was the original sleeping lodge, the restaurant building was the original eating cabin, and one of the original guest cabins still houses visitors. The structures are authentic examples of turn-of-the-20th-century Adirondack style. Their spacious rooms are rich with knotty-pine paneling, grand stone fireplaces, and handmade furniture. From their broad porches you can enjoy a gorgeous view.

Two lodges (Mountain House and Lake House) and the Wawbeek Restaurant stand on a bluff that juts into the lake, and a third lodge (Carriage House), and several log cabins either overlook the water or are tucked into the woods. Mountain House and Lake House are perfect for large family gatherings: Mountain House has a large common room with knotty-pine paneling and a stone fireplace, along with a small kitchen, dining area, six bedrooms (each with private bath), and double-deck porches; Lake House—whose eight bedrooms each have a separate sitting area, fireplace, and jetted tub—has connecting rooms on the main floor that can become a living/dining area when the entire lodge is booked. In the Carriage House are four bedrooms with private entrances. Cabins have one or two bedrooms each, as well as kitchens and screened porches, making them especially suitable for families. All guest accommodations are furnished in Adirondack style— patchwork quilts on the beds, stained woodwork, sturdy wooden chests and tables, pullout sofas in the sitting rooms. The overall look goes well with the fabulous views of the mountains and piney woods from decks and windows.

Dining at the Wawbeek Restaurant is excellent and so popular that, even if you are staying at the resort, you must make reservations. The menu, which changes with the seasons, exploits local products such as Adirondack-raised goat cheese, venison, rainbow trout, and rabbit, along with expertly finished grilled or sautéed beef, chicken, and seafood dishes. A vegetarian "bark eater" platter is always on the menu, too. The North Country cuisine suits the dining-room architecture to a T. Dark wood paneling, walls of windows overlooking the lake in the foreground and mountains beyond, and a stone fireplace with a recessed hearth large enough for two banquettes give the room a backwoods tone. Upstairs but open to the dining room, the lounge is dominated by an enormous mounted moose head, which according to resort lore is a trophy of one of Teddy Roosevelt's hunting trips.

In winter you can cross-country ski or snowshoe on trails that begin right at the doorstep of the lodges and cabins. After a day in the snow and a hearty dinner, you'll probably want to settle in front of the fireplace with a book or a favorite person—or both. In warmer months, the wooded trails are perfect for hiking and mountain biking, and a ¼-mi-long nature walk follows the lakeshore. If you'd rather be in or on the water, laze on the quiet beach or play with the fleet of canoes, pedal boats, sailboats, kayaks, rowboats, and motorboats. You can also use the boat launch if you prefer to bring your own craft. On the lake you can go fishing, or just putter around admiring the scenery. Whatever you choose to do at the Wawbeek, you are bound at some point to find yourself swinging in a hammock strung between two birch trees, picnicking in a shady grove, sitting around a campfire, or staring into the night sky from an Adirondack chair. And you are likely to agree that the movers and shakers who first "camped" in the Adirondacks a century or more ago had the right idea.

Tip *The Adirondack Park Visitor Interpretive Center, about 20 mi north of the Wawbeek in the town of Paul Smiths, offers all kinds of free* *programs, from lectures on bear behavior and birds of prey to maple-sugaring outings and regularly scheduled interpretive trail walks.*

⇱ 20 rooms, 12 cabins ⦿ Full breakfast, restaurant, bar, picnic areas, some kitchens, some kitchenettes, some microwaves, some refrigerators. **Recreation**: bird-watching, fishing, hiking, horseback riding (nearby), mountain biking, beach, lake swimming, boating, canoeing, kayaking, rowing, sailing, golf privileges, 2 tennis courts, cross-country skiing, downhill skiing (nearby), sledding, snowshoeing, basketball, billiards, croquet, horseshoes, Ping-Pong, volleyball, board games. **Services**: boats, sleds, snowshoes, and mountain bikes provided; boat launch; dock. ⎙ In-room fireplaces, private balconies and decks, some pets allowed (fee); no a/c, no room phones, no room TVs ▦$125–$570 ▭ AE, MC, V.

⌂ *553 Hawkridge, Tupper Lake, NY 12986* ☎ *518/359–2656 or 800/ 953–2656* 🖶 *518/359–2475* ⊕ *www.wawbeek.com.*

North Carolina

EARTHSHINE MOUNTAIN LODGE
Family Hideout

Pisgah National Forest covers more than 500,000 acres in the mountains of western North Carolina. It is a woodland of conifers, maples, oaks, poplars, and fir trees, inhabited by bear, fox, deer, wild geese, and wild turkey. In this old, old forest, Indian paintbrush and trillium sprinkle the ground with color. Hikers make their way along trails past lakes and streams, rock climbers clamber up cliffs, and kids play on Sliding Rock, a natural waterslide.

On 88 acres at the edge of the national forest, overlooking the Blue Ridge Mountains, about 10 mi from Brevard, Earthshine Mountain Lodge is an outdoor education center that welcomes school groups most of the year but opens to families from Memorial Day to mid-August and on some weekends and holidays the rest of the year. The property includes a 10-room, 1½-story cedar-log lodge and a cottage with three separate suites. Dominated by wood beams and big picture windows, guest rooms are designed for families, with queen-size log beds, upstairs lofts with double beds and small balconies, quilts, and wood floors covered with throw rugs. All of your meals are provided, so you can immerse yourself completely in the lodge's activities. You can order a picnic lunch from the kitchen if your activities will keep you away from the lodge during the day.

One of the first things you should do when you arrive is sign up for your choice of activities on the board in the dining room. Programs, including discovery sessions in Cherokee Village, are offered at scheduled times in the mornings and afternoons. Hidden in the trees, Cherokee Village is the scene of corn-grinding and bead-making. At the lodge's re-created Pioneer Village, you and your children can watch demonstrations of blacksmithing, candle making, cider pressing, and wool spinning. Take a guided hike through thick rhododendron to King's Falls, or venture out on your own down another trail that crosses the property. Test your confidence and overcome fear on Flight Through the Treetops, the exhilarating zip-line course that takes you into the treetops and sends you flying above a pond. Trek down to the barnyard to help feed the goats, ducks, and sheep, or just find an empty hammock and swing.

Passionate and well trained, the staff—mostly graduates of nearby Brevard College's Wilderness Leadership and Experiential Education program—know how to make you feel safe during adrenaline-pumping activities, even as they encourage you to push your boundaries. They inject a lot of fun into the living history programs by playing Indian and pioneer characters with names like Aspen, Moe, Weasel, and Oaknot.

You are bound to burn a lot of energy at Earthshine, but you'll be well nourished by straightforward, home-style cooking at three square meals a day. Breakfast might be pancakes and sausage or scrambled egg burritos; lunch might include barbecued chicken or veggie burgers and potato salad; and for dinner you might have catfish or prime rib with baked potato. A salad bar and just-baked bread are plentiful with lunch and dinner, and peanut butter and jelly sandwiches are available around the clock—as are sodas, lemonade, tea, and coffee. From-scratch treats, such as brownie sundaes and banana split pie, are for dessert. Meals are served in the main lodge, where a fire burns in the dining room's stone fireplace. You can sit at one of the long wooden tables and benches overlooking the mountains, in the upstairs Vulture's Roost under a large antler chandelier, or outside on the terrace. No alcohol is served at the lodge, but if you want to bring your own spirits, the lodge has bar setups.

In the evening, horses, sheep, and goats grazing on the grassy hillside make a peaceful scene. But things don't wind down at night if you don't want them to: a typical evening might feature a magic show, campfire storytelling, or a sing-along with a mountain music band. Sneak away for a quiet game of checkers if you prefer; the slapping of the lodge's screen door or the chirping of crickets is the only sound you're likely to hear.

Tip *Each summer the Brevard Music Center, 15 mi away, hosts musicians from around the country during a seven-week festival. Daily rehearsals and performances are open to the public for free.*

🛏10 rooms, 3 suites ⏢American plan, dining room, picnic area, kitchenette. **Recreation:** bird-watching, fishing, hiking, horseback riding, wildlife viewing, sledding, horseshoes, recreation room. Nearby: mountain biking, rock climbing, rafting, river swimming, kayaking, 18-hole golf course. **Services:** fishing equipment, babysitting, shop. **Classes and programs:** guided hikes, guided nature walks, entertainment, sing-alongs. ♿ No room phones, no room TVs, no smoking 💲$170 💳D, MC, V.

🏠 *1600 Golden Road, Lake Toxaway, NC 28747* ☎ *828/862–4207* 🌐 *www.earthshinemtnlodge.com.*

THE LODGE ON LAKE LURE
Romantic Retreat

Built in the 1930s, this lakeside mountain lodge is the only inn on Lake Lure. With 27 mi of shoreline, 1,000-acre Lake Lure is stocked regularly with bass and is full of trout. Deer, bears, bobcats, bald eagles, gray herons, and ducks live along its shores. The community of Lake Lure, 45 minutes southeast of Asheville, is a sleepy burg where boathouses are decorated with colorful window boxes and potted plants. It's the kind of place people return to year after year. Tucked away from the summerhouses on 6 acres of grounds thick with rhododendron, poplar, hickory, and dogwood trees, the lodge has views of Bald Mountain and Shumont Mountain.

Guest rooms are spacious, with contemporary fabrics, lots of books, and notable antiques from one of the owner's collections, including a Chinese temple table (in the Cove Room) and several English pieces throughout. Most rooms have private balconies, and many of the bathrooms have claw-foot tubs with separate showers. Beds are made up with luxury linens, down pillows, and fluffy duvets. Finished in wormy chestnut wood paneling and hand-hewn ceiling beams, the cocoon-like Great Room is dominated by a stone fireplace on one end and an Asian copper screen on the other. Lush Oriental rugs, antiques, and down-filled furniture make this an inviting spot to sit down with one of the inn's photographic nature books. A fine place for sunbathing or for sipping wine in the evening, the large deck is flanked by trees. The dining room is open for dinner from Thursday through Saturday nights, by reservation only; typical dishes include salmon and beef tenderloin.

Breakfast is served in the dining room, which looks out over the lake. The lodge's boathouse offers canoes to guest. No Jet Skis are allowed on the lake, though ski boats are. If you don't feel like splashing around in the lake, take a scenic drive on the Blue Ridge Parkway, go horseback riding at a local stable, or do some tubing on the nearby river. A few miles from the lodge, 1,000-acre Chimney Rock Park has four hiking trails, from an easy 15-minute loop to a strenuous two-hour trek. In addition to the eponymous 500-million-year-old rock, the park has a 404-foot waterfall. Sightings of yellow-throated warblers, belted kingfishers, scarlet tanagers, peregrine falcons, and high-elevation birds such as darkeyed junco and common raven are possible.

Tip *For the best rates, avoid busy July, August, and October, and ask about package deals.*

🛏 17 rooms ⃝🅾⃝ Full breakfast, dining room, bar. **Recreation:** birdwatching, fishing, lake swimming, canoeing, piano. Nearby: waterskiing, boating, hiking, horseback riding, mountain biking, rock climbing, tubing (water), kayaking, 18-hole golf course, golf privileges, tennis courts, cross-country skiing, sleigh rides, playground. **Services:** canoes provided, dock, business services, Internet access, meeting rooms. ⚲ Cable TV with movies, in-room VCRs, some jetted tubs; no kids under 8, no smoking 🔲 $149–$245 ▭ AE, D, MC, V.

🖃 *Box 519, Lake Lure, NC 28746* ☎ *828/625–2789 or 800/733–2785* 🖷 *828/625–2421* ⊕ *www.lodgeonlakelure.com.*

FALLING WATERS RESORT
Laid-Back Adventure ~ Rustic Escape

Imagine sitting on your private deck while leaves drift down from sun-dappled oak, tulip poplar, and hemlock trees. The sound of a nearby waterfall lulls you. Perhaps you've spent the day hiking a trail in Great Smoky Mountains National Park, or rafting down white-water rapids, or driving along winding mountain roads to admire the changing foliage. It's late afternoon now, and you've returned to your yurt and all its modern comforts.

Inspired by the shelters used by the Mongols of central Asia, yurts are circular tents with conical roofs. At Falling Waters Resort, 75 mi from Asheville, the yurts are made of high-tech canvas wrapped around a Douglas-fir lattice frame. You might call a stay here "soft" camping: your yurt is outfitted with a hardwood floor, adjustable skylight, queen-size bed, futon, and electricity to run your ceiling fan, space heater, refrigerator, coffeemaker, and radio/CD player. It's appointed with colorful area rugs, a decorative bedstead, and even pictures on the wall. To reach your deck, just open the French doors. You are more than comfortable, yet you are not separated from nature: fresh, fir-scented air fills your room, and at night you can hear crickets singing all around you and bullfrogs announcing their reign over the nearby ponds. You'll want to bring a citronella candle or two for the evenings you sit out under the stars.

Falling Waters occupies 22 acres on a former homestead, where an old logging road leads to Fontana Lake, ½ mi from the yurts. The largest lake in the Southeast, Fontana is ringed by steep, forested slopes. On its shores live wild turkeys, deer, bears, and bald eagles, and in its waters you can fish for bass or bluegill. If you catch anything, bring it back to your yurt and cook it over the flames of a fire ring or grill. You're on your own for all of your meals, including breakfast, so bring bagels or cereal and snacks. Down a path are an outdoor hot tub, four full bathrooms, and a laundry room.

Stay near home and swim or canoe in Fontana Lake, or take advantage of Falling Waters' central location in an area of plentiful natural attractions. For rafting adventures down the Nantahala Gorge (with mellow rapids that are great for kids and senior citizens), walk across the road to the local outfitter. Fish for rainbow and brown trout in the Nantahala River (3 mi away), or go horseback riding through Nantahala National Forest. Joyce Kilmer Forest is filled with huge, prehistoric trees and mosses, and Cherohala Skyway scenic highway passes quiet picnic spots and interpretive exhibits.

Only 12 mi away lies 800-square-mi Great Smoky Mountain National Park. Thought to be the most biologically diverse area in the world, the park has 1,600 types of wildflowers, more than 100 species of trees and shrubs, and 120,000 acres of old-growth forest. The park service is working to restore the red wolf and the eastern river otter to the mountains. The Appalachian Trail runs along the crest of the Smokies; you can hike there or hike or ride horseback on 800 mi of other trails in the park. While you're out and about you might see cedar waxwings, turkeys, and hawks in fall and winter or American goldfinches and indigo buntings in summer. Year-round, northern cardinals, Carolina chickadees, and tufted titmouse flit through the trees.

Tip *The most private yurts are Numbers 7 and 8. They are also the farthest from the bathhouse, which you might find inconvenient. Yurt 8 has excellent views of Fontana Lake, and Numbers 1 and 6 sit on the edge of a pond.*

↪ 8 yurts ❢❍❢ Grills, picnic area, refrigerators. **Recreation:** birdwatching, fishing, hiking, running, wildlife viewing, boating, playground. Nearby: biking, horseback riding, pool, lake swimming, river swimming, swimming hole, tubing (water), canoeing, jet skiing, kayaking, rafting, sea kayaking, driving range, 18-hole golf course, tennis courts, basketball, miniature golf, in-line skating, soccer, softball, volleyball. **Services:** outdoor hot tub, laundry facilities, shop, meeting room. **Classes and programs:** white-water kayaking and rafting clinics (Class I–III rapids), and jeep tours. ♿ No a/c, no room phones, no smoking 🖃 $80 ⊟ D, MC, V.

✉ Box 190, Almond, NC 28702 ☎ 828/488–2384 or 800/451–9972 🖷 828/488–9130 ⊕ www.fallingwatersresort.com.

SNOWBIRD MOUNTAIN LODGE
Romantic Retreat

Putter around in your socks and warm your toes by a crackling fire in this stone-and-wood lodge built in 1941. On 100 acres overlooking Snowbird Mountain Range in western North Carolina, 88 mi from Asheville, Snowbird Mountain Lodge is a throwback to a sleepier, more casual time. Hand-crafted furniture, creaky screened doors, the scent of wood smoke, and that old-house smell transport you to another era. Overlooking Nantahala National Forest, the lodge has mountain views on one side and woodland views on the other. You can take it all in from a rocker on the front porch or an Adirondack chair on the lawn. Hundreds of poplar, red maple, oak, and chestnut trees surround the lodge, and in winter the backdrop of bare tree branches makes the leather couches, hand-cut chestnut beams, butternut paneling, and book-filled shelves all the more attractive.

Reflected in tall, grand windows, a fire burns in the dining room's stone fireplace, softly lighting its wild cherry paneling and crisp white linens. Four-course dinners here are memorable: almond-crusted trout, coq au vin with gnocchi and root vegetables, corn bread pudding, chocolate crème brûlée. You'll have to bring your own wine, though, because this is a dry county. Breakfast is quite a spread, with a buffet of oatmeal, yogurt, fruit salad, breads, and muffins, as well as a hot entrée—perhaps buckwheat pancakes with walnut butter or scrambled eggs with ham and mushrooms. Picnic lunches, with fancy sandwiches and homemade cookies, make daily outings easy.

The guest rooms in the two-story main lodge are paneled in different hardwoods and include many of the original beds, chests, and luggage racks created by local craftsmen, as well as quilts. A few yards away, the Wolfe Cottage has two guest rooms, each with fireplace, whirlpool tub, and mountain views. On the other side of the main lodge, in a more secluded area, the Chestnut Lodge houses guest rooms with fireplaces, wet bars, steam showers, whirlpool tubs, and mountain views. Simply framed photos of leaves, waterfalls, and other nature scenes decorate the entire lodge.

Lots of little outdoor nooks entice you to sneak away with a book or cup of tea. Along one of the trails on the grounds, the sunrise deck looks down over 14,000-acre Santeetlah Lake. You can swim or canoe in the lake (3 mi away), or choose a destination from the lodge's file of hiking, biking, and driving suggestions. The mountain bikes that the lodge provides are great for exploring more than 50 mi of gated, low-traffic Forest Service roads, some of which begin ¼ mi away. Drive a few minutes to Joyce Kilmer Memorial Forest, where the Cherohala Skyway scenic highway starts. The road winds through Cherokee and Nantahala national forests and past numerous lookout points.

Tip *The lodge offers special programs such as wine dinners, winter holiday cooking classes, and a week in fall when professional storytellers continue the Appalachian tradition of handing down lore.*

23 rooms ⁨🍽️⁩ American plan, dining room, some minibars. **Recreation:** biking, bird-watching, hiking, mountain biking, running, wildlife viewing, lake swimming, badminton, tennis courts, horseshoes, library. Nearby: fishing, horseback riding, tubing (water), waterskiing, boating, canoeing, rowing, 18-hole golf course. **Services:** bikes, canoes, and fly-fishing equipment provided; massage; guided fishing trips; shop; busi-

ness services; Internet access. **Classes and programs:** guided hikes, natural history programs, cooking classes, storytelling. ⚓ Some in-room hot tubs; no a/c in some rooms, no room phones, no room TVs, no kids under 12, no smoking ▨ $210–$350 ▭ MC, V.

📖 *4633 Santeetlah Rd., Robbinsville, NC 28771* 📠 *828/479–3433 or 800/941–9290* 📠 *828/479–3473* 🌐 *www.snowbirdlodge.com.*

THE SWAG
Tranquil Outpost

The Swag serves up nature on ice with a twist. A swanky, swishy getaway, this 250-acre property sits atop a 5,000-foot ridge that runs along one side of Great Smoky Mountain National Park, 13 mi north of Waynesville and 50 mi west of Asheville. Once you arrive, after slowly wending your way up the 2½-mi-long driveway that climbs 1,110 feet, you can survey the view from the inn's porch. The term "swag" refers to a dip between two mountain peaks; the dip that gives the inn its name creates dimensional views of the Great Smoky Mountains, the Blue Ridge Parkway, and Cold Mountain.

The inn's six hand-hewn log buildings were reassembled from Appalachian structures. The main living room, formerly a Tennessee Baptist church, has cathedral ceilings (of course). A huge white-tailed and mule-deer antler chandelier, stone fireplace, and bearskin wall hanging set the scene around the small tables where breakfast is served. Breakfast is a casual buffet of hot tea (served in your own individual pot) and spice muffins, with cider-simmered oatmeal or a western omelet.

Usually packed to go in a backpack or basket, depending on your request, lunch is beyond ordinary: fresh salads come from the inn's organic garden, and other treats might include tomato pie and rich chocolate–peanut butter bars. Service at dinner is more formal, though attire remains casual. Hors d'oeuvres on the porch are followed by four courses, accompanied if you like by BYOB wine (this is a dry county). Place cards indicate where you and your chatty dinner companions will sit around the two large tables; upon request honeymooners or anniversary couples may be seated at private tables for two. A mix of young and old, the people who frequent the Swag are an active group: svelte 80-year-olds are sure to pass you on the trails.

Such care has been taken with the guest rooms that you may find it difficult to leave yours. Even the smallest of them are lovely, with ceiling beams or hewn log walls, easy chairs, and original artwork. Most rooms have views and wood-burning fireplaces; many also have balconies or private porches, towel warmers, a sauna, hand-crafted cabinetry, and wrought-iron accents. Common to all are steam showers, refrigerators stocked with trail mix and juices, coffeemakers with whole coffee beans and a grinder, and CD players/digital audio receivers with more than 100 channels. Step outside, and you'll find hammocks and swings scattered around the property, as well as a spring-fed pond.

In the morning, when you open your curtains to see a brilliant silver mist hovering above the mountains, you'll likely be eager to grab your freshly carved walking stick (compliments of the inn) and get going. The inn's guest naturalists lead trail excursions throughout the year. A mile on glorious Hemphill Bald Trail takes you through woodlands and open pasture, up to awesome views of Cataloochee Divide and Maggie Valley. There, a stone table makes the perfect picnic spot. You can hike onward to a waterfall trail or a less strenuous, 3-mi nature trail with markers; or simply go through the gate that opens onto Great Smoky National Park's extensive trail system. If you prefer to go fishing, you might try the Cherokee Indian Reservation. A guide from a local outfitter can show you some of the prettier and less-known spots.

Tip *Ask about the weeklong furniture-making workshop, where the craftsman who built Central Park's rustic bridges and gazebos demonstrates how to make landscape furniture of branches and twigs.*

🛏 10 rooms, 3 cabins ⏀ American plan, dining room, picnic area, refrigerators. **Recreation:** bird-watching, hiking, running, swimming hole, golf privileges, badminton, billiards, croquet, horseshoes, racquetball, library, piano, recreation room. Nearby: biking, fishing, horseback riding, mountain biking, rock climbing, wildlife viewing, tubing (water), canoeing, kayaking, rafting, 18-hole golf course. **Services:** massage, sauna, guided fishing trips, helipad, laundry service, shop, business services, concierge, Internet access, meeting rooms. **Classes and programs:** guided hikes, guided nature walks, arts and crafts classes, cooking classes, birding and wildflower talks, entertainment, singalongs. ♿ In-room safes, some jetted tubs; no a/c, no smoking 💳 $330–$700 ⊟ AE, D, MC, V.

🗐 *2300 Swag Rd., Waynesville, NC 28785* ☎ *828/926–0430 or 800/789–7672* 🖷 *828/926–2036* ⊕ *www.theswag.com* ☉ *Closed Dec.–mid-Apr.*

North Dakota

EAGLE RIDGE LODGE
Romantic Retreat

Being casual and relaxed is the western way. Nowhere is this more apparent than at Eagle Ridge, where hosts Joann and Paul Douglas won't let you in the front door unless you can prove you have at least one pair of jeans in your bag. Perched on a bluff on the edge of North Dakota's badlands in the far western part of the state, 7 mi from Medora, this modern lodge is in one of the least populous areas in the nation. Out here in the Western Dakotas, sometimes called America's Outback, some places are measured in square miles per person rather than people per square mile. This is ranch country, where livestock can outnumber inhabitants—sometimes by a hundred to one or more.

Homemade furnishings, country details, and nature-inspired names like Bear Paw and Gumbo Lily give the seven guest suites an unpretentious, woodsy charm. The rooms are spacious and uncluttered, accented by a few pieces of furniture made from logs and rough-hewn wood, lightly sanded and varnished. The furniture is handmade by Paul; the thick quilts covering the log-frame beds are sewn by Joann. Each room has its own fireplace, and four of the suites have claw-foot bathtubs.

The views from the guest rooms, and from anywhere else in the lodge, are incredible—sandy badlands buttes and rolling prairie, unscarred even by fence posts, extending into the distance. The Great Room, where most of the lodge's talks and educational programs take place, has a giant two-story window overlooking juniper-clad hills and horse and cattle range. Its finished hardwood furniture is somewhat more refined than that in the bedrooms, lending the room a casual country elegance that contrasts with the hewn-log staircase and the antique wagon wheel above the stone fireplace. The programs that take place in the Great Room cover topics related to the surrounding wilderness. An employee of nearby Theodore Roosevelt National Park might give a talk on recent fossil finds in the badlands, or an astronomer from one of the colleges in Bismarck might give a lecture. Joann, who is known in the area for her quilting, teaches regular (and well-attended) classes at the lodge.

Little Missouri National Grasslands covers 1 million acres of public and private land surrounding the lodge. The Maah Daah Hey Trail, a 100-mi developed path that traverses the grasslands and Theodore Roosevelt National Park, is also nearby: the southern trailhead is about 6 mi northeast of the lodge. Hikers, horseback riders, and mountain bikers can see wildlife such as coyotes, golden eagles, red-tailed hawks, and bison along this trail, which passes through both prairie and rocky badlands. The terrain is for the most part relatively smooth and flat, though inclement weather can wreak havoc on trail conditions any time of year.

Joann tries to vary the lodge's breakfast menu daily and usually takes requests if you're staying more than one night. Standard fare consists of western favorites: ham, sausage, scrambled eggs, dark coffee, and fruit juice. Some of Joann's more creative dishes include casseroles. You also receive a complimentary steak dinner with your stay, though you can choose shrimp, pork chops, or chicken. Be sure to try the ribs if your visit falls during barbecue season.

Tip *Trail rides are available from outside outfitters who offer daylong excursions. If you want to camp out overnight, the outfitters will provide all of your gear and will cook authentic cowboy cuisine for each meal.*

⮧ 7 suites ᴼ Modified American plan, restaurant, lobby lounge. **Recreation:** bird-watching, hiking, mountain biking, wildlife viewing. **Services:** horse boarding. **Classes and programs:** natural history programs; arts and crafts classes; astronomy, archaeology, history, and environmental talks. ♿ No room phones, no room TVs, no kids under 13, no smoking ⌨ $165–$200 ▭ MC, V.

✉ *P.O. Box 331, Medora, ND 58654* ☎ *701/623–2216 or 866/863–2453* ⊕ *www.eagleridgelodge.com.*

MISSOURI RIVER LODGE
Tranquil Outpost

Right on the Missouri River, 70 mi from Bismarck, this bed-and-breakfast is part of a 2,000-acre working cattle ranch between Bismarck and Lake Sakakawea. The several miles of land bordering the river on the ranch's property include part of the Lewis and Clark Trail, so you can see the landscape and wildlife that the famous explorers saw—a river island, rocky bluffs rising from the water's edge, bald eagles nesting in cottonwoods, magpies scavenging along the river. Interpretive signs along the trail display expedition journal excerpts that document their observations.

You can hike, bike, or ride a horse on any part of this trail. Horseback riding is especially popular. Many of the trail's sights are right on the ranch's property, so there is plenty to see within a two-hour round-trip walk. In the area, members of the Lewis and Clark expedition found numerous bird species, many of which had never been scientifically observed or reported before. Today you can see the same creatures seen by the Corps of Discovery, including northern flickers, western kingbirds, and western meadowlarks. There are also many raptors, such as the red-tailed hawk, golden eagle, and American kestrel. The best time of year for birding is probably May, when migratory species begin to move back into the area—they leave again in September. There are, however, many birds that live here through the winter, when naked trees and white ground make spotting them easier. In warm weather, head down to the private sand beach on the riverbank. You can bring your own watercraft, or you can rent canoes, kayaks, pedal boats, and motorized boats from the nearby dock.

Constructed of native stone and wood, the lodge fits in well with its surroundings. The interior, on the other hand, is more sophisticated. Native stone graces the fireplaces, but the style of the furnishings is refined. Elegant hardwood armchairs are arranged neatly around the grand fireplace in the sitting room; wrought-iron and glass tables distinguish the dining room, which is candlelit for dinner. Guest rooms are decorated with wallpaper to match the spreads on the brass or iron beds. Three of the seven rooms are suites with at least two full-size beds; the single rooms are smaller and have one full-size bed. The suites have private entrances and exclusive access to the lodge's large porch and sitting room.

Tip *Around here, April is known for blizzards, and May is damp and cool. The only truly warm months are June, July, and August. Temperatures drop again in early September, when the leaves start to fall and snow is likely to appear.*

🛏 4 rooms, 3 suites ⏐◎⏐ Continental breakfast, dining room, lobby lounge. **Recreation:** bird-watching, fishing, hiking, mountain biking, wildlife viewing, beach, river swimming, boating, canoeing, kayaking, rowing, cross-country skiing. **Services:** boat and mountain-bike rentals, Internet access, business services. ⌂ Satellite TV, some pets allowed; no smoking ▱ $60–$85 ▭ AE, D, MC, V.

🏠 *140 42nd Ave. NW, Stanton, ND 58571* ☎ *701/748–2023 or 877/ 480–3498* ⊕ *www.moriverlodge.com.*

221 MELSTED PLACE
Romantic Retreat

Many residents of northeastern North Dakota bear the names—and, in some cases, the accents—of their Scandinavian ancestors, who settled the prairie around here in the 19th and early 20th centuries. The town of Mountain (population 133), less than 30 mi from Canada and Minnesota and 1¾ hours from Grand Forks, was founded by Icelandic immigrants, some of whom built grand Victorian homes. Among the grandest of these, 221 Melsted Place is now a bed-and-breakfast.

Melsted Place was built in 1910 in the middle of farmland, 2 mi from the tiny community of Mountain. Wheat fields, woodlands, and prairie surround the home. Much of the wetlands and forests that once blanketed the northeastern corner of the state were cleared away by pioneer farmers, though you can see oak woodlands and marshes at the edges of some farms. A piece of this "wild" land is preserved at Icelandic State Park, about 15 mi northeast of Melsted Place.

The inn has antique Victorian furnishings throughout. A grand staircase with heavy rails and banisters leads upstairs to the four guest rooms. Each of the rooms has unusual decorative touches. The Ancestral Garden Suite, for instance, has floral curtains and bedding, and the Melsted Master Suite has two large bay windows and a smaller stained-glass window, all facing east to admit the early-morning sunlight. The Matriarchal Suite is the grandest bedroom; its hallmark is a king-size bed with elaborate gold-leaf headboard. The innkeepers are proud to tell you that then-President of Iceland Olafur Grimsson stayed in this room when he visited the area in 1999.

A full breakfast with meats, fruits, and eggs is served in the ornate dining room every morning. You can make advance arrangements for other meals, as well. A large hardwood table, draped lightly with a lace tablecloth, is the focal point of the room. Plenty of light streams though the windows for breakfast; dinners are lighted by a crystal chandelier and taper candles on the center of the table.

Tip *Melsted offers some evening activities. Try your hand at torch-lit croquet, or find out if there will be a bonfire later in the night. The outdoor hot tub in the back garden is available year-round.*

🛏 4 rooms � Full breakfast, dining room, lobby lounge. **Recreation:** biking, bird-watching, running, wildlife viewing, downhill skiing (nearby), croquet. **Services:** outdoor hot tub, massage. **Classes and programs:** sightseeing tours. ♿ No room phones, no room TVs, no kids, no smoking 💲 $80–$120 💳 AE, D, MC, V.

✉ *Box 221, Mountain, ND 58262* ☎ *701/993–8257* 🌐 *www.melstedplace. com.*

Ohio

THE INN AT CEDAR FALLS
Tranquil Outpost

The route to the Inn at Cedar Falls, 1¼ hours from Columbus, is a circuitous one. You'll drive roads that twist and turn through the Hocking Hills, negotiating switchbacks that hug rocky outcroppings and descend into sandstone gorges. You won't go any faster than 45 mph, considerably less in the winter. Arriving in the Hocking Hills will slow you down, and that is precisely the reason to visit.

A modern, barn-shape structure sided with weathered, salvaged wood, the inn looks right at home in the hardwood forest. On the porch, you can settle into a rocking chair under a quilt and look out upon the Hocking Hills. Deer and other wildlife often wander past the inn and its cottages. Birds nest in the branches overhead and peck at the seeds in the feeder hanging from the eaves. At dusk, get comfortable on the veranda and watch the sunset, or head for an Adirondack chair under the shade tree.

You can stay in the inn itself, which is decorated with locally crafted tin-punch lanterns, Shaker-style furniture, wood-burning stoves, and easy chairs. Or you can reserve one of the cabins or cottages on the grounds. The six cabins, constructed in the 1800s of 18-inch logs, now contain 21st-century creature comforts such as a full kitchen, spacious bath, and lots of living space. The modern cottages are smaller and include kitchenettes. Each cottage occupies its own 2-acre plot of land and comes furnished with a Jacuzzi, a wood-burning stove, and a bookshelf crammed with books, and board games.

Three 1840s log houses were joined and modernized to create the inn's restaurant. In warmer weather dine outside on the patio and watch hummingbirds in the daytime or starlit skies in the evening. Inside, a large wood-burning stove will warm you on cool days while you watch chef Erik Keller and his crew creating the day's meals in the open kitchen. Whenever it's in season he uses locally grown produce; many ingredients come straight from the vegetable and herb garden outside.

You'll find little reason to refuse a decadent dessert after a day of exploring the region. Surrounded by nearly 2,500 acres of the Hocking Hills State Parks, you might spend your time seeking out the myriad waterfalls and hidden caves that punctuate the local gorges, or you might go canoeing and fishing on the Hocking River. Winter is a magical time to visit the region. By mid-January frigid temperatures freeze the hills' trickling waterfalls in place, forming solid, icy cascades in some areas and giant ice stalactites and stalagmites in others. After a walk in the brisk winter air, there's nothing more enjoyable than heading back to your cabin, taking a soak in the Jacuzzi, and enjoying a glass of wine before dinner.

Tip *Although the inn welcomes children, inn rooms and cottages sleep only two. If you plan to bring your family, reserve a log cabin, with accommodations for four.*

9 rooms, 6 cabins, 12 cottages ⦿ Full breakfast, restaurant, some kitchens, some kitchenettes, some refrigerators. **Recreation:** hiking. Nearby: fishing, horseback riding, rock climbing, lake swimming, canoeing, kayaking. **Services:** massage, shop. **Classes and programs:** guided hikes and nature walks; mushroom hunting; cooking, wine tasting, and holiday wreath-making classes. Some jetted tubs; no room phones, no room TVs, no smoking $89–$259 AE, MC, V.

21190 St. Rte. 374, Logan, OH 43138 740/385-7489 or 800/653-2557 740/385-0820 *www.innatcedarfalls.com.*

MAUMEE BAY RESORT
Family Hideout

Along the Lake Erie shoreline, dune grass can grow up to 6 feet high and a stiff northern lake breeze keeps the air fresh and cool on even the hottest summer days. Colonies of 12-foot-tall plume canes sway as their feathery heads whisper in the breeze, and butterflies dance around the fragrant white flowers of buttonbushes. An abundance of deep purple wild irises blooms in the spring, the best time to spy songbirds and waterfowl that rest here before completing their spring migration north to Canada. All this happens within the borders of Maumee Bay State Park, a place of beaches, marshland, wet woods, meadows, and, of course, the lake.

Immerse yourself in this world by staying in the park, at Maumee Bay Resort, which has cabins and a lodge. Quilter Lodge stands a few hundred feet from Lake Erie's shore. Throughout its common areas, rockers and lounge chairs cluster before the three-story windows that look out over unbroken views of lake and sky. In the Water's Edge Restaurant, there's scarcely a reason to ask for a window table—nearly every seat in the house has gorgeous views of the lake. Crystal glassware and navy linens evoke the sparkling blue water outside, and the menu includes steak, chicken, and seafood.

Most of the guest rooms at the lodge have magnificent water views; those that don't look over the golf course and 1,300 acres of state parkland. All rooms have a patio or balcony from which you can enjoy magnificent sunsets. A quarter mile away, the resort's cabins are well spaced, surrounded by dune grass and woods, and exceptionally quiet. Cabins vary in size, with some sleeping as many as 11. All are equipped with a full kitchen, a grill, a picnic table, and an outdoor hot tub. Around the cabins in late spring you're likely to see scores of Canada geese, with mothers leading their broods of fuzzy goslings and hissing at those who get too close.

The resort has recreational activities galore, from organized craft sessions for the kids to basketball, racquetball, swimming, and jet skiing. But the park's true appeal lies farther afield. A 2-mi boardwalk on its eastern end meanders through marshland alive with birds. Bordered on the east by Mallard Club Marsh Wildlife Area and Cedar Point and Ottawa National Wildlife Refuges, Maumee Bay is permanently buffered from lakefront development. In spring, all of this land attracts one of the nation's largest populations of migratory songbirds. For even greater birding, drive east about 10 mi to Magee Marsh Wildlife Area on Route 2. If you're just looking for some exercise, head to the western end of Maumee Bay State Park, where there are 8 mi of hiking and biking trails. Walk or bike along the Lake Erie shoreline, and then head inland on trails that wend their way through wildflower meadows and woods and past several small lakes and ponds. In winter the largest pond becomes an ice-skating rink.

Tip *If you stay in the lodge, ask for an upper-level room for the most spectacular scenery. Take a lower-level poolside room if you're traveling with kids.*

120 rooms, 24 cottages Restaurant, snack bar, room service, lounge, some kitchens, some kitchenettes, some microwaves, refrigerators. **Recreation:** biking, bird-watching, fishing, hiking, running, wildlife viewing, beach, pool, indoor pool, lake swimming, boating, canoeing, jet skiing, kayaking, rowing, sailing, 18-hole golf course, tennis court, cross-country skiing, basketball, in-line skating, racquetball, volleyball, Ping-Pong, video-game room, playground. **Services:** basketballs, volleyballs, and tennis and racquetball rackets provided; bicycle, boat, canoe, Jet Ski, and kayak rentals; gym; hot tub (lodge); sauna; dock; marina; pro shop; laundry facilities; shops; business services; meeting rooms. **Classes and programs:** children's programs (ages 5–12), movies. Cable TV with movies, in-room safes, no-smoking rooms $111–$305 AE, D, DC, MC, V.

⌂ *1750 Park Rd., No. 2, Oregon, OH 43618* ☎ *419/836–1466 or 800/ 282–7275* 🖷 *419/836–2438* ⊕ *www.maumeebayresort.com.*

MURPHIN RIDGE INN
Romantic Retreat ~ Tranquil Outpost

On 140 hilltop acres in Ohio's Appalachian foothills, surrounded by Amish homesteads and farms about an hour from Cincinnati, Murphin Ridge Inn is a revelation for those who've forgotten what quiet sounds like, or how dark a nighttime sky can be, or what fun it is to catch fireflies, or what to do with yourself when there's nothing that really needs doing. Innkeepers Sherry and Darryl McKenney love to see how their guests slowly unwind in this peaceful place an hour from Cincinnati. You can start by parking yourself on the front porch to take in views of the mountains and wildlife. At dusk, white-tailed deer graze in the wheat field and rabbits do their best to steal goodies from the kitchen garden.

The modern, barnlike guesthouse is decorated simply but comfortably. Unique Shaker-influenced furniture designed and handcrafted by local designer David T. Smith furnishes each room. The Shaker theme extends to the cabins, each of which also has a two-sided gas fireplace, a two-person whirlpool tub, and a two-person shower. Each cabin's front porch is outfitted with rocking chairs or a porch swing. Whether you stay in the guesthouse or a cabin, fluffy bathrobes, upholstered recliners, and fabulous views of the Appalachians may tempt you to remain in your room during your entire stay.

Refresh yourself with a walk along one of the footpaths that criss-cross the Murphin Ridge property. Darryl is happy to show you his favorite haunts if you like, or you can invite the resident pooch, Red Dog, to accompany you. (Gray Cat would rather just sleep.) Explore the wildflower fields and hardwoods that cover the hills, and look for the headstones of a 19th-century cemetery that's been swallowed up by forest. Take out the croquet set and set your course for the yard's towering maples and oaks, or play a lazy game of shuffleboard. If you venture off the grounds, do a little shopping from Amish farmers and furniture makers. Keep in mind that, although children are welcome at Murphin Ridge, you and your younger kids will feel most comfortable if you come in summer, when there are plenty of ways to burn off energy. In cooler months, when activity shifts indoors, youngsters will find little to do here and will soon be bored by the decidedly quiet and adult atmosphere.

When mealtime comes around, treat yourself to dinner at the inn's restaurant. The homey dining room is housed in an 1808 log cabin joined to an 1820s brick house. In the kitchen, the chef bakes his own bread daily and incorporates produce from the kitchen garden—lettuce in spring and early summer, tomatoes in late summer, beets in autumn—into the meals. All of the herbs come from the inn's garden, too. The menu's remaining produce is purchased from Amish farmers in season. Continental dishes are served with local flair—Amish sweet corn–crusted chicken breast; Will's harvest pizelle with garden vegetables. The hearty breakfasts typically include locally grown fruit in season, cinnamon French toast, Foggy bottom pancakes, and breakfast sausage.

🛏 10 rooms, 9 cabins ⭕ Full breakfast, restaurant, some refrigerators. **Recreation:** Biking (nearby), bird-watching, hiking, wildlife viewing, pool, tennis court, croquet, shuffleboard, recreation room. ♿ Wireless internet, some jetted tubs; no room TVs, no smoking 💲 $104–$225 ▭ MC, V, D, AE.

🏠 750 Murphin Ridge Rd., West Union, OH 45693 ☎ 937/544–2263 or 877/687–7446 📠 937/544–8151 ⊕ www.murphinridgeinn.com.

Oklahoma

CANDLEWYCK COVE RESORT
Tranquil Outpost

Drive past a country store and through a gate in a wooden fence. Follow a narrow, winding road through tall trees and past a gazebo. This is how you get to Candlewyck, a gated 7-acre resort on the shore of Grand Lake O' the Cherokees in northeastern Oklahoma. The cottages, spread out in a semicircle along the banks of quiet Paris Cove, were built in 1996 with horizontal lines reminiscent of Frank Lloyd Wright's prairie-style homes.

The resort, in the foothills of the Ozark Mountains, is so quiet that you are likely to see deer and their young grazing on the grounds in the afternoon. Landscaped lawns slope down to 450 feet of private shoreline. From the patio of the main house, water trickles down a waterfall into Honey Creek. At night, lights twinkle in the trees. When you arrive, you'll receive a basket of fruit. Your room will be in a four-plex cottage, unless you rent the honeymoon cottage, a two-bedroom cottage with a kitchen, or the three-bedroom house that sleeps up to 12. Each unit is light and airy, the four-plexes decorated with white woodwork and pine furnishings and the honeymoon cottage with a four-poster bed. All accommodations have a fireplace and a private balcony or deck. There are two grills on the grounds where you can cook the catch of the day, and you can buy locally grown vegetables at produce stands in Grove five minutes away and from farmers who often sell sweet corn and other produce from the backs of their pickups.

In the morning, you can walk down to the gazebo to sip your coffee and watch the deer amble by. If you're feeling energetic, you can amuse yourself on the lake. Paris Cove offers excellent fishing for crappie, bass, catfish, and channel cat; cast from the dock, or hire a fishing guide at a nearby marina. You can also rent a boat from a marina and moor it at one of the dock's three slips. It's fun to explore the lake's serpentine 1,300-mi shoreline and its islands and coves by boat, foot, or car. Around the lake, you can reach many restaurants by boat as well as by car. Away from the lake on the outskirts of Grove is Lendonwood Gardens. The botanical garden has more than 1,500 types of plants, a Japanese teahouse, a koi pond, and an enclosed Zen garden with 80 exquisitely formed bonsai. Grass pathways wind among towering oaks, 500 varieties of daylilies, waterfalls, roses, and flowering trees.

Tip *Step aboard one of two* Cherokee Queen *paddle wheelers for a leisurely tour of Grand Lake O' the Cherokees from Sailboat Bridge. Daytime and moonlight excursions (some with meals) run March 15–October 31. Call 918/786–4272 for times and prices.*

🛏 8 rooms, 4 suites, 5 cottages, 1 house �’❘❘ Some kitchens, grills, microwaves, refrigerators. **Recreation:** bird-watching, fishing, wildlife viewing, lake swimming, pool, hot tub, boating, waterskiing, sailing, 18-hole golf course (nearby). **Services:** pontoon rental. ⛲ In-room fireplaces, some in-room VCRs, some jetted tubs, private balconies and patios; no room phones, no smoking 💳 $99–$500 ▭ AE, D, MC, V.

🗺 *59800 E. 307 La., Grove, OK 74344* ☎ *918/786–3636* ⊕ *www. candlewyckcove.com.*

INN AT JARRETT FARM
Romantic Retreat

In the heart of the Osage Indian Reservation in northeastern Oklahoma lies the 3,600-acre Woolaroc Ranch, Museum & Wildlife Preserve, where Native American art and history are presented side by side in a stunning natural setting. This was once the country estate of Frank Phillips, founder of Phillips Petroleum, who made up the name by combining the words "woods, lake, and rocks." When you arrive at Woolaroc you receive a map and guide to help you identify the animals you'll see in the ponds and meadows. And you will see animals: the preserve is home to 750 critters, including water buffalo, African pygmy goats, bison, emus, llamas, peacocks, ostriches, longhorn cattle, and four-horned sheep. You can explore Woolaroc on foot, along miles of trails, and climb an observation tower to see the land from on high. Then have lunch (on weekends April–October) in the glassed-in dining room, which overlooks streams, flowers, trees, and a lake beyond.

A 30-mi drive from Woolaroc, the 120-acre Inn at Jarrett Farm is closest to this wondrous slice of nature. Built in 1984 as a residence, the hilltop property became an inn in the late 1990s. The main house, five modern duplex cottages, and single stand-alone cottage are just off the highway, but you'll feel miles away. In summer the soft-yellow buildings with their cool, pale-blue-and-white interiors are a soothing refuge from the sun. In winter twinkling lights outside and holiday decorations inside give the inn a welcoming glow. The cottage suites, and the huge suite in the main house, are spacious, pastel-painted, and luxuriously furnished with soft couches and chairs, a fireplace, and large windows. Artwork hangs on the walls beneath vaulted ceilings. Chocolates, a mini-refrigerator stocked with bottled water, a coffeemaker, bathrobes, and a CD player will help you feel at home.

Your day starts with a two-course breakfast. Warm fruit (in winter) or a fresh fruit smoothie, occasionally made from blackberries picked on the property, wakes up your palate. Then comes the main course, which may be the inn's signature soufflé-like breakfast casserole of meat, cheese, and eggs. You'll eat overlooking manicured lawns, a white picket fence, the pool and hot tub, and the thick trees that encircle the inn. Such attention is paid to detail that if you are seated in one room for breakfast, you will be welcomed to another room for dinner. On the evening menu are finely wrought dishes such as tenderloin of beef fillet. Desserts such as apple dumpling topped with pecan-praline sauce and ice cream completes the menu. A fire blazes on the hearth in winter, and live piano music accompanies dinner on special occasions.

The first-class hospitality extends outdoors—even the hiking trails are meticulously groomed. The grounds also include a stocked fishing pond. Take a swim in the pool or just relax in one of the high-backed rockers on the porch, and watch the sun set over the Osage Hills.

Tips *Ask to sit in the solarium for breakfast. The wicker chairs and views through the French doors will help get your day off to a pleasant start. And be sure to make reservations for dinner.*

🛏 12 suites 🍽 Full breakfast, restaurant, refrigerators. **Recreation:** bird-watching, fishing, hiking, wildlife viewing, pool, library. **Services:** massage, outdoor hot tub, meeting rooms. ♿ In-room fireplaces, in-room VCRs, jetted tubs, no smoking rooms; no room phones 💳 $185–$295 ▭ AE, D, MC, V.

🏠 *38009 U.S. 75 N, Ramona, OK 74061* ☎ *918/371–1200* 🖷 *918/ 371–1300* ⊕ *www.jarrettfarm.com.*

QUARTZ MOUNTAIN RESORT ARTS AND CONFERENCE CENTER
Family Hideout

One of the country's oldest mountain ranges, the Wichita Mountains of southwestern Oklahoma were formed millions of years ago, after an explosion inside the Earth pushed granite thousands of feet upward. The sharp peaks were worn down over the millennia, and eventually the rounded mountains provided water and winter shelter to bands of Kiowa, Comanche, and Cheyenne-Arapaho Indians. Today, a piece of the mountains is protected by a 4,500-acre state park with a lodge.

Cradled by soft mountains on three sides and Lake Altus on the other, Quartz Mountain Lodge was built on a circular plan that echoes the council ring of the Plains Indians. The lodge entrance is oriented according to Kiowa principles, and reds, blues, and yellows of ceremonial significance to the tribe are used throughout. In the lobby, high cathedral windows illuminate a bronze sculpture titled *As Long as the Waters Flow,* and Mission-style furniture is grouped before a heavy stone fireplace. Each guest room has a lake or river view and is decorated in a western, Native American, or southwestern theme. An easy chair and ottoman are next to the French doors that lead to your balcony or patio. Leave the French doors ajar at night and you'll be lulled to sleep by cicadas and the soft lap of waves against the shore. The lodge also maintains nine cabins and a 64-person bunkhouse. In the Sundance Café you can start the day with biscuits and gravy and end it with cedar plank salmon, in front of a fireplace or on a deck overlooking the lake.

Children's activities make the lodge a great retreat for families, though you're just as likely to see couples taking a morning walk around the lake or heading toward the hiking paths armed with binoculars. A good place to start your exploration is the Quartz Mountain Visitor/Nature Center, where exhibits focus on the animals, plant life, and geologic history of the area. Guided nature programs, including stargazing and hiking, are offered daily during summer and on weekends off-season. Year-round, you can fish for bass, crappie, walleye, and trout. On Baldy Point, experienced rock climbers can try more than 50 routes. And there are many hiking trails through the park: Sunrise Trail climbs Quartz Mountain, Twin Peaks Path is ideal for bird-watching, and the Wichita Interpretive Trail is set up with brochures that discuss the plants and animals you might see. Starting in May, 80 species of wildflowers begin to bloom; you can see blossoms until October. White-tailed deer, wild turkeys, coyotes, bobcats, and birds from blue jays to bald eagles inhabit the park.

Two beaches and an indoor pool give you plenty of opportunity to swim, and the lodge's courtyard has space for lawn games. Spend some time in the arts-and-crafts center—you might be inspired by the original art on display throughout the lodge and in the art gallery. The artwork is here because the park is the home of the Oklahoma Arts Institute, which sponsors occasional workshops, concerts, and performances. A conference and performing arts center sits unobtrusively across a ¼-mi bridge.

Tips *Quartz Mountain State Park is one of the region's best spots to sight migrating bald eagles, especially in January and February. The park organizes sighting programs each winter. For details, call 580/563–2238.*

118 rooms, 2 suites, 11 cabins, 64-person bunkhouse ❙❙ Restaurant, lounge, some refrigerators. **Recreation:** bird-watching, fishing, hiking, rock climbing, wildlife viewing, lake swimming, boating, canoeing,

18-hole golf course, boccie, croquet, horseshoes, miniature golf, volleyball, library. **Services:** hot tub, meeting rooms. **Classes and programs:** guided hikes and nature walks, natural history programs, children's programs (ages 4–12). ☼ Satellite TV, wireless Internet, some in-room fireplaces, private balconies and patios; no smoking. 💳 $69–$169 ▭ AE, D, DC, MC, V.

🏠 *22469 Lodge Road, Lone Wolf, OK 73655* ☎ *580/563–2424 or 877/999–5567* 📠 *580/563–2422* ⊕ *www.quartzmountainresort.com.*

SHILOH MORNING INN
Romantic Retreat

On 73 acres northeast of Ardmore in south-central Oklahoma, Shiloh Morning Inn is surrounded by the year-round green of cedar trees. The gate at the entrance symbolically holds the outside world at bay. Birdhouses are placed throughout the property, and hammocks swing beside walking trails. As you stroll through woods and meadows to the pond, it's hard to believe that all this lies only a few minutes from I–35.

Bob and Linda Humphrey spent a decade planning the perfect inn. The result, the two-story Shiloh Morning Inn, sits on a hill, with grand views from its upstairs and downstairs porches. On foul-weather days, you can kick back in the library with a game of backgammon in front of the fireplace, or choose one of more than 300 videos and watch a movie in your suite. Each room is unique. The luscious rose Hummingbird Suite has its own private reading room and fireplace; the Pelican's Perch is decorated in Caribbean blues; and the yellow Butterfly Suite has Asian accents. All have a king bed, a private balcony or deck, a sitting area, monogrammed bathrobes, and a stocked mini-refrigerator. You'll have either a whirlpool tub for two or a private hot tub; either way, you can see your fireplace while you soak. Four private cottages nestled back in the trees have all the amenities of the suites in the main house, plus screened-in porches with hot tubs.

At breakfast, you sit at a table for two. Linda attended school to learn European baking techniques, and she makes all the inn's baked goods, including biscotti and English muffins. Her three-course breakfasts usually start with a fresh-fruit smoothie and move on to both savory and sweet courses—smoked Gouda–and-onion quiche, miniature waffles stuffed with bacon and cheese, crepes, or pecan waffles with blueberry coulis and Devonshire cream. Linda also grows her own herbs, and she prepares dinners by reservation. Her repertoire includes pecan-crusted trout fillets, oven-roasted quail, grilled pork tenderloin with vermouth sauce, and slow-cooked baby back ribs. Packed in insulated carriers, the salads, bread, entrée, dessert, and carafe of wine or iced tea are easy to take back to your deck or balcony or to another location of your choice.

You may feel no need at all to leave the inn grounds, but if you feel like exploring, head for the Arbuckle Mountains and Lake of the Arbuckles. The 77 foot waterfall in Turner Falls Park has been a popular attraction since the park opened in 1868. In Chickasaw National Recreation Area, eastern woodland meets mixed-grass prairie to create a patchwork of ecological zones that support red-tailed hawks, bison, coyotes, roadrunners, quail, wild turkey, deer, bobcats, and beavers. You can explore on hiking, biking, and horse trails; go boating; or test the waters at the mineral springs.

Tip *If you want to order dinner, give Linda two days' notice. Whoever places the first order gets to choose that evening's entrée.*

📭 5 suites, 4 cabins 🍽 Full breakfast, dining room, some microwaves, refrigerators. **Recreation:** bird-watching, fishing, hiking, horseback riding (nearby), wildlife viewing, boating (nearby), board games, video-cassette/DVD library. ♨ In-room data ports, in-room fireplaces, some in-room jetted tubs, private balconies; no kids 📶 $139–$269 💳 AE, D, MC, V.

🏠 R.R. 1, Ardmore, OK 73401 ☎ 888/554–7674 or 580/223–9500 📠 580/223–9615 🌐 www.shilohmorning.com.

SIMPLER TIMES INN
Romantic Retreat

Life slows down on the Duck Creek arm of Grand Lake O' the Cherokees in northeastern Oklahoma. On Grand Lake O' the Cherokees, 66 mi long and sprawling into four Oklahoma counties, you can plunge into just about any kind of lake activity imaginable.

Cindy and Pat Belford chose this site for their inn because they had vacationed on the property for 30 years. They welcome you to stroll along their 220 feet of private shoreline or to fish from the dock; a complimentary boat slip makes the inn a popular lodging for boaters. Built of rock, the main house commands splendid views of the cove from its deck and screened-in porch. There's a gathering room downstairs and a parlor upstairs. Classical music plays in the background.

Four of the five guest rooms face the lake, and all separate cottages have a deck or balcony. Inside, you can take in lake views from your jetted tub, with flickering light from your gas fireplace. The TV/VCR is hidden inside an armoire, and a coffeemaker sits on a neat breakfast tray near French doors that lead outside. Each room has a different look and individual features, such as the roomy covered deck of Christopher's Cove, or, in the Heritage Room, the quilt made by Cindy's grandmother and memorabilia such as the primer books her mother used to teach second grade. Up under the eaves, Angel's Alcove has a king bed, bunk beds, and a big-screen TV. The cottage also has a kitchenette.

You breakfast on Cindy's blueberry-pecan French toast in front of the fireplace in the lake-view dining room, at the table for two in your room, or on your balcony. If you breakfast in your room, a tray will be left outside your door. Later in the day, you can cook over the large fire pit and eat at picnic tables along the cove, or dine at one of several restaurants on nearby Monkey Island.

Tip *Fall is wonderful at the inn, with colorful foliage and off-season rates.*

🛏 5 rooms, 1 cabin 🍴 Full breakfast, picnic area, some kitchenettes. **Recreation:** fishing, horseback riding (nearby), lake swimming, waterskiing, boating, jet skiing, kayaking, sailing, 36 hole golf course (nearby). **Services:** dock, Internet access. ♨ In-room fireplaces, in-room VCRs, jetted tubs, private balconies; no room phones, no kids under 12 (unless you rent the entire house), no smoking ⚏ $90–$130 ⊟ AE, MC, V.

🗐 *450920 E. 317 Rd., Afton, OK 74331* ☎ *918–782/9742 or 888/233–7480* 🖷 *918/782–9799* 🌐 *www.simplertimesinn.com.*

Oregon

MT. ASHLAND INN
Laid-Back Adventure ~ Romantic Retreat

Surrounded by 40 acres of wilderness on the 5,500-foot-high ridge crest of Siskiyou Mountain, 30 mi south of Medford, this hand-crafted log lodge has spectacular views of terrain that's teeming with wildlife. Bird-watchers may spot the pileated woodpecker, the great horned owl, the Cassin's finch, or the red-breasted nuthatch. Signs of bobcats, black bears, coyotes, and foxes abound. White-tailed deer are frequently sighted.

Summers here in Southern Oregon's Rogue Valley, 5 mi north of the California border, are great for hiking, mountain biking, white-water rafting, and fishing. The inn sits only 200 feet from the Canada-to-Mexico Pacific Crest Trail. The Oregon portion of the trail, one of the easiest stretches, leads to mountain lakes, through forest, and past meadows. Literally outside the inn's back door, the trail is open to hikers and bikers. There's white-water rafting on the nearby Rogue, Klamath, and North Umpqua rivers, whose rapids range from Class I to Class V. Here, you can also go for steelhead, salmon, trout, and bass. In winter, the inn's proximity to trails and open space makes it a perfect base for cross-country skiing and backcountry snowshoeing. Mt. Ashland Ski Resort, 3 mi up the road, is something of a local's secret—with no lift lines and moderately priced lift tickets. At the end of the day, you can warm up in the inn's sauna or the patio hot tub, where the view is endless sky, forest, and lofty 9,500-foot Mt. McLoughlin to the northeast. Later, take a moonlight snowshoe tour, compliments of the inn.

The five suites are furnished with homemade log furniture, hand-sewn quilts, and finely preserved antiques. An elaborate breakfast—the innkeepers pride themselves on never serving guests the same meal twice—is part of the package and is often created from one of innkeeper Laurel Biegert's personal recipes. Oregano shrimp timbale, anyone? You're on your own for lunch and dinner, but the cookie jar is always filled with goodies and the sitting room buffet well stocked with snacks and hot drinks.

The hardest part about figuring out where to have lunch and dinner is that there are so many good places to eat nearby. Ashland is 14 mi away, and the Rogue Valley is a wine-growing region where food and culture are valued. In historic Jacksonville, old brick storefronts house boutiques, cafés, and antiques shops, and the outdoor concert venue Britt Fest draws singers, comedians, and bands all summer long. And, of course, Ashland is the site of the Oregon Shakespeare Festival, a seasonal lineup of contemporary and Shakespearian plays performed in five indoor and outdoor theaters.

Tip *Let the innkeepers guide you to the best place in town to pick up a food basket, and then sneak off for a picnic in Grouse Gap. This spot in the woods has views of Mt. Shasta and a valley of wildflowers.*

🛏 5 suites ❀ Full breakfast, microwaves, refrigerators. **Recreation:** bird-watching, hiking, mountain biking, cross-country skiing, snowshoeing, board games. Nearby: fishing, rafting, downhill skiing. **Services:** cross-country skis and snowshoes provided; outdoor hot tub; sauna. ♿ In-room fireplaces, jetted tubs; no a/c, no room phones, no room TVs, no kids under 10, no smoking 💳 $160–$200 🛏 D, MC, V.

🏠 *550 Mt. Ashland Rd., Ashland, OR 97520* 📠 *541/482–8707 or 800/830–8707* 🌐 *www.mtashlandinn.com.*

COOPER SPUR MOUNTAIN RESORT
Laid-Back Adventure

Although only 23 mi south of Hood River and 50 mi east of Portland, north-central Oregon's Cooper Spur Mountain Resort occupies a piece of mountain so ethereal that the hustling modern world may as well be on another planet. Smack on the north side of Mt. Hood, on 750 acres of private forest at 3,500 feet, the resort has views of Mt. Hood, Mt. Adams, and Mt. Rainier and a sea of ponderosa pine, Douglas fir, and meadows.

Nearly 120 years ago, young explorer David Cooper opened the first "hotel"—in reality a seasonal tent camp—in this area, hoping to draw others to the mountain he loved. He succeeded. With his wife and children as staff, the young Cooper played host to scientists studying Mt. Hood, hunters, and intrepid travelers hungry for a taste of the new frontier out west. Years later, skiers built a ski jump and rope tow. In 1953 the little ski hill was officially crowned Cooper Spur Mountain Resort. Today the resort is a winter home base for skiers and boarders who come to enjoy the white stuff at the family-oriented Cooper Spur ski area and the larger Mt. Hood Meadows 12 mi to the south. Winter weekends and holidays, overnight guests at Cooper Spur can buy $25 lift tickets for Mt. Hood Meadows. Midweek, the tickets are free. In summer, the mountain turns green, and bikers and hikers roam its trails, lured by mountain-bike jumps and obstacles, an interpretive trail, and an abundance of wildflowers. And, as in winter, three hot tubs bubble for end-of-the-day soaks.

You'll sleep in log cabins or lodge condominiums, each with a stone fireplace, log walls, wood paneling, and a spiral staircase to a loft. If you have a large group, reserve the log house, a four-bedroom, two-bath home with its own hot tub. Dinner is served in the Pioneer Dining Room, where vintage pictures of the ski area and lodge decorate the wood walls and the menu is a mix of comfort food and fancier fare like steak, prime rib, and West Coast clam chowder.

Thriving Hood River, at the heart of the Columbia River gorge, is popular among windsurfers and kite boarders. This region is also noted for its endless orchards, mom-and-pop wineries, and waterfalls. The scenic 35-mi Fruit Loop leads to a number of wineries and family fruit stands. Kayak and rafting excursions and guided fishing trips are available on Hood River and other nearby rivers, and the historic Mt. Hood Railroad offers excursions across the Hood River valley. Pack a picnic lunch for the four-hour scenic ride, or take the dinner or brunch train to eat a four-course meal in a 1940s-era lounge car.

Tip *Don't miss the Hood River Saturday Market, held rain or shine in downtown's Cascade Avenue City Parking Lot.*

6 rooms, 6 cabins, 3 condos, 1 house Dining room, lounge, kitchens, refrigerators, microwaves. **Recreation:** hiking, mountain biking, tennis court, downhill skiing, sledding, snowshoeing, telemark skiing. Nearby: fishing, horseback riding, river swimming, tubing (water), waterskiing, windsurfing, boating, canoeing, kayaking, 18-hole golf course. **Services:** outdoor hot tub, massage. Some pets allowed (fee); no a/c, no smoking $99–$269 AE, D, MC, V.

10755 Cooper Spur Rd., Mt. Hood, OR 97041 541/352–6692 541/352–3506 www.cooperspur.com.

CRATER LAKE LODGE
Tranquil Outpost

Almost 8,000 years ago, southern Oregon's Mt. Mazama volcano catastrophically erupted, then collapsed into itself, forming a giant volcanic depression known as a caldera. A few hundred years later, this caldera filled with snow and rain and became what we know today as Crater Lake. The 1,932-foot-deep lake is the deepest lake in America (and the seventh-deepest in the world). Filled by snowmelt from the surrounding Cascades, the lake is also one of the clearest lakes around. Since 1902, the lake has been protected within Crater Lake National Park. It's about 60 mi from Klamath Falls and 50 mi from Medford.

The wood-and-stone Crater Lake Lodge, built in 1915, has spectacular vistas of this famously brilliant sapphire lake. Over the years, the severe winters and ongoing neglect had taken their toll, and in 1989, engineers reported the old building might well collapse. Because of the enormous cost of repairing and preserving it, the park service considered demolishing the lodge, but public outcry put a stop to that. Now heroically restored, the grand mountain roost is one of the gems of the national park system. Rooms are simply furnished, but half have lake views, and the public spaces, such as the Grand Hall, are stunning, all Douglas fir floors, thick, exposed wood beams, stone fireplaces, and columns rough-cut from tree trunks. You can sip coffee on the veranda in the morning and cocktails in the Great Hall in the afternoon—either way, the lake is always at your feet.

You can explore the surrounding area by car on the 33-mi Rim Drive that encircles the lake, winding through forests of hemlock, fir, and pine. The road leads to views of the lake from every angle, as well as to pull-offs for wildlife viewing and trailheads. Offshore, you can take an interpretive boat tour of the lake, with stops at Wizard Island, a cinder cone jutting up from lake bottom. Although half a million people visit the park every year, it's easy enough to find solitude in its 184,000 acres and on its 90 mi of hiking trails. The trails range from easy to strenuous, leading to overlooks of the lake, tracking through forest, and climbing the rocky face of the sharp, snowcapped cliffs of the Cascades. Deer and elk inhabit this region, which is also along the early-summer migration route of a herd of pronghorn. Smaller critters include pine martens, squirrels, and rabbits. Not far away is the Volcanic Legacy Scenic Byway, which meanders past rivers and mountain lakes and through canyons and dense forests of pines, hemlocks, and firs to the Oregon-California border.

Tip *July and August are best weather-wise, but in June and September the park sees fewer visitors. In June you'll probably find snow still on the ground—and even more may be falling. In September, the weather is likely to be milder, though at 7,100 feet, conditions are unpredictable.*

⬐ 71 rooms ❑ Dining room, restaurant, picnic area. **Recreation:** biking, bird-watching, fishing, hiking, horseback riding (nearby), wildlife viewing, cross-country skiing, snowshoeing. **Classes and programs:** interpretive walks, guided hikes, natural history programs. ♿ No room phones, no room TVs, no smoking ⊟ $130–$255 ⊟ AE, D, DC, MC, V.

⬐ *1211 Avenue C, White City, OR 97503* ☎ *541/830–8700* 🖷 *541/830–8514* ⊕ *www.craterlakelodges.com.*

METOLIUS RIVER RESORT
Tranquil Outpost

Five miles off scenic U.S. 20 in Central Oregon's Cascade Mountains, 40 mi east of Redmond, a group of luxury cabins stands amid ponderosa pines only steps from the Metolius River, a premier fly-fishing spot and a National Scenic and Recreational River. Here in the heart of the Deschutes National Forest and the Metolius Recreational Area, trails for hiking, biking, and horseback riding wind by mountain lakes, along rivers, and through forests of ponderosa pine and larch. Deer, foxes, golden mantle ground squirrels, spotted owls, bald eagles, woodpeckers, warblers, and hummingbirds all make their home here, and critter sightings are your reward if you're quiet and observant.

Cabins at Metolius River Resort are cedar shingled, with stone chimneys, paned windows, and decks. Ranging in size from 840 to 1,100 square feet, they are privately owned, so their interiors vary. In one you might find Persian rugs and designer furniture, in another, retro appliances and a mountain country theme. River-rock fireplaces, cathedral or beamed ceilings, loft bedrooms, and knotty-pine paneling are typical features. Each cabin has a full kitchen, and there are communal grills on the grounds. If you don't feel like cooking you can take out from the nearby Camp Sherman deli (where can get your morning espresso) or try the fresh Oregonian cuisine—trout, salmon, local produce, duck, homemade bread—at the Kokanee Café, a hop and a skip from your cabin doors.

It's just a short walk to the headwaters of the Metolius, the place where the river—the largest spring-fed river in the United States—bubbles to life from below. On nearby Suttle Lake, you can fish, water-ski, and sail. Or visit the Wizard Falls Fish Hatchery, hidden deep in the forest (but an easy drive on paved roads). Atlantic and Kokanee salmon as well as brook, brown, trophy, and rainbow trout swim in open tanks awaiting handouts from the 25¢ fish-food machines. Don't be surprised if an eagle or osprey swoops in low. There are also rare blue rainbow trout—their color is a fluke of nature that makes them easy prey.

In winter, this area is snow country. At the resort you can snowshoe and cross-country ski from right outside your cabin door. Small Hoodoo Ski Area has quiet, uncrowded easy and intermediate downhill slopes nearby. Sixty-odd miles away is Mt. Bachelor, with 350 inches of annual snowfall, 3,700 acres of trails, 3,365 feet of vertical drop, and 56 km of groomed Nordic trails.

Tiny Sisters, population 1,000, is roughly 15 mi southeast of the resort. Small though it may be, it's activity-packed, with top-ranked golf courses, riding stables, and river rafting. Main Street brims with shops and galleries, most specializing in the fine art and folk art of cowboy country (magnificent painted landscapes, carved-wood wildlife, skillfully crafted quilts). July's Sisters Outdoor Quilt Show is huge. The small city of

Bend, another 20 mi southeast, is a center for fishing, rafting, boating, hiking, biking, rock climbing, skiing, horseback riding, and golf. The thriving cultural scene means outdoor concerts at Drake Park summer nights, downtown art galleries, and High Desert Museum, showcasing regional history.

Tip *Remember that the key to dressing comfortably here is layering. Summer days are generally hot, but mornings often start out cool. Likewise, winters are generally cold and brisk, but some days can be surprisingly mild.*

🗦 11 cabins ⏍ Restaurant, grocery store, grills, kitchens. **Recreation:** biking, fishing, hiking, wildlife viewing, cross-country skiing, snowshoeing. Nearby: waterskiing, horseback riding, mountain biking, river swimming, boating, canoeing, jet skiing, kayaking, rafting, 18-hole golf course, tennis courts, sledding, snowmobiling, telemark skiing. ☒ Some satellite TVs with movies, in-room fireplaces, in-room VCRs, private decks; no a/c, no kids (some cabins), no smoking ☒ $165–$195 ⊟ MC, V.

🗌 25551 S.W. Forest Service Rd. 1419, Camp Sherman, OR 97730 ☎ 800/818–7688 or 541/595–6281 🖷 541/595–6281 ⊕ www.metoliusriverresort.com.

SEA QUEST BED & BREAKFAST INN
Romantic Retreat

On the central Oregon coast, where the forest meets the sea about 3 hours from Portland, innkeepers Elaine Ireland and George Rozsa have created a guest home as whimsical and laid-back as nearby Yachats itself. Antiques share space with puzzles, toys, a piano, a tremendous book collection, and oversize chairs. In the great room, a brick pillar twists from floor to ceiling by a fireplace of agates and local rocks. Every guest room has a private entrance from the beach; furnishings are a modern reflection of the maritime wilderness. Nearly every space in the sprawling, two-level, cedar-and-glass B&B has a commanding ocean view. You'll have front-row seats to all the action at sea, including the formidable winter storms, when the ocean works itself into a dramatic fury.

Days at the inn begin with Elaine's breakfast buffet—vegetarian dishes, salad, smoked salmon, a huge selection of fruit, homemade granola, roasted potatoes, and pastries. The beach here is great for agate hunting and peaceful strolls. Low tide reveals tidal pools full of crabs, starfish, sea anemones, and sea cucumbers. Afternoons bring two herds of elk for grazing, and deer, raccoon, wild ferret, and mink are drawn to dine on the briny grass of the salt-spray meadows by the inn. From the bluff, which wraps around the ocean side of the house and ranges from 3 to 12 feet above the beach, you might spot whales, a sea lion, or even a dolphin. On Ten Mile Creek, on the south side of the property, you'll see river otters, pelicans, herons, osprey, and eagles. Nights are for listening to the ocean waves lap and splash, and watching the stars and the blinking lights of fishing boats chugging home from sea.

Two and a half miles north of the inn is Strawberry Hill, accessible only at low tide. Between its fingerlike rock formations, seawater collects in inlets that attract marine life, including sea lions and seals. A little farther north, the Cape Perpetua Scenic Area showcases the dramatic side of the Oregon coast. Nowhere is the state's rough terrain more accessible than in the preserve's Sitka spruce rain forest, wildflower meadows, and stands of old-growth spruce. There are 23 mi of hiking trails ranging from short and gentle to longer, expert climbs. The easy climb from the visitor center to the lookout point, roughly a 20-minute walk, offers an awesome view of the seascape below. Other trails lead from sea to rain forest, providing access to tidal pools and a protected Marine Garden. You can see the Spouting Horn, a rock formation that channels seawater into a spout that shoots high into the air, and Devil's Churn, a gap in the rocks where the ocean crashes and swirls in a mighty display.

Just north of Cape Perpetua is the town of Yachats (pronounced ya-*hots*), a tiny enclave of artists and artisans. Another 25 mi north is bustling oceanfront Newport, site of the Oregon Coast Aquarium and the Yaquina Head Outstanding Natural Area. Oregon Dunes National Recreation Area is roughly 40 minutes south of Sea Quest, with hidden lakes, rain forest, rivers, and the opportunity to bird-watch, view wildlife, pick berries, swim, fish, picnic, or hike.

Tip *If you're interested in sea lions, head 20 mi south of Sea Quest on U.S. 101 to Florence, where some 200 wild Stellar sea lions live at Sea Lion Caves. Formed 25 million years ago, the cavern is roughly the height of a 12-story building and the length of a football field. When the sea lions are in, it's raucous, lively, and smelly; when not, there isn't much to see. Call ahead (541/547–3111) for a status report.*

🛏 5 rooms, 1 suite ⬛ Full breakfast. **Recreation:** bird-watching, fishing, hiking, wildlife viewing, horseshoes. Nearby: horseback riding, boating, sailing, sea kayaking. ⬥ Some jetted tubs, private decks, board games, library, piano; no a/c, no room phones, no room TVs, no kids under 12, no smoking ▭ $170–$400 ▭ MC, V.

📍 95354 U.S. 101, Yachats, OR 97498 ☎ 800/341–4878 or 541/547–3782 ⊕ www.seaq.com.

TU TU' TUN LODGE
Tranquil Outpost

Southwestern Oregon's Tu Tu' Tun Lodge is on the banks of the Rogue River, one of the first rivers in the United States to earn Wild and Scenic designation by Congress, and it's all about the river. Here, local jet-boat guides will pick you up for a ride on the water, with black bear, bald eagles, blue heron, osprey, fox, deer, and turtles on the shores. Or take off downriver for a gentle glide in one of the inn's kayaks. Or make the 7-mi drive to the oceanfront town of Gold Beach and explore the 27-mi stretch of beach that connects Gold Beach to Brookings, the southernmost town on the Oregon coast, where you can beachcomb for agates; scan tidal pools for sea anemones, sea cucumbers, crabs, starfish, and mussels; fly a kite; or take a hike over the coastal headlands and around the dunes.

But even if you never left the property of Tu Tu' Tun Lodge (pronounced tu-*too*-tun), you would still have plenty to do: swim in the heated outdoor lap pool; play croquet, horseshoes, or pitch-and-putt golf; or enjoy an in-room massage. Innkeepers Laurie and Dirk Van Zante excel at providing laid-back luxury living in the wilds of Oregon. Guest rooms and two suites overlook the river, each with private balconies or patios, slate or cast-iron fireplaces, terra-cotta entries, and granite bath counters. There are also two houses: the Garden House, which has an outdoor hot tub, stone fireplace, and views of the forested hills, and the River House, where every room has a view of the Rogue. Mornings begin with a tray of coffee, freshly squeezed orange juice, and the *Oregonian* at your door. In the afternoon there's a complimentary refreshment bar on the Herb Terrace; evenings, when the fire pits glow on the deck and stars glitter above, you can snack on complimentary hors d'oeuvres and sample the innkeeper's collection of regional red and white wines.

Restaurants in town are few, but you have the option of paying extra for the inn's meal plan, which includes breakfast and dinner. Along with a breakfast buffet bar of homemade pastries, yogurt, granola, and fresh fruit, the inn serves hot entrées such as eggs Saratoga (scrambled with cream cheese) with cottage potatoes, pepper bacon, and cornmeal toast. The meal plan's four-course dinner might include salmon, marinated beef fillet, stuffed chicken breast, grilled sturgeon, popovers, grilled vegetables, and chocolate mocha pie for dessert.

Tip *Ask for directions to the secret beach, a spot along the ocean not readily visible to casual passersby, and plan a picnic.*

⤳ 16 rooms, 2 suites, 2 houses ⏣ Modified American plan (extra charge), lounge, grills, picnic area. **Recreation:** fishing, hiking, wildlife viewing, pool, river swimming, boating, kayaking, putting green, croquet, horseshoes, golf, lawn chess. **Services:** kayaks, fishing poles, horseshoes, and croquet equipment provided; massage; guided fishing trips. ♿ In-room fireplaces, private balconies and decks, library; no a/c, no room TVs, no smoking ▨ $165–$425 ⊟ D, MC, V.

🏠 *96550 North Bank Rogue, Gold Beach, OR 97444* ☎ *541/247–6664 or 800/864–6357* 🖷 *541/247–0672* ⊕ *www.tututun.com.*

WALLOWA LAKE LODGE
Tranquil Outpost

As you drive along the backcountry Highway 82 in northeastern Oregon, about 1½ hours from La Grande, there comes a moment when the two-lane road emerges from the hills and farmland and rounds a corner, and there, like a mirage, lies Wallowa Lake, stretching dark and cool as far as the eye can see. Travel a few more miles, past the boats, the anglers, the parasailers, and the water-skiers, and you'll glimpse the Wallowa Lake Lodge, a grand old wood-frame building, three stories tall and set front and center on the south shore of the lake.

The lodge was built in the 1920s as a place for the well-heeled, who traveled by boat from the opposite end of the lake to dine and dance. Back then, it was one of the few places in the area with electricity and was quite the place to stay. In those days, developers had high hopes that Wallowa Lake would become the Northwest's premier vacation spot. Those dreams never panned out, but the lodge survived and is today a popular place to enjoy the outdoors. Guest rooms are finished in early-20th-century style; the more rustic lakeside cabins have knotty-pine paneling and stone fireplaces. Like all great old lodges, this one comes with a large public living room filled with easy chairs, pine furniture, and a stone fireplace. The dining room, where breakfast and dinner are served, is casual; you'll hear live piano music on Friday and Saturday nights. You might start your day with biscuits and gravy or hazelnut pancakes with marionberry butter, and end it with rib-eye steak or Alaskan halibut.

Fishing for Kokanee salmon and lake trout and boating—small motorized boats, rowboats, and kayaks are permitted—are the obvious draw. But in this area, which has been called the Little Switzerland of America, hikers and horseback riders find plenty to do. Eagle Cap Wilderness Pack Station rents horses for rides in the Eagle Cap Wilderness area less than ½ mi from the lodge. One mile from the lodge, three hiking trails lead into the wilderness. The Chief Joseph, Aneroid, and West Fork trails pass over rivers and by waterfalls, wildflower meadows, and mountain lakes, with views of local valleys. Experienced hikers can make the trek to the top of the 10,000-foot summit of Chief Joseph Mountain. Trails start at 4,000 feet, and most hikes can be accomplished in a day or with one overnight. For mountaintop views without the work, hop on the Wallowa Lake Tramway (a five-minute walk up the Joseph/Wallowa Lake Highway) for a 10-minute, 3,700-foot ascent to the top of 8,150-foot Mt. Howard, where short groomed trails yield spectacular views of the towns of Joseph, Enterprise, Lostine, and Wallow and the peaks of the Wallowa Mountains.

Tip *A sign on the lodge's front door reminds you that deer are wild animals with hooves and teeth. No doubt as you read the sign, you'll be under*

*the watch of one or two deer nibbling grass nearby. Chances are, in a short
time you'll have spotted so many deer you almost won't notice them anymore.*

🛏 22 rooms, 8 cabins 🍽 Restaurant. **Recreation:** bird-watching,
wildlife viewing. Nearby: fishing, hiking, horseback riding, lake swimming, parasailing, waterskiing, boating, jet skiing, cross-country skiing,
sledding, snowmobiling, snowshoeing. ♿ No a/c, no room phones,
no room TVs, no smoking 💳 $89–$150 ⊟ D, MC, V.

🏨 *60060 Wallowa Lake Hwy., Joseph, OR 97846* ☎ *541/432–9821*
🖷 *541/432–4885* ⊕ *www.wallowalake.com.*

Pennsylvania

CLARION RIVER LODGE RESORT & SPA
Tranquil Outpost

This is a room with a view. The balcony doors of your suite, which is perched high above a bend in the Clarion River, show off steep, forested hills spreading left and right as far as the eye can see. In the morning, mist rises off the river to shroud the trees; later in the day, drifting clouds make shadow puppets on the dense canopy. At the Clarion River Lodge, the views are everywhere: the tent sheltering a massage table on a sky-high deck has one side open to the vista. The cabana, where a summer barbecue treats you to chicken and ribs and live music, offers the brilliant sight of thousands of stars. A shady nook along the riverbank is the perfect place to nap in a lawn chair surrounded by green.

The lodge, in the northwestern Pennsylvania town of Cooksburg, about 100 mi from Pittsburgh, sits on the doorstep of the 7,182-acre Cook Forest State Park and on the banks of the Clarion River. Close to 30 mi of hiking trails wind through the forest; several paths lead to the Forest Cathedral, where primeval white pine and eastern hemlock grow 200 feet tall. One of the largest stands of old-growth forest in Pennsylvania, the Forest Cathedral is a Natural National Landmark. The Clarion River, a Wild and Scenic River, has made a remarkable transformation from polluted (by mining) to pristine; and bald eagles are once again being sighted in the area. The river also lures swimmers, and anglers come for the trout, warm-water game fish, and panfish. If you'd like to canoe, the inn will provide lunch and a local outfitter will ferry you upstream so you can paddle back to the lodge.

Once a private retreat, the contemporary lodge has cathedral ceilings supported by oak beams and lined with cherry paneling. In the guest rooms, faux painting, tea staining, stamping, and draping make the accommodations more homey than hotel-like. Beyond the queen and king beds, each room is different. MeadoWood, for example, takes a quaintly creative approach to French Provincial style. Briarwick has a log headboard and walls painted like embossed leather. Each of the river-view suites has a fireplace, jetted tub, full kitchen, and sofa bed—you might want to switch rooms so you can sleep in front of the fire, with the balcony door wide open. The space feels like a well-appointed family room with its durable carpet, casual wood furnishings, and a kitchen counter with high stools, just right for snacking.

After a trip to Ireland, innkeeper Ellen O'Day decided to re-create the Dingle Pub on her property. A neighbor donated cherrywood for the handsome bar and shadowboxes, which are filled with mementos from guests. The talented singers and guitar players on the staff now entertain on some weekends while guests sing along. The River Room restaurant is family-friendly and quality-conscious: seafood is bought fresh in Pittsburgh, pasta is homemade, and the beef is Black Angus. The full-service River Winds Spa offers a Clarion River Stone Therapy treatment with hot basalt and cold marble to promote well-being. A weekend at this lodge will do the same.

Tip *The nearby Sawmill Center for the Arts has a May-to-October schedule of festivals, theater productions, fly-fishing instruction, and other events. Classes teach dulcimer-making and wood carving, and there's a field trip to forage for wild edibles and herbs in Cook Forest.*

↰ 20 rooms, 12 suites ⊚ Continental breakfast, restaurant, room service, bar, pub, grills, some kitchens. **Recreation:** river swimming, canoeing, golf privileges, sleigh rides, board games, library. Nearby: biking, fishing, hiking, horseback riding, mountain biking, cross-country skiing, ice-skating, sledding, snowmobiling. **Services:** spa, babysitting, laundry facilities, business services, Internet access, meeting rooms. **Classes and programs:** guided nature walks. ⟁ Satellite TV, in-room data ports, some in-room fireplaces, some jetted tubs, some private decks, some pets allowed, no-smoking rooms 🛏 $109–$250 ⊟ AE, D, MC, V.

⌂ HC 1 (Box 22 D), Cooksburg, PA 16217 ☎ 814/744–8171 or 800/648–6743 🖷 814/744–8553 ⊕ www.clarionriverlodge.com.

GLENDORN
Luxurious Resort

Cross a bridge, announce yourself, and pause—the estate's gate will slowly open. Before you drive the mile down the private road to the Big House, one of Bambi's cousins may pause to watch you pass before hopping away into Allegheny National Forest. Frogs may linger on the stone footbridge that leads to your cottage in the woods, steps away from a rushing stream. You're 80 mi—and light-years away—from Buffalo, New York.

For the inventive and nature-loving Dorn family, five generations of whom vacationed together at 1,280-acre Glendorn, life was a fairy tale, a rags-to-riches story of patriarch Clayton Glenville Dorn and his son, Forest, who made millions in oil drilling. In 1929 C. G. Dorn purchased acreage that included his favorite fishing camp on the banks of a trout stream. He built an all-redwood lodge in the style of the great camps of the Adirondacks and added cottages for each of his children. Now the retreat has become a resort. Have a cocktail in front of the Great Hall's two-story hearth and watch the chipmunks scamper through. At breakfast, your personal camp counselor asks what activity you'd like to try today. Your cookie jar is constantly refilled, and your dinner menu might list French onion soup with smoked Gouda or poached lobster tail in a champagne-and-grapefruit butter sauce, exquisitely prepared by chef Jason Gulisano.

Activities director Damon Newpher can turn any city slicker into the outdoorsy type. With patient instruction, he initiates novices to the pleasures of skeet shooting and fly-casting. A certified Orvis guide, he takes more experienced anglers on trips down the Allegheny River. On your own, you can hike or snowshoe through the forest of birch, beech, and black cherry. Start with an easy walk to Bondieu Lake, where you might see muskrats, mink, or beaver. For something more challenging, make the steep hike up Cherry Path to a hut for a chef-prepared picnic.

At Glendorn, Pennsylvania's only Relais & Châteaux property, friendships are formed over banana pancake breakfasts on the terrace and croquet games on the lawn. You'll feel like you're a guest in someone's home—albeit a grand one—and that your hosts will soon walk through the door. The accommodations are plush—Aveda bath products, CD players, twice-a-day housekeeping, and bedding so delicious you'll want to buy the same sheets for your home. But rooms are also personal: a daughter's jewelry still sits out on her dresser; a grandfather's favorite books line the shelves. The Big House has two rooms and two suites, sophisticated spaces with historic touches. The Green Suite's fireplace is framed by 18th-century Dutch tiles depicting stories from the Bible. The Dorn Suite, where President and Mrs. Taft once spent a weekend, has carved white-oak paneling and a sunporch. Cabins are scattered about the property, nestled among hemlocks and maples; one overlooks bass-filled Skipper Lake, and the most secluded, the Forest Hideout, can be reached only via a winding, unpaved road. The one- to four-bedroom cabins, are paneled with chestnut and knotty pine and warmed by wood-burning fireplaces (there are 41 fireplaces for the 30 guests). Several have wet bars, his-and-hers bathrooms, spacious dressing rooms, and screened porches. With the windows open, you can hear birds chirping, raindrops falling, and streams running.

Back in the lodge, guests who have stayed in some of the world's best hotels whisper to each other about how perfect and special Glendorn is, perhaps keeping their voices hushed so that the spell of enchantment is not broken.

Tip *From Memorial Day to Labor Day, Glendorn's "100 Days of Summer" entices families with canoe races, nature walks, movies on the lawn (blankets and popcorn provided), and a lakeside barbecue and bonfire with s'mores (the marshmallows are homemade) and fine champagne.*

🛏 2 rooms, 2 suites, 6 cabins 🍽 American plan, dining room, ice-cream parlor, room service (in main lodge), picnic area, some kitchens. **Recreation:** biking, fishing, hiking, pool, canoeing, rowing, golf privileges, 2 tennis courts, cross-country skiing, sledding, snowshoeing, basketball, boccie, croquet, shuffleboard, sporting clays, volleyball, piano, recreation room, videocassette library, playground. **Services:** bicycles, fishing rods, cross-country skis, tennis equipment and snowshoes provided; gym; massage; guided fishing trips; tackle shop; babysitting; dry-cleaning service; laundry service; airport shuttle; car rental; business services; Internet access; meeting rooms. **Classes and programs:** guided nature walks; skeet- and trap-shooting and fly-fishing lessons. ⛄ Some in-room fireplaces, in-room VCRs, some private patios, some pets allowed (fee); no a/c in some rooms 💲 $495–$795 💳 AE, DC, MC, V.

📬 *1000 Glendorn Dr., Bradford, PA 16701* ☎ *814/362–6511 or 800/843–8568* 📠 *814/368–9923* 🌐 *www.glendorn.com.*

INN AT STARLIGHT LAKE
Laid-Back Adventure

Perhaps it was the mist rising off spring-fed Starlight Lake, ringed by acres of forests and meadows, that prompted one guest to call the Inn at Starlight Lake her Brigadoon. This waterside Adirondack-style inn in the lake district of northeast Pennsylvania's Appalachian Mountains, 5 mi southwest of Hancock, New York, and 150 mi (2¾ hours) from Manhattan, welcomed its first guests in 1909. Those summer boarders arrived on the Erie Railroad, which passed through Hancock. They came to enjoy the clean air and untouched forests. Happily, the area is still undeveloped; Starlight isn't even on most maps. The railroad is long-abandoned, but its bed is just right for biking, hiking, and cross-country skiing. The crystal-clear lake beckons, even on chilly mornings. Children can safely swim in the enclosed dock area, and stronger swimmers have the entire lake to explore.

Jim and Sari Schwartz and Joan Roy keep this harmonious inn. The antiques-furnished sunroom and parlor lobby are informal rather than fancy; they invite ease, like a grandmother's house where you don't have to be on your best behavior. The main building and adjacent cottages house the snug guest rooms, all fresh with their white coverlets, ruffled curtains, pastel floral walls, and mix-and-match furniture. There are no phones or TVs to interrupt your daydreams. Settle into one of the rockers on the lakefront porch to start your day with a cup of coffee before heading to the dining room for blueberry pancakes or homemade granola. The kitchen serves excellent dinners of chicken piccata or linguini with clam sauce, broiled seafood, or smoked teriyaki baby-back ribs, followed by pecan pie with maple-walnut ice cream.

Fly-fishers come to the upper Delaware River to try for large, wild stream-bred rainbow trout, brown trout, and shad. A nearby Orvis shop offers fishing instruction, guides, and equipment. Many other local outfitters package adventures for grown-ups. You can be picked up for guided canoe and kayak trips on the river (where eagle sightings are frequent) or for escorted mountain-bike tours through state game lands and countryside. The inn is the booking agent for a self-guided inn-to-inn mountain-bike tour of Wayne and Susquehanna counties; routes cover 15 to 30 mi a day over country roads and abandoned railroad beds. In winter, strap on a pair of snowshoes and take a moonlight walk or a full-day backcountry excursion. For skiers, the inn is a place of respite after a day at Elk Mountain, Pennsylvania's best ski area, or at nearby Mt. Tone, where you can also try snow tubing.

Tip *If you're planning to visit in summer, reserve way ahead. This corner of the state is home to many summer camps, and all of them list the Inn at Starlight Lake as a great place to stay on visiting day.*

🛏 22 rooms, 1 suite 🍽 Restaurant, bar. **Recreation:** Biking, fishing, hiking, lake swimming, tubing (water), canoeing, rowing, tennis court, cross-country skiing, snowshoeing, downhill skiing (nearby), billiards, horseshoes, Ping-Pong, shuffleboard, volleyball, piano, recreation room, playground. **Services:** bikes provided, babysitting. ♿ No-smoking rooms; no a/c, no room phones, no room TVs 💲 $140–$255 💳 MC, V.

🏠 *Box 27, Starlight, PA 18461* ☎ *570/798–2519 or 800/248–2519* 📠 *570/798–2672* 🌐 *www.innatstarlightlake.com.*

SKYTOP LODGE
Family Hideout

This imposing Dutch Colonial stone manor sits on a plateau overlooking a perfectly manicured golf course, sweeping greens clipped for lawn bowling, and 5,550 acres of wilderness laced with trout streams and waterfalls. The setting is formal and grand, and if you close your eyes and spin the globe, you might think you have landed in a British hill station in India, the kind of place where colonials took refuge from the sweltering summers on the subcontinent—though you're just 90 mi from Manhattan.

In the prosperous Roaring '20s, Skytop was built as a members-only golf club, and the lodge still has an air of refinement and privilege. Families dine together at breakfast, lunch, and dinner, and though the dining room might seat as many kids as Romper Room, it's surprisingly civilized. At dinner, guests are dressed "appropriately" (men wear jackets). Under watchful parental eyes, children don't splash each other with the lemon-scented water in their finger bowls, which arrive after their macaroni and cheese—or their rock-lobster risotto or potato-crusted ahi tuna.

There's a full schedule of what curmudgeons might call mandatory fun: hayrides, sand volleyball games, archery, and other activities. Since 1928, guests have gathered in the Pine Room on Saturday nights for the Elimination Dance, a combination of a conga line and musical chairs. Winners lead a Grand March; everyone holds hands and weaves in and out of the room. This time warp is seductive, and families come back year after year.

The guest rooms and minisuites in the lodge have been dressed up in English country style, with sunny yellow walls and floral printed bedding in shades of red and green. TVs are hidden in highboys, moldings are ornate, and bathrooms have been modernized. The rooms are oddly shaped, long and skinny or in an "L," because baths that were once down the hall are now en suite. Even with improvements, the rooms reveal their vintage. By contrast, the 20-room Inn at Skytop, a golf resort built in 1998, is a spiffy youngster with gas fireplaces, private balconies, and luxurious bathrooms. You can also stay in standard cottages with four interconnecting bedrooms that can be configured to accommodate up to 14 people. With their small refrigerators, VCRs, and washer-dryer units, these cottages are great for families.

An on-site spa offers private Pilates sessions, instructor-guided yoga walks and power walks, and Watsu (water shiatsu), in which you lie in warm water while you're gently stretched. Booklets point out botanical wonders along Trout Stream Trail on the way to a magnificent waterfall by a hemlock-rhododendron-blueberry swamp, or to Goose Pond, the lodge's least-visited wilderness. Guided hikes are also on the roster. If you meet any wildlife on your walks, you can add them to the posted list of recent animal sightings, which may include bald eagles, black bears and their cubs, rattlesnakes, or voles. On selected nights each week, a local astronomy teacher takes guests to the summit of Skytop Mountain and sets up his high-powered telescope to show the moon's craters and the Milky Way's arch across the night sky. Here on the pitch-black mountaintop away from city lights, with a clear view of thousands of stars, you'll discover the real privilege that comes with a stay at Skytop Lodge.

Tip *The lodge schedules nostalgia weekends with various themes, such as Big Band ballroom dancing, celebrity chefs, and country weekends with sing-alongs and Buffalo Bill contests. Literary weekends celebrate Dickens with a Mrs. Cratchit's dinner party.*

🛏 110 rooms, 35 suites, 12 cottages ⑩ American plan. Deli, 2 restaurants, ice-cream parlor, room service, lobby lounge, pub, picnic area. **Recreation:** fishing, hiking, horseback riding (nearby), mountain biking, wildlife viewing, pool, indoor pool, lake swimming, canoeing, kayaking, rowing, driving range, 18-hole golf course, 2 putting greens, 7 tennis courts, cross-country skiing, downhill skiing, ice-skating, sledding, snowshoeing, archery, badminton, basketball, billiards, croquet, horseshoes, lawn bowling, miniature golf, paddle tennis, Ping-Pong, shuffleboard, sporting clays, volleyball, library, piano, recreation room, video-game room, videocassette and DVD library, playground. **Services:** bicycle, boat, tennis, fishing rod, paddle-tennis and sport-clay rentals, gym, hot tub, spa, pro shop, tackle shop, ski shop, babysitting, dry-cleaning service, laundry service, shop, business services, meeting room. **Classes and programs:** guided hikes; guided nature walks; tennis competitions; golf; fly-fishing, skiing, and tennis lessons; fitness and yoga classes; children's programs (ages 4–10); astronomy talks; dances; movies. ☄ Cable TV, some in-room safes, in-room VCRs, wireless Internet, some jetted tubs, no-smoking rooms 🖂 $395–$720 ▭ AE, DC, MC, V.

🗋 *1 Skytop, Skytop, PA 18357* ☎ *570/595–7401 or 800/345–7759* 🖷 *570/595–9618* ⊕ *www.skytop.com.*

Rhode Island

ATLANTIC INN
Tranquil Outpost

Aboard the ferry as it glides into its slip on Block Island, you are treated to a stunning view: a row of restored Victorian inns stretches along Water Street and onto a knoll overlooking Old Harbor. On a hill above the busy harbor is Atlantic Inn, a graceful, three-story white clapboard structure with a row of dormer windows on its mansard roof and a veranda running the length of the facade. The inn's location removes it from the hub-bub of the town while giving it sweeping views of the island and the sea. At sunset, folks gather on the veranda for cocktails and tapas. The veranda, which overlooks much of the inn's 6 surrounding acres of lawn and gardens, is also a perfect vantage point for parents to watch their kids playing in a child-scale replica of the 1879 inn.

Innkeeper-owners Anne and Brad Marthens have personally and individually decorated each guest room. Rooms aren't large or grand, but the cheerful wallpaper patterns and antique furnishings (mostly original) make them appealing. Sea breezes keep rooms fresh and cool, so air-conditioning is unnecessary. There are no TVs on the premises, but a puzzle is always under construction in the foyer. Flowers from the cutting garden appear throughout the public rooms, and the bounty of the herb garden and grape arbor makes its way into dishes at the restaurant, which offers some of the best food on the island.

Block Islanders have bent over backward to protect their corner of paradise, setting aside nearly 40% of the land (so far) with conservation easements so plants and wildlife can thrive and people can continue to enjoy them. The Nature Conservancy maintains the Greenway, 25 mi of hiking trails that are open to the public, and offers guided nature walks from mid-June through Columbus Day. Thousands of migratory birds head north or south along the Atlantic Flyway overhead; shorebirds congregate on beaches and salt marshes, and birds of prey hover near ocean-facing cliffs.

Shaped like a pork chop, Block Island is only about 4 mi across at its widest and no more than 7 mi long. The topography includes sand dunes, pastures, some 365 ponds, and 17 mi of beach. Self-guided bike tours, ranging from 3½ mi to 8 mi long, take you past island sights such as Great Salt Pond, New Harbor, 150-foot-high Mohegan Bluffs, and, of course, fabulous ocean vistas. Narrow country lanes around the island meander past weathered-shingle homes, most with trimmed lawns and pretty flower gardens and often with stone fences, a pond or two, or acres of meadow. Kayaking or canoeing on Great Salt Pond is another way to explore the sheltered shoreline.

The town of Old Harbor is where the action is between mid-June and Labor Day, when Block Island's population swells from about 850 year-round residents to nearly 15,000 vacationers. People arrive by ferry or private boat for the day, a weekend, or longer. But don't let high season scare you: once you're a block from the waterfront at the Atlantic Inn, serenity reigns.

Tip *Leave your car at home. Although the Block Island ferry accommodates cars, you really don't need one. The island is fairly flat, and bicycles or mopeds are common modes of transportation. (Rentals are available near the ferry landing.)*

🛏 21 rooms 🍴 Continental breakfast, restaurant, lobby lounge. **Recreation:** 2 tennis courts, croquet, board games. Nearby: biking, birdwatching, hiking, beach, boating, canoeing, kayaking. ♿No a/c, no room TVs, no smoking 💳 $159–$279 ▭ D, MC, V.

🏠 *High St. (Box 1788), Block Island, RI 02807* 📞 *401/466–5883 or 800/224–7422* 📠 *401/466–5678* 🌐 *www.atlanticinn.com* 🚫 *Closed Nov.–mid-Apr.*

CANAL BOAT SAMUEL SLATER
Romantic Retreat

The cheery red Canal Boat *Samuel Slater* is a B&B that is truly unique. Docked on the quiet, tree-lined Blackstone River in Central Falls, 4 mi north of Providence and smack in the middle of the most densely populated part of Rhode Island, the 40-foot British-made boat is similar to the historic canal boats that ply London's River Thames. Launched in May 2000 as part of the millennium celebrations, it was named for the man widely regarded to be the father of the American Industrial Revolution, which arguably began down the road at Slater Mill. The only boat of its kind plying American waters can be yours for a night—or longer.

The two cabins (one double stateroom and two bunks in the salon) sleep up to four people with all the comforts of a floating home, including a fully equipped galley and a head with shower. After a day exploring the Blackstone River valley, you can sit on deck and watch the stars or get cozy down below. There's a logbook in which previous guests have recounted their stays, and you're welcome to add your own narrative. At a prearranged time in the morning, a quiet knock at the hatch means your breakfast has arrived: juice, coffee and tea, maybe eggs and bacon or pancakes.

A morning or evening cruise on the canal boat ($65 for up to four overnight guests) is a must. As a boatman steers you along the placid river for an hour and a half, you'll probably see waterfowl swooping into the nearby marsh and maybe some turtles. The scene is lovely in spring and summer but particularly spectacular when the leaves turn in early fall. A paved bikeway parallels the river for 7 mi, beginning north of the canal boat dock at Central Falls and continuing to Lincoln. Besides biking, you can jog, walk, cross-country ski, and in-line skate along the bikeway. Eventually, the bikeway will stretch between Providence, Rhode Island, and Worcester, Massachusetts. The portion completed so far is a fairly flat and shady path past former and existing farms. You'll also come across millponds and the old towpath and locks of the canal, as well as derelict Industrial Revolution–era mills partially hidden behind the trees that line the riverbank.

The river, the canal remnants, and the bikeway are part of the Blackstone River Valley National Historic Corridor, a 400,000-acre greenbelt extending 47 mi between Providence and Worcester. The harnessing of power from the Blackstone River was one of the events that launched America's "Second Revolution" in the late 18th century. Starting in 1828, freight and passengers were transported between Providence and Worcester on horse-drawn boats that traveled a hand-dug canal parallel to the river. The river itself was not navigable because it made a 438-foot drop along its course, and it was blocked by 34 dams that powered riverfront mills. By 1848 new technology—the railroad—made the canal obsolete. At Slater Mill Historic Site, you can learn how the river powered the mill and see what life and work were like in the 1830s. It wasn't pretty. But today, with the mills gone, the river that for 200 years was used, abused, and then neglected is once again clean and hospitable for birds, fish, and people who enjoy canoeing, kayaking, rowing, and catch-and-release fishing.

Tip *You can rent a bike at Blackstone Valley Surrey, 175 Main St. in Pawtucket (401/724–2200.)*

⇰ One 2-cabin boat ⭗ Full breakfast, kitchenette, microwave. **Recreation:** Nearby: biking, bird-watching, fishing, hiking, boating, canoeing, kayaking. ⟐ In-room VCR; no smoking 🖾 $179 ▭ AE, D, MC, V.

⌂ *c/o Blackstone Valley Visitor Center, 175 Main St., Pawtucket, RI 02860* ☎ *401/724–2200 or 800/454–2882* 📠 *401/724–1342* ⊕ *www.tourblackstone.com/canal.htm* � *Closed Nov.–Mar.*

South Carolina

DEWEES ISLAND
Rustic Escape

On the 20-minute ferry ride to 1,206-acre Dewees Island from the Isle of Palms (about 12 mi northeast of Charleston), the stress of daily life tends to slip away. Dewees has no busy roads, no cars, no high-rises, no golf courses, no stores or restaurants—and few people—and is accessible only by boat or air. More than 90% of the island remains undisturbed; of its 65 homes, 10 are available for rent through Island Realty, and all are carefully tucked amid the vegetation and barely visible. Wildlife is the only thing here that's abundant and, in fact, is the island's main attraction: Dewees Island even has its own environmental education director, Arla Jessen.

Arla, who makes it a point to meet all newcomers, is an enthusiastic resource, answering questions about bait and the best fishing holes, teaching novices how to throw a cast net, leading birding field trips and marsh walks, and, perhaps, recruiting you to monitor turtle nests. Other than spreading your towel on the nearly empty beaches, you can go fishing, clamming, shrimping, and crabbing; spy on blue herons and pelicans; and paddle a canoe. Cocktail hour is inevitably spent on the beach, perhaps near a loggerhead turtle nest about to hatch.

Homes on the rental program have views of the ocean, tidal creeks, marshes, or maritime forest. All have plenty of porches and are open to ocean breezes and sunlight. Otherwise, each house is different; ask if your kitchen has staples, condiments, and other basics. Transportation along the sand roads is via a complimentary golf cart. It's easy to spend an entire day exploring the island by cart, jumping on and off to poke along the paths, swim in the ocean, examine tidal pools, climb observation towers, or just walk down the island's docks for a closer look at the hermit crabs and marsh hens.

Dewees is a bona fide back-to-nature experience—there's no staff manicuring hedges or sweeping spiderwebs out of sight. The Huyler House—with a hands-on nature center, screened-porch recreation room, outdoor pool, and tennis courts—is the closest thing to an activity center; you may find yourself stopping by to pore over reference books to determine what kind of bone or animal track you came across that morning, or popping in to borrow a video or board game. Kids love dumping their pails of marsh goodies on the wet lab floor, where Arla helps identify their treasures.

Though you may wish you were stranded here, you're not. The ferry arrives at and departs the island every half hour from early morning to about 11 or 12 each night, so if you forget something you can hop over to the marina store. If you just don't feel like cooking dinner, try one of the restaurants not far from the ferry dock.

Tips *Bring a high-powered flashlight, shoes for wading, binoculars, and bug spray. Fall means fewer bugs, more birds, more fish, and more shells.*

⟿ 10 houses ⎟◎⎟ Grills, picnic area, kitchens. **Recreation:** bird-watching, fishing, wildlife viewing, beach, pool, river swimming, canoeing, sea kayaking (nearby), 18-hole golf course (nearby), 2 tennis courts, billiards, handball, Ping-Pong, basketball, shuffleboard. **Services:** massage, helipad, babysitting, grocery shopping, meeting rooms. **Classes and programs:** guided nature walks, natural history programs, arts and crafts classes, nature talks. ♿ Some VCRs available; no phones in some rooms, no TVs in some rooms, no smoking ▨ $500–$816 ▭ AE, D, MC, V.

⎙ *Island Realty, 1304 Palm Blvd., Isle of Palms, 29451* ☎ *843/886–8144 or 800/707–6434* 🖷 *843/886–5131* ⊕ *www.islandrealty.com.*

RED HORSE INN
Tranquil Outpost

The Red Horse Inn stands in the middle of fox-hunting country in what you might call the hamlet of Gowensville, near the town of Landrum in the Upcountry on 190 acres of pastureland. Four horses and a donkey graze near the inn, and the Blue Ridge Mountains stretch off in the distance.

From the inn and its five Victorian-style cottages, you can always see the mountains. Guest rooms in the main building have whirlpools, fireplaces, and kitchenettes with a small fridge, microwave, and coffeemaker. Each white-clapboard, green tin–roofed cottage is equipped with a kitchen, and some have a loft. Warmed by a fireplace and illuminated by tall windows, the cottages are all hardwood floors, cathedral ceilings, and cheerful fabrics. After a day of hiking in fresh mountain air, you might collapse in front of the TV in your loft, or just return to your porch rocker and keep time with the swish of horse tails.

In the morning, sunlight fills your cottage and filters through the drapes around your bed. Take your muffins and fruit out onto your front porch rocker. Once you're alert and well fed, ask owners Roger and Mary Wolters to share their collection of flyers and directions for scenic walks and hikes, drives, and antiquing. With nine state parks nearby, you can follow a plan or just roam Devils Fork State Park, which lies on the south shore of Lake Jocassee, a 7,500-acre lake filled with trophy small-mouth bass and rainbow and brown trout. Along its 75 mi of shore-line, a wildflower called Oconee Bell grows; foxes, wild turkeys, deer, and birds such as tanagers, vireos, warblers, and eagles make their home. The bass, bream, and crappie fishing is fine on Lake Keowee, where Keowee–Toxaway State Natural Area's dramatic rock outcrop-pings stand amid rhododendron and mountain laurel. Within Moun-tain Bridge Recreation and Wilderness Area, Caesar's Head and Jones Gap state parks contain two of South Carolina's best fly-fishing streams and a challenging network of mountain trails. Caesar's Head, inhab-ited year-round by hawks, ravens, and turkey vultures, draws bird-watchers, especially in September, to admire migrating broad-winged hawks. In November ospreys, red-tailed hawks, peregrine falcons, and other species pass by.

Hike to one of the area's many waterfalls, or head down one of the wooded trails on the inn's property, either on foot or on one of the inn's horses. The Wolters maintain the trails, which meander among dog-woods, mountain laurel, wild azaleas, mimosas, wild rose, ligustrums, and tiny wild iris. The Middle Tiger River spans the lower portion of the property. Down the road, a nice walk away, is Campbell's covered bridge, the last one remaining in South Carolina. Since fox-hunting groups often follow the chase right across the Wolters' property, you might see equestrian action from your cottage. For a truly dreamy segue into dinner, ask the Wolters's son, Ben, to take you for a ride in the inn's vis-à-vis—a Cinderella-style horse-drawn carriage.

Tips *The cottages—especially the Hayloft, which has a private garden with a pond—are more romantic than the inn rooms. With notice of a day or two, the inn's owners will whip up a three-course meal for you.*

🛏 6 rooms, 5 cottages ❙◯❙ Full breakfast, dining room, kitchens. **Recreation:** fishing, sledding. Nearby: bird-watching, hiking, rock climbing, lake swimming, boating, 18-hole golf course, tennis courts, ballooning, miniature golf, playground. **Services:** massage, meeting rooms, business services, Internet access. ♿ Some satellite TVs, in-room VCRs/DVDs, some pets allowed (fee); no smoking 💳 $125–$250 ⊟ D, MC, V.

🏠 *310 N. Campbell Rd., Landrum, SC 29356* ☎ *864/895–4968 or 864/ 909–1575* 📠 *864/895–4968 *51* ⊕ *www.theredhorseinn.com.*

RICE HOPE PLANTATION
Tranquil Outpost

The back roads that lead here from 40-mi-distant Charleston travel through stands of pine, across rivers, alongside marshy creeks, and past little country towns. When you arrive in the Low Country at the sprawling, two-story Rice Hope, its circular driveway and grounds shaded by gigantic oaks dripping with moss, you're likely to be greeted by the heehaws of Chico, the inn's resident donkey. You'll probably spot the peacocks just about the time Lucy the dog comes tearing around the corner.

On about 7 acres on the edge of the Cooper River, Rice Hope is a former rice plantation. The original part of the house dates to 1840; additions were made in the early 1900s. Though paint and wallpaper are peeling in some places and the windows need washing, there is an authentic, genteel shabbiness to the inn. It is filled with antiques, worn Oriental rugs, and a motley collection of vintage artifacts. The library, with a porch off to one side, houses finds from local shipwrecks and objects picked up around the grounds—porcelain fragments, field hoes, locks, and parts of the old rice trunks that controlled water levels in the fields. The inn has four working fireplaces, and many rooms overlook the river and gardens, including the dining room, where a bird theme prevails—down to the details on china, candlesticks, and paintings. In the guest rooms, throw rugs cover the hardwood floors; the suite has a huge sitting room and a private porch.

Your hosts—owner Lou Edens, her son Jamie, and daughter-in-law Katie—add warmth and humor. Jamie tends the barnyard animals, propagates seedlings, and cooks a mighty breakfast with fresh eggs he gathers from the chickens.

Rice Hope advertises that it's "inconveniently located in the middle of nowhere," but that doesn't mean there's nothing to do. The inn's patio, its bricks edged with green moss, leads you into a garden of 200-year-old camellia and azalea bushes. The garden, in turn, slopes down to a waterfront swing beneath a canopy of huge oaks. You can take a canoe or kayak out to the former rice fields, now a shallow, swamp-like ecosystem, or walk to Childsbury, a 90-acre historic site where a village thrived in pre-Revolutionary times. Or take a short drive to peaceful Mepkin Abbey, also a former rice plantation, whose friendly monks welcome visitors to their sweeping, well-tended riverfront gardens.

A quarter-million acres of swamps, huge oaks, and little lakes (thought to have been formed by falling meteors), nearby Francis Marion and Sumter National Forest is the habitat of deer, wild turkeys, bobcats, and the red-cockaded woodpeckers; trees with woodpecker nests are marked. Miles of hiking, horseback riding, and cycling trails meander through the preserve; one leads to a shell mound that marks the site of a former Indian village.

But you don't have to go anywhere at all. It's enough just to sit on the patio, looking out over the water, watching the wind make the Spanish moss dance languidly on outstretched oak limbs, and listening to the woodpeckers. At dusk the peacock parade begins as, one by one, young peacocks follow their mother into the front yard's oak tree to roost.

Tip *The area's quiet back roads and hidden historic sites are great for biking—but bring your own. There are no rentals in the vicinity.*

5 rooms Full breakfast, picnic area. **Recreation:** bird-watching, fishing, running, wildlife viewing, canoeing, kayaking, tennis court, badminton, basketball, boccie, horseshoes, library. Nearby: hiking, horseback riding, river swimming, scuba diving. **Services:** canoes and kayaks provided, dock, Internet access. In-room VCRs; no phones in some rooms, no smoking $110–$155 AE, MC, V.

206 Rice Hope Dr., Moncks Corner, SC 29461 800/569–4038 *843/884–5020 www.ricehope.com.*

South Dakota

THE BARN BED & BREAKFAST
Tranquil Outpost

When this bright red barn was built in the south-central part of South Dakota in 1924, the surrounding country was thoroughly rural. The nearest town, Geddes, was 3 mi away, and even the few neighboring farms were a mile distant. Since then, some things have changed. The barn has been completely renovated and, instead of lodging horses and dairy cows, it now houses a four-room inn. The stables of the lower levels are gone; scythes and leather saddles that once lay on wooden rails, waiting for their next use, now serve as decoration. However, much is still the same—neighbors are far and few between, the roads are dirt, and Geddes (population 252) is the nearest town.

The worn wood posts of a tie stall, once used to keep livestock from running away, now separate the kitchen from the dining room, where you breakfast on eggs, bacon, pancakes, waffles, and almost anything else you'd care to order. A lounge upstairs has plenty of seating and a satellite television, and the open loft above it has a kitchenette, several beds, a pool table, and board games. The adjacent four bedrooms are furnished with antiques and themed. For example, you'll find a saddle, spurs, and a bridle in the Cowboy Room and a dream catcher and star quilt in the Native American Room. Privacy is paramount at The Barn. Although you can opt for a one-room rental, innkeeper Judy Parker offers inexpensive packages that give you the run of the entire bed-and-breakfast for your stay.

Once the sun comes up, wander over to the grove of mulberry and plum trees and pick some ripe fruit. If you'd like to get to know the farm's animals, you can feed the potbellied pigs, or spend some time with Leroy the miniature donkey and Buford the pony, who wander the farmyard like faithful dogs. Or, if you want to try your hand at farmwork, go and pick eggs from the roosts in the henhouse. You are free to do any of this on your own, though the staff is happy to help if you ask.

You can explore the surrounding farmland on foot or by bike, which you can rent in Mitchell (70 mi northeast) or Sioux Falls (140 mi northeast). Or visit the banks of the Missouri just 5 mi down the road. Take your fishing poles and spend the afternoon under a tree catching walleye and trout in the Mighty 'Mo, or grab a swimsuit and dive into the lazy waters. A 20-mi drive south brings you to Lake Francis Case, where developed beaches and picnic areas are plentiful and uncrowded. Several Hutterite colonies are nearby, as well. The Hutterites, part of South Dakotan culture since 1870, value simple living in harmony with the land (although with some kinds of technology); they live communally and regard farming as very important. You can take a tour of one of these colonies—pick up some fresh produce and meat while you're there, bring it back to The Barn, and you can grill dinner on the back porch.

Tip *In August Geddes celebrates Fur Traders Day with go-kart races, a rodeo, and an antique-tractor pull.*

 4 rooms Full breakfast, dining room, lobby lounge, grills, picnic area, kitchenette. **Recreation:** biking, bird-watching, hiking, horseback riding, running, wildlife viewing, cross-country skiing, billiards. Nearby: fishing, beach, river swimming, lake swimming, waterskiing, boating. **Services:** horse boarding, kennel. Some pets allowed; no a/c in some rooms, no room phones, no room TVs, no smoking $75 MC, V.

 37191 284th St., Geddes, SD 57342 605/337–2483 www.bbonline. com/sd/thebarn.

BLACK HILLS HIDEAWAY BED & BREAKFAST
Tranquil Outpost

When George Armstrong Custer led an army expedition through the Black Hills in 1874, he set into motion a series of events that would drive the Lakota Sioux from their lands, spark the country's last great gold rush, and lead to his own death. But out of the turmoil was born one of the Wild West's legendary boomtowns: Deadwood, in the extreme western part of the state. Miners, muleskinners, madams, gunslingers, and gamblers flocked to this wild and woolly settlement, forging wagon trails through the rocky gulches and piney hillsides. Black Hills Hideaway sits along one of these ancient roads, tucked away in the ponderosa forest but only 7 mi from bustling Deadwood.

Although this mountain chalet is mammoth, the 67 acres of creek-carved canyons, soaring granite cliffs, and towering trees that surround it make it feel smaller. The countryside is well suited for hiking or mountain biking, and owners Kathy and Ned Bode supply complimentary bikes and directions for the chalet's forest or to the surrounding Black Hills National Forest, a 1.2-million-acre emerald oasis that rises from the plains of South Dakota and Wyoming. An alpine-meadow golf course, two ski slopes, snowmobile trails, caves, the Badlands, and Mount Rushmore are only a short drive away.

The chalet's guest rooms have amenities like a whirlpool tub in the bathroom or a private deck with a hot tub. There are no televisions in the rooms (though there is one in the living room), nor are there telephones (though you may request one). Each room is simply and pleasantly decorated in a different motif—Asian or Caribbean or southwestern or European. The fanciest rooms evoke the Black Hills with pine furniture, wrought-iron details, and fireplaces.

Breakfast here is typically hearty and western—thick pancakes, meats, eggs, and fruit. Depending on the season, you can sit outside on the deck or in the dining room. The staff will pack you a small sack lunch for an additional fee, if you wish—a smart option if you want to spend the day exploring. Refreshments are provided every evening, so you can relax with a drink and hors d'oeuvres by the fireplace at day's end.

Deadwood, on the National Register of Historic Places, has been meticulously restored, and now looks as it did during the gold rush, its brick streets lined with Victorian facades. Museums, art shows, and costumed Wild West actors entertain you during the day, and casinos, saloons, and concerts make the nightlife hot.

Tip *The owners of Black Hills Hideaway also keep a cabin on a large lake several miles to the south. The Bodes' Abode on Pactola Lake sleeps two to six people and has a kitchen, a washer and dryer, a deck, and a TV with a VCR. There is a two-night minimum stay.*

⮌ 8 rooms ⧖ Full breakfast, dining room, lobby lounge. **Recreation:** bird-watching, hiking, mountain biking, running, wildlife viewing, sledding. Nearby: horseback riding, rock climbing, indoor pool, lake swimming, tubing (water), waterskiing, boating, jet skiing, rowing, 9-hole golf course, 2 tennis courts, cross-country skiing, downhill skiing, snowmobiling, basketball, billiards, horseshoes, miniature golf, softball, volleyball, playground. **Services:** mountain bikes provided. ♿ Some jetted tubs; no room phones, no room TVs, no smoking ▱ $105–$179 ▭ MC, V, D.

🏠 11744 Hideway Rd., Deadwood, SD 57732 ☎ 605/578–3054 🖷 605/578–2028 ⊕ www.enetis.net/~hideaway.

SYLVAN LAKE LODGE
Family Hideout

Sylvan Lake has been the crown jewel of the Black Hills since 1895, when the region's first hotel was built only yards from the shoreline. About 7 mi north of Custer in the central Black Hills, it was a favorite haunt for South Dakota's upper class until a fire burned the structure to the ground 40 years later. Architect Frank Lloyd Wright heard about the tragedy and came here to design a new resort. Wright chose a location high in the trees above the lake, but before he could draft plans, political bickering forced him to withdraw from the project.

Although the new wood-and-stone Sylvan Lake Lodge wasn't designed by Wright, it sits in his suggested location above the lakeshore, facing a breathtaking panorama of sapphire waters and towering Harney Peak. The stone veranda that snakes around the lodge's back side has some of the best views in the Black Hills. Above, the canopy of stars is just as magnificent after dark.

Next to the veranda, the dining room serves pheasant breast, buffalo prime rib, and grilled trout. Trophy mounts keep watch over the nearby lobby, which also contains a stone fireplace, wrought-iron chandeliers, and buffalo leather couches.

Decorated much like those in a mid-range hotel, rooms upstairs sleep up to six people. The cabins, just down from the lodge near the lakeshore, are similarly furnished. More like small log homes, most cabins have a kitchen, and a porch where you can eat while admiring the lake and the evening sky. Although all rooms and cabins have TVs, you may never turn yours on. After all, Sylvan Lake Lodge is at the heart of 71,000-acre Custer State Park, South Dakota's premier outdoor playground.

The park's hiking paths to the top of Harney Peak, the highest point in the United States east of the Rockies, begin from Sylvan Lake. The trail to Harney connects with others that lead around the Needles, sheer granite spires that attract serious rock climbers from all over the country. Area outfitters, who cater to novices and experts alike, often teach classes here. The park's thick forests and grassy meadows are home to bison, elk, antelope, bighorn sheep, mountain goats, deer, wild turkeys, and a small pack of friendly burros. Park rangers run nature hikes, gold-panning trips, candle-making demonstrations, and woodcutting classes. Locally there are also chuck-wagon suppers, short horseback trips, and mountain biking. You can take a jeep safari to see bison or take in a musical at the Black Hills Playhouse, a log auditorium in the pines.

Tip *From the Honeymoon Cabin's isolated perch on a ledge above the lake, the sight of morning's pink light dancing across the granite Needles is unforgettable.*

🛏 35 rooms, 31 cabins 🍴 Snack bar, restaurant, room service, lobby lounge, grocery store, picnic area, some kitchens, some kitchenettes, some microwaves, some refrigerators. **Recreation:** bird-watching, fishing, hiking, wildlife viewing, beach, lake swimming, rowing. Nearby: horseback riding, mountain biking, rock climbing. **Services:** rowing rentals, guided fishing trips, tackle shop, laundry facilities, laundry service, shop, meeting rooms. **Classes and programs:** guided hikes, natural history programs, photo safaris, fly-fishing lessons, children's programs (ages 7–12). ☖ Some pets allowed (fee), no smoking; no a/c in cabins ▦ $95–$235 ▭ AE, D, MC, V.

⌂ HC 83 (Box 74), Custer, SD 57730 ☎ 605/255–4772 or 800/658–3530 🖷 605/255–4706 ⊕ www.custerresorts.com.

VALIANT VINEYARDS AT BUFFALO RUN RESORT
Tranquil Outpost

Hundreds of thousands of acres of farmland dominate largely flat eastern South Dakota, producing everything from corn and wheat to soybeans and sugar beets. With crops planted in rows that stretch to the horizon, it's difficult to tell one farm from the next. However, outside the town of Vermillion in the far southeastern corner of the state, 6 oddball acres of fertile farmland on a bluff above the Missouri and Vermillion rivers grow a fruit not usually found in this snowy northern climate. Grape vines creep along the stone pathways and up the short fences at Valiant Vineyards, South Dakota's first winery.

When "cold-hearty" grapes, bred to withstand cold winters, were introduced to the Dakotas in the early 1990s, Valiant Vineyards (named for one of the grape species) was among the first to grow the fruit. In 2000 the concern moved its operations to this ridge above the Missouri River and built a Bavarian-style winery with banquet rooms, a restaurant, and a bed-and-breakfast. The Vineyard produces several different red, white, blush, and dessert wines, some flavored with wild berries.

Although the B&B looks old and weathered, the interior sparkles. Here, Europe meets the American West. Faux-marble columns, cherry-finished end tables, and brass candelabra contrast with unfinished pine chairs and bronzed wild mustangs. A mural of charging buffalo keeps company with leather furniture, stone planters carved with grapes, and log pine tables draped with white tablecloths and topped with large glass vases of fresh seasonal flowers.

Each of the five bedrooms has its own theme. Three have a more antique feel, and two are more contemporary. The Native American room features modern furniture with contemporary American Indian art, and the USD room shows off University of South Dakota memorabilia. Bathrooms are distinctly modern, as are the amenities. All but one room comes with a whirlpool tub, candles, and a bucket for chilling wine, and you can arrange for a massage in your room.

Daily winery tours explain the wine-making process and end with tastings. Afterward, you can relax on the porch with a bottle of one of the vineyard's creations, or find your own private spot in the vineyard and have a picnic. Either way, you're guaranteed an excellent view of the river below and the Nebraskan farmland beyond. Or your hosts at Valiant can have Missouri River Expeditions take you down the Mighty 'Mo in a kayak or canoe on a half-day, full-day, or multi-day trip. Some guides are trained ornithologists, astronomers, or Native American researchers and give educational talks in the evening.

Valiant's very own bistro serves lunch and dinner by request for groups of 10 or more. For dinner, take the 2-mi stroll or bike ride into the town of Vermillion (population 9,765). While you're there, walk around the University of South Dakota campus; its W. H. Over Museum houses the state's largest collection of artifacts relating to South Dakota's natural and cultural history.

Tip *Make an appointment in advance to tour the winery. Tours are generally at 10:30 AM and 3 PM except holidays.*

⇨ 5 rooms ⏺ Full breakfast, dining room, restaurant, lobby lounge. **Recreation:** biking, bird-watching, hiking, running, wildlife viewing. Nearby: fishing, river swimming, canoeing, kayaking. **Services:** massage, shop, meeting rooms. ⟁ Cable TV; no smoking ▱ $95–$105 ▱ AE, D, MC, V.

⬁ *1500 W. Main St., Vermillion, SD 57069* ☎ *605/624–4117* 🖶 *605/624–8823* ⊕ *www.buffalorunwinery.com/*

WAKPAMNI BED & BREAKFAST
Romantic Retreat

The Wakpamni Bed & Breakfast occupies the southern edge of the Pine Ridge Indian Reservation, in southwesternmost South Dakota, 2 mi from the Nebraska border. Still the working family farm of innkeeper Larry Swick, the Wakpamni is made up of several structures. The Folks House, a Depression-era farmhouse, is now a three-bedroom guest home. The Main House is newer and larger, with more elaborately decorated rooms. Behind the houses are three tepees where you can sleep. A small gallery sells western and Native American art.

The dominant feature of the inn, however, is its garden. In the vast stretch of grasslands along the Nebraska border, trees and blossoming flowers are few and far between. If the average rainfall here were a fraction of an inch less, this isolated region would be desert. Yet Larry, a farmer, and his wife, Betty, have cultivated a flourishing collection of towering cottonwoods, spruces, and junipers, as well as a sizable garden of bright flowers. Paths encourage you to stroll—and the scattered chairs or benches invite a snooze.

Rooms are furnished with antiques. A few rooms honor the farmers and pioneers from whom Larry descended; the Lakota Room is dedicated to the people who first inhabited the land. The only room with a king-size bed, the Lakota Room is also the most lavish; the art that covers the walls—pipes of medicine men, sacred buffalo skulls—reflects the culture of the Oglala Sioux, the people who govern the reservation. The tepees behind the houses bring you closer to nature and give you a taste of the culture native to the region as well. They are for the most part traditional, but not entirely: the floors are wood rather than dirt, and king-size bedding can be provided on request.

Guest rooms are stocked with locally flavored reading material—books on Lakota culture in the Lakota Room, a book of cowboy humor in the Cowboy Room. You can find more to read, as well as a satellite television, in each house's common room. The common room of the larger Main House also has a piano and pool table.

A few miles away from the inn, you're in the center of the Oglala Sioux Nation. There are powwows, rodeos, and festivals almost every weekend in summer. Unless you're a Lakota, you'll find that you're in the minority here. Visitors occasionally observe the cultural celebrations, but Pine Ridge isn't a major destination; these are Lakota ways, and nothing is catered for tourists. However, the Swicks are happy to explain local customs and tell you about upcoming celebrations.

If you want to get even farther away from civilization, drive about 1½ hours north from the inn to Badlands National Park—the preserve of rattlesnakes, coyotes, a few stray buffalo, and the occasional sagebrush.

Tip *Despite temperatures in the 90s and 100s, August is a good time to visit if you want to see the modern Lakota way of life. The first weekend of the month brings the annual Oglala Nation Powwow and Rodeo in nearby Pine Ridge. Also from June to August, the Red Cloud Indian School Art Show attracts well-known Native American artists from all over the United States and Canada.*

🛏6 rooms, 3 tepees 🍽Dining room, lobby lounge. **Recreation:** birdwatching, hiking, horseback riding, running, wildlife viewing, library, piano, recreation room. **Services:** Lakota tour guide, exercise room, outdoor hot tub, shop. **Classes and programs:** horseback-riding lessons. ♿ No room phones, no room TVs, no kids under 12, no smoking 💳 $60–$100 ▭ AE, MC, V, D.

📧 *HC 64 (Box 43), Batesland, SD 57716* ☎ *605/288–1800* 📠 *605/288–1868* 🌐 *www.wakpamni.com.*

Tennessee

BLACKBERRY FARM
Family Hideout ~ Luxurious Resort

If you like your nature in measured doses accompanied by generous helpings of creature comfort, Blackberry Farm might be the perfect country getaway. In the foothills of the Great Smoky Mountains, 25 mi from Knoxville, Sam Beall has created a retreat that resembles an English country estate, all wildflower meadows and wooded hillsides, promising ever-so-civilized relaxation.

Topped with gables and stone chimneys and bulging with copper-roofed bay windows, the two-story stone inn looks like a large Georgian cottage. Pathways through the semiformal flower garden invite strolling. From the veranda, you have a fine view of the forest, which is especially lovely when the maples and hickories turn crimson and gold in fall. Inside, the common room is furnished with easy chairs and warmed by a fireplace. Guest rooms, decorated with chintz, have fluffy featherbeds. On the walls hang oil paintings of English scenes. Curtained windows overlook the manicured grounds. Exuberant fresh flower arrangements add a finishing touch.

Three times a day, southern-inspired cuisine is served in a wood-paneled dining room hung with English hunt paintings. At breakfast, choices include blackberry griddle cakes and cornmeal pudding with maple cream cheese. Lunch might be sweet tea–brined fried chicken or grilled quail. For dinner, consider pumpkin seed–crusted pork tenderloin, tea-smoked rack of lamb, or marsala-marinated breast of Muscovy duck. There is also a chef's tasting menu. Whatever you order, you can pair it with a bottle from the extensive wine cellar.

When you're not eating, you can explore the farm's 4,200 acres, hiking the trails that crisscross the property. Or hire a gentle Rocky Mountain horse, specially bred for mountain riding, from the stables and see the land from horseback. Between late March and mid-October, seek out the meadows carpeted in wildflowers. Or polish your casting skills in a fly-fishing lesson and let expert fishing guides show you the best trout streams. They may even take you there on horseback. Not up for anything strenuous? Have a game of croquet.

Your kids can have fun, too, at Camp Blackberry during family time and holidays. Supervised activities such as cooking classes, scavenger hunts, swimming, and fishing keep young ones busy while you sign up at the cooking school or go for some serious pampering in the Farmhouse Spa, housed in an 1870s farmhouse. Have a facial or a full-body treatment with blackberry-infused moisturizer. Relaxation, deep tissue, and hot stone massages are also available, in the farmhouse or in the comfort of your room.

Tip *The inn frequently hosts wine-tasting dinners and guest chef dinners. Sign up for the mailing list to receive updates.*

↩ 23 rooms, 16 suites, 2 cottages ⑩ American plan, restaurant, room service, some kitchens. **Recreation:** biking, bird-watching, fishing, hiking, horseback riding, mountain biking, running, wildlife viewing, pool, 4 tennis courts, basketball, croquet, volleyball. **Services:** spa, guided fishing trips, tackle shop, laundry service, shops, airport shuttle, business services, Internet services, meeting rooms. **Classes and programs:** guided nature walks, children's programs (ages 3–12), cooking classes. ♿ In-room data ports, some in-room fireplaces; no smoking ▦ $645–$1,145 ▭ AE, MC, V.

⌂ *1471 West Millers Cove Rd., Walland, TN 37886* ☎ *865/984–8166* 📠 *865/681–7753* ⊕ *www.blackberryfarm.com.*

BUCKHORN INN
Tranquil Outpost

On 25 private acres less than a mile from the entrance to Great Smoky Mountains National Park, Buckhorn Inn has welcomed visitors since 1938. The meadows and pine-and-hemlock forest that hide the inn from the outside world also shelter deer, raccoons, and other wildlife. Ducks float on the pond while thrushes and wrens fill the woods with their music. After dark, the cries of owls and whippoorwills drift through the night air.

On the inn's grounds, there's a wooded trail through the woods that takes about one hour to walk. Markers name trees and shrubs along the path, including one that you may not know: Fragrant Cloud, a rare dogwood variety, was discovered by the inn's founder, Douglas Bebb, who gave it the evocative name. Continue on your walk and listen to the frogs at a deep mountain pond. In a meadow of wildflowers is Rachael's Labyrinth. One of the largest meditation labyrinths in the United States, the native fieldstone pathway is 60 feet in diameter. Starting at its outside edge, walk the circular route to the center while insects and birds twitter all around you.

The two-story, white clapboard inn presents a rather plain face, but it's surrounded by azaleas, dogwoods, and other flowering trees and shrubs. Matching cottages are arranged along walkways a few yards away. The spacious guest rooms have contemporary furnishings, with brightly patterned bedspreads and upholstery. Some bedsteads are brass. Several rooms, in both the inn and the cottages, have a working fireplace and a Jacuzzi. In the inn's main room, a stone fireplace warms a sitting area, and a book-lined wall overlooks a grand piano where impromptu sing-alongs sometimes break out. At the other end of the room is the dining area, where you can eat a hearty country breakfast or lunch while taking in a view of Mt. LaConte, the highest peak in Tennessee.

The evening meal is a four-course affair that might include panfried rainbow trout and summer greens or rack of lamb with roasted potatoes. Desserts, such as peach-blueberry tart and triple chocolate pudding pie, have a strong southern accent. After dinner, settle into one of the rocking chairs on the covered flagstone terrace and watch the sky melt from russet to indigo over the mountaintops. As the heavens fade to black, millions of glittering stars appear, undimmed by city lights.

Less than a mile from the inn, Great Smoky Mountains National Park fairly bursts with more than 100 species of trees and shrubs. Approximately 120,000 acres are old-growth forest, and groves of rhododendron line the mountain ridges. On the 800 mi of trails and along the several scenic drives, you might see ruffled grouse, wild turkeys, and white-tailed deer. You can rent a horse or a bike for trail riding, go fishing below a waterfall, or join one of the many excellent ranger programs offered daily. And as afternoon slips into evening, you can catch a whiff of wood smoke from the campgrounds as you make your way back to the inn.

Tip *Buckhorn Inn doesn't serve wine, beer, or spirits, but you may BYO. Visit in April and you can smell the special dogwoods.*

9 rooms, 7 cottages, 3 guesthouses ❙◎❙ Dining room, some microwaves, some refrigerators. **Recreation:** bird-watching, fishing, hiking, wildlife viewing, library, piano. Nearby: biking, horseback riding. **Services:** business services, Internet access. Some in-room fireplaces, in-room VCRs, some jetted tubs; no smoking $115–$160 AE, D, MC, V.

2140 Tudor Mountain Rd., Gatlinburg, TN 37738 ☎ *865/436–4668 or 866/941–0460* 🖷 *865/436–5009* ⊕ *www.buckhorninn.com.*

FALL CREEK FALLS STATE RESORT PARK
Laid-Back Adventure

One of the tallest waterfalls east of the Rockies, Fall Creek Falls shoots over the edge of a cliff and plunges 256 feet to a sheltered pool below. Nearby, rushing streams carve gorges in the dense woodland, and cascades tumble over rocky outcroppings. In the humid, shady gorges, hemlock and tulip poplar replace the oak and hickory that grow on the ridges. Mountain laurel and rhododendron blanket the hillsides with flowers in spring and cover them with deep green foliage the rest of the year in 21,000-acre Fall Creek Falls State Resort Park.

Give yourself a few days—or longer—to soak up the views and the fresh air by booking one of the park's cabins or a room at the Fall Creek Falls Inn. The contemporary glass-and-wood inn is perched on the edge of the park's 350-acre lake. Rooms are standard hotel-style, but most have a wall of sliding glass doors that open onto a private balcony or patio overlooking Fall Creek Lake. Cabins, which are equipped with kitchens and grills plus working fireplaces, stand lakefront or on a hillside overlooking the lake. Each has a small deck and can sleep 8 to 10. In the inn's large, casual restaurant, food is southern-style—biscuits and gravy, grits, and sausage at breakfast and fried catfish and chicken at lunch and dinner. In season, blackberry or peach cobbler may be on the dessert menu.

Well-marked trails, ranging from relatively flat and easy to steep and challenging, lead to scenic overlooks in the park. The Woodland Trail is the main route to the Nature Center (where you can learn about the flora, fauna, and geology of the park) and to Fall Creek Falls Overlook. From the Nature Center, the Paw Paw Trail climbs a hill to excellent views of Cane Creek Falls and Cane Creek Gulf, before looping back to its starting place. Follow Piney Falls trail to a spot where you can watch Piney Falls; then head back across a swinging wood-and-rope bridge over a deep, tree-lined gorge. You can pedal a paved 3-mi bike path or two mountain-bike trails, or challenge yourself on the 18-hole forest-rimmed golf course. Rent pedal boats or canoes to explore the lake, and you may spot a kingfisher skimming along just above the water or hawks perched on overhanging tree branches.

Tip *Watch out for poison ivy—it's prevalent throughout the park.*

 145 rooms, 20 cabins, 10 villas Snack bar, restaurant, grills, picnic area, some kitchens. **Recreation:** biking, bird-watching, fishing, hiking, mountain biking, wildlife viewing, pool, canoeing, 18-hole golf course, recreation room, video game room. **Services:** bike rental (April–October), pro shop. **Classes and programs:** guided nature walks, natural history programs. Some in-room fireplaces, private balconies and patios, some pets allowed, no-smoking rooms $64–$200 AE, D, MC, V.

 2009 Village Camp Road, Pikeville, TN 37367 423/881–5298 or 800/250–8610 423/881–5103 www.state.tn.us/environment/parks/ parks/FallCreekFalls.

Texas

BLISSWOOD
Tranquil Outpost

To understand what Blisswood is about, you need only watch owner Carol Davis trot her South American *paso fino* (fine gaited) horse across the lush meadows of her south-central Texas ranch. The horse's resplendent mane and tail ripple in the breeze while a black Labrador retriever lopes nearby. Carol grew up as a fourth-generation Texas rancher but moved to Houston, 65 mi east of here, as an adult. Blisswood's 650 acres of tall grass and oak forest represent a return to the life she has always loved—a life connected to nature.

Blisswood, part of the Lehmann Legacy Ranch near Cat Spring, about 50 mi west of Houston, looks much as it did on April 29, 1872, when the Austin County District Court issued a property deed to the original owner, Julius Cornelius. The centuries-old live oak trees, whose gnarled, twisting branches still shade the property, were witnesses to the history of the Old West. Historical Accommodations of Texas has already recognized the ranch as one of the "great stays of Texas" even though Carol has welcomed guests to her bed-and-breakfast sanctuary only since late 2002. Your privacy is fiercely protected while you're here: you won't even get directions to the ranch until you book.

Accommodations are meticulously maintained houses and cabins, some dating from the 19th century and authentically furnished with country antiques. There is a Southern-style two-story dwelling with a front-porch swing, the dormered Texas Farmhouse, the two-story Log Cabin, the spacious Dog-Trot House with a pool, and the enormously popular one-bedroom Writer's Cabin, snuggled in exquisite seclusion among the oak trees. Each has a porch or deck where you can lounge and gaze out over the ranch. Continental breakfast is provided each morning in your own kitchen. When it's time for lunch or supper you can cook your own or eat in Carol's at Cat Spring Cafe, where chef Doug Atkinson prepares barbecued scallops with creamy grits and green chili broth. Housed in an old agricultural society hall, the restaurant has leather-covered walls. At "branding parties" here, local ranchers bring their cattle brands (some in their families for generations) and sear their marks right into the walls.

Around the ranch are secret gardens where you can sit for hours, ponds where geese glide gracefully, and an arching white bridge that leads to a vine-covered gazebo where country weddings sometimes are conducted. You can roam hay fields surrounded by white picket fences or fish for catch-and-release bass in the ponds. Llamas, miniature donkeys, bison, Corriente cattle, and fallow deer graze in the meadows. A vineyard shelters red and white wine grapes. Horseback riding is popular, and you can take riding lessons on a gentle and well-trained paso fino or thoroughbred horse.

Tip *Need a break from the peace and quiet? Not far away are a collection of early farmhouses, antiques shopping, and an 18-hole golf course.*

🛏 3 cabins, 5 houses, 1 suite ⏹ Continental breakfast, grills, picnic area, kitchens. **Recreation:** biking, bird-watching, fishing, hiking, horseback riding, mountain biking, running, wildlife viewing, pool, lake swimming, swimming hole, rowing, archery, badminton, carriage rides, croquet, horseshoes, sporting clays, board games. Nearby: driving range, 18-hole golf course, putting green, ballooning, hang gliding. **Services:** archery equipment and bicycle rentals, massage, guided fishing trips, babysitting, grocery shopping, horse boarding, kennel, laundry facilities, airport shuttle, business services, Internet access, meeting rooms. **Classes and programs:** guided hikes, guided nature walks, photo safaris, horseback-riding lessons, yoga and cooking classes, history and nature talks. ♿ Some in-room fireplaces, some jetted tubs, private decks, some pets allowed (fee); no room phones, no room TVs, no smoking 💲 $125–$350 💳 MC, V.

🏠 *13300 Lehmann Legacy La., Cat Spring, TX 78933* ☎ *713/301–3235 or 800/753–3376 (weekdays)* 📠 *979/865–8010* 🌐 *www.blisswood.net.*

CANYON OF THE EAGLES LODGE & NATURE PARK
Family Hideout ~ Tranquil Outpost

Every winter, bald eagles nest in the area around 30-mi-long Lake Buchanan, 70 mi northwest of Austin. The lake is popular with boaters and anglers in search of trophy striped bass. But it never seems crowded, especially in the 940-acre nature preserve managed by the Lower Colorado River Authority, which the Texas Legislature established in 1934 for purposes of conservation and land reclamation. The lodge in this preserve is the lake's prime sanctuary for human visitors.

At Canyon of the Eagles Lodge, you can boat, fish, and hike to your heart's content. The Vanishing Texas River Cruise leaves from the dock for lake-to-shore views of waterfalls, cliffs, and birds of the Colorado River Canyon. Feeling lazy? Hang out on the dock or along the 5 mi of private lakeshore. Or gather with family and friends at the barbecue pits and fire pits along the waterfront. Canyon of the Eagles has some of the darkest skies in Texas, so the Austin Astronomical Society hosts several star parties here monthly. The softly glowing electronic lights of the many telescopes can make the observation area resemble a mass UFO landing site. Outdoor lighting is kept low to minimize light pollution.

Tiny lights on your room keys illuminate your way along gravel trails that loop through mesquite, juniper, and other native vegetation to the lakeside lodge and cottages. With their unpretentious elegance, the accommodations here are far superior to the spartan cabins you usually find along recreational lakes. Arranged in clusters, lodge and cottage rooms are furnished with old-fashioned quilts and country furniture. Poured concrete floors are polished to a high sheen and topped with area rugs; canvas curtains and black-and-white photographs of early bird-watchers and explorers complete the uncluttered look. Each room has a covered wooden deck or porch with rocking chairs, where you can take in panoramic views of the shimmering lake.

The lodge's Canyon Room Restaurant puts a Continental twist on Texas favorites with dishes like Texas-style crab cake, or baked Brie with mission-fig chutney. Saturday and Sunday brunch includes traditional choices such as pancakes and exotic fare such as grilled eggplant Benedict.

Your most intimate encounters with the area's special geology, vegetation, and wildlife likely will take place on the five hiking trails through the preserve. White-tailed deer and armadillos might show up as you walk, and you might see endangered birds such as the black-capped vireo and the golden-cheeked warbler. Bird nesting areas may be closed off at certain times of the year, but in winter you're still likely to hear the rush of wings overhead, announcing the arrival of a magnificent northern bald eagle.

Tip *Bring a regular flashlight with you, especially if you plan to make any nighttime excursions around the grounds. Otherwise, you just might trip over an armadillo along the way.*

🔁 64 rooms 🍽 Restaurant, grocery store, grills, picnic area, some microwaves, some refrigerators. **Recreation:** biking, bird-watching, fishing, hiking, mountain biking, running, wildlife viewing, beach, pool, boating, canoeing, kayaking, rowing, sailing, horseshoes, volleyball, recreation room. Nearby: horseback riding, waterskiing, jet skiing. **Services:** canoe, kayak, sailboat, and inner-tube rentals; massage; dock; helipad; tackle shop; babysitting; laundry service; concierge; business services; Internet access; meeting rooms. **Classes and programs:** guided hikes, guided nature walks, natural history programs, photo safaris, canoe races, triathlons, sailing and kayaking lessons, art and crafts classes, photography classes, nature and history talks, movies, sightseeing tours. ⟨⟩ In-room data ports, private terraces, some pets allowed (fee); no room TVs, no smoking ⌷ $10–$179 ⊟ AE, D, MC, V.

⟨⟩ *16942 Ranch Rd. 2341, Burnet, TX 78611* ☎ *512/756–8787 or 800/ 977–0081* 🖷 *512/715–9718* ⊕ *www.canyonoftheeagles.com.*

CHISOS MOUNTAINS LODGE
Laid-Back Adventure

Return guests at Chisos Mountains Lodge know there is only one place in the world where you can see the perfect sunset. It's right here, from the balconies of the west-wing rooms. They overlook one of Big Bend National Park's famous formations—the Window. Ask for one of these rooms (they don't cost extra) and check in before sunset. Then settle into a lounge chair on your balcony and watch the flaming sun sink below a notched mountain peak. If it's been a stormy day, you're in for an especially dazzling view, scented by freshly dampened juniper. A pinpoint of sun breaks through a tiny hole in the clouds. Celestial rays spray in all directions against the dark backdrop. You might be forced to abandon your perch for a few moments to dash out the front door of your room and photograph a radiant rainbow settling upon the main lodge building. Another quick snap of the camera captures a nearby hill glowing red in the waning light. Then it's back to your balcony just in time for the last of the show. A distant, lone tree stands in silhouette as the sky fades to purple.

But don't despair if all of the west-wing rooms are booked. To take in the glorious sunset you can always hike the ½ mi Window View Trail. Chisos Mountains Lodge isn't so much about what it is (a fairly ordinary motel) but about where it is. The only lodge within the almost mind-boggling 801,163-acre expanse of Big Bend National Park stands amid juniper and piñon forest high in the Chisos Basin, about 135 mi from Fort Stockton. You are likely to spot a small white-tailed deer of a breed that lives only within this desert-surrounded "sky island" in the national park and adjacent areas in Mexico. Birders come here to track more than 450 species. Unusual vegetation includes an evergreen called the Texas madrone, whose flesh-colored bark and red berries grow naturally in only a couple of spots in the United States—the Chihuahuan Desert of Big Bend and Guadalupe Mountains National Park in West Texas.

Rooms at the lodge are not distinctive, except, of course, for their views. But they are relatively inexpensive and well maintained, with decorative touches such as prints of blooming cacti on walls. The six stone cottage rooms don't differ that much from other accommodations, except that they are a bit larger and have three double beds. The lodge restaurant has both basic American and a few more creative menu items—fresh mint leaves flavor the chocolate mousse—but its real specialty is the view. Some of the finest views appear in spring, when the desert plants flower.

Besides hiking some of the trails from the lodge through the forested area for views of valleys below, check out the park's Santa Elena Canyon Trail, accessible via Ross Maxwell Scenic Drive or Old Maverick Road, 8 mi west of Castolon. This almost 2-mi round-trip crosses Terlingua Creek for a view of steep cliffs jutting from the Rio Grande. Birders consider the Rio Grande Village Campground a must-see: colorful visitors such as the scarlet vermilion flycatcher flit among groves of cottonwood trees. Outfitters based in nearby Terlingua and Lajitas offer four-wheel-drive excursions, river rafting, mountain-bike touring, horseback riding, and guided hikes. Park rangers conduct daily slide shows, talks, and walks featuring natural or cultural history.

Tip *The rare colima warbler has only one home in the United States, right here in the Chisos Basin near the lodge. Look for a white eye ring and dark gray head as you hike trails into higher elevations, where the warbler is found. If you plan to visit, book as much as a year in advance. By contrast, you can usually walk in without a reservation in summer since the sometimes intense heat is considered the off-season.*

🛏 72 rooms ❚◯❚ Restaurant, grocery store, mini-refrigerators, microwaves. **Recreation:** bird-watching, hiking, running, wildlife viewing. Nearby: biking, fishing, horseback riding, mountain biking, rafting. **Services:** Shop. ♿ Some private balconies; no room phones, no room TVs, no smoking 🚭 $76–$94 (per person) 🖃 AE, D, DC, M, V.

✉ *Basin Rural Station, Big Bend National Park, TX 79834* ☎ *432/477–2291* 📠 *432/477–2352* ⊕ *www.chisosmountainslodge.com.*

CIBOLO CREEK RANCH
Luxurious Resort

In no way is this west Texas property, on the National Register of Historic Places, a typical guest ranch. Don't expect organized sing alongs around the campfire, staged cattle roundups, or other dude ranch clichés—although there are trail rides. There are no family-oriented activities or children's programs. Nor does Cibolo Creek Ranch maintain a huge staff to cater to your every whim. Nonetheless, facilities are decidedly upscale, and the guests are often A-list. The ranch—which is 3½ hours from Midland/Odessa and El Paso—does no significant marketing or advertising, relying instead on word-of-mouth to attract the likes of Julia Roberts, Bruce Willis, Tommy Lee Jones, and Mick Jagger. But even these celebrities likely carry their own baggage, because there are no porters. Sure, a wrangler might dash over to assist if your load of luggage is huge. But Cibolo Creek is, after all, a real working ranch, sprawled across a breathtakingly immense 30,000 acres. You're in for a real ranch experience in glorious isolation.

Most working ranches, though, don't have the ultra-sophisticated flourishes of the fortlike structures here. Lodgings stand where the ranch's original owner built forts in the 19th century to ward off attacks from Indians and bandits. The main lodge building and hacienda, El Cibolo, has 22 guest rooms that were built from the ruins of an original fort. La Cienega, which has its own chef and 12 bedrooms around a courtyard, has cottonwood beam ceilings and the original adobe walls of an old fort. In both El Cibolo and La Cienega, kiva fireplaces, handmade quilts, wrought-iron beds, and Mexican and Spanish antiques give each room distinction. Telephones and televisions are in common areas; El Cibolo has a fully equipped guest office.

All alone in its own small valley several miles from the hacienda, La Morita is a primitive one-bedroom cottage lighted only with oil lamps. A propane-powered stove can supply heat, but there is no electricity—hence, no air-conditioning and no real kitchen facilities. The cottage is, however, furnished with the same southwestern touches found in the regular accommodations. It also has hot and cold running water and a bathroom. You can drive several miles to La Cienega for meals or request that the chef provide seasoned meats that you can grill outside the cottage. Some honeymooners prefer this cottage, because not even the housekeeping staff comes by unless requested.

Included with your room rate are six daily meals. When you consider the superb quality of food served here, the room rate seems almost a bargain. Dinner might include mesquite-grilled antelope or quail, topped off with a dessert of chocolate fondant. In the dining rooms and other common areas, vigas carved from cottonwood warm the ceilings. While you lounge in the day room and porch in the main hacienda you'll have views of the ranch and its small, spring-fed lake without the inconvenience of sweating, shivering, or swatting insects. The ranch's own museum display artifacts of early pioneers and Native Americans in the Big Bend area.

You can ride horseback with a wrangler. You also can take a guided trail ride or jeep tour, or try your hand at skeet shooting. On a hot day, you might prefer just to doze in a pedal boat on the property's small lake. After dinner in the evenings, you can sit around a campfire. Not far away are Big Bend National Park, the McDonald Observatory at Fort Davis, and the town of Marfa (home of the Marfa Lights phenomenon).

Tip *Ask the staff where you can find Native American relics, such as ancient pictographs, around the property.*

🛏 34 rooms, 1 cottage ⏹ American plan, dining room, bar, picnic area. **Recreation:** biking, bird-watching, fishing, hiking, horseback riding, mountain biking, running, wildlife viewing, beach, 2 pools, billiards, sporting clays, board games, library, recreation room, videocassette library. **Services:** bicycles, pedal boats, and shotguns (for skeet shooting) provided; ATV rentals; rifle and pistol range; spa; exercise room; 2 outdoor hot tubs; massage; airstrip; helipad; laundry facilities; shop; airport shuttle; business services; Internet access; meeting rooms. **Classes and programs:** guided hikes, guided nature walks, natural history programs, off-road tours, photo safaris, movies, sightseeing tours. ♿ In-room fireplaces, some jetted tubs, some private terraces, some pets allowed (fee); no room phones, no room TVs, no smoking 💳 $450–$600 ▭ AE, D, DC, MC, V.

✉ *HCR 67 (Box 44), Marfa, TX 79843* ☎ *432/229–3737 or 866/496– 9460* 🖷 *432/229–3653* ⊕ *www.cibolocreekranch.com.*

THE INN ABOVE ONION CREEK
Romantic Retreat

When you pull onto this inn's one-lane country road off Highway 150 in Hill Country, about 25 mi southwest of Austin and about 45 mi northeast of San Antonio, you start to ponder: what mystery lies beyond the dense veil of oak trees and cedar elms? A flurry of color greets you when you reach the Inn Above Onion Creek as hundreds of butterflies flit among the gardens and greenery. Inside, a glass of decaf raspberry iced tea awaits in the dining-and-kitchen area. While you sip this refreshing cooler you feel your shoulders straighten and relax.

Up in your second-story room, you can see views of distant hills and meadows. The plump, soft featherbed beckons—when was the last time you took an afternoon nap? Filled with whimsical decorative touches such as country hats, an antique desk, and fresh flowers, most rooms have a two-way gas fireplace, a huge jetted tub, and a separate shower. Separate from the inn in its own wooded area is the two-bedroom, two-bath Thelma's House, which accommodates up to six in style. Painted concrete floors give way to wall-to-wall carpeting in the bedrooms. You can sit and read in absolute solitude for hours on the covered porch. The house has a full kitchen and a trail to the inn, where meals are served. At dinner, the menu includes organically grown okra, eggplant, and other luscious treats picked fresh from the inn's garden. Organic produce also comes from local farmers. It's part of the inn's "green" mission, which also includes water conservation through means such as drip irrigation, spare water use, and recycling.

Be sure to explore the trails on the inn's 100 unspoiled acres of meadows and trees. One leads to Onion Creek itself. Some friendly cattle might greet you along the way and even follow you a short distance in hopes you've arrived to feed them. Circling back to the lodge, stop by the garden, where a black-and-white cat reclines in a gazebo constructed of rough-hewn sticks. Scarlet hollyhock and fragrant, yellow honeysuckles are in bloom in spring, and lush roses and yellow and orange cosmos grace the gardens throughout the summer.

Except for dormant months, primarily December and January, the garden flutters with queen butterflies, who resemble monarchs with their brilliant orange wings thickly lined in black. John Orr, who owns the inn along with his wife, Janie, has made sure the creatures have a good home here. Following his lifelong passion for butterflies, he designed the garden specifically to attract these colorful visitors. Birds such as western kingbirds and purple martins also find the garden attractive.

If you are a garden aficionado, consider driving 25 mi northeast to Austin to visit the Lady Bird Johnson Wildflower Center (4801 LaCross Ave., 512/292–4100), where nature trails give access to 60 acres of hill country terrain bursting with more than 500 different native plant species and flowers. Or just stay around the lodge. The paved drive of almost a mile is popular with joggers and bicyclists seeking a smooth path through thick woods. Nearby, the spring-fed San Marcos River is fine for swimming, snorkeling, and inner-tubing.

Tip *If you prefer not to dine with other guests, the inn will prepare a meal tray that you can take to your room. Many guests like to breakfast outdoors—just ask for a tray.*

🛏 9 rooms, 1 house 🍽 Modified American plan, dining room, picnic area, some microwaves, some refrigerators. **Recreation:** biking, birdwatching, hiking, running, wildlife viewing, pool, golf privileges, horseshoes, board games, library, videocassette/DVD library. Nearby: river swimming, swimming hole, tubing (water), boating, canoeing, kayaking, rafting, rowing, driving range, 18-hole golf course, putting green. **Services:** massage, business services, concierge, Internet access, meeting rooms. **Classes and programs:** guided hikes, guided nature walks, natural history programs, cooking and writing classes, storytelling, astronomy talks, concerts. ⚴ Satellite TV with movies, in-room fireplaces, in-room VCRs/DVD players, some jetted tubs, private balconies; no kids under 12, no smoking 💳 $200–$450 ⊟ AE, MC, V.

🏠 *4444 Hwy. 150 W, Kyle, TX 78640* ☎ *512/268–1617 or 800/579–7686* 🖷 *512/268–1090* ⊕ *www.innaboveonioncreek.com.*

LANTANA LODGE
Family Hideout

Huge portions of Texas food and hospitality are served at this lodge, one hour north of Dallas, where views of Ray Roberts Lake filter through thinned stands of tall cedar and oak trees. The lodge motto might as well be "Eat, drink, and be merry," for there's an easygoing camaraderie among staff, guests, and locals visiting from nearby Pilot Point. Staff continually urge you to go outside and enjoy the scenery, particularly the sunsets that reflect off the wide expanse of lake. You have many choices of how to spend your days at the lodge, from horseback riding, bird-watching, and hiking along some 26 mi of trails to fishing and enjoying water sports on the lake. Plus, there is an array of organized events such as trail rides and barbecues, campouts, campfire sing-alongs, horseback rides, and nature walks.

Remodeled in 2003, the lodge looks like a huge log-cabin home on the outside. Inside, it's decorated with deer-antler chandeliers and lighting fixtures shaped like Texas state-flag stars. Guest rooms have a taupe-and-blue color scheme and patchwork quilts. Some have antique furnishings, and many have great views.

You'll need to get up and out of your room to work off the meals presented by chef Heron Barbosa. Prime rib might be accompanied by pesto, and desserts such as strawberries and cream à la mode are often works of art. Locals come in droves to the lodge's family-friendly Bronze Buffalo Grill; lodge manager James Craig jokes about the three parking areas—one for vehicles, one for boats, and one for horses. Area residents often ride in on horseback or motor in by boat, and tie up at the guest dock. On chef's nights, held periodically, Barbosa displays both showmanship and skill in a cooking exhibition while preparing a five-course meal. By arrangement, the kitchen staff will serve you a "gazebo" dinner by the water. During a trail-ride meal break, you can take part in a hands-on demonstration (and eat your fill) of Dutch-oven cooking—corn bread and cobblers prepared this way are especially delicious. At chuck-wagon dinners, there are country guitar serenades and recitations of cowboy poetry.

Of course, the real reason to come to Lantana Lodge is to enjoy the great outdoors, especially man-made Ray Roberts Lake, a reservoir that helps serve the municipal water needs of Dallas. Covering 30,000 acres, the lake is at the center of a 20-mi corridor of wetlands and waterfowl sanctuaries. Opened for boating and fishing only since 1990, the lake is a favorite of anglers, who come to cast for largemouth bass, white bass, white crappie, flathead catfish, channel catfish, and other quarry.

Tip *Feeling romantic? Ask for your dinner to be served on the lodge's lakeside gazebo. But note that the lodge is BYO.*

🛏 30 rooms, 1 suite 🍽 Restaurant, room service, picnic area. **Recreation:** biking, bird-watching, fishing, hiking, horseback riding, mountain biking, running, wildlife viewing, 3 pools, lake swimming, parasailing, croquet, horseshoes, Ping-Pong, volleyball, library. Nearby: beach, boating, canoeing, kayaking, basketball. **Services:** boathouse, boat launch, dock, guided fishing trips, helipad, horse boarding, business services, Internet access, meeting rooms. **Classes and programs:** guided hikes; guided nature walks; natural history programs; off-road tours; photo safaris; roping, riding, and fishing competitions; dances; sightseeing tours; sing-alongs. 🛗 Cable TV; some in-room VCRs; some private balconies, decks, patios, and terraces; no smoking 💲 $85–$249 💳 AE, D, DC, MC, V.

2200 Farm Rd. 1192, Pilot Point, TX 76258 ☎ 940/686–0261 or 866/ 526–8262 🖷 940/686–5659 ⊕ www.lantanalodge.net.

9E RANCH BED & BREAKFAST LOG CABINS
Rustic Escape

The Lost Pine Forest, an odd region 30 mi east of Austin, is one of nature's anomalies. Its 70 square mi of towering loblolly pines lie about 100 mi from Texas's only other loblollies, which stand near the far eastern state border. The trees stranded in central Texas are relics from eons ago, when a wetter climate prevailed. As rainfall decreased, the trees should have died out, but in this spot sandy soil and an underground water supply continued to support the evergreens. The 9E Ranch lies on 300 acres in this forest. Artist Joan Bohls inherited the ranch from her father, a country doctor, and preserved a portion of his beloved hideaway by converting it to a bed-and-breakfast in 2000. If you truly want a taste of unadorned, down-home ranch life as it was decades ago, this is the place.

You can stay in the DeColores Art Barn, which has the same rough-hewn appearance it had when it served as the ranch's real barn. The inside, however, has been extensively remodeled, with a wood-burning stove, modern conveniences, and decorative touches like the tiny cowboy boots Joan wore as a little girl, now bronzed. South American knickknacks reference the classic song "De Colores," about the many colors of nature. DeColores sometimes serves as an art studio, and workshops are conducted on the screened porch. The cedar Texas Lone Star Cabin has pine floors and its own front porch and yard with a lovely garden. Inside are a wood-burning stove and an extra twin bed in the loft (children will love the glow-in-the-dark stars pasted onto the ceiling). Both DeColores and Texas Lone Star sleep up to four.

Private and modern in the heart of the forest is the Eagle's Nest, which sleeps two. The snug cedar-and-pine hideaway has an antique footed tub as well as a regular shower. You don't even have to stroll onto the porch to enjoy close-up views of stately pines and meadows where cattle and deer graze. The living area juts right out into the trees. A pair of binoculars rests on the windowsill.

On the ranch you can be splendidly alone in your cabin and hardly see another guest. Joan and Kent bring a breakfast basket to your porch on weekends but never intrude—a knock at the door lets you know your food has arrived. On weekdays, your breakfast is in the cabin refrigerator so that you can warm it up in the microwave at your convenience. If you're looking for some companionship, you're likely to find it on the back porch of the main house, which is lined with lawn chairs. You're free to roam the property, pet the horses, stroll by the lily pond, or sit in the gazebo. In three ponds, you can fish (catch-and-release) for bass. To see more of the Lost Pine Forest, go hiking in Bastrop and Buescher state parks.

Tip *Want to get hitched? Kent Bohls is a Lutheran pastor*

⇥ 3 cabins ⏌◎⏌ Full breakfast, grills, picnic area, kitchens. **Recreation**: biking, bird-watching, fishing, hiking, mountain biking, running, wildlife viewing, canoeing, putting green, disc golf, board games, videocassette library. Nearby: horseback riding, beach, 2 pools, lake swimming, river swimming, boating, rafting, rowing, driving range, 18-hole golf course, tennis courts, ballooning, carriage rides. **Services**: rowboat provided, massage, horse boarding, laundry service, airport shuttle, concierge, Internet access, meeting rooms, travel services. **Classes and programs**: guided hikes, guided nature walks, photo safaris, concerts, sightseeing tours, sing-alongs. ♿ Some in-room fireplaces, in-room VCRs, private decks, some pets allowed; no smoking ⊟ $95–$145 ⊟ MC, V.

⌂ *2158 Hwy. 304, Smithville, TX 78957* ☎ *512/497–9502* ⊕ *www.9er-anch.com.*

Utah

BOULDER MOUNTAIN LODGE
Tranquil Outpost

Perched on a crown of rolling earth surrounded by mountains to the north and west and canyons and deserts to the south and east, the town of Boulder is one of the most isolated in the Lower 48. Here stands Boulder Mountain Lodge, a surprisingly sophisticated hostelry, 4½ hours from St. George, 4 hours from Moab—truly in the middle of . . . well, nowhere.

The lodge's timbered, western-style stucco buildings cluster near a 15-acre lake sanctuary for ducks, coots, and other waterfowl. Horses graze nearby. A large outdoor hot tub overlooks the lake and bird sanctuary, and a stone fire pit sends the fragrance of burning pine wafting through the crisp evening air. In the lodge's common area you can sit before a fire in the big sandstone fireplace. A gallery displays the work of local artists. Your spacious room is furnished in contemporary style with western accents, perhaps with a sofa for lounging or a kitchenette for your convenience. Puffy comforters and duvets top the beds—some of them king-size.

Each day you can choose to play in the mountains or explore canyon country. If you'd like a little help on your adventures, the folks at the lodge will arrange for guide services. On your own, you can head for the hills by driving north on Highway 12, where you can see why the National Scenic Byways Program has named this highway one of only 20 All-American Roads. The route takes you up and over Boulder Mountain, through a cool, alpine region. At turnoffs, you'll take in spectacular views of plateaus and canyons stretching across the horizon.

Just a few hundred yards from the lodge, you can drive onto the Burr Trail, which leads into landscape of otherworldly geological formations such as the dramatic Waterpocket Fold. From the heights of the trail you have breathtaking views of brilliantly colored cliffs, canyons, buttes, mesas, plateaus, and mountain peaks. Drive south on narrow, winding Highway 12 into Grand Staircase–Escalante National Monument to a hogback of rock that commands views of the truly vast preserve. The drive is not for the faint of heart, but is definitely worthwhile. South of the hogback, stop at Calf Canyon Recreation Area for a 5½-mi round-trip hike to a 126-foot waterfall that shoots off a cliff. A few miles farther south, you can hike for miles in wild, rocky desert land along the Escalante River. Bureau of Land Management rangers can guide you to some of the West's best hidden slot canyons.

After a day of exploring you'll no doubt be ready for dinner at the lodge's Hell's Backbone Grill. Owners Blake Spalding and Jen Castle use only local organic foods that have a historic foundation in the area, so you might find buffalo on the menu, but never salmon. Their creations are inspired by Native American, western range, southwestern, and Mormon pioneer recipes. Vegetables come from the lodge's garden. The food is excellent, and on a mild evening it's especially enjoyable on the patio overlooking the pond.

Tip *Plan your trip around a full moon and arrange to take a guided moonrise hike—a truly memorable experience.*

🛏 20 rooms 🍴 Restaurant, some kitchenettes, microwaves, refrigerators. **Recreation:** bird-watching, hiking, horseback riding, mountain biking, rock climbing (nearby), running, wildlife viewing, badminton, croquet, horseshoes, soccer, volleyball. **Services:** hot tub, massage, laundry service. **Classes and programs:** guided hikes, guided nature walks, photo safaris. ♨ Satellite TV, laundry facilities 💲 $69–$168 💳 AE, D, MC, V.

🏠 *Hwy. 12, Boulder, UT 84716* ☎ *435/335–7460 or 800/556–3446* 📠 *435/335–7461* 🌐 *www.boulder-utah.com.*

CAMELOT LODGE
Laid-Back Adventure

You can't often say that "there is no other place like this in America," but in the case of Camelot Lodge, it's true. At this adventure lodge, 18 mi from Moab, camel trekking in the desert is the specialty. Here, two camel treks, ranging from three to four hours, take you deep into the desert, winding through canyons and over sand dunes. Depending on the trek you select, you may learn camel commands and camel handling, including how to saddle your own camel. While you sway atop your mount, you can hear about the history of the camel in North America. It is an experience not to be missed.

If you don't have a four-wheel-drive vehicle, the only way to Camelot is to catch a ride in the lodge's four-wheel-drive shuttle or on its jet boat. The jet boat takes you to the lodge through the steep-walled canyons of the Colorado River, where American bald eagles, red-tailed hawks, and peregrine falcons soar overhead. Take the land route instead, and you're likely to see desert bighorn sheep, coyotes, and mule deer. Or take the shuttle in one direction and the boat in the other.

The modern adobe lodge stands near the sandy shores of the Colorado River, backed by red-rock bluffs. Surrounding it are large expanses of public land, including Canyonlands National Park, so there isn't a bad view in the house. Each of the guest rooms opens onto the deck, where you can sit and watch the sun over land and water. Furnished simply in contemporary southwestern style, each room holds a queen or two twin beds. A woodstove warms the common living-dining room, where hearty home-style meals are served at a large communal table. At night, a million stars sparkle above the lodge.

The river beach is yours for the swimming, and the land around the lodge is great for hiking and mountain biking. Owner-operator Terry Moore is happy to show you ancient Native American tool-chipping sites and the sandstone formations known as the Catacombs. Not far from the lodge is thousand-year-old rock art left by ancestral Puebloan peoples.

Tip *Spring and fall are the best times to come to this isolated desert retreat. Spring is wildflower season, and cactus and other desert flora bloom in wild colors. Summer is brutally hot, especially July and August. The camels don't mind the heat, but most people do.*

5 rooms ❍ American plan. **Recreation:** bird-watching, hiking, mountain biking, rock climbing, running, wildlife viewing, beach, river swimming, boating, canoeing, kayaking, rafting (nearby). **Classes and programs:** guided hikes, guided nature walks, photo safaris, camel treks, camel-handling lessons. No room phones, no room TVs, no smoking $125.

 Box 621, Moab, UT 84532 435/260–1783 www.camelotlodge.com.

SORREL RIVER RANCH
Luxurious Resort

People around Moab are certain that few places on earth are as beautiful as the canyon country surrounding their town. Sorrel River Ranch, on the banks of the Colorado, makes the most of that beauty. Whether you choose a mountain view or river-view room, you will see only stunning scenery from your window. Second-story spa suites overlook the Colorado River and have private decks with swings, where you can watch the cliffs change color with the setting sun; in these digs, even the large, deep therapy tubs share the view. All of the elegantly western guest rooms are furnished with hefty log beds and ironwork designed especially for Sorrel.

Horses graze in their corrals near the lodge; the ranch offers guided trail rides into the surrounding red-rock wilderness. You can put a kayak into the Colorado right in front of the lodge and float downriver to Moab, and ranch staff will pick you up and shuttle you back. The mountain biking and hiking in the area are superb, and outfitters offer white-water rafting and 4x4 tours. Arches and Canyonlands national parks are close by. In the Sorrel's spa, a full menu of services is available, including massages of all types. In the tandem massage, two therapists simultaneously perform their magic on your fatigued muscles; in the couples massage, the two of you receive treatment at the same time; in the desert stone massage, hot stones are used. You can gaze at the river and red-rock spires during your pedicure or manicure.

The regionally renowned River Grill serves three exquisite meals a day, before a fireplace beneath soaring ceilings and on a deck with spectacular views. The contemporary American cuisine ranges from fresh fish to buffalo ribs, and a spa menu offers vegetarian fare.

Tip *The ranch hosts several concerts during the Moab Music Festival, usually in early to mid-September. For two weeks, top-flight classical, jazz, and world musicians perform in the ranch's outdoor pavilion.*

🛏 57 rooms ▐◎▌ Restaurant, room service, kitchenettes, microwaves, refrigerators. **Recreation:** bird-watching, hiking, horseback riding, running, wildlife viewing, pool, tennis courts, playground. Nearby: rock climbing, rafting, 18-hole golf course. **Services:** mountain-bike and inflatable-kayak rentals, gym, hot tub, massage, salon, sauna, spa, babysitting, horse boarding, laundry facilities, laundry service, shop, business services, concierge, meeting rooms. **Classes and programs:** guided horseback rides, horseback-riding and tennis lessons, yoga classes. ♨ Satellite TV, in-room VCRs, jetted tubs; no smoking 🍽 $279–$459 ☰ D, MC, V.

🖅 *Box K, Moab, UT 84532* ☎ *435/259–4642 or 877/359–2715* 📠 *435/259–3016* ⊕ *www.sorrelriver.com.*

SNOWBERRY INN
Romantic Getaway

A big log cabin that looks like a barn, the Snowberry Inn overlooks Pineview Reservoir in northern Utah's Ogden Canyon, about one hour from Salt Lake City. Around here, life is all about the outdoors. Any time of year, you can explore the mountains: hiking, mountain biking, water sports, and winter sports.

Innkeepers Pat and Sherrie Dohrer will make you feel right at home. Jump-start your morning with some premium coffee and the Snowberry's signature cream cheese–stuffed French toast. In the afternoon, sit on the front porch with Pat and Sherrie to sip some wine and nibble on hors d'oeuvres. The inn does not serve dinner, but your hosts can recommend excellent restaurants in the canyon. For special occasions, they may cook a big pot of soup.

In the evening, you can soak in the hot tub beneath starry skies or play the well-tuned piano or a game of chess in one of several common areas. There are two nooks where you can watch television or a movie. When you retreat to your room, comforters and quilts make snuggling easy. Furnished with antiques, each room has a private bath with a hand-crafted pottery sink. The Alaskan Room, with a claw-foot tub, is the house favorite. Friends traveling together choose one of the downstairs suites or the apartment, where you can spread out and stow your ski gear. The Snowberry accepts youngsters only selectively in an effort to maintain a peaceful mood.

Two ski resorts, Powder Mountain and Snowbasin, are nearby. Snow-mobiling, snowshoeing, cross-country skiing, and ice fishing are also pop-ular. From a helipad within walking distance of the Snowberry, you can take off for backcountry skiing. In warmer seasons you can hike into the foothills or mountains; Skyline Trail is a favorite of Pat and Sher-rie. Take a swim or go boating, sailing, or fishing in Pineview Reservoir. Each August, the local Balloon and Art Fest fills the sky with colorful hot-air balloons morning and evening for a weekend. During fall foliage season (usually mid-September to early October) Ogden Canyon and the hillsides behind the inn blaze with gold, orange, and fiery red.

Tips *November is quiet at the Snowberry. You are almost guaranteed a dusting of snow in the mountains. Fall is the best time for wildlife viewing.*

🛏 7 rooms 🍴 Grills, picnic area. **Recreation:** biking, bird-watch-ing, fishing, hiking, mountain biking, running, wildlife viewing, lake swimming, waterskiing, windsurfing, boating, jet skiing, rowing, sail-ing, cross-country skiing, downhill skiing, sleigh rides, sledding, snow-mobiling, snowshoeing, telemark skiing, badminton, horseshoes, volleyball, library, piano, recreation room. Nearby: horseback riding, rock-climbing, 18-hole golf course, tennis court, tubing (snow), bas-ketball. **Services:** outdoor hot tub, massage, spa, ski storage. **Classes and programs:** yoga and tai chi classes. ♿ Satellite TV, no smoking; no a/c, no room phones, no room TVs 💳 $119–$159 ☰ MC, V.

📍 *1315 N. Hwy. 158, Eden, UT 84310* ☎ *801/745–2634 or 888/746–2634* 🌐 *www.snowberryinn.com.*

SUNDANCE
Family Hideout ~ Luxurious Resort

The fragrance of pine, juniper, and fir wafts through the air. Wildflowers bloom outside your door. Birds wake you in the morning and mule deer amble through the woods. Sundance Resort, set on the eastern slopes of 11,750-foot Mt. Timpanogos, about 53 mi from Salt Lake City, is a place where nature is woven into every moment. Owned by actor Robert Redford, the 6,000-acre resort is committed to the environment, outdoor exploration, and artistic expression.

Constructed from cedar, fir, pine, and stone, Sundance was developed without disturbing the original landscape, so the wilderness remains front and center. A group of buildings at the heart of the resort houses the restaurants, shops, and the base lodge for the resort's ski area. One- to three-bedroom guest cottages stand on hillsides along paths that wind through stands of old-growth pines, groves of aspen, and along clear mountain streams. The cottages' rough-hewn beams, wood trim, and richly textured, colorful fabrics don't make a lavish statement, but everything is so well executed that an air of understated luxury prevails. Suites have a stone fireplace or woodstove, a deck, and either a full kitchen and dining area or kitchenette. The cushier two- to five-bedroom mountain homes have large baths, and some have private hot tubs.

No matter the season, you'll find abundant recreational opportunities. When there's no snow, ride the ski lifts into the high country and take a solitary hike. Trails range in difficulty and length, from a 1½-mi nature trail to a 7½-mi trek through steep terrain to a series of waterfalls. There are more than 25 mi of ski lift–accessed mountain-biking trails. Many of the Sundance hiking and biking trails connect with others in the adjacent Uinta National Forest. You can also fish for trout in the Provo River, or take a ride with the wranglers at Sundance Stables.

In winter, Sundance turns into a white wonderland with some 450 acres of alpine skiing and snowboarding and the requisite lifts. And 24 mi of cross-country trails wind through open meadows and groves of aspen; Nordic skiing by torchlight is unforgettable.

Year-round, relax in the Spa at Sundance, or at the Artisan Center and Gallery, a.k.a. the Art Shack, take a lesson in silversmithing, pottery throwing, painting, and jewelry making. Film screenings and workshops are held throughout the year, and in January the Sundance Film Festival showcases independent films at the resort and in nearby Park City.

Meals at Sundance are as much of a treat as is the bucolic setting. The Tree Room serves seasonal mountain cuisine, and the wine list makes oenophiles smile. The Foundry Grill specializes in authentic western cooking on a large wood-burning grill and rotisserie, before incredible views of Mt. Timpanogos. The Owl Bar, with its worn plank floors, stone fireplace, and 1890s rosewood bar, is an intimate place to hear live music and have a cocktail after dinner.

Tip *Cottages along the Mandan Loop path are particularly private.*

⇨95 studios and suites and 11 mountain homes ⦿Snack bar, 2 restaurants, room service, bar, grocery store, some kitchens, some kitchenettes. **Recreation:** bird-watching, hiking, horseback riding, mountain biking, running, wildlife viewing, cross-country skiing, downhill skiing. Nearby: fishing, rafting, ballooning, soaring, snowmobiling. **Services:**

fly-fishing equipment provided with tours; ski, snowboard, and mountain-bike rentals; spa, ski shop, laundry service, shops, business services, concierge, Internet access, meeting rooms. **Classes and programs:** guided hikes, guided nature walks, fly-fishing lessons, skiing lessons, yoga classes, children's programs (ages 8 and up), art and crafts classes, photography classes, concerts, movies. ⚓ Cable TV, in-room fireplaces, in-room VCRs/DVDs, some jetted tubs, some private decks and patios, no-smoking rooms ▭ $265–$1,425 ▭ AE, D, DC, MC, V.

🐾 *R.R. 3 (Box A-1), Sundance, UT 84064* ☎ *801/225–4107 or 800/892–1600* 📠 *801/226–1937* 🌐 *www.sundanceresort.com.*

ZION PONDEROSA RANCH RESORT
Family Hideout

Snuggled against the boundary of Zion National Park, about 150 mi from the Las Vegas airport, this out-of-the-way family resort overlooks the park's majestic cliffs. Your kids will accuse you of being lost before you finally reach the turnoff for Zion Ponderosa Ranch Resort, but once they've settled into your cabin and discovered the swimming pool, climbing wall, and horses, you'll really score some points. The ranch is an all-inclusive resort that aims to please every member of your family.

Horseback rides, guided ATV tours, fishing, or mountain biking will keep you busy if you like. Try your hand at archery, or get messy with a game of paintball. Grown-ups can work out in the recreation barn or sign up for a massage. While older children learn rappelling or riflery, Camp Ponderosa keeps the little ones busy. Memorial Day to Labor Day, they can take pony rides, try the lower reaches of the climbing wall, work on art projects, or go swimming under the watchful eye of camp counselors experienced with young children. Farther afield, take advantage of the ranch's location by hiking into Zion National Park from the top down. Most park visitors approach the trails from the floor of Zion Canyon and hike up the steep, rigorous trails. Hiking in from the ranch, you end up at the bottom of the canyon, and resort staff will pick you up to shuttle you back to the resort.

You can stay in a cabin suite or a cowboy cabin, or you can set up a tent in the campground. The cabins are log, each with a front porch; all have simple, functional furnishings. Cabin suites have one bedroom and a fold-out couch in the living room; cowboy cabins are one-room affairs that share bathing facilities. The resort also offers some sensational log rental homes—including a luxury home in the woods, away from the activity—for larger groups. Whichever accommodations you choose, the price of your stay includes all meals and recreation at the resort. You get three rib-sticking meals a day, with dinner entrées such as barbecued chicken, halibut, or rib-eye steak with a big baked potato on the side. Meals are served in the main lodge; for an additional fee, you can participate in a chuck-wagon dinner during peak season. At the end of a busy day, put the kids to bed and take a soak in the hot tub, gazing up at the Milky Way in one of the darkest night skies in America.

Tip *In off-peak season (early September through late May), lodging-only rates are available.*

16 cabin suites, 8 cowboy cabins, 12 log homes ¡©¡ Modified American plan, dining room, snack bar, grills, picnic area, some kitchens, some kitchenettes, some microwaves. **Recreation:** biking, bird-watching, hiking, horseback riding, mountain biking, running, wildlife viewing, pool, tennis court, archery, basketball, disc golf, horseshoes, Ping-Pong, volleyball. Nearby: downhill skiing, snowmobiling, fishing, rock climbing. **Services:** sports equipment provided, hot tub, massage, guided fishing trips, laundry facilities. **Classes and programs:** guided hikes, guided nature walks, off-road tours, rock-climbing and rappelling lessons, mountain-biking lessons, children's programs (ages 3–11), art and crafts classes, sightseeing tours. Some in-room fireplaces, private porches; no phones in some rooms, no TV in some rooms $85–$565 AE, D, MC, V.

Box 5547, Mt. Carmel, UT 84755 800/293–5444 or 435/648–2700 435/648–2702 *www.zionponderosa.com.*

Vermont

BLUEBERRY HILL INN
Tranquil Outpost

A creaky, blue Federal-style farmhouse dating from 1813 is the centerpiece of a 120-acre wilderness retreat in 22,000-acre Moosalamoo Nature Preserve (part of Green Mountain National Forest). An hour from Burlington, and 3½ hours from Boston, it's just about smack in the middle of Vermont at the end of a long, dirt road. Once you arrive amid the fabulous gardens, miles of hiking and cross-country skiing trails, and tasteful but unfussy accommodations, you may not want to venture beyond the grounds. It doesn't hurt that Blueberry Hill Inn has one of the state's most acclaimed small restaurants.

Although within the forest, Blueberry Hill isn't a dark, shadowy woodland retreat. Clear and open meadows afford long views and lots of sunlight. You can access dense stands of hardwood trees nearby via hiking trails through the property. You can also opt for a gentler stroll beside the stunning herb and flower beds and fruit trees, or around the small millpond in back. Adirondack chairs set strategically about tempt you to sit back and listen to the chatter of songbirds. You are welcome to explore a large greenhouse to the side of the inn.

The inn is best known for its cross-country skiing center, which occupies a cavernous barn just across the dirt road from the inn, rents skis in winter and mountain bikes in summer, and provides detailed maps of its 60 mi (97 km) of trails. Upstairs is a lounge warmed by a woodburning stove. The wood-fired sauna, set inside a small building on the edge of the spring-fed millpond, is an invigorating and relaxing place to unwind after a day of cycling or skiing.

The main house, built as a way station for 18th-century loggers and travelers, contains a few guest rooms, but most are out back in an addition; there's also a cottage with one queen bed and two twins. If it's the trappings of colonial living you want, choose a room in the main house, with its wide-plank floors and period-style wallpaper and fabrics; in these rooms big windows overlook the seemingly endless fields of wildflowers and the forested mountains beyond. Rooms in back are either off a plant-filled solarium-style hallway, or in an adjacent wing overlooking the pond. They feel newer despite their antiques, braided rugs, and quilts. There's more privacy here but a little less character, and some of the bathrooms—though clean and functional—could stand updating. In general, although furnishings are well-chosen and graceful they're not sumptuous, so it's easy to focus on what's truly exquisite about this place: the surroundings.

The menu of contemporary cuisine, which focuses on regional produce and ingredients, changes nightly. Typical meals might include halibut baked with tomatoes, cilantro, and a hint of saffron over jasmine rice, or twice-baked goat cheese soufflé. Dinner is served in a room with a prodigious stone fireplace and rafters hung with dried herbs. You can have your full and hearty breakfast here or out in the brick-floor greenhouse, where tall windows overlook still more fields and forest.

Tip *On weekdays except in fall, you can book a room that includes breakfast but no dinner for $20 less per person—sensible if you want to sample the area's great restaurants.*

🛏 11 rooms, 1 cottage ⦿ Modified American plan, restaurant. **Recreation:** bird-watching, fishing, hiking, mountain biking, running, wildlife viewing, lake and pond swimming, cross-country skiing, snowshoeing, lawn games, library. **Services:** cross-country ski rentals, sauna, ski shop. 🐾 Some pets allowed; no a/c, no room phones, no room TVs, no smoking 💲 $250–$320 💳 AE, MC, V.

🏠 *1307 Goshen-Ripton Rd., Goshen, VT 05733* ☎ *802/247–6735 or 800/448–0707* 📠 *802/247–3983* ⊕ *www.blueberryhillinn.com.*

THE INN AT BUCK HOLLOW FARM
Tranquil Outpost

After driving for several miles up winding Buck Hollow Road in the sparsely populated northwest corner of the state, about 35 minutes from Burlington, it's easy to be distracted by the views. It's even easy to miss the entrance to Buck Hollow Farm, a low-key B&B that looks like just another farm—albeit one anchored by an especially dapper yellow colonial house.

Things don't get any more formal after you park your car and knock on the door of Brad Schwartz's inn, which is surrounded by a 400-acre working farm, complete with a long barn in the back and horses and sheep sauntering about the paddocks. Schwartz is a former New York attorney who decided to move to farthest Vermont and run a farm and antiques business. He opened the B&B as a sideline but runs it with great warmth.

Sure, the rooms have antiques, and the inn has just enough creature comforts to remind you you're on vacation: a hot tub, 40-foot pool, in-room satellite TV, CD/clock radios, and a two-person jetted tub in the only shared bathroom. But life on the farm is without cares, and you are encouraged to bring kids of any age as well as pets. If you don't have your own four-legged traveling buddy, you're welcome to pal around with one of the two dogs or five cats who live on the property—all of them warm up quickly to strangers.

In addition to the reasonable rates and comfy digs, Buck Hollow offers miles of trails for strolling during the warmer months and cross-country skiing from November through April. The trails pass through farm fields, alongside a babbling brook, and into dense thickets of woodland; you have to walk only a relatively short ways from the farmhouse before it's well out of view.

Summer and fall are favorite times to visit. When it's warm you can laze by the pool, which has a small waterslide, or wander out by the barn, perhaps to pet the sheep. But winter can be even more rewarding, when Buck Hollow Farm is covered with snow, and a plume of smoke rises daily from the sugarhouse out back, where you can watch Schwartz boil down sap to make maple syrup. Inside, you can curl up in the sunroom, a contemporary space with a slate floor, high beam ceilings, tall windows, and a big stone fireplace.

The sunroom, which overlooks the pool and fields, acts as a bridge of sorts between the main house and the restored 1790s carriage house, which contains the accommodations—two rooms on each floor with private baths on the first floor and a shared bath on the second floor. Folk furniture fills the three guest rooms and one large suite (which can accommodate six in its queen bed, sofa bed, and two rollaways). Three rooms have canopy beds piled high with country quilts, and one has a private deck.

Tip *Visiting from nearby Québec? You can save big from November through June, when Buck Hollow accepts Canadian dollars at the same value as U.S. dollars; just book directly with the inn.*

⇨ 3 rooms, suite ᛁ◉ᛁ Full breakfast. **Recreation:** bird-watching, hiking, mountain biking, wildlife viewing, pool, cross-country skiing, carriage rides. **Services:** laundry facilities, laundry service, shop, business services, wireless Internet access, meeting room. **Classes and programs:** maple syrup–making demonstrations. ⍨ Satellite TV, some jetted tubs, some private decks, some pets allowed; no room phones, no smoking ▨ $78–$99 ▤ AE, D, MC, V.

🏠 *2150 Buck Hollow Rd., Fairfax, VT 05454* ☎ *802/849–2400 or 800/ 849–7985* 🖷 *802/849–9744* ⊕ *www.buckhollow.com.*

INN AT SHELBURNE FARMS
Tranquil Outpost

The towns just south of Burlington, including Shelburne, are becoming increasingly suburban. But the area's 1,400-acre Shelburne Farms preserves one of the great agricultural tracts in New England. The property is not only a working dairy farm and a treasured cultural center, but also home to a sumptuous country inn hidden down a long driveway and overlooking Lake Champlain.

The 35-room mansion, with its steep-pitched roof and towering red chimneys, is gorgeous inside and out, with stunning wood paneling, Oriental rugs, and Victorian settees in the grand lobby and sitting rooms. The inn occupies one of New England's most impressive summer "cottages," originally the home of William Seward (President Lincoln's secretary of state) and his wife, Lila Vanderbilt Webb (daughter of William Henry Vanderbilt).

The inn strikes a genial balance between dignified and easygoing. You pull up in your car under a large portico, where a casually dressed bellhop greets you with a smile and whisks your luggage inside. Many rooms are staggeringly proportioned and contain museum-quality antiques, but you won't feel out of place in relaxed summer attire. This is neither a country club nor a stuffy resort.

Some guest rooms are lavish, with unobstructed lake views, ornamental fireplaces, and furnishings original to the house, if not the room they're in now. These top-of-the-line accommodations have large bathrooms with marble-sink basins and clawfoot tubs. But many of the building's original work areas and servants' quarters have been turned into smaller and more modest rooms, some that share bathrooms, and these can be had for a fraction of what the fanciest rooms cost. The variety of accommodations and rates brings together an eclectic group.

Landscape architect Frederick Law Olmsted, co-creator of New York City's Central Park, designed the magnificent grounds. From Adirondack chairs set along the broad and neatly maintained lawns and hedges, you have clear views of Lake Champlain and, in the distance, the Adirondack Mountains. The shoreline is rocky and windswept, with steady breezes on even the hottest summer afternoons. Trails through the property, ranging from $\frac{1}{4}$ mi to $4\frac{1}{4}$ mi, pass through hardwood forests, across farm fields, and beside bountiful organic gardens. The short Lone Tree Hill Loop is especially rewarding—it climbs to the highest point on the farm, affording unsurpassed views of both the Adirondacks and Green Mountains.

A highlight of a stay here is a guided tour of the property, which takes in the farm outbuildings, the petting zoo, and the cheddar cheese–making facility. Not surprisingly, the inn's restaurant serves stellar regional cuisine made with local ingredients. You might try a salad of greens grown in the farm's garden, with a maple-ginger vinaigrette, and Vermont lamb or grilled tenderloin of beef. There's also a marvelous Sunday brunch. In warm weather you can dine on a patio overlooking the water.

Tip *Shelburne Farms hosts a variety of concerts and events, including the Harvest Festival in late September with hayrides, farm exhibitions and demonstrations, and a pie-baking contest.*

➭24 rooms ⍾Restaurant, bar. **Recreation:** bird-watching, fishing, hiking, running, wildlife viewing, beach, lake swimming, boating, sailing, tennis court, billiards, croquet, library. **Services:** meeting room. **Classes and programs:** guided farm tours, concerts, lectures. ♿No heat or a/c, no room TVs, no smoking ▦$135–$395 ▭D, DC, MC, V.

⌂ *1611 Harbor Rd., Shelburne, VT 05482* ☎ *802/985–8498* ▤ *802/ 985–8123* ⊕ *www.shelburnefarms.org* ⊘ *Closed mid-Oct.–mid-May.*

ROARING BRANCH
Rustic Escape

The heady aroma of pines and the sound of the Roaring Branch River permeate the crisp air at this holiday colony of six log cabins in southwestern Vermont's Green Mountains, 1¼ hours from Albany, New York. One of the finest stands of eastern white pine trees in Vermont (most more than 200 years old) and plenty of hemlocks, oaks, and white birch shelter scarlet tanagers, partridges, and the occasional pileated woodpecker. The 36 acres of towering woods are also home to raccoons, deer, and chipmunks and are sometimes visited by black bears. Running 20 to 50 feet below the granite ledge where most of the cabins stand, the river offers bountiful fly-fishing and is a tributary of the nearby Battenkill, one of New England's great trout streams.

You don't have to rough it at Roaring Branch, but neither will you find much in the way of modern luxuries. Indeed, it feels a bit like sleep-away camp without the rules and structure, and without the noise. The log cabins, which have critter-inspired names like Possum and Bobcat, are all at least 100 feet from one another. Cabins come in two styles: rustic units that date to the compound's construction in 1913 and modern cabins built since the late 1980s. Dripping with old-time funkiness—and draftiness, for that matter—the rustic cabins have quaintly slanted floors and, often, their original lodgepole furniture and stair railings. The modern cabins feel more plush, with TVs (but minimal reception), VCRs, and dishwashers; some have skylights.

All cabins have a living room with a stone fireplace, a fully equipped kitchen with electric range and oven, a separate dining area, one bathroom, and one to three bedrooms. Each has a charcoal grill outside and blankets on the beds; you bring your own bed linens and towels. For the most part cabins are rented Saturday to Saturday, but in June, September, and October the minimum stay in the rustic cabins is only three nights. Modern cabins sleep six, rustic cabins five to eight.

Roaring Branch is popular with artists and writers, who hole up for weeks on end, taking advantage of the isolation, but there's enough here to keep kids happy, too. Set far enough away from the log cabins to maintain their tranquil air, a recreational area has two clay tennis courts, a game room and library, and a large lawn. You can play or swim in the river, or just sun on the rocks that line its banks. For some solitary exercise, make the 15-minute stroll to the old Chiselville Covered Bridge, just down the country road from the driveway. Farther afield but still very close by, you can hike, canoe, bike, ride horseback, kayak, or golf. And it's pretty easy to spend an afternoon shopping and dining in Manchester, 10 mi north. But at the end of the day, you get to return to this charmed log-cabin village, which feels lost in the 1940s, just outside the Vermont village that Norman Rockwell once called home.

Tip *If you're with preteens, book one of the handful of cabins with an open sleeping loft. These snug aeries are always a huge hit.*

6 cabins Grills, picnic area, kitchens, some microwaves. **Recreation:** hiking, fishing, mountain biking (nearby), wildlife viewing, river swimming, 2 tennis courts, badminton, basketball, horseshoes, Ping-Pong, volleyball, library, recreation room. Some in-room VCRs, some pets allowed; no a/c, no phones in some rooms, no TVs in some rooms, no smoking $120–$130 (per cabin, per day) No credit cards.

Box 8, Arlington, VT 05250 802/375–6401 www.roaringbranch. com Closed Nov.–May.

Virginia

MARRIOTT RANCH
Tranquil Outpost

Against the backdrop of the bluish-gray Blue Ridge Mountains, the dreamy Blue Ridge foothills of northern Virginia are threaded with designated scenic Virginia Byways. The serpentine roadways, canopied by 100-foot trees, are bordered by lush ferns, flowering mimosas, and graceful dogwoods. Some roads take your breath away as they rise and fall like a roller coaster; some cross tributaries of the mighty Shenandoah River. By the time you reach Marriott Ranch, 55 mi from Washington, D.C., you are far removed from your everyday world.

A working 4,200-acre farm where you'll see cattle, sheep, and wheat fields, Marriott Ranch was the private retreat of hotel magnate J. Willard Marriott Sr. He bought the property in 1951 because it reminded him of his boyhood home in Utah. But this land is distinctly Virginian, with undulating hills, pastures, hardwood forests, and fences of black wood and stacked stone. Near the center of property is the Inn at Fairfield Farm, a bed-and-breakfast in a manor house, carriage house, and log cottage. James Marshall, the brother of Supreme Court Justice John Marshall, built the manor in 1814. Standing beneath white ash trees and framed by boxwood hedges, the stately structure transports you to a gentler era as soon as you step over the threshold. A library, a living room, and a sitting porch invite reading and quiet conversation. In the dining room and piano room, large Monticello-style windows take in views of grazing cattle, horses, and gorgeous sunrises or sunsets over the mountains. The porch is a good place for drinks.

Guest rooms in the manor house are furnished with queen-size poster or sleigh beds and have fireplaces and private baths; some have a Jacuzzi. The rooms in the 20th-century carriage house have two double beds and their own outside entrances, and the carriage suite has a king-size bed. The Baroness Cottage, an early-1800s log cabin, was modernized during World War II by Baroness Jeanne von Reininghaus Lambert of Belgium, and is well suited to families or visitors on extended stays. A family room with fireplace, a large eat-in kitchen, and a spacious bedroom with full bath occupy the ground floor, and upstairs are two smaller bedrooms with a shared bath. Whichever accommodations you choose, you will have access to all the amenities of the manor house. In the morning you are served a hearty three-course breakfast, and in the afternoon there's a traditional tea and complimentary wine in the dining room. Formerly used for smoking ham and wild turkey, the SmokeHouse Public Room in the Carriage House has a fireplace, wood-burning stove, and smoke-darkened beam ceiling. It serves as a small lounge, but bar service is available only for group events.

Getting out into the gorgeous countryside on horseback is revitalizing. Just as Marriott once rode the ranch with U.S. presidents Ronald Reagan and Dwight Eisenhower and with business leaders from around the world, you, too, can ride the trails; the 50 horses suit any skill level. You can also hike the expansive property or tour it by jeep. Off the ranch, you might go canoeing, rafting, kayaking, or tubing on the Shenandoah River or take in a polo match or steeplechase race at Great Meadows, 20 mi away. Also in the area are eight wineries, Skyline Caverns, and the antiques shops of Front Royal's historic district.

Tip *Even if you've never ridden before, you can climb into the saddle here. You'll be matched with a horse suited to you and guided on trail rides. Don't forget jeans and sturdy, closed-toe shoes.*

⤵ 10 rooms, 1 suite, 1 log cottage, 1 carriage house ¶◎¶ Full breakfast, restaurant, pub, grills, picnic area, some kitchens, some refrigerators. **Recreation:** bird-watching, fishing, hiking, horseback riding, running, wildlife viewing, croquet, horseshoes, shuffleboard, volleyball, library. Nearby: river swimming, canoeing, kayaking, rafting, rowing, 18-hole golf course. **Services:** horse boarding, business services, concierge, meeting rooms. **Classes and programs:** guided hikes and nature walks; fishing, horseback-riding, and western dance lessons; sing-alongs. ⌂ Some pets allowed (fee); no room TVs, no smoking ▱ $125–$400 ▭ AE, D, MC, V.

⌖ *5305 Marriott La., Hume, VA 22639* ☎ *540/364–2627, reservations 877/324–7344 Ext. 1* 🖷 *540/364–3564* ⊕ *www.marriottranch.com.*

PEAKS OF OTTER LODGE
Tranquil Outpost

Possibly the most famous mountains in Virginia, Harkening Hill, Sharp Top, and Flat Top are known collectively as the Peaks of Otter. Thomas Jefferson once pronounced that the three Blue Ridge mountains, which reach elevations of 3,375 to 4,001 feet, were "of greater height than any in our country, perhaps North America." That was before he sent Lewis and Clark on their expedition.

Snuggled between two of the mountains at Milepost 86 on the Blue Ridge Parkway (29 mi northeast of Roanoke), the Peaks of Otter

Lodge is the only year-round lodging on the National Park Service–administered scenic route. Like the road itself, the lodge is surrounded by magnificent alpine vistas and hardwood forests of beeches, birch, buckeyes, and spruce firs that are especially lovely during fall foliage season and spring flowering. It's alongside Lake Abbott, with a group of rocking chairs near the entrance. Rooms have wooden furniture and quilted bedspreads, and all have a lake view. The lodge restaurant, which serves standard American fare, is popular for its Friday seafood buffet and Sunday breakfast buffet. Breakfasts are hearty, and lunch and dinner menus include salads, sandwiches, pasta, steak, ribs, southern fried chicken, roast turkey, and rainbow trout, plus warm cobblers, cheesecake, bread pudding, and pie for dessert.

Swimming, wading, boating, and ice-skating are forbidden in and on Lake Abbott, but you can walk its shoreline—an easy stroll of about a mile—and fish for the lake's catfish, smallmouth bass, golden shiners, sunfish, and bluegill. The lake lies within Jefferson National Forest, where you can hike in the mountains and access the 2,144-mi Maine-to-Georgia Appalachian Trail. The summits of Flat Top and Harkening Hill are each a relatively short but strenuous 1½- to 2-mi walk from the lodge; Sharp's Top is a 1½-mi hike straight up. If you don't feel like hiking, take the bus up to Sharp Top for a 360-degree view of the mountains. In the Peaks of Otter Visitor Center (Blue Ridge Parkway Mile Post 86), natural history walks and lectures are offered. A drive about 30 mi south from the lodge leads to Smith Mountain Lake, Virginia's second largest, with 500 mi of waterfront. Here you can get your fill of water sports and fish for many species of bass.

Tip *Book a year in advance if you want to visit when fall foliage is peaking, generally during a two-week period between mid-October and mid-November. Another busy time is early June, when the mountain laurel and rhododendron are in bloom.*

63 rooms ♭○┤ Coffee shop, restaurant, lounge, grocery store, grills, picnic area. **Recreation:** bird-watching, fishing, hiking, rock climbing, running, wildlife viewing. Nearby: lake swimming, parasailing, boating, canoeing. **Services:** shop, business services, meeting rooms, travel services. ♿ No-smoking rooms; no room phones, no room TVs ▭ $66–$156 ▭ MC, V.

Box 489, Bedford, VA 24523 ☎ 540/586–1081 or 800/542–5927 ᕔ 540/586–4420 ⊕ www.peaksofotter.com.

WESTMORELAND STATE PARK
Family Hideout ~ Rustic Escape

Some 63 mi east of burgeoning, historic Fredericksburg, and 8 mi southeast from Richmond, peace and quiet reign on the 90-mi, million-acre peninsula that Virginians call the Northern Neck. The wide Potomac River flows on the north side of the peninsula and the Rappahannock River on the south side, both emptying into the briny Chesapeake Bay at the peninsula's eastern end. Numerous inlets from the rivers and the bay give the Northern Neck a ragged coastline that entices anglers and water-sports lovers.

Westmoreland State Park, built by the Civilian Conservation Corps (CCC) in 1936, lies on a 1½-mi stretch of the Potomac. Hiking trails wind through marshlands, woods, meadows, and along the river, which you can view from Horsehead Cliffs. You can fish for striped bass, spot, and bluefish in the brackish river and go after catfish, bream, bass, and crappie in Rock Spring Pond or rent a kayak, pedal boat, or rowboat. Displays at the visitor center, open in summer, provide historical and ecological perspective on the coastal plain.

Scattered through the park, the cabins are constructed from log, wood frame, and cedar siding, and most have either one or two bedrooms, plus air-conditioning and heat, modern bathrooms, a working fireplace, and plain wooden furniture. The Potomac River Retreat, a house with five bedrooms and five baths, accommodates 16. Fronting the Potomac, its deck has tables, chaise longues, and a charcoal grill.

If you want a change of pace from all the nature activities in the park, take a five-minute drive to Stratford Hall, birthplace of Robert E. Lee and boyhood home of two signers of the Declaration of Independence. Washington's Birthplace National Monument, a working farm with a museum and replica house, is 10 minutes from the park. Ingleside Plantation Vineyards is about 10 mi away.

Tip *There's no restaurant in the park and only a couple nearby (the dining room at the Inn at Montross, on Route 3, is excellent), so bring your favorite staples from home, and don't forget the dishwashing supplies. Nearby Heathville, Kilmarnock, and Warsaw have full-service supermarkets. In summer, roadside stands and farmers' markets sell just-picked local produce.*

🛏 32 cabins, 1 house 🍽 Snack bar, grills, picnic area, kitchens. **Recreation:** fishing, hiking, beach, pool, river swimming, boating, kayaking, playground. **Services:** kayak, pedal boat, and rowboat rentals; boathouse; boat launch; laundry facilities. **Classes and programs:** guided hikes, guided nature walks, guided kayak trips, natural history programs, children's programs (ages 6–12). ♿ Some pets allowed (fee); no room phones, no room TVs 💲 $51–$321 💳 MC, V.

🏠 *1650 State Park Rd. (Rte. 1, Box 600), Montross, VA 22520* ☎ *804/ 493–8821 or 800/933–7275* 📠 *804/493–8329* 🌐 *www.dcr.state.va.us/ parks/westmore.htm.*

Washington

ALTA CRYSTAL RESORT
Laid-Back Adventure ~ Tranquil Outpost

About 60 mi and less than two hours from Seattle, Alta Crystal Resort seems a world away. Nestled on 22 acres of the Mt. Baker–Snoqualmie National Forest, it's surrounded by 150-foot-tall firs. You're 7 mi from the Crystal Mountain ski area and a five-minute drive from the Sunrise Entrance to Mt. Rainier National Park.

You'll stay in one of three chalets, in a suite updated in the late 1990s with pleasant country furnishings. Larger quarters are bi-level with a bedroom and bathroom on the main floor and an open sleeping loft and second bathroom upstairs; the smaller ones have one bedroom and bathroom, and a futon in the living room suitable for two young children. If it's just the two of you, go for the spacious honeymoon cabin, which has a loft bedroom and a creek right outside the window. All accommodations have a fireplace and a kitchen. The resort also has a minigrocery store, where you can stock up on basics; lodge staff is happy to pick up a few things for you on their daily run into town.

You can hike, bike, ski, and snowshoe right from your door. Play volleyball and horseshoes on the resort's open grass field. Swim in the outdoor heated pool or soak in the outdoor hot tub (both open year-round), and check out the restored 1920s log lodge, which serves as a recreation center. Or venture farther out, to Crystal Mountain, Mt. Rainier, and the surrounding forest lands. When the road is open (it closes for snow and is generally closed all winter), drive from Mt. Rainier's Sunrise Entrance to the park's highest drivable point, at 6,400 feet, for spectacular views. Steve Cademotori, who owns Alta Crystal with his wife, Vivian, has climbed Mt. Rainier and is knowledgeable about the area, including the best trails to hike and sights to see.

Steve's and Vivian's love for where they live and what they do is evident. At night you can join them and your fellow guests for a bonfire, held several times a week depending on the season, and roast marshmallows, make s'mores, have a beer or some hot chocolate, and chat about your day's adventures. This is the kind of place where many guests choose to return every year and some wish they never had to leave.

Tip *In Greenwater, check out the Wapiti Woolies store for local huckle-berry products, hiking gear, and the namesake wool hats lined with polar fleece. You can also get an espresso drink or fruit smoothie.*

⤺ 23 suites, cabin ⑩ Grocery store, picnic area, grills, kitchens, microwaves. **Recreation:** biking, bird-watching, hiking, mountain biking, running, wildlife viewing, pool, cross-country skiing, snowshoeing, croquet, horseshoes, Ping-Pong, volleyball, recreation room. Nearby: fishing, horseback riding, rock climbing, downhill skiing, sledding, telemark skiing, tobogganing, tubing (snow). **Services:** bicycle rentals, outdoor hot tub, ski storage, grocery shopping, meeting rooms. **Classes and programs:** guided hikes, guided nature walks, natural history programs, nature talks, movies. ⛄ Cable TV, in-room data ports, in-room fireplaces, in-room VCRs, private balconies and decks; no a/c, no smoking ▨ $150–$240 ▭ AE, MC, V.

⌂ *68317 Hwy. 410 E, Greenwater, WA 98022* ☎ *360/663–2500 or 800/277–6475* 🖷 *360/663–0728* ⊕ *www.altacrystalresort.com.*

FREESTONE INN
Family Hideout ~ Luxurious Resort

It's not surprising that the Freestone Inn has been hugely popular since it opened in the the mid-1990s. It has a spectacular setting, stylish accommodations, excellent food, and a refined but unpretentious sensibility. With 21 rooms and 15 cabins (some dating back to the 1940s) on a ranch of more than 100 acres, surrounded by 2.1 million acres of public land, the resort gives you more than enough room to roam—by foot, bike, skis, or snowshoes—without feeling crowded.

Here in north-central Washington's Methow Valley, three to five hours from Seattle and 15 mi from Winthrop, the North Cascade mountains lie within sight of the lodge, and lakes and rivers beckon with rafting, fishing, and other water sports. Trails in the valley are abundant and well used by hikers, mountain bikers, runners, and horseback riders in spring, summer, and fall. In winter, you can cross-country ski and snow-shoe more than 200 km of groomed trails, go snowmobiling and sledding, take a sleigh ride, or heli-ski in the North Cascades. For an aerial view of the valley, take an early-morning hot-air balloon ride or flight-seeing tour by helicopter.

So many choices may seem overwhelming, but the recreation specialists at the inn's activity center, Jack's Hut, will help you out with tips; set you up with outfitters; rent you bikes and other equipment; sell you supplies for fishing and hiking; and lend equipment for playing volleyball and other games right on-site. The activity center also has a Ping-Pong table and outdoor heated pool (closed in winter).

Freestone Inn offers special programs for kids, too, including nature hikes and arts and crafts. The Kidventure program runs 4:30–7:30 PM and includes dinner, so you can enjoy some time off and some good food in the inn's restaurant. Executive chef Stuart Holm's impressive creations are based on local produce and herbs, and homemade honey, jam, and other products. Though the dinner menu may be too fancy for your kids, the whole family can enjoy the hearty breakfasts together.

Close to Early Winters Creek and framed by trees, the cabins are often visited by deer. Stay in one of the larger ones and you'll have your own fully equipped kitchen. Bring groceries from home, or stop in Winthrop's grocery store or the smaller but closer convenience store in the little town of Mazama. The cabins are convenient for families who want more space and the privacy of a separate bedroom for the children. The large living rooms have a sturdy dining table and fireplaces for warming up in winter. You can soak under the stars in the creekside hot tub, or in the tub by the inn. Two of the inn's suites have their own jetted tub, and all have a gas fireplace. There's also a three-story stone fireplace in the lobby of the inn. In the library, you can borrow board games and see photos of local history.

Tip *Bargain prices prevail in November (except Thanksgiving weekend), December 1–15, and April.*

📫 17 rooms, 4 suites, 15 cabins, 3 lodges 🍽️ Café, restaurant, room service, some kitchens, some kitchenettes, some microwaves, refrigerators. **Recreation:** biking, bird-watching, fishing, hiking, running, wildlife viewing, beach, pool, lake swimming, cross-country skiing, sleigh rides, sledding, snowshoeing, tobogganing, tubing (snow), badminton, croquet, horseshoes, paddle tennis, Ping-Pong, volleyball, library, recreation room. Nearby: horseback riding, mountain biking, rock climbing, tubing (water), waterskiing, boating, canoeing, kayaking, rafting, sailing, 9-hole golf course, tennis court, ballooning, hang gliding, downhill skiing, ice climbing, ice-skating, snowmobiling, telemark skiing, carriage rides, disc golf, miniature golf, soccer, playground. **Services:** volleyball, croquet, horseshoes, badminton, football, and Frisbee equipment and sleds provided; bicycle, bike trailer, helmet, cross-country ski, snowshoe, water-tube, day-pack, and fishing equipment rentals; 2 outdoor hot tubs; massage; guided fishing trips; tackle shop; shop; meeting rooms. **Classes and programs:** guided nature walks, children's programs (ages 6–15). ♿ Cable TV; in-room data ports; in-room fireplaces; in-room VCRs; some jetted tubs; private balconies, decks, and patios; no smoking 💳 $125–$595 💳 AE, MC, V.

🏠 *31 Early Winters Dr., Mazama, WA 98833* 📞 *509/996–3906 or 800/639–3809* 📠 *509/996–3907* 🌐 *www.freestoneinn.com.*

LAKE QUINAULT LODGE
Tranquil Outpost

On the road between Washington's capital, Olympia, and Lake Quinault Lodge, you'll encounter several miles of clear-cut timberland. Keep driving: one car length into Olympic National Forest and the cathedral of thick old-growth firs and cedars on either side of the road stands as a majestic welcome to lush and verdant rain forest. Magically light-dappled on a sunny day, the towering moss-covered trees are eerily shadowed under clouds. Lake Quinault Lodge, an old-timey retreat, blends so well with the national forest's pristine greenery it's hard to tell where the buildings end and the forest begins. To protect the lush environment, the lodge relies on a water conservation program, and environmentally friendly cleaning products. Staff works with the U.S. Forest Service to maintain ecologically sensitive areas. Little wonder that, for many who return year after year, the lodge is the very heart of the rain forest.

Standing almost exactly as it did on opening day in August 1926, the cedar shake and shuttered lodge is unpretentious—a sort of grand lady among the lake's other resorts and homes. A broad wooden deck, old Adirondack chairs, and a wide lawn add a hint of East Coast. Inside, vintage photographs from the lodge's past hang on the walls. Period wicker and upholstered furniture, a grand brick fireplace, and ceiling beams painted with Native American designs cast a spell in the great room, tempting you to stay up late reading, playing games, and chatting over wine and coffee from the fireside bar. Don't look for fussy service, opulent suites, or a spa—Lake Quinault Lodge stands out for its small and decidedly homey rooms, creaky stairs, low-key staff, and trees so large around you could fit your family inside.

With upward of 140 inches of rain each year, the rain forest around Lake Quinault rarely see temperatures below freezing or over 80°F. On the south shore of Lake Quinault, swimming, fishing, kayaking, and horseshoes are summer absolutes. Olympic National Park is a short drive away. The federally protected Quinault River valley and its surrounding rain forest contain awesome Sitka spruce and western hemlock forests—some of the finest in the Lower 48—as well as record-size Douglas fir, western cedar, big-leaf maple, and vine maple. The forest resembles a jungle, with plants growing in, on, and around each other. Mere steps from the lodge front door, well-maintained trails put you nose-to-bark with age-old trees—some 300 feet tall and 20 feet in diameter.

After a day of paddling or hiking, head back to picnic on the lawn, sip wine on the deck, or enjoy Northwest cuisine in the Roosevelt Room restaurant, in what was originally the lodge's covered sunporch. Fresh Northwest salmon and other fish, free-range meats, and Washington-grown produce are restaurant staples.

Tip *Take along* The Tree People *and* The Listening Ones, *two popular mystery novels set in Lake Quinault and written by local author Naomi M. Stokes. Warning: they are not for the faint of heart.*

⌨ 92 rooms, 1 suite ▯◯▯ Restaurant, lobby lounge, picnic area. **Recreation:** bird-watching, hiking, running, wildlife viewing, indoor pool, lake swimming, river swimming, tubing (water), boating, canoeing, kayaking, rowing, sailing, billiards, croquet, horseshoes, Ping-Pong, board games, library, piano, recreation room, video game room. Nearby: biking, fishing, mountain biking, beach. **Services:** lawn games provided, boat rentals, massage, sauna, boat launch, dock, guided fishing trips, meeting rooms. **Classes and programs:** guided hikes, guided nature walks, natural history programs, movies. ♿ Some in-room fireplaces; some private balconies, decks, and patios; some pets allowed; no-smoking floors; no a/c, no room phones, no TVs in some rooms ▭ $117–$255 ▭ AE, DC, MC, V.

⌂ *Box 7, Quinault, WA 98575-0007* ☎ *360/288–2900 or 800/562–6672* 🖷 *360/288–2901* ⊕ *www.visitlakequinault.com.*

OCEAN CREST RESORT
Tranquil Outpost

When visiting Washington's coast, most of the state's residents head to the busy beach town of Ocean Shores, which came to life in the 1960s and has grown by leaps and bounds since. The town gets close to 3 million visitors yearly and as many as 50,000 a day on weekends. To skip all this and find the untrammeled coast, continue north another 20 mi. The town of Moclips was one of Washington's first beach destinations for vacationers, and it has several older resorts and motels, the best of which is Ocean Crest. Surrounded by trees, the inn overlooks verdant landscape that gives way to a sandy stretch of beach washed by the Pacific.

The resort has been around for more than 50 years, and it's neither fancy nor sleek. From the outside, its age and era show, but the rooms have been kept up; you'll find pleasant furnishings and modern conveniences like microwaves and coffeemakers. There's no need for air-conditioning—the windows let in the sea breezes and the roar of the waves. The resort is right off the two-lane highway, but you're not likely to be bothered by traffic sounds, since the road dead-ends just 12 mi north on the Quinault Indian Reservation.

The ocean view from your balcony is especially dramatic during storm-watching season—late fall through early spring—when the fireplace also comes in handy. There are one- and two-bedroom units with kitchens as well as large studios, with king beds that face the ocean, and sleeper sofas. If you prefer to save your pennies, stay in one of the standard motel rooms—they lack the ocean view, but you'll be outdoors most of the time anyway.

The resort's capacious recreation center across the street has a gym, hot tub, indoor pool, sauna, and massage services. The beach is down a series of stairways through the forest—132 steps in all. North of the Ocean Crest on Highway 109, you can learn more about the area's history at the Museum of the North Beach or head to Ocean Shores to horseback ride or to the Quinault rain forest to hike and explore.

The resort's restaurant has stunning views of the ocean. Breakfasts are best and the desserts are great (try the blackberry cobbler); stick with the simplest entrées at dinner. Another option is the Windjammer restaurant a few miles south in Pacific Beach at the Navy's Pacific Beach Resort. It's open to the public and has dinner and breakfast buffets and live entertainment on weekends.

Tip *If you get a kitchen unit, load up on groceries in nearby Aberdeen.*

9 rooms, 16 studios, 12 1-bedroom units, 8 2-bedroom units ⑩ Restaurant, lounge, some kitchens, some kitchenettes, some microwaves, some refrigerators. **Recreation:** bird-watching, running, wildlife viewing, beach, indoor pool, playground. Nearby: fishing, hiking, horseback riding. **Services:** health club, hot tub, massage, laundry facilities, shop, meeting rooms. **Classes and programs:** aqua-cise classes. ⚙ Cable TV, in-room data ports, some in-room fireplaces, some private balconies and patios, some pets allowed (fee); no a/c, no smoking ▣ $59–$165 ▭ AE, D, MC, V.

⌂ *Box 7, Moclips, WA 98562* ☎ *360/276–4465 or 800/684–8439* 🖷 *360/276–4149* ⊕ *www.oceancrestresort.com.*

RUN OF THE RIVER
Laid-Back Adventure ~ Romantic Retreat

As you pull into the flower-bordered driveway at Run of the River, you may imagine that the deer in the nearby meadows are greeting you. Old bikes and snowshoes and other whimsical odds and ends decorate the lodge's exterior and landscape. A friendly Airedale meets you at the door. Clearly, this place is charmed.

Open since the mid-1980s, the inn underwent a major renovation in 2001 that added smart details to the suites: heated-tile bathroom floors, river-rock hot tubs for two, river-rock fireplaces, hand-hewn log-frame king beds with luxury linens, and double-headed showers. Northwest landscapes and Native American art adorn the walls, and each suite comes with binoculars for bird-watching, birdseed for the bird feeders, a private outside entrance, and a deck with a log swing and bubble-blowing toys. Next to the TAKE A HIKE sign on your deck, walking sticks, a backpack, and a picnic basket are provided.

A sense of pampering prevails in the suites. The refrigerator is stocked with complimentary beverages, a fancy Capressa coffeemaker grinds the coffee beans right before brewing, bath salts are placed by the Jacuzzi, and a complimentary Burt's Bees kit is packed with lotions and other body balms. A basket of fruit and wine awaits when you arrive. The four suites on the top level of the two-story inn have "play lofts," great for reading or napping, with couches and views of the mountains and river.

The Great Room is seasonally decorated with mountain and country touches; the long dining table is set festively for breakfast, prepared by owners Monty and Karen Turner. The feast includes fruit, energy drinks, fresh-baked pear-huckleberry crumble, cinnamon breakfast cake, and the signature sourdough breakfast bowls filled with jambalaya, peppers, and sausage. Much of the produce is locally grown, and the Icicle River Blend coffee is roasted locally.

Breakfast is the time to meet your fellow guests, share stories, and get fueled for an active day. The Turners can give you advice on the area and help set you up with all you need for a day's adventure. The inn provides mountain bikes, helmets, and even a tandem bike free of charge; in winter you can strap on a pair of their snowshoes and tromp through the snow. The grounds are bordered on two sides by a bird refuge, and you may see deer, coyote, elk, and even bears.

Tips *For a great lunch, bike 3 mi southeast to Sleeping Lady Mountain Retreat (a conference facility), whose Kingfisher Dining Hall is often open to the public by advance reservation (800/574–2123). The lunch buffet ($15) features fresh produce, some from Sleeping Lady's organic garden, and Northwest meats, poultry, and fish. Stroll the grounds for a look at artwork such as the glass-blown Chihuly Icicles. In summer, there are free chamber music concerts on many Saturday afternoons.*

🛏 6 suites 🍴 Full breakfast, dining room, refrigerators. **Recreation:** biking, bird-watching, hiking, running, wildlife viewing, river swimming, snowshoeing. Nearby: fishing, horseback riding, mountain biking, tubing (water), boating, canoeing, jet skiing, kayaking, rafting, rowing, sailing, three 18-hole golf courses, putting green, cross-country skiing, dogsledding, downhill skiing, ice-skating, sleigh rides, sledding, snowmobiling, telemark skiing, tobogganing, tubing (snow), miniature golf. **Services:** mountain bikes, helmets, snowshoes, backpacks, and hiking sticks provided; outdoor hot tub; ski storage; shop. ⛄ Satellite TV, in-room data ports, wireless Internet, in-room fireplaces, in-room VCRs/DVDs, jetted tubs, private balconies and patios; no kids, no smoking 💲$205–$245 ▭ D, MC, V.

🏠 *9308 E. Leavenworth Rd. (P.O. Box 285), Leavenworth, WA 98826* ☎ *509/548–7171 or 800/288–6491* 🖷 *509/548–7547* 🌐 *www. runoftheriver.com.*

West Virginia

CANAAN VALLEY RESORT STATE PARK
Family Hideout ~ Laid-Back Adventure

Lying at 3,200 feet in the Allegheny Mountains of northeastern West Virginia is the Canaan Valley. Fourteen miles long and 5 mi wide, it is the highest valley of its size east of the Rockies. The Blackwater River meanders through it, and wetlands such as swamps, marshes, and bogs support black bears, white-tailed deer, wild turkeys, grouse, snowshoe hares, cottontail rabbits, and a variety of squirrels. Humans find the valley attractive, too, and come here to go skiing, rock climbing, mountain biking, fishing, hiking, backpacking, tubing, and white-water rafting.

Within 6,000-acre Canaan Valley Resort State Park, the land itself—with the solitude you can find there—is the biggest attraction. In winter, chairlifts access 37 snowy slopes with a vertical drop of 850 feet and runs of up to 1¼ mi. The park also maintains 18 mi of cross-country ski trails, plus ice-skating and snow-tubing areas. In spring, summer, and fall, you can go hiking, biking, and horseback riding on the trails or access hundreds more miles of marked trails in the adjacent million-acre Monongahela National Forest.

The park is great for families. In ski season, Canaan Resort offers half- and full-day children's ski programs for two age groups (3–4 years and 5–12 years) that includes ski rental, lift ticket, and lessons. Children's crafts sessions go on year-round in the lodge's activity center, and park rangers lead walks for kids.

At the end of the day, take a sauna in the fitness center and return to your cabin or lodge room. The clapboard cabins have decks and stone fireplaces. In the contemporary stone-and-wood lodge, guest rooms are spacious motel-style units. For a cocktail, stop by the Laurel Lounge and settle in before the fireplace or big-screen TV. Then have some dinner in the Hickory Room, whose glass walls let in views of the valley and mountains. The dinner menu might include potpie of the day, buffalo meat loaf, chicken bruschetta, and Canaan surf and turf—brown sugar–glazed salmon and house-marinated flank steak with a bourbon-mushroom sauce.

The area surrounding Canaan Valley Resort State Park is full of natural attractions. Canaan Valley National Wildlife Refuge, managed by the U.S. Fish and Wildlife Service, protects the valley's beaver ponds and bogs. In the sunken bogs grow sphagnum moss, cranberries, and the insect-eating sundew plant (more typical of northern Canada than of West Virginia). In the Dolly Sods Wilderness Area, named for the Dalhe family's "sods" (where sheep grazed in the mid-1800s), you can hike along nine trails; pick your way over rocky plains, around bogs, through hardwood forests and laurel thickets; and look out over sweeping valley vistas. In the summer you can pick blueberries. Guided tours of Seneca Caverns, West Virginia's largest, show off spaces such as the 60-foot-long, 30-foot-wide, and 70-foot-high Grand Ballroom. Nearby, Smoke Hole Cavern has the trout-filled Crystal Cave Coral Pool, the likes of which exists in only one other cavern in the world. Rock climbers scale 900-foot Seneca Rocks, one of the best climbs in the East.

Tip *For more hiking, head to nearby Canaan Mountain, Blackwater Falls State Park, or Otter Creek Wilderness Area.*

 250 rooms, 23 cabins Snack bar, 2 restaurants, lounge, sports bar, picnic area, some refrigerators. **Recreation:** biking, bird-watching, fishing, hiking, climbing wall, paintball, Eurobungy, geocaching, mountain biking, running, wildlife viewing, pool, indoor pool, swimming, driving range, 18-hole golf course, putting green, 2 tennis courts, cross-country skiing, downhill skiing, ice-skating, snowshoeing, tubing (snow), miniature golf, recreation room, playground. Nearby: rock climbing, horseback riding, canoeing, kayaking, rafting. **Services:** snowboarding, skiing, ice-skating, golf, and tennis equipment rentals; health club; hot tub; sauna; pro shop; ski shop; laundry facilities; shop; Internet accesss; meeting rooms. **Classes and programs:** guided hikes; natural history programs; skiing, snowboarding, and golf lessons; children's programs (ages 3–12). Cable TV, no-smoking rooms $64–$234 AE, D, DC, MC, V.

 Rte. 32 (HC 70, Box 330), Davis, WV 26260 *304/866–4121 or 800/622–4121* *304/866–2172* *www.canaanresort.com.*

GLADE SPRINGS RESORT
Luxurious Resort ~ Family Hideout

On 4,100 acres in West Virginia's Allegheny Mountains, Glade Springs Resort shares its landscape of mountain laurel and wildflowers with wild turkeys, deer, and couples and families who spend their days walking, biking, and horseback riding on 26 mi of trails; canoeing, kayaking, and fishing on Mallard Lake; luxuriating in the full-service spa; or white-water rafting on the renowned rivers nearby.

Scattered around the wooded property are southern colonial-style buildings, some with white columns and porches, others of pink brick with a quartet of chimneys. You can reserve everything from a hotel-style room to a six-bedroom lodge with a kitchen and dining room. The Small Talk Café, a casual eatery, is open for breakfast, lunch, and dinner, and in the evening Robert's restaurant serves creative, exquisitely plated dinners; soft-shell crabs, yellowfin tuna, rock shrimp, game, or duck are accompanied by live piano music. Afterward, sink into an easy chair in the lounge and warm your feet by the fire.

You're in the lap of luxury at Glade Springs, but your kids won't feel out of place. If they're under 17 they stay free and may participate in free tennis, golf, and fishing clinics. Throughout the year, the resort's Equestrian Center operates trail rides suitable for all ages and ability levels. Folks under 52 inches tall favor the pony rides, and the genteel set can take carriage rides. Work on your casting skills with a fly-fishing lesson, or sharpen your aim at the sporting-clays facility. Framed by mature trees, the resort's two superlative golf courses are laid out over naturally hilly terrain; there are clay and hard courts indoors and out. Not far from Glade Springs are skiing, llama trekking, and jet-boat river tours.

Southern West Virginia is premier white-water country, home of the New River Gorge National River (a 53-mi portion of the river) and Gauley River National Recreation Area (a 25½-mi stretch of water). All-day rafting trips from the resort are fun even for novices. The New River flows past rocks up to 330 million years old and through a craggy, 1,300-foot-deep canyon known locally as the Grand Canyon of the East. The river also flows beneath the world's longest single-span arch bridge. The Upper Gauley has more than 100 major rapids, with big drops along the way—children under 12 are not allowed. The Lower Gauley takes you on at least 45 roller-coaster rapids and you must be at least 15. A good choice for families with children at least six years old is the more placid Upper New River, where you can bob along mild rapids and idle in calm pools. Two kinds of float trips are available, via standard raft or in inflatable kayaks.

Tip *If you're planning to take a white-water rafting trip, you can bring your own wet suit, booties, and paddle jacket or rent them from the rafting company. Life vests and helmets are included.*

▷ 134 rooms ▢ 2 restaurants, bar, lounge, some kitchens. **Recreation:** biking, bird-watching, fishing, hiking, horseback riding, mountain biking, running, wildlife viewing, pool, lake and river swimming, canoeing, kayaking, rafting, driving range, two 18-hole golf courses, putting green, 8 tennis courts, basketball, playground. Nearby: rock climbing, cross-country skiing, downhill skiing, snowshoeing, tubing (snow). **Services:** bicycle, fishing pole, and golf- and tennis-equipment rentals; health club; hot tub; spa; guided fishing trips; pro shop; dry-cleaning service; laundry facilities; laundry service; shop; business services; concierge; meeting rooms; Internet access. **Classes and programs:** guided hikes; guided nature walks; fly-fishing, golf, and tennis lessons; fitness and yoga classes; children's programs (infant–17), dances. ♿ Cable TV, no-smoking rooms ⌨ $99–$509 ▭ AE, MC, V.

🏠 *200 Lake Dr., Daniels, WV 25832* ☎ *304/763–5200 or 800/634–5233* 🖷 *304/763–3398* ⊕ *www.gladesprings.com.*

Wisconsin

CANOE BAY
Luxurious Resort ~ Romantic Retreat

Hidden in Chetek, a northern Wisconsin town otherwise spotted with bait shops and supper clubs, Canoe Bay is a sumptuous place just for couples, nestled amid 280 unspoiled wooded acres, some two hours from Minneapolis. Your surrender to tranquillity begins the moment you turn down the winding drive. At Canoe Bay nature frees your mind from worldly worries.

A member of the Relais & Châteaux group, Canoe Bay stands out for its quality, amenities, and attentive care. Going to every length to ensure privacy for their guests, owners Dan and Lisa Dobrowski deliver driving directions only when confirming your reservation.

The commitment to discreetness extends throughout your stay. Staff members (often the owners themselves) deliver victuals to your room via specially outfitted electric golf carts that are silent so that a resident doe and her fawn hardly twitch as a cart passes by. A quick ring of a bell announces your meal's arrival; then the porters slip silently away. Even when all six suites and 15 cottages are full, you may never spot another soul as you wander the trails to discover the two hidden lakes, lounge on the pier with a book from the resort's expansive library, or paddle across the mirror-smooth water in a canoe. And though the cabins seem close together, they are situated so that balconies are completely private, leaving the soothing views, Wisconsin wildlife, and genteel Lake Whadoon to you alone.

The cabins and other buildings reflect the owners' fondness for the clean lines and natural materials characteristic of the architecture of Frank Lloyd Wright. Smooth woods and rough stone make the interiors lush but not ornate. As the sun sets and the stars emerge, you can sit before a roaring fire and watch a recent theatrical release on your state-of-the-art audiovisual system. The wet bar is carefully stocked with candy, specialty snacks, soft drinks, water, coffee, and teas. If you order a cheese plate and a bottle of wine ahead of time, it will be waiting for you (along with fresh fruit, flowers, and bottled water) when you arrive. The bath is equipped with a whirlpool tub for two, plus specialty toiletries, fluffy towels, and warm robes. At night, a king-size bed with smooth Egyptian cotton linens pampers you like royalty. The staff has simply thought of everything, including small bowls of mints on nightstands, near telephones, and in other spots.

Breakfast is included, picnic lunches are available upon request, and the dining room is open every night except Tuesday. Off the property, consider a spring jaunt through area antiques stores, a summer hike at the nearby Chippewa Moraine Ice Age Center, a fall drive over the rolling Blue Hills, or a winter glide along local cross-country ski trails. Afterward, you will have to decide which does more to restore the spirit: the serene setting, the exquisite service, or the indulgent rooms. Perhaps it is the perfect combination of all three.

Tip *Bring your bug spray. But keep in mind that Canoe Bay operates in harmony with nature and the owners prefer eco-friendly sprays and lotions.*

🛏 6 suites, 15 cottages 🍽 Continental breakfast included in room rate, full breakfast available for additional fee, dining room, picnic area, wet bars, microwaves. **Recreation:** bird-watching, fishing, hiking, running, wildlife viewing, lake swimming, canoeing, kayaking, library, snowshoeing. Nearby: biking, 18-hole golf course, cross-country skiing, sleigh rides, library. **Services:** canoes and kayaks provided, gym, massage, shop, Internet access. ♿ Cable TV with movies, in-room DVD players; no room phones, no kids, no smoking 💳 $325–$1,800 🏧 AE, D, DC, MC, V.

✒ *Box 28, Chetek, WI 54728* ☎ *715/924–4594* 📠 *715/924–2078* 🌐 *www.canoebay.com.*

SILVER STAR INN
Tranquil Outpost ~ Laid-Back Adventure

Nature takes top billing at the Silver Star Inn. This post-and-beam bed-and-breakfast is hidden amid bucolic farms and wooded hills near the Wisconsin River in Spring Green about an hour from Madison and 2½ hours from Milwaukee. This part of the state is known as the Driftless Area because it escaped the wrath of two great glaciations that otherwise leveled the countryside. Here you can get lost in quiet valleys, tickle your toes in spring creeks (which happen to be excellent spots for fly-fishing), or career down one of the longest stretches of barrier-free waterways in the Midwest.

The 10 suites are decorated with country antiques and contemporary art and photos. The owner is a photographer, so room names recall individuals or things significant to photography, such as the Aperture. A hearty breakfast of fresh fruit, cereals, and seasonal homemade baked goods will remind you that simple fare is often the greatest luxury. Overall, the accommodations are not lavish, but they are more than adequate and provide a quiet, restful, and convenient home base for exploring the idyllic countryside.

The patchwork hills, limestone outcroppings, scenic bluffs, and rivers attract bikers, paddlers, skiers, and wildlife watchers. Silver Star is in the heart of it all. Its 340 acres include some manicured gardens and lawns, but most of the property is either heavily wooded or former farmland that's now prairie. You can sip your morning tea on the deck while watching for woodpeckers, bobolinks, eagles, herons, or cranes; more than 35 species have been counted on the grounds. You can also walk through the trails surrounding the inn. Deer are so populous that spotting two or three together is unremarkable, and don't be surprised if a wild turkey ambles across your path.

Governor Dodge State Park, just minutes away, offers more than 5,000 acres of challenging hiking as well as two quiet lakes for boating (only electric motors are allowed), and cross-country skiing and snowshoeing in winter.

If you like a little civilization along with your scenery, spend an evening at the American Players Theater, which presents Shakespeare, Chekhov, and other classics in an outdoor amphitheater atop a grassy knoll in Spring Green. Also minutes from the inn is Taliesin, Frank Lloyd Wright's Wisconsin studio. Spend just a few minutes in this incredible pocket of natural wonder and it is easy to appreciate his inspiration.

Tip *Ask for the Stieglitz-Steichen Suite; it is the only room with a whirlpool bath.*

🛏 10 suites 🍽 Continental breakfast. **Recreation:** bird-watching, hiking, running, wildlife viewing, cross-country skiing, snowshoeing. Nearby: biking, fishing, river swimming, canoeing, kayaking, 9-hole and 18-hole golf courses, downhill skiing, ice-skating, library. ♿ No room phones, no smoking 💵 $110–$150 🛏 D, MC, V.

🏠 *3852 Limmex Hill Rd., Spring Green, WI 53588* ☎ *608/935–7297* 🌐 *www.silverstarinn.com.*

SPIDER LAKE LODGE
Romantic Retreat

Once a fishing camp accessible only by boat, Spider Lake Lodge is now the perfect blend of contemporary comfort and Northwoods nostalgia. Tucked amid towering pines and contrasting birch trees on a hilltop at the very end of a serpentine road some 150 mi from the Twin Cities, this log-cabin B&B takes you back to lake life of yesteryear. "Here, there is no time," says a sign above a handless clock. And it's true. The hours seem to hang in the damp, earthy air, refusing to go anywhere fast. These are the long, lazy days most people only dream of.

The lodge has a long history on the lake. In 1923 Ted Moony, an avid fisherman, built the structure from hand-hewn tamarack and cedar with help from Native American lumberjacks. Anglers who came for the great fishing stayed for the raucous fun. The property changed hands over time, eventually landing with current owners Craig Mason and Jim Kerkow, who have filled the retreat with memorabilia from the fishing-camp days: stuffed animal trophies, massive stone fireplaces, twisted twig furniture, and other retro bric-a-brac. There are some surprises, too, like the orchids blooming beneath antler chandeliers, the posh velvet couches, and the scrumptious breakfasts that begin with dessert.

In the seven themed guest rooms, kitsch meets comfort. The Bear's Den features a bearskin throw for the bed along with pillowcases, framed pictures, decorative boxes, and decorative touches dedicated to the Royal Canadian Mounted Police. The Moonhanis pays homage to Indian maidens, and the Let'er Buck brings a rodeo theme. Mason and Kerkow clearly had fun with the interiors and admit that *maybe* they went a little over the top. Yet guests love the nostalgic feel of the place.

Big Spider Lake is a Class "A" Musky lake, but there are plenty of other options besides fishing. You can drift out onto the placid lake in a rental pontoon, or stroll near the lodge to look for deer, elk, and foxes. Although sightings are rare, rumor has it that bears still pay an occasional visit. After the sun sets you can gather by the bonfire and listen for wolves and coyotes howling in the distance. As night falls, resident loons wail and call until the sunrise welcomes another peaceful day. This is the perfect place to get close, but not too close, to what is left of the Wisconsin wilderness.

If you're looking for more adventure, you can hike in summer or snowshoe in winter in Chequamegon National Forest, just minutes from Spider Lake Lodge. Canoeing, kayaking, and rafting are popular on the Chippewa Flowage and the Namakagon River. Sure, you can work up a sweat, but the roaring fires, cushy beds, and easy charm of Spider Lake Lodge may make you wonder why you would want to.

Tip *Ask for Moody's Camp when you make your reservation. Although it's not a suite, this corner hideaway is ideal for those wishing to nod off to a lakeside lullaby heard through the sliding door that opens to the waterfront deck. Plus, Moody's lower-level quarters have the lodge's only whirlpool tub.*

🛏 7 rooms ⑩ Full breakfast. **Recreation:** bird-watching, 9-hole golf course, fishing, hiking, wildlife viewing, lake swimming, canoeing, cross-country skiing, ice-skating, library. Nearby: biking, horseback riding, running, boating, rowing, 18-hole golf course, snowmobiling, snowshoeing, bowling, miniature golf. **Services:** canoes provided, boat rental assistance, dock. ♿ No room phones, no room TVs, no kids under 12, no smoking 💳 $139–$179 🟰 AE, MC, V.

🏠 *10472 W. Murphy Blvd., Hayward, WI 54843* ☎ *715/462–3793 or 800/653–9472* 📠 *715/462–9691* ⊕ *www.spiderlakelodge.com.*

Wyoming

BROOKS LAKE LODGE
Laid-back Adventure ~ Luxurious Resort

The colossal peaks of the Pinnacles form a backdrop to the jewel-blue waters of Brooks Lake, which is surrounded by lush green mountain meadows. Here, deep in the heart of the Shoshone National Forest 21 mi northwest of Dubois, Brooks Lake Lodge has cosseted travelers since 1922. With a nearly one-to-one staff-to-guest ratio and a maximum capacity of 36 guests, the lodge combines seclusion with service.

You can take a room in the main lodge, part of which dates from the resort's founding or reserve an intimate cabin for two or a large log cabin for the whole family. All accommodations have down duvets and Egyptian cotton sheets on lodgepole-pine beds. In the lodge rooms, walls are stripped-log and ceilings knotty-pine. All the cabins have a wood-burning stove. The family cabins have two bedrooms, each with private bath, and a loft with well-stuffed couches and a variety of games.

An extensive network of hiking trails gets you into the forest, either on foot or by mountain bike (bring your own) or on horseback. This is grizzly country, but there is no need to fear the animals so long as you remain somewhat alert and maintain your composure should you come across one. If you feel uncomfortable hiking the Pinnacles, fishing on the lake, or horseback riding alone, the lodge will provide a guide.

If you feel like taking it easy, head for the spa for a massage or an exercise class. Or mosey over to the historic section of the lodge for a game of chess in the great room or shuffleboard or darts in the Diamond G Bar. In the afternoon, tea is served in the lodge or on the flagstone patio, where you can soak up the cool mountain air as you gaze over the lake. A fireplace takes the chill off cool summer evenings in both the tearoom and the dining room. At dinner you can sit with fellow guests at large tables or request a private table for two (as many honeymooners do). Each evening the chef carefully explains the menu choices, which might include filet mignon or trout; there is always a vegetarian entrée. After dinner, go for a soak in the outdoor hot tub as you watch the moon rise over the Pinnacles.

Tip *The Lodge Spa has treatment and workout rooms, but the single greatest feature is its large outdoor hot tub, where you can soak while watching the stars or listening to birds calling, coyotes howling, or elks bugling.*

⇨ 6 lodge rooms, 1 suite, 8 cabins |◎| American plan, dining room, bar. **Recreation:** bird-watching, fishing, hiking, horseback riding, running, wildlife viewing, canoeing, rafting, cross-country skiing, sledding, snowmobiling, snowshoeing, tubing (snow), archery, badminton, horseshoes, paddle tennis, Ping-Pong, shuffleboard, volleyball, library, piano. **Services:** exercise equipment, outdoor hot tub, sauna, spa, guided fishing trips, tackle shop, ski shop, babysitting, laundry service, airport shuttle, business services, meeting rooms. **Classes and programs:** guided hikes and nature walks, natural history programs, horseback-riding and fly-casting lessons, children's programs, yoga and arts and crafts classes, concerts, sing-alongs. ♿ Some jetted tubs; no a/c, no room phones, no room TVs, no smoking 🏷 $200–$350 per person; family cabins $1,500 per night ▭ AE, D, MC, V.

🖰 *458 Brooks Lake Rd., Dubois, WY 82513* 🕾 *307/455–2121* ⊕ *www. brookslake.com.*

JENNY LAKE LODGE
Tranquil Outpost

From the rocking chair on the front porch of your log cabin at Jenny Lake Lodge, you can see the magnificent peaks of the Grand Tetons; watch moose, elk, or fox wander past; and smell the wildflowers of Grand Teton National Park. The cabins are scattered through the pine forest and connected by gravel walkways. Each has a big bed with extra pillows, bright quilts, down comforters, and electric blankets. Rooms come with a phone only on request, but a walking stick is standard, and you have use of a 1950s-style bicycle to get from your cabin to the main lodge, which holds the dining area, gift shop, and a sitting area. At this most exclusive of the national park's resorts, children of all ages are welcome, but the lodge is better for older kids and adults.

Many hiking trails meander out from the lodge. Take an early-morning or late-evening stroll around Jenny Lake itself, or cross the road to paths that lead to String Lake and spectacular Cascade Canyon. If you want a full day of hiking, take a sack lunch and make your way to Mystic Falls and Inspiration Point. This is a busy area of the park, in fact the most-used trail in Grand Teton, but once you've passed Inspiration Point, you'll leave most of the other hikers behind. Impressive views of Jackson Hole and a glimpse of wildlife such as songbirds, marmots, chipmunks, deer, and possibly even black bears will be your reward. In late spring and fall, you might also hear the distinctive sound of a bull elk bugling for a mate. For a change of pace, take a horseback trail ride across Jackson Hole, or pedal along Teton Park Road. Those activities are included in the price of your stay.

You can have a casual breakfast in the dining room and lunch on soup or sandwiches there as well, or have the kitchen pack you a lunch to eat as you explore the park. For dinner, jackets are suggested for men— appropriate considering it's a six-course affair that might include elk, breast of pheasant, or roast prime rib of buffalo and delectable desserts such as blackberry sorbet. Summer evenings are cool at Jenny Lake, so you might want to throw on a jacket or sweater for your evening stroll or if you plan to read a book on your porch.

Tip *Visit in early June or September to avoid summer crowds.*

⟿ 37 cabins ⑩ Modified American plan, restaurant, refrigerators. **Recreation:** biking, bird-watching, fishing, hiking, horseback riding, rock climbing, running, wildlife viewing, lake swimming, boating, canoeing, library. **Services:** shop, airport shuttle, Internet access, concierge. ⌂ No a/c, no room TVs, no smoking ▣ $475–$700 ▤ AE, MC, V.

🖃 *Box 250, Moran, WY 83013* ☎ *307/733–4647* 🖷 *307/543–3143* ⊕ *www.gtlc.com* ⊘ *Closed early Oct.–late May.*

PARADISE GUEST RANCH
Family Hideout ~ Laid-Back Adventure

Nestled in a valley and surrounded by the Big Horn National Forest, Paradise Guest Ranch is well insulated from the outside world. Once you've driven the winding 4-mi gravel road that leads to the ranch from U.S. 16, park your car and forget about it. For the next week you'll be living in a log cabin on a hillside above French Creek. You can turn your attention to watching moose in the willows along the creek, exploring the surrounding forest on horseback or on foot, learning how to fly-fish, and spending quality time with your kids.

Your week starts with a gathering in the French Creek Saloon, where you meet the staff and other families visiting the ranch. Kids often strike up new friendships before the evening is out. A short orientation session follows dinner, and then it's time to settle in. The guest cabins, all of them with views of Fan Rock, stair-step their way up the hillside. Most cabins have one or two bedrooms, a fireplace, laundry facilities, and a kitchenette; a few larger cabins have a full kitchen and up to four bedrooms. Each cabin has a deck or porch, and all have western-style furniture, a small dining table, and limited drink supplies such as coffee, tea, and hot chocolate mix.

You can spend your week at Paradise however you like, but horseback riding is certainly the main attraction. On your first full day at the ranch a basic horseback-riding lesson prepares you for your time in the saddle. After that, you choose from rides at different skill levels, from gentle walks to rides that mix in some trotting to lopes across the mountain meadows. You can ride for a couple of hours or a full day, be sure to take at least one all-day ride so you can savor the full flavor of this high-mountain country. A full-day ride takes you across open plateaus, through deep pine forests, and along mountain streams or to high-country lakes, where you can stop for a picnic or a nap in the grass. At every level of ability, you'll ride with a wrangler. Don't feel like riding? Try fly-fishing, even if you have never fished before; guides will show you how, or hike along the horse trails, or follow the path along French Creek in and out of pine forest. Some trails, the main road to the ranch, and routes to nearby trails serve mountain bikers.

The children's programs are outstanding. Activities for children include arts and crafts, fishing, and horseback riding. One afternoon a week, there's a horseback competition in the arena, along with wheelbarrow and three-legged races and other games. Kids ages 13–17 can take an overnight pack trip. Adults and families who want to sleep in a tent and hike and fish in remote mountain areas can take multiday pack trips.

For most meals, you fill your plate at a buffet in the log dining hall, but one evening you'll hike ¼ mi to the ranch picnic area for a campfire meal, and on another night you'll ride horseback, or go on a hay wagon, to a different mountain spot for a chuck-wagon dinner. Each evening, gather in the French Creek Saloon for kid-friendly sing-alongs, square dancing, storytelling, and other entertainment.

Tip *Summer at Paradise is family-oriented, but in September the ranch hosts only adults. One week focuses on activities for women, such as fly-fishing clinics, cooking classes, and horse-packing instruction.*

⮌ 18 cabins ⦿⦿ Dining room, bar, picnic area, some kitchens, some kitchenettes, some microwaves. **Recreation:** biking, bird-watching, fishing, hiking, horseback riding, mountain biking, running, wildlife viewing, pool, river swimming, tubing (water), basketball, billiards, croquet, horseshoes, Ping-Pong, softball, volleyball, library, piano, recreation room, video game room, playground. **Services:** fishing-equipment rentals, hot tub, massage, guided fishing, tackle shop, babysitting, grocery shopping, laundry facilities, shops, airport shuttle, business services, Internet access, meeting rooms. **Classes and programs:** guided hikes and nature walks; natural history programs; photo safaris; fly-casting and horseback-riding lessons; fitness, cooking, photography, and writing classes; children's programs (ages 3–17); concerts; dances; entertainment; movies; sightseeing tours; sing-alongs. ⌂ No-smoking rooms; no a/c, no room phones, no room TVs ▦ $1,675 per wk adults, $525–$1,275 per wk children ▭ No credit cards.

⌂ *Box 790, Buffalo, WY 82834* ☎ *307/684–7876* 🖷 *307/684–9054*
⊕ *www.paradiseranch.com* ☯ *Closed late Sept.–late May.*

SPIRIT WEST RIVER LODGE BED & BREAKFAST
Tranquil Outpost

Outside the tiny community of Riverside (population 86) in south-central Wyoming, Spirit West River Lodge sprawls beside the Encampment River. Among the cottonwoods and other trees surrounding the lodge and in the ranch pasture and natural-grass meadow that lies nearby, a resident herd of white-tailed deer and a family of raccoons (who regularly visit the lodge's back deck) make their home. In this woodland setting, the only sounds you're likely to hear are the rustle of aspen leaves in fall and the gurgle of the river as it flows past your room.

The center of activity at the one-story lodge is the great room, dominated by a lichen-covered stone fireplace and a wall of windows. Several seating areas and a bar invite you to linger, especially on cold days and in the evening. The great room, like the rest of the lodge, is a showcase for oil paintings, limited-edition prints, and bronze sculptures by R. G. Finney, a western and wildlife artist and his wife, Lynn, lodge keeper of Spirit West. The Finneys see to it that you feel at home in one of the four guest rooms. A large room decorated with mountain-man attire has big windows overlooking the river and grounds, plus a stone shower large enough for two. One room has a Jacuzzi tub, and another is decorated with memorabilia of Lynn's great-uncle Gee-String Jack Fulkerson, who made his reputation freighting supplies to copper mines in the nearby Sierra Madre in the early 1900s. The fourth room, with two double beds, is all buffalo, with buffalo hides and appropriate artwork. All the rooms share a riverfront deck. Near the lodge stands a three-bedroom, two-bath guesthouse, with its own kitchen.

Breakfast is served in the lodge dining room or, if weather permits, on the deck overlooking the river. Lynn's breakfast specialties range from caramelized apple French toast to breakfast enchiladas to eggs sardou. They are melt-in-your-mouth good, yet healthful, since Lynn cooks with low-fat ingredients as much as possible. The occasional campfire breakfast, cooked outside next to the river and near the lodge tepee, features hearty fried potatoes, eggs, bacon, or pancakes.

The lodge's mile of Encampment River frontage allows you to cast for rainbow trout from outside your room. Within five minutes of the lodge a trail leads to the Indian Bathtubs, a natural landmark with a spectacular view of the Encampment River valley. Seven miles west of town, you can explore the Sierra Madre in Medicine Bow National Forest on skis in winter and on foot in summer. Also near the lodge, 13 mi west of town, is a major trailhead of the Continental Divide National Scenic

Trail. Elsewhere in the area, off-trail snowmobiling is popular in winter, and river kayaking on the Encampment livens up early spring.

Tip *Lynn Finney is a native of the area and a senior (50-plus) Olympian who has won numerous gold medals in cycling. An avid cross-country skier, she can provide you with the latest details on trails and trail conditions.*

☞ 4 rooms, 1 guesthouse ⃝ Full breakfast, dining room, bar, picnic area. **Recreation:** biking, bird-watching, fishing, hiking, canoeing, kayaking, rafting, cross-country skiing (nearby), snowshoeing, snowmobiling, horseback riding (nearby), library, piano. **Services:** exercise equipment, business services. ⃝ Movies, satellite TV, no a/c, no room phones, no room TVs, no smoking ⃝ $85 rooms, $250 guesthouse ⃝ AE, D, MC, V.

⃝ *Box 605, Encampment, WY 82325* ⃝ *307/327–5753* ⊕ *www. spiritwestriverlodge.com.*

TWIN CREEK RANCH
Laid-Back Adventure

A working cattle ranch 24 mi southeast of Lander, Twin Creek lets you help with a cattle drive and the branding of livestock, groom a horse or fix a fence, or gather eggs and feed the chickens down by the barn. A vacation here immerses you in Wyoming ranch life.

The drive to the ranch, the last 8 mi of it on a gravel road, takes you past a rock outcrop, Shipwreck Rock, that looks like a ship in heavy seas. On the ranch, the landscape includes both sagebrush-covered hillsides and grassy hay land. Twin Creek's own 5,000 acres, plus an additional 10,000 acres of leased and federally managed land, offer lots to see, from petroglyphs to wildflowers to wild birds.

A three-level log lodge is the heart of guest life on the ranch. The living, dining, and kitchen areas are on the second floor in a big, open space with a piano in one corner. Artwork and photographs of ranch activities decorate the walls, and large windows provide views of the ranch. Guest rooms are on the ground floor, where two large rooms share a shower, and in the third-floor loft, where two smaller rooms share a large bathroom with a claw-foot tub and an outdoor deck with a view of Twin Creek. Each room is furnished with a set of bunk beds and a king bed, all covered with quilts. Rag rugs soften the wood floors.

You can choose a package that includes all meals or book at a bed-and-breakfast rate. All meals are served at a long, heavy wood table, using plates, glasses, and cups that are stacked on split-log shelves when they aren't in use. Most of the food served at Twin Creeks is organically produced and locally grown, and some—such as the hen's eggs and goat's milk—even comes from the ranch. The ranch's "beyond organic beef," all-natural meat from range-fed cattle, is carefully aged for flavor and tenderness. But the menu here goes well beyond beef: black bean quesadillas with roasted red peppers and ancho chili hollandaise; gazpacho; and a chocolate mole tart with tamarind crème anglaise might appear. For breakfast, look for ranch-raised eggs and whole-grain bread, scones, muffins, and biscuits.

Some weeks, the entire ranch is devoted to special programs. The Environmental Restoration Adventure in October teaches environmental stewardship. Another week is for women and includes yoga sessions, therapeutic massage, and writing workshops.

Tips *If you visit the ranch at winter solstice, you can attend a party with dance music from a local western band. You will also witness ranch life in winter, when feeding cattle is the primary activity. At any time of the year, note that the entrance to the lodge, framed by boulders, is over rough ground.*

⟿ 4 rooms |○| American plan, dining room. **Recreation:** bird-watching, fishing, hiking, horseback riding, mountain biking, running, wildlife viewing, snowshoeing, horseshoes, library, piano. **Services:** massage, guided fishing trips, horse boarding, laundry facilities, laundry service, airport shuttle, business services, meeting room, travel services. **Classes and programs:** guided hikes and nature walks; natural history programs; photo safaris; horseback-riding and fly-fishing lessons; yoga, arts and crafts, cooking, photography, and writing classes; nature restoration talks; dances; sightseeing tours. ⚘ Some pets allowed (fee); no a/c, no room phones, no room TVs, no smoking ✉ $190 (per person) ▭ MC, V.

⌂ *768 Twin Creek Rd., Lander, WY 82520* ☎ *307/335–7485* 🖷 *307/ 335–7485* ⊕ *www.twincreekranch.com.*

Escape to Nature in Canada

Alberta

AURUM LODGE
Laid-Back Adventure ~ Romantic Retreat

Overlooking the turquoise waters of Lake Abraham and the North Saskatchewan River valley is an inn that provides country comfort in harmony with the surrounding ecology. Just 30 minutes north of Banff National Park, Aurum Lodge is a world away from the mobs of tourists that crowd Banff Townsite. It stands in the Bighorn Wildland, an irreplaceable habitat for grizzlies and other wildlife. A four-hour drive from either Calgary or Edmonton, the preserve is an unspoiled wilderness, with no roads or motorized access into many parts of the area.

Aurum, the Latin word for gold, accurately describes this treasure of an inn. The owners of the lodge do everything they can to reduce its impact on the environment, using solar power to generate heat and electricity, maximizing energy efficiency, and choosing eco-friendly products whenever possible. Their efforts have earned Aurum Lodge the five green leaf eco-rating (the highest possible) from Audubon-Green-leaf, an award reserved for world leaders in environmental performance.

The lodge's appeal does not stop there. Built with blond timber and topped with a red roof, the lodge is a welcoming sight in the wilderness. Inside, the spacious great room with rock-clad fireplace, Scandinavian-style wood furniture, and artifacts from around the world has an airy and open feeling that matches the expansive outdoor landscape. Picture windows offer spectacular views and channel light into the lodge. You can make yourself at home in the library (with books in English and German) or on the sundeck. Guest rooms, designed for two, have pine beds and warm duvets. For even more privacy you can take the apartment, where you can cook for yourself, or choose one of two log cottages that have a fireplace and a full kitchen. If you stay in the lodge you'll get breakfast, which includes a selection of cereals, juices, home-style breads, and eggs made to order. Available upon request, evening meals feature a light, healthful menu that focuses on fresh vegetables and fruits, accompanied by Canadian wine.

With no alarm clocks, phones, televisions, or small children to disturb you, you can rise with the sun. In between, take a walk or a hike, sit and ponder, or read, all amid some of the most pristine alpine scenery in Alberta. For some excitement, try ski-joring (in which sled dogs pull you on skis) or canoeing, or take a day trip to Banff National Park or Lake Louise. When the evening shadows darken the waters of Lake Abraham, take a moment to admire the darkest of night skies; then indulge yourself by diving under your duvet.

Tip *Bring some good hiking or walking shoes if you want to explore the wilderness that surrounds the lodge. It is only a five-minute walk from the lodge to some waterfalls near the edge of Lake Abraham.*

🛏 5 rooms, 2 cottages, 1 apartment ❡◎❙ Full breakfast (lodge only), dining room, picnic area, some kitchens. **Recreation:** biking, birdwatching, fishing, hiking, mountain biking, running, wildlife viewing, library. Nearby: horseback riding, rock climbing, canoeing, kayaking, cross-country skiing, dogsledding, ice climbing, snowshoeing. **Services:** meeting room. ♿ Some in-room fireplaces, some pets allowed; no a/c, no room phones, no room TVs, no kids, no smoking ▦ C$110–C$220 ▤ D, MC, V.

✉ *Box 76, Nordegg, AB T0M 2H0* ☎ *403/721–2117* 📠 *403/721–2118* ⊕ *www.aurumlodge.com.*

KILMOREY LODGE
Tranquil Outpost

Surrounded by mountain peaks on the shore of Waterton Lake's Emerald Bay, 165 mi (265 km) south of Calgary near the Montana and British Columbia borders, this rambling old lodge in Waterton Lakes National Park is one of the few park accommodations with direct lake views. The 1920s log inn is one of Waterton Village's original buildings and is filled with photographs and artifacts that chronicle some of the history of the park. Each of the guest rooms is uniquely decorated and outfitted with antique furniture and soft eiderdown comforters.

In the southwest corner of Alberta, Waterton Lakes National Park is a rare find: a quiet, uncrowded national park with breathtaking scenery. You won't find yourself elbow-to-elbow with your fellow humans while you discover spectacular mountain hiking trails, waterfalls and lakes, rare wildflowers, and an abundance of wildlife. And you will see animals: in the park, the prairie meets the mountains and runs up their slopes, creating large, open areas ideal for viewing wildlife. Because you can see animals from a distance on this kind of terrain (bring your binoculars and your zoom lenses), you are more likely to catch a glimpse of a mountain sheep, elk, white-tailed deer, mule deer, or grizzly or black bears than you would be in a heavily forested park. Yet you need not intrude upon them, and as a result you stay safer.

Come here in summer, and you'll be able to fish, swim, bike, and play golf. See the backcountry on a scenic Waterton Lake cruise to adjoining Glacier National Park in Montana. Summer is peak season, so the shops of alpine Waterton Village sometimes bustle with activity. In winter, many of the cabins and shops of the village are boarded up; the Kilmorey is one of only a handful of establishments that remain open once the snow flies. Quiet descends, deer and bighorn sheep run freely through the town, and herds of elk numbering in the hundreds frequent the hillside pastures. Winter or summer, the wine list at the lodge's Lamp Post Dining Room—one of the best restaurants in the area—offers the largest selection of Canadian wines in Alberta. After a quiet dinner there, you might just be tempted by the sofa and fieldstone fireplace in the lobby library.

Tip *Winter, when you have the park almost to yourself, is a romantic time to visit Waterton. The Kilmorey offers special winter packages that include classes in Canadian cooking, wine and beer tastings, and meals.*

📡 19 rooms, 4 suites 🍽 Café, restaurant, room service, lounge. **Recreation:** bird-watching, fishing, hiking, running, wildlife viewing, lake swimming, golf privileges, cross-country skiing, snowshoeing, board games, videocassette library. Nearby: biking, horseback riding, mountain biking, rock climbing, scuba diving, canoeing, rowing, driving range, 18-hole golf course, putting green, tennis court, ice climbing, ice-skating, softball, playground. **Services:** snowshoe rentals, ski storage, shop, business services, Internet access, meeting rooms. **Classes and programs:** guided hikes and nature walks, cooking classes. ♿ Some jetted tubs, no-smoking rooms; no a/c, no room phones, no room TVs 📼 C$98–C$227 🖃 AE, D, DC, MC, V.

📪 *Box 100, Waterton, AB T0K 2M0* ☎ *403/859–2334 or 888/859–8669* 📠 *403/859–2342* 🌐 *www.kilmoreylodge.com.*

NUM-TI-JAH LODGE
Laid-Back Adventure

Bow Lake glistens like an iridescent turquoise jewel beside Num-ti-jah Lodge, a place that promises sanctuary for the soul. Here, 30 mi (48 km) north of Lake Louise, the mountains rise steeply from the water's edge, and the blue ice of the Crowfoot and Bow glaciers is visible above the azure water. Spend a few days here, and your mind is likely to become as clear as the lake's smooth glacial waters.

Num-ti-jah has all the character of an authentic backcountry lodge, with a few added luxuries. Built in the 1930s by eccentric mountain man Jimmy Simpson, it was one of the few Canadian Rockies lodges of the time that were not financed by the Canadian Pacific Railway. The four-story log-and-stone lodge is octagonal, and both exterior and interior stonework integrates hundreds of mineral crystals that Simpson collected on forays into the surrounding mountains. A large, hand-built stone fireplace is the focal point of the library. The interior of the lodge is adorned with trophy mounts, paintings, objects, and photographs, the legacy of Simpson's glory days—even his six-shooter is on display. In winter, a fireside heritage chat series includes stories from Simpson's colorful life.

"If you listen, the wilderness can teach you," Simpson once said. At the lodge, you have ample opportunity to listen to nature. The rooms have no phones or televisions, and the focus is on spending time outdoors. In summer you can go hiking in the mountains or fishing on Bow Lake. Wildlife such as birds, deer, elk, and small mammals abound in the area, although you are unlikely to see the elusive, nocturnal pine marten, or *num-ti-jah,* as it is called in the Stoney Indian language. Winter days are made for cross-country skiing and snowshoeing around the lodge or downhill skiing at Canada's largest ski area, Lake Louise, only a 30-minute drive away.

After a day in the great outdoors, soothe your muscles in the outdoor wood-burning sauna or flop into a hammock stretched between two pine trees. Complimentary coffee or tea is always available to warm you up in the Great Room. Each evening regionally inspired cuisine is served fireside in the dining room; on some winter weekends, food and wine tastings and culinary classes are part of the scene. After dinner, try your hand at billiards in the lounge or play chess by the fire in the library. By the time you burrow under the fluffy duvet in your room, the pressures of your "real" life will seem a million miles away.

Tip *There are several good hiking trails not far from the lodge. Ask the restaurant to prepare you a hiker's lunch complete with trail mix.*

25 rooms Restaurant, picnic area. **Recreation:** bird-watching, fishing, hiking, running, wildlife viewing, cross-country skiing, ice-skating, sledding, snowshoeing, tobogganing, billiards, library, piano, recreation room. Nearby: biking, horseback riding, mountain biking, rock climbing, canoeing, rafting, downhill skiing, ice climbing, sleigh rides, snowmobiling, telemark skiing. **Services:** massage, sauna, tackle shop, ski storage, babysitting. **Classes and programs:** arts and crafts classes, cooking classes, nature and heritage talks. No a/c, no room phones, no room TVs, no smoking C$110–C$285 MC, V.

Box 39, Lake Louise, AB T0L1E0 403/522–2167 403/522–2425 *www.num-ti-jah.com.*

RAFTER 6 RANCH RESORT
Family Hideout

More than half of Kananaskis Country's roughly 2,500 square mi (4,000 square km) of foothills and mountains are protected wilderness. This region of Alberta, 50 mi (80 km) west of Calgary and 30 mi (50 km) east of Banff National Park, was named by explorer John Palliser, in honor of a legendary Indian known as Kin-e-ah-kis, who was famous for fending off an ax attack. The spirit of the Wild West lives on in Kananaskis Country, where you can explore virtually untouched hills, plains, and rivers. One of the best ways to do it is on horseback, and a great base is Rafter 6 Ranch Resort. Here, on almost 100 acres overlooking the Kananaskis River valley, the rich traditions of Canada's ranching past are alive and well.

This is a rustic, family-friendly place with a relaxed atmosphere, where people of every age can slow down and step back in time. Early mornings (6–7 AM) and early evenings (6–7 PM) in warmer months, you can see an old-fashioned horse roundup. When you're finished watching the ranch hands at work, take a trail ride or wagon ride, or go hiking, fishing, swimming, and river rafting. Cowboy Church is held on Sunday from May through October, in a church with Gothic windows, a cathedral ceiling, a bell, and a mountain view. In winter, life on the ranch slows down. Sleigh rides, horseback riding in the snow (when temperatures permit), and stargazing might draw you outside, or you might prefer to stay indoors and perfect your pool or Ping-Pong game. Not far away are several major ski areas where you can go downhill or cross-country skiing, and you can find winter activities like ice fishing and dogsledding nearby.

The ranch's Mad Trapper Dining Room specializes in rib-sticking cowboy cuisine; you can also chow down at special outdoor barbecue suppers held throughout summer. Your accommodations are decorated with handcrafted western-style furnishings, and murals painted by Ray Cowley adorn the walls in many rooms. Stay in a lodge room, or spread out in a log cabin or chalet. Cabins and chalets have stone fireplaces and cast-iron bathtubs; one of the larger cabins has a full kitchen, and the chalets have kitchenettes. Fancy it's not, but your room has everything you need to enjoy some cowboy comfort at the end of the day.

Tip *Bring some hot dogs and have a weenie roast in one of the ranch's outdoor fire pits.*

18 rooms, 8 cabins, 4 chalets ‖◎‖ Coffee shop, restaurant, bar, lounge, picnic area, some kitchens, some kitchenettes. **Recreation:** bird-watching, fishing, hiking, horseback riding, running, wildlife viewing, pool, river swimming, rafting, cross-country skiing, sleigh rides, billiards, carriage rides, horseshoes, soccer, softball, volleyball, library, piano, recreation room, videocassette library, playground. Nearby: biking, mountain biking, rock climbing, canoeing, kayaking, rowing, 9-hole golf course, dogsledding, downhill skiing, ice climbing, ice-skating, snowmobiling, snowshoeing, telemark skiing. **Services:** soccer balls provided, hot tub, massage, babysitting, shop, laundry facilities, laundry service,

airport shuttle, business services, meeting rooms. **Classes and programs:** horseback-riding lessons, dances, entertainment. ♿ Some in-room fireplaces, no-smoking rooms; no a/c, no room phones, no room TVs ▱ C$159–C$345 ▭ AE, MC, V.

✉ *P.O. Box 100, Exshaw, AB T0L 2C0* ☎ *403/673–3622 or 888/ 267–2624* 🖷 *403/673–3961* ⊕ *www.raftersix.com.*

TEKARRA LODGE
Family Hideout

For millions of years, water, ice, and wind have worked together to sculpt the landscape of Jasper National Park. The result is a work in progress, a landscape of jagged mountain peaks, deep valleys, and rough-hewn canyons. In the heart of the park, 3 mi (5 km) from busy Jasper Townsite, Tekarra Lodge stands on a bluff overlooking the confluence of the Athabasca and Miette rivers. Giant pines surround the lodge, mountains tower behind it, and cabins are scattered through the forest. Elk sometimes graze on the grounds, and the occasional black bear ambles through.

Constructed in 1946, this log-cabin resort centers on a main lodge that houses the restaurant and bed-and-breakfast rooms. Whether you stay in the lodge or in a cabin, you have access to a hospitality room with soft sofas, books and magazines, and a log fireplace. The cabins, which can sleep two to seven people, have wooden porches, stone fireplaces, full kitchens or kitchenettes, and a draped sleeping area.

There's plenty to do at the lodge, from hiking to mountain biking. Nearby, you can try white-water rafting or play some golf in a spectacular mountain setting that might just distract you from your game. Explore Jasper National Park on a day trip to Mt. Edith Cavell, Miette Hot Springs, Maligne Lake, the Whistler's Mountain tram, or the Columbia Icefields. If you need a dose of civilization you can find it in Jasper Townsite's restaurants, shops, movie theater, and aquatic center.

In the lodge, Tekarra Restaurant will give you another taste of civilization. One of the finest restaurants in Jasper National Park, the restaurant presents regionally inspired contemporary cuisine in a candlelit, mountain-casual dining room and on a patio in the shadow of the mountain peaks. It's been in operation since 1952 and has served its share of celebrities, including Marilyn Monroe. While filming *River of No Return* in Jasper in 1953, the actress stayed at Tekarra Lodge after she was asked to leave the elegant Jasper Park Lodge for repeatedly "dressing inappropriately for dinner." Things are more relaxed at Tekarra, and that is a big part of its appeal. Another draw is the lodge's solitude. You might find that all you want to do is put your feet up in front of your fireplace, listen to the rushing river waters, or snuggle into bed under a warm duvet.

Tip *When you stay at the lodge you can get discounts on boat and bike rentals at Pyramid Lake Resort, Tekarra's sister property. The resort is also a good option if you come to Jasper in winter, when Tekarra is closed.*

⇨ 10 lodge rooms, 43 cabins ⦿ Full breakfast (lodge rooms only), restaurant, grills, picnic area, some kitchens, some kitchenettes. **Recreation:** biking, bird-watching, fishing, hiking, mountain biking, running, wildlife viewing, croquet, horseshoes, board games, library, playground. Nearby: horseback riding, rock climbing, canoeing, kayaking, rafting, rowing, driving range, 18-hole golf course, putting green, carriage rides, skate park. **Services:** bicycle rentals, babysitting, laundry facilities, meeting room. **Classes and programs:** natural history programs. ♿ Some in-room fireplaces, some private porches, some pets allowed (fee), no-smoking rooms; no a/c, no room phones, no room TVs ▭ C$75–C$214 ▭ AE, D, DC, MC, V.

⬆ *Highway 93 A South, Jasper, AB T0E 1E0* ☎ *780/852–3058 or 888/ 962–2522* 🖷 *780/852–4636* ⊕ *www.maclabhotels.com/leisure_tekarralodge. htm* ☺ *Closed Oct.–Apr.*

British Columbia

APRIL POINT RESORT & SPA
Laid-Back Adventure

Quadra Island, accessible only by air (from Seattle, via Kenmore Airlines) or by ferry or water taxi (from Campbell River, 100 mi [160 km] north of Nanaimo on Vancouver Island), is one of hundreds of thickly forested, thinly populated islands in the sheltered Strait of Georgia, off the east coast of Vancouver Island. Hiking and biking trails lace the old-growth fir and cedar forests, pebble beaches punctuate the shores, and the surrounding waters are alive with whales, dolphins, seals, and huge salmon. Long home to members of the Kwakwaka'wakw First Nation, this 16-mi-long (26-km-long) island is rich in native culture. Many artists—native and non-native alike—live on the island and open their studios to visitors.

April Point Lodge, occupying a 15-acre point on the island's southwest coast, started out as a fishing lodge in the 1950s. Refurbished from the ground up in 1998, it is now a modern eco-tourism resort, complete with a fleet of fishing boats. There's plenty to do here, but a giant outdoor chess board in the middle of it all serves as a subtle reminder to slow down to "island time."

The resort's centerpiece is a pale-green cedar-sided lodge built on pilings over the water, in the style of B.C.'s coastal fishing villages. Guest rooms are in the lodge and in a variety of duplex, three-plex, quad-plex, and eight-room units spread across the point. All rooms are bright and spacious, with pine furniture, duvets, coffeemakers, and forest-green fabrics. The two-, three-, and four-bedroom guesthouses have fireplaces and full kitchens. Wherever you stay, you'll have a deck with a view of the ocean and the mountains beyond. Honeymooners usually opt for Room 23, a little log cabin that stands on its own at the end of the property.

The main lodge holds not only accommodations but also a restaurant, a fireside lounge, and the activity center. With wall-to-wall windows and a wide deck over the water, the restaurant makes the most of the view; inside are log pillars, an open-beam ceiling, and local art. The menu appeals to fresh air–fueled appetites: lunch is burgers, salmon, and halibut, and dinner is steak, chicken, pork, and, of course, more seafood. A sushi bar showcases the freshest of fish and shellfish, most of it from local waters (as is the rest of the restaurant's seafood). The bread and desserts, including ice cream, are all made in-house.

The folks at April Point's activity center can set you up with mountain bikes to explore the island's miles of traffic-free roads and forest trails; sea kayaks to paddle the sheltered coves; and even motor scooters, handy for visiting local crafts studios or finding a private picnic spot. On one of the resort's wildlife or whale-watching tours you may spot a breaching whale, or a black bear combing a deserted beach. Take an ocean-rapids tour and you can ride the white water created by the turn of the tide, or explore nearby islands and mountain peaks by helicopter. True to April Point's origins, sportfishing is also a big draw. The waters near Quadra Island produce some of the world's largest Chinook and spring salmon, and 30-pounders are not uncommon. But you don't have to catch the fish to admire them: guides can take you snorkeling with the salmon.

Tip *April Point's owners also operate Painter's Lodge, a resort 10 minutes across the water on Vancouver Island. You are welcome to hop on the resort's free water taxi and use the pool, tennis courts, hot tubs, and restaurant at Painter's Lodge.*

🛏 49 rooms, 8 guesthouses ❙◎❙ Restaurant, lounge, grills, picnic area, some kitchens, some kitchenettes. **Recreation:** bird-watching, fishing, mountain biking, wildlife viewing, snorkeling, rafting, rowing, sea kayaking, badminton, boccie, croquet, horseshoes, Ping-Pong, volleyball, piano. Nearby: hiking, horseback riding, pool, scuba diving, 18-hole golf course, 2 tennis courts, skate park, playground. **Services:** scooter, mountain-bike, and sea-kayak rentals; massage; dock; guided fishing trips; helipad; marina; babysitting; grocery shopping; laundry facilities; shop; business services; meeting rooms. **Classes and programs:** guided hikes, natural history programs, sea-kayaking lessons, sightseeing tours. ♿ Cable TV, some in-room fireplaces, some in-room VCRs, private decks, some jetted tubs, private decks, some pets allowed (fee); no a/c, no room phones, no smoking 🖾 C$145–C$319 ▤ AE, DC, MC, V.

🏠 Box 248, Campbell River, BC V9W 4Z9 ☎ 250/285–2222 or 800/663–7090 🖷 250/285–2411 ⊕ www.aprilpoint.com ⊘ Closed early Oct.–early May.

CLAYOQUOT WILDERNESS RESORTS & SPA
Luxurious Resort

One of the world's last remaining temperate rain forests and home to thousand-year-old trees and thriving populations of black bears, eagles, and whales, the Clayoquot Sound UNESCO Biosphere Reserve on Vancouver Island is among the most diverse and pristine ecosystems in North America. Within the reserve, Clayoquot Wilderness Resorts' 16-room floating lodge is moored in sheltered Quait Bay. Ferries or a direct charter flight is the only means of direct access to the lodge.

With a wraparound deck and water views from virtually anywhere on board, the lodge is reminiscent of a fine yacht. The soft-golden walls, country floral fabrics, and local First Nations art in the guest rooms exude the kind of warmth you need after a damp day in the rain forest. Each room has sliding glass doors opening onto a private deck, where you can sip your morning coffee and watch for passing whales.

Clayoquot's lodge may seem like a boat, but Quait Bay is its permanent port of call. Just across the gangplank are 250 acres of private rain forest laced with hiking, riding, and mountain-biking trails and enhanced by two lakes, a waterfall-fed swimming hole, and a traditional First Nations sweat lodge. Also on shore is the Healing Grounds Spa, where you can unwind in a sauna filled with a rain forest–like mist and take a raft of treatments, from shiatsu and hot-rocks massage to detoxifying wraps using pure British Columbian glacial mud.

Return to the lodge at the end of the day and curl up with a drink by the big river-rock fireplace in the great room, or watch the chef at work in the open kitchen, preparing dinner from organic produce and local ingredients such as Clayoquot Sound oysters, house-smoked wild Pacific salmon, steamed Dungeness crab, or Vancouver Island–raised free-range Muscovy duck. Dinner, served at a big family-style table, at candlelit tables for two, or, on fine evenings, under the stars on deck, is a five-course, wine-paired affair. You can choose from a number of options, including vegetarian dishes, for each course. Later on, the lower lounge beckons with games and satellite TV, but the hot tub on the deck is the best place for stargazing.

You'll probably want to spend at least some of your Clayoquot time at the resort's Wilderness Outpost, 20 minutes across the water. The outpost lies within the biosphere reserve, on the edge of Vancouver Island's mountainous Strathcona Provincial Park. Though you sleep and eat in tents here, this is not camping as you might imagine it. Instead, think high-end safari or, as the owners did, the Rockefeller's "summer camp." Accommodations are in private, roomy prospectors' tents on raised wooden platforms. Not only are they equipped with electricity, fireplaces, and river-view porches, but they are also graced with such Rockefelleresque touches as Oriental rugs, down duvets, thick terry robes, and handmade Adirondack-style furniture.

At the outpost you can stroll along cedar boardwalks through the woods to the three massage tents, the lounge and game tents, and the detached but private shower facilities. Days here are spent biking, fishing, kayaking, whale- and bear-watching, canoeing, and horseback riding. Meals are served in the dining tent, where fresh seafood, local produce, and fine wine are served on china and crystal, reflecting the standards set at the main lodge. Evenings wind down with a massage, a soak in one of the wood-fired hot tubs, a session in one of the saunas, or stargazing over drinks by the outdoor communal fire.

Whether you stay at the lodge or the outpost, take at least one of the resort's marine excursions to outlying sea caves, waterfalls, beaches, and hot springs (with whale-watching en route). If you ride, check out the equestrian excursions: the resort's landing craft takes horses and riders to remote locations for day and overnight treks. All of the excursions offer a delicious taste of nature. The guided excursions are one of the few things you might pay extra for at Clayoquot, because the resort takes the all-inclusive approach. Three-, four-, and seven-night packages include flights from Vancouver; transfers from Tofino; all meals, snacks, and alcohol; and unguided activities. Spa packages also include all spa services, and activities packages also include guided activities.

Tips *Most guests who spend a week here split their time between the two properties—four nights at the lodge and three at the outpost, or vice versa. If you fly into Tofino, the resort's shuttle will pick you up at the airport.*

 16 lodge rooms, 18 outpost tents American plan, dining room, room service, lounge. **Recreation:** bird-watching, fishing, hiking, horseback riding, mountain biking, wildlife viewing, lake swimming (lodge only), swimming hole (lodge only), surfing (nearby), canoeing, sailing, river and sea kayaking, library, recreation room. **Services:** all sports equipment and outerwear provided, gym (lodge only), outdoor hot tubs, massage, sauna, spa, dock, guided fishing trips, helipad, shop, business services, Internet access, meeting rooms. **Classes and programs:** guided hikes and nature walks, fly-fishing lessons, yoga classes, sightseeing tours. Some in-room fireplaces, private decks and porches; no a/c, no room phones, no room TVs, no smoking Lodge: C$850–C$1,100 per person; Outpost: C$1,350–C$1,600 per person AE, MC, V.

 Box 130, Tofino, BC V0R 2Z0 *250/726–8235 or 888/333–5405* *250/726–8558* *www.wildretreat.com* *Lodge closed Nov.–Mar.; Outpost closed Oct.–Apr.*

EAGLE NOOK OCEAN WILDERNESS RESORT
Romantic Retreat

No roads reach this sound on Vancouver Island's west coast, so getting to Eagle Nook Ocean Wilderness Resort is a thrill in itself. From the fishing village of Ucluelet (110 mi [175 km] west of Nanaimo), where the highway ends, Eagle Nook's catamaran whisks you on a 45-minute journey through a watery wilderness, past rocky islets draped with lounging sea lions and evergreens top-heavy with eagles' nests. En route, you'll pass the edge of the Broken Group Islands. Part of the Pacific Rim National Park Reserve, this sheltered archipelago of forested islets, transparent seas, and abundant marine life is one of the world's most renowned sea-kayaking destinations.

Your first sight of the lodge will be from the sea. Set on a private 70-acre peninsula, Eagle Nook is bounded by water in front and back and by forest on either side. Hand-peeled log trim on the low-slung cedar-sided structure helps it blend into the landscape. Inside, one grand room holds a scattering of sofas and leather wing chairs, wooden wildlife sculptures, a stone fireplace (lighted on all but the warmest evenings), and the dining area, where tables are set before floor-to-ceiling water-view windows.

Thanks to the location, every guest room has a water view. The large, hotel-style lodge quarters have tall windows, lean-out (rather than step-out) balconies, pine furniture, an autumnal color scheme, and exceptionally comfortable beds. The two log cabins have separate bedrooms, woodstoves, kitchenettes, and plenty of privacy. And although Eagle Nook may be isolated, it's not spartan: call it soft adventure with the emphasis squarely on "soft." Service is informal but attentive, with such pampering as morning coffee delivered to your room, cocktails served at the waterside hot tub, and after-dinner massages (Swedish and aromatherapy are all on the spa menu).

Although you don't have to leave the lodge to spot wildlife—a telescope in the great room is trained on a neighboring eagle's nest, and seals frequently pop up in the bay—you'd be depriving yourself if you didn't take a marine nature tour. Your guide, Charlie Everard, has named many of the 170 eagle pairs in the area. He'll show you which rocks the sea lions like best, and though he can't guarantee whale sightings, he knows their habits. On your own, you can kayak in pond-smooth Jane Bay next to the lodge. A better option, though, even if you've never kayaked before, is to paddle with the resort's kayak guide in the national park, where the clear, calm waters reveal a wealth of marine life. If you book ahead, a helicopter can fly you out for a day of hiking on mountain and coastal trails, or for a tour of glacial lakes, mountain peaks, and small islands.

Closer to the lodge you can explore trails cut through the rain forest to nearby pebble beaches. You may bump into the chef collecting oysters for an outdoor oyster roast, or sea asparagus and watercress for your dinner. The local bounty—wild salmon, perhaps?—makes the lavish four-course meal an event, complete with wine from the well-stocked cellar. Afterward you can relax by the fire or step out on the deck to admire the phosphorescence in the water and the canopy of stars overhead.

Tip *Rain and mist can sock in the sound at any time of year, so bring a book, or several. Bad weather shouldn't keep you from exploring, though, since the lodge provides gear for wet-weather trips.*

🛏 23 rooms, 2 cabins ⏐◎⏐ American plan, dining room, bar. **Recreation:** bird-watching, fishing, hiking, wildlife viewing, sea kayaking, billiards, library, recreation room. **Services:** kayaks and paddleboats provided, outdoor hot tub, sauna, spa, dock, guided fishing and kayaking trips, laundry service, shop, Internet access, library, DVD library, meeting rooms. **Classes and programs:** boat and helicopter sightseeing tours. ⏚ No a/c, no room phones, no room TVs, no smoking ▭ C$699–C$863 per person, including transfer from Ucluelet and Wild Life cruise. There is a two-night minimum stay. ▭ AE, MC, V.

🏛 *120 W. Dayton, Suite B6, Edmonds, WA 98020* ☎ *250/723–1000 or 800/760–2777* 🖷 *425/771–4518* ⊕ *www.eaglenook.com* ⊙ *Closed Oct.–late May.*

ECHO VALLEY RANCH & SPA
Luxurious Resort ~ Romantic Retreat

Part dude ranch, part Thai spa, this resort in British Columbia's faraway Cariboo ranching country brings together Eastern and Western spa treatments, philosophies, and even architecture. Owners Norm and Nan Dove, hailing from the United Kingdom and Thailand respectively, have welcomed guests at their ranch in the Marble Mountains since 1995. A 4½-hour drive from Vancouver and 30 miles (50 km) from Clinton, the nearest town, Echo Valley enjoys some of the clearest skies and purest air on the continent. Norm and Nan chose this spot for the ranch partly because it is the meeting point of four distinct ecosystems. The ranch itself sits among montane forests of pine and Douglas fir, home to deer, black bears, and rich birdlife. Rolling grasslands extend to the north, while to the east are the alpine peaks of the Marble Range and to the west is a dramatic, gorge-cut desert.

The main lodge, guest lodge, and cabins are of spruce log construction, with vaulted ceilings. Lodge rooms are spacious, with duvets on the beds and throw rugs on hardwood floors. Some have sleeping lofts, many have balconies, and all have great views. The ranch-house cabin is big enough for four, and two smaller cabins are just right for two. Romantics usually opt for the honeymoon cabin, which has its own hot tub, a fireplace, a canopied four-poster bed, and a private setting overlooking a creek. Whichever room you choose, you'll book it as part of a package that includes not only meals but all manner of amenities. Different packages, such as the classic, spa, or honeymoon options, include different amenities and services, from gold-panning trips to personal fitness instruction. Packages are offered for three, four, or seven days.

Nan works closely with spa director Jaranya Hanoi to make the vision of "East meets West" a reality at the ranch's spa. The specialty here is Thai massage, but all manner of treatments are available in a facility that includes an indoor swimming pool. For complete immersion in Eastern wellness traditions, book the guest suite in the ranch's authentic Baan Thai (Thai house), which commands great views from a hillside near the main lodge. Built in the Royal Thai style using western woods, it is the only building of its kind in North America. The luxe Thai-style guest suite is furnished with hand-carved teak furniture. On the lower level you can take classes in *Ruesri Dut Ton,* an ancient form of yoga practiced in Thailand. The house also contains a spa treatment room.

Explore the surrounding landscape by hiking on your own or with a guide, biking along deserted country roads, rafting in the fast-flowing Chilcotin or Fraser rivers, riding in an air-conditioned four-wheel-drive vehicle, or boarding a small plane for a flightseeing tour. Tennessee walking horses—famous for their easy gait—and experienced wranglers can take you into the rolling hills and along forest trails. Sometimes, experienced riders help herd cattle on the open range. For another up-close animal encounter, watch a demonstration of the noble sport of falconry.

Meals, taken family-style in the main lodge, include produce, meat, and poultry raised organically on the ranch; wild mushrooms, herbs, and berries gathered from the surrounding forest; and plenty of home baking. If you like, the chef will tailor your meals according to "Dr. D'Adamo's Eat Right for Your Type" diet, favored by Norm and Nan. The regular menu of haute but healthful cuisine gives way at least once a week to a traditional Thai feast or a cowboy cookout. Either way, East meets West in the evening. About once a week, cowboy songs or graceful Thai dances are performed under clear, starry skies.

Tip *Though normally not allowed at the resort, kids under 13 are welcome at Elkhorn for two weeks each summer.*

15 lodge rooms, 1 suite, 4 cabins American plan, dining room, picnic area, some minibars. **Recreation:** bird-watching, fishing, hiking, horseback riding, mountain biking, wildlife viewing, indoor pool, rafting (nearby), sleigh rides, snowshoeing, billiards, horseshoes, shuffleboard, recreation room. **Services:** snowshoes provided, mountain-bike rentals, health club, outdoor hot tub, sauna, spa, steam room, airstrip, guided fishing trips, laundry service, shop, meeting rooms, wireless Internet. **Classes and programs:** guided hikes; photo safaris; fly-fishing and riding lessons; fitness, yoga, and cooking classes; concerts; dances; entertainment; sightseeing tours. Some in-room fireplaces, some jetted tubs, some private balconies; no a/c, no room TVs, no kids under 13, no smoking C$234–C$885 per person AE, MC, V.

Box 16, Clinton, BC V0K 1K0 ☎ 250/459–2386 or 800/253–8831 📠 250/459–0086 🌐 www.evranch.com ☾ Closed early Nov.–mid-Dec. and early Jan.–late Mar.

STRATHCONA PARK LODGE & OUTDOOR EDUCATION CENTRE
Family Hideout ~ Laid-Back Adventure

A lakefront nature center and wilderness retreat 125 mi (200 km) northwest of Nanaimo, this resort is a great place for kids and adults to try their hand at rock climbing, canoeing, kayaking, and more. Myrna Boulding and her late husband, Jim, nutrition and phys ed teachers respectively, founded the lodge on the edge of Strathcona Provincial Park in 1959. Now widely regarded as one of Canada's leading outdoor education centers, the lodge is still run by the Boulding family. The staff includes about 40 enthusiastic guides and instructors. In the off-season, school and other groups visit often, but come summer this bucolic complex in the mountainous heart of Vancouver Island morphs into a summer camp for people of all ages. All of the camp icons are here: canoes and beach volleyball, lake swimming, hiking trails, and a chance to push your personal envelope in a safe, supportive, and scenic environment.

You (and the kids) might start the day by tackling the ropes course, whizzing down the zip line, or climbing a rock face, before exploring Treasure Island by canoe—all with the help of skilled and patient guides. Older kids can sign up for the teen camps, but there are no separate children's activities: the idea is for families to spend time together. Kid-free couples and solo adults are welcome, too, and women and senior citizens particularly seem to enjoy the positive vibe of the place. Overnight forays into the wilds, called Wilderness Out-Trips, offer adults, and sometimes families with teens, more intense adventures, including sea kayaking off the coast and trekking through the island's alpine heart. Evening programs are typically something you've never tried before: kayak soccer and bannock (fry bread) barbecues, anyone? Grown-ups can chill out and watch the sunset from the Hi-Bracer Lounge.

Strathcona Park Lodge is a rustic-looking complex stretching across 160 acres of flower-dotted and wooded hillside. Every corner of the property has magnificent views of the lake and its backdrop of glacier-topped peaks, some reaching above 7,000 feet. From the original log-and-timber lodge to the modern post-and-beam Preece Cottage, most of the resort's structures were built individually rather than as part of a master plan. As a result, accommodations vary. Options include lakefront log cabins with kitchens, woodstoves, water-view decks, and a mix of handmade and hand-me-down furniture; capacious lodge rooms with adze-cut log beams, low-slung beds topped with duvets, and lake-view balconies; and simpler rooms with shared baths.

A whale skull is suspended above the picture windows in the Whale Room, where you line up for hearty, healthful buffets of salads, ethnic dishes, soups, and casseroles. Grab a tray and pull up a pew (the seats were rescued from a demolished church) inside, or come early on fine days to claim a seat on the deck, for front-row mountain views. Next door at the Canoe Club Café, the table-service menu offers local and exotic cuisine, including fresh seafood. Both eateries give you a choice of vegan, wheat-free, gluten-free, and omnivorous dishes. Chances are, though, your lunch will be a picnic on a deserted lake island or quiet mountaintop.

Tip *The all-inclusive, weeklong Family Adventure package has parents and their 6- to 13-year-olds swinging on a zip line, learning survival techniques, and camping out on a canoe trip together. There's also a package specifically for grandparents and grandkids.*

⮑ 37 rooms, 10 cottages �🍽 2 restaurants, lounge, picnic area, some kitchens, some kitchenettes. **Recreation:** hiking, rock climbing, beach, lake swimming, boating, canoeing, kayaking, sailing, sea kayaking (nearby), basketball, volleyball. **Services:** massage, sauna, dock, laundry facilities, shop, meeting rooms. **Classes and programs:** guided hikes; natural history programs; canoeing, kayaking, mountaineering, rock-climbing, and orienteering lessons; natural history, nutrition, navigation, wilderness survival skills, and minimum-impact camping talks. ⛄ Some private balconies and decks; no a/c, no room phones, no room TVs, no smoking 🖼 C$55–C$365 ▭ MC, V.

⌂ *Box 2160, Campbell River, BC, V9W 5C5* ☎ *250/286–3122* 🖨 *250/286–6010* ⊕ *www.strathcona.bc.ca* ⊘ *Dining room and restaurant closed Nov.–mid-March; lounge closed Sept.–June.*

WEST COAST WILDERNESS LODGE
Laid-Back Adventure

Fjord-cut, mountain-backed, and deeply forested, the Sunshine Coast of British Columbia north of Vancouver is a surprisingly untrammeled place. An easy ferry or seaplane ride from the city, the area is popular with artists and outdoorsy types but has not yet opened its doors to mass tourism or luxury-resort developers. It's here, 75 mi (121 km) from Vancouver on a bluff overlooking the confluence of two inlets, that Paul and Patti Hansen built their eco-friendly lodge. Paul, an outdoor educator, has made a career of introducing city folks to the wilder side of B.C. At the lodge, the Hansens strive to make the wilderness accessible and affordable to everyone. Women's retreats, corporate retreats, and family reunions are all popular here, especially in the off-season. Summer brings singles and couples of all ages as well as families with school-age children.

The post-and-beam lodge and cedar-sided guest cottages, built with recycled wood and timber cleared from the land, sit high above the water. Relaxing in the window-lined restaurant or on the wide, sunny deck, you can look out over an islet-dotted inlet rich in marine life and lined by the wooded slopes and glacier-topped peaks of the Coast Mountains. A forest trail leads down to the waterfront, where the grassy shore is perfect for readying your kayak, tossing a beach volleyball, or sitting around the campfire after a day out on the water. To ensure that you're never far from the view, the wood-fired sauna on the water's edge has a picture window.

Your days here might include an easy paddle through the clear waters of Sechelt Inlet, a canoe excursion on a freshwater mountain lake, or a kayak trip to see Frail Falls, one of the highest waterfalls in B.C. A short hike will take you to the dramatic Skookumchuck rapids: here, at the turn of the tide, seawater churning through a narrow channel creates the fastest-moving tidal rapids in the world. Closer to the lodge, you can have a go at one of the resort's natural climbing walls (or watch your friends climb while you have a drink on the deck), take a turn on the woodland ropes course, or try your hand at archery. All of the activities, except hiking, are guided, so you can be as active, or not, as you like. For an extra splurge, you can book a helicopter or seaplane flight to a glacial lake deep in the mountains.

Rooms are in five mini-lodges perched on the bluff. Each of the lodges has a shared living room and four guest rooms with private bath. Accommodations range from doubles with king beds and picture windows to extra-large units with log bunks for the kids. Rooms are bright, airy, and uncluttered, with tall windows, skylights, white walls, pine wainscoting, soft cotton-covered duvets, and a mix of 20th-century antiques and rough-hewn handmade bed frames. Guest rooms have no TVs, although they can be rented from the front desk for watching videos.

Dinner, served on white tablecloths before two-story-high windows, usually includes fresh local seafood and organic produce. Vegetarian options and "go on, you earned it" desserts are always on the menu. The kitchen opens early, so there's time after dinner to catch the sunset and spot wildlife during an evening boat cruise around the islands. After that there's stargazing from the hot tub, games in the rec room, or maybe an oyster barbecue down at the campfire.

Tip *Just 30 mi (50 km) from the lodge is Princess Louisa Inlet, a narrow, glacier-carved fjord with up to 60 waterfalls (depending on the season) plunging down its sheer, 7,000-foot walls. It's one of the outstanding scenic wonders of the province. Paul and Patti can arrange a visit by boat, seaplane, or helicopter.*

⊃ 20 rooms ⦿ American plan, restaurant, lounge, some refrigerators. **Recreation:** bird-watching, fishing, hiking, mountain biking, rock
climbing, wildlife viewing, sea kayaking, canoeing, archery, badminton,
billiards, boccie, horseshoes, Ping-Pong, volleyball, piano, recreation
room. Nearby: scuba diving, 9-hole golf course. **Services:** canoes,
kayaks, mountain bikes, and rock-climbing equipment provided; outdoor hot tub; massage; sauna; guided fishing trips; dock; meeting
rooms. **Classes and programs:** guided hikes and nature walks; orienteering, sea-kayaking, yoga, and rock-climbing lessons; sightseeing
tours. ⏚ No a/c, no room phones, no TV in some rooms, no smoking ▧ C$115–C$185 ⊟ AE, MC, V.

✉ *General Delivery, Egmont, BC V0N 1N0* ☎ *604/883–3667 or 877/
988–3838* 🖷 *604/883–3604* ⊕ *www.wcwl.com.*

WICKANINNISH INN
Tranquil Outpost

The extreme western edge of Vancouver Island, pummeled by Pacific
surf and blanketed with old-growth rain forest, is a striking setting. Here,
near the tiny village of Tofino (140 mi [225 km] west of Nanaimo),
Dr. Howard McDiarmid, the local general practitioner, built his weathered cedar inn. Though it dates to only 1996, the inn is already an in-
stitution in this part of the world, and it has played a major role in
redefining this out-of-the-way region as an eco-tourism destination.

The 1½-mi (2½-km) expanse of hard-packed, driftwood-strewn beach
before the inn is a place for taking solitary jogs or meditative walks, beachcombing, and enjoying the almost mystical juxtaposition of ancient rain
forest against open ocean. The Pacific Rim National Park Reserve, just
down the road, has an extensive network of hiking trails, and the whole
area is popular for fishing, kayaking, and surfing. The staff at the inn
can arrange games of golf and excursions to nearby forested coves and
islands, including one with hot springs–fed pools. The whale-watching is great here, especially during the gray whales' February-to-May
migration up the coast from Mexico to Alaska.

The Wick, as it's known locally, lets you enjoy the wilderness in comfort. Two three-story buildings, set on a promontory at the ocean's edge,
hold rustically elegant guest rooms, a full-service spa, and one of western Canada's most innovative dining rooms. The original building is home
to the restaurant, spa, and 45 ocean-view rooms. A newer building, called
the Wickaninnish on the Beach, holds a mix of standard rooms and
multi-level suites. Rooms in both buildings are large, and each has a fireplace and a private balcony. Interiors echo the seascape outside, and
creative design touches show up everywhere. Thoughtful details include
driftwood chairs, adze-cut mantels, and bathtubs set before ocean-
view windows. In the 900-square-foot Canopy Suite, fiber optics in the

ceiling replicate the local night sky, faithfully showing the correct star positions.

At the inn's Ancient Cedars Spa, every visit starts with a fireside foot soak using salts from the Dead Sea. You can opt for a hot-stone massage or body wrap, or indulge in a massage for two in a separate cedar building. Retire to the library, which houses a first edition of the journals of Captain George Vancouver, the first European explorer in the area. Linger over cocktails in the beach-view lounge, whose bar is fashioned from a gigantic tree root. When it's time to eat, move on to the glass-enclosed Pointe Restaurant, poised on an outcrop over the sea. The chefs here make the most of such local delicacies as oysters, gooseneck barnacles, wild mushrooms, Dungeness crab, and Pacific salmon, and there are always plenty of vegetarian options on the seasonally changing menu. The maître d' can match your entrée selection with a good wine—many are locally produced and hard to find elsewhere.

Tip *Book well ahead for the Wick: even in winter it's busy, as people come to watch the dramatic storms that lash the coast. In spring the rooms fill with whale-watchers.*

🛏 63 rooms, 12 suites ᵀ◎ᶦ Restaurant, room service, lounge, some kitchens, minibars, microwaves. **Recreation:** beach, library, recreation room. Nearby: fishing, hiking, wildlife viewing, surfing, sea kayaking, 9-hole golf course. **Services:** fitness room, bicycle rentals, spa, steam room, airport shuttle, business services, meeting rooms. ♿ Cable TV, in-room fireplaces, private balconies, some pets allowed (fee); no a/c, no smoking ☑ C$260–C$1,500 ▭ AE, DC, MC, V.

✉ *Box 250, Tofino, BC V0R 2Z0* ☎ *250/725–3100 or 800/333–4604* 🖷 *250/725–3110* ⊕ *www.wickinn.com.*

Manitoba

BISCUIT HARBOUR RESORT
Laid-Back Adventure

Biscuit Harbour, a three-hour drive north of Winnipeg, is a protected cove near the narrows of Lake Winnipeg, the 14th-largest freshwater lake in the world. Towering white cliffs surround the harbor, which got its name from the layered limestone's resemblance to a layered tea biscuit. The shoreline is scattered with pinkish-white shale limestone and the occasional flat, truck-size rock perfect for a private picnic. Tall poplars, pine, and ground spruce grow here, and pinecones carpet the soft forest floors.

Ever since Geiri and Anne Johnson started the business in 1962, the family has run Biscuit Harbour Resort with casual friendliness. On the deck of the restaurant, where trees grow right through the floor, transplanted Kiwi waitresses joke easily with American and European anglers, local hydro-line workers, and the odd canoe group coming off the Bloodvein River across the narrows. At hand-carved jack-pine tables, they serve barbecued bison sandwiches and pickerel burgers made from fresh fish caught by commercial fishermen down the road.

You can stay in the main lodge or in a cabin; either way your accommodations are functional rather than sumptuous, but all are spacious and homey. Cedar cabins stand a few hundred yards from the main lodge. Although the cabins are lakefront, dense forest in most cases blocks the lake view. Each cabin has a deck with a barbecue for grilling fish from the "fish house" in Pine Dock. Inside, kitchens are supplied with basic equipment as well as an electric griddle, microwave, and toaster oven. Once you get the fireplace going, you can enjoy it from the jetted tub. Cabins are heated for winter and have ceiling fans and cooling units for summer.

You can explore the 20 mi (32 km) of Biscuit Harbour coastline on your own or, if you request it in advance, with a guide. Paddle around the harbor to small beaches or tea biscuit cliffs, or set up a campfire in the breakwater pit—it's like having a fire in the middle of the lake. Look for fiddlehead ferns and wild irises along Caterpillar Creek, or hike for two or three hours around Bushy Point (ask for directions to the trailhead at the end of the airstrip), where you'll find empty beaches and fine views across the lake. In winter, lake-effect snow dumps mounds of the fluffy stuff on the area, making it an ideal place to snowshoe or cross-country ski.

For a truly Manitoban experience, drive about 15 minutes north of Pine Dock, watching for the right-hand turnoff onto the winter road; then drive east a few miles across the frozen lake. It's about 10 miles to the aboriginal town sites of the Bloodvein First Nation. There are no organized facilities for visitors, but you can have a look around. Another great half-day trip is to funky Matheson Island, population 151. To get there, drive north past Pine Dock to the end of the road—literally—and take the two-minute ferry ride to the island. Like nowhere else in the prairie province of Manitoba, the crib dock–lined shorefront, fishing boats, and net flags lend the island a strong maritime feel. Pick up a snack at Island Delight or Bern's Bakery, and dine alfresco at one of the picnic tables lining the shorefront. Alternatively, book a full-day boat tour to McBeth Point to see limestone cliffs, seabirds, and fossil-lined beaches.

Tip *Book a floatplane from Biscuit Harbour for C$250 per person round-trip, and fly in to a basic but snug cabin on stunning Sasaginnigak Lake. Peppered with hundreds of islands, the lake is a great place to fish or simply to enjoy rich forest surroundings.*

5 rooms, 2 suites, 3 cabins ⃝ Restaurant, lounge, some kitchenettes. **Recreation:** bird-watching, fishing, hiking, wildlife viewing, beach (nearby), boating, canoeing, cross-country skiing, snowmobiling, snowshoeing, videocassette library. **Services:** pedal boat, motorboat, and canoe rentals; airstrip; dock; guided fishing trips; marina; Internet access. **Classes and programs:** guided nature walks, photo safaris, sightseeing tours. Some in-room fireplaces, some in-room VCRs or DVD players, some jetted tubs, some private decks, some pets allowed; no a/c in some rooms, no phones in some rooms, no smoking C$90–C$265 AE, DC, MC, V.

Box 119, Arnes, MB R0C 0C0 ☎ *204/276–2084 or 888/536–5353* *204/276–2181* ⊕ *www.biscuitharbour.com.*

ELKHORN RESORT, SPA & CONFERENCE CENTRE
Tranquil Outpost

Straddling Manitoba's western spine 60 mi (36 km) north of Brandon, Riding Mountain National Park is elevated 1,400 feet (420 meters) above the Manitoba Lowlands. The reserve protects 1,200 square mi (3,000 square km) of aspen parkland, hardwood forest, grassland, and wetlands. Thousands of moose and elk, hundreds of black bears, and 250 bird species live here, and wildlife enthusiasts come to hike, bike, horseback ride, snowshoe, and ski the park's 186 mi (300 km) of ever-changing trails.

Next door to the park, Elkhorn Resort is a convenient base from which to explore the area. Hotel-style guest rooms in the main lodge and A-frame chalets overlooking the stables and lawn are outfitted in oak or cherrywood and subdued fabrics and have bright, modern bathrooms. Double-sided chalets (book the one-bedroom side, the two-bedroom side, or both sides for three bedrooms) are nestled in the woods away from the lodge. Set up in separate cul-de-sacs of three or four chalets, they face the golf course or the forest and are very private. Here you can feel completely immersed in nature while enjoying the comforts of fine furnishings, designer lighting, and tiled floors. You can cook in your chalet or head to the lodge for meals in the warmly decorated restaurant. Windows on three sides overlook the herbal garden and the ranch next door, while a mixed crowd of family vacationers and conference goers dines on such morsels as tender roast elk.

One floor down from the lobby, the Solstice Spa will relax you as soon as you step inside, with the sounds of quiet music and falling water. From the changing area, you can gaze out at the horses while sipping lemon water. A beguiling limestone cliff-and-waterfall sculpture stands in the middle of the doughnut-shape mineral pool outside. To re-create seawater from 400 million years ago, crystals found 3,000 feet (900 meters) below the Canadian prairies are dissolved in the mineral pool. Plan to spend a few hours in the spa for a pine-needle or cinnamon-clove soak, marine algae wrap, or massage and pedicure. A Seasonal Festivity for Couples package offers simultaneous massage and aromatherapy treatment.

There's plenty to do outdoors, as well. Get a hiking map from the Park Visitor Centre on Wasagaming Drive in town and take an early-morning hike on the 2½-mi (4-km) Bead Lakes Trail—you may even see a moose or two. If you prefer guided hikes, check with the visitor center or the resort's on-site outfitter. For a wheeled outing, borrow the resort bikes and cycle along Wasagaming Bike Trail or take an excellent sunset ride on Lakeshore Trail. Or ride less than a mile into the park town of Wasagaming, a treasure of Victorian wooden structures and towering conifers.

In winter, much of the town is closed, but cross-country ski trails within a five-minute drive of the resort are groomed and open. Arrowhead and Brule trails suit beginning skiers, while veteran skiers may prefer the 11-mi (17½-km) Grey Owl Trail. Watch for woodpeckers, great gray owls, and hawks. You'll have the trails almost to yourself, and ample inspiration for romance.

Tip *Prime wildlife-viewing season is September 1 to October 20. Book a wildlife safari with Elkhorn partner Earth Rhythms to learn about the area's biodiversity. For birding, come during spring migration, mid-May to late June, for fabulous warbler viewing.*

🛏 54 rooms, 3 suites, 29 chalets ¶◎¶ Restaurant, room service, lounge, some kitchens, some microwaves, refrigerators. **Recreation:** biking, hiking, horseback riding, indoor pool, 9-hole golf course, sleigh rides, billiards, horseshoes, Ping-Pong, shuffleboard, volleyball, recreation room. Nearby: bird-watching, fishing, wildlife viewing, beach, lake swimming, boating, canoeing, kayaking, 18-hole golf course, tennis court, cross-country skiing, snowmobiling, snowshoeing. **Services:** badminton, baseball, croquet, football, horseshoe, soccer, and volleyball equipment provided; bicycle and golf-club rentals; gym; hot tub; outdoor hot tub; salon; sauna; spa; steam room; dry-cleaning service; laundry service; business services; Internet access; meeting rooms. **Classes and programs:** guided hikes, guided nature walks, natural history programs, photo safaris, yoga classes. ♿ Cable TV, some in-room data ports, some in-room fireplaces, in-room DVD players, some jetted tubs, some private balconies, some private decks, no-smoking rooms 💳 C$80–C$600 ▤ AE, DC, MC, V.

✉ *Box 40, Onanole, MB R0J 1N0* ☎ *204/848–2802 or 866/355–4676* 🖷 *204/848–2109* 🌐 *www.elkhornresort.mb.ca.*

FALCON TRAILS RESORT
Rustic Escape

In the southeastern corner of Whiteshell Provincial Park, 100 mi (165 km) east of Winnipeg, wildflowers create an ever-changing carpet between rugged granite outcroppings. Loons call across still lakes, and beavers amble out of their watery domain along paths of their own making. Atop a mantle of 2-billion-year-old bedrock capped with lush forest, Falcon Trails Resort's wooden cabins look out over the uninhabited east side of Falcon Lake, one of almost 200 clear, rock-edged lakes in the 965-square-mi (2,500-square-km) park.

The Whiteshell, as it is called by locals, beckons with dozens of trails, including a portion of the Trans-Canada hiking trail, and 186 mi (300 km) of connected waterways. You can hike directly from the resort along paths lined with saskatoon bushes, wild plum trees, and chokecherries. Delicate nodding trillium and sarsaparilla sway in the breeze. Warblers, raptors, and waterfowl are plentiful, depending on the season. Outside the park, a hike past the resort's biathlon range takes you to Pine Ridge lookout. Canoes are moored at the dock of some cabins; paddle to outlying islands to try to see fox, deer, or beavers. At Falcon Ridge Ski & Recreation Area, ski, snowboard, or snow-tube on a hill with a T-bar and three tows. Or wax up and head off on groomed cross-country trails. Horseback riding is available about 30 minutes from the resort at Falcon Beach Riding Stables.

The resort's post-and-beam chalet-style cabins are on the lakefront and have stunning views of the shoreline and nearby islands. Chalets are well spaced, five of them within a few hundred yards of the Welcome Center (lobby) and another three about ½ mi (1 km) away. If you come with children in winter, ask for a cabin close to Falcon Ridge Ski & Recreation Area. From just about any window in any chalet, you won't see any other chalets. The walk from your car to your chalet can range from 20 to 200 feet (6–60 meters). It may be a chore to haul your luggage to your cabin in wheelbarrows or sleds, but separation from the parking lot lends your accommodations the tranquillity necessary for rejuvenating your mind and soul.

Each cabin's wood-burning stove is flanked by enormous windows overlooking the sapphire lake. Pine floors, cathedral ceilings, and open sleeping lofts with captains' ladders create a casual mood. Whip up a meal in your fully equipped kitchen or on the grill on your large screened-in porch. Later, pop a complimentary movie into the VCR or wrap yourself in a fluffy towel and step outside to your three- or four-person hot tub. On a winter night, pour some wine, light a few candles, and slip from the freezing air into the warm, bubbling water. As you gaze at the white slash of moonlight across the lake, the quiet will be punctuated by the sound of wind through the pines and perhaps a plaintive wolf howl from one of the resident packs.

If Falcon Trails isn't quiet enough for you, stay at one of the High Lake Cabins, wilderness eco-havens within walking or skiing distance of the main resort. Solar power supplies the electricity, propane fuels the refrigerator and stove, and wood-burning fireplaces heat the rooms. Filtered, potable water is gravity-fed, and toilets are composting and odor-free. You may arrange for an ATV or snowmobile to haul your gear in and out at the beginning and end of your stay. Either of the large post-and-beam cabins is perfect for sharing with another couple or family. Paddle around the points to fish, or read a novel on the long deck with almost invisible floor-to-ceiling screens. You'll hear nothing but the chickadees in the pines.

Tip *When you make your reservations, also book a massage with a local masseuse, who will come to your chalet to work the soreness out of your weary muscles.*

3 rooms, 11 chalets Kitchens, some microwaves, refrigerators. **Recreation:** bird-watching, fishing, hiking, mountain biking, running, wildlife viewing, lake swimming, canoeing, cross-country skiing, downhill skiing, snowshoeing, tubing (snow), board games, library, videocassette library. Nearby: horseback riding, rock climbing, boating, 18-hole golf course, sleigh rides, ice-skating, snowmobiling. **Services:** canoes provided, bicycle rentals, outdoor hot tub, dock, business services, meeting rooms. **Classes and programs:** biathlon, mountain-biking, and skiing competitions; biathlon lessons. In-room fireplaces, private porches; no a/c, no room phones, no TV in some rooms, no smoking C$55–C$250 AE, MC, V.

📫 *Box 130, Falcon Lake, MB R0E 0N0* ☎ *204/349–8273* 🖷 *204/349–3287* ⊕ *www.falcontrails.mb.ca.*

INVERNESS FALLS RESORT
Rustic Escape

Deep in the heart of Whiteshell Provincial Park, Inverness Falls Resort lies beside tiny (for Manitoba) Brereton Lake, 85 mi (137 km) east of Winnipeg. This wild sanctuary shelters visiting birds such as chickadee, pine grosbeaks, redpolls, and nuthatches, so many of them that they eat 2,500 pounds (1,125 kg) of seed every season. Fox, beaver, and deer are frequently seen downstream from the resort. At Alf Hole Goose Sanctuary, about 8 mi (13 km) south of the resort, migrating birds abound in fall and goslings hatch in spring. When you come to Inverness Falls Resort, be sure to bring your binoculars.

You can hike from the resort to the 3-mi (5-km) Amisk Trail, which will lead you through forests of white spruce, balsam fir, aspen, and poplar. Bunchberry and wild lily of the valley line the paths. Depending on the season, you may hear or see warblers, raptors, or waterfowl. On early spring mornings, take the rowboat 300 yards (270 meters) out from the shoreline for great walleye (pickerel) fishing, or borrow a canoe below the falls and paddle down Rennie River to explore or fish. Come summer, swim or relax on the resort's sandy beach or take a canoe or pedal boat out on the lake. When leaves and grasses turn yellow in fall, eerie morning mists rise from the lake, wild rice is ripe for harvesting, and mushrooms thrive under falling leaves. Hoarfrost may dust the landscape white, and the snowmobilers haven't got their sleds out yet. In winter, 6 mi (10 km) of groomed cross-country novice ski trails run through a red pine plantation, and 125 mi (200 km) of groomed snowmobile trails crisscross Whiteshell Provincial Park. You can borrow snowshoes at the resort office and follow High Rock Ridge Trail.

A stream flows through the resort property, separating the lakefront cottages from the creekfront chalets by a footbridge. One of the cottages contains two suites, but otherwise accommodations stand alone. All of the suites, cottages, and chalets have living rooms with fireplaces, stereos, fully equipped kitchens, and decks with propane barbecues. Furnishings are a mix of functional wood and upholstered pieces. Some of the luxury cottages and chalets, set among spruce groves or near the falls, have two-person jetted tubs surrounded in rich wood paneling.

Book the secluded War Eagle Lake Wilderness Retreat—the honeymoon cabin—and a 1,400-square-foot, handcrafted log cabin, complete with log-hewn staircase and a canoe, is yours, all yours. Note, however, that it's not for the faint of heart (though it has 24-hour emergency radio contact with the resort). Your expedition starts with a guided 90-minute ATV ride from the resort, followed by a 20-minute canoe ride across

War Eagle Lake with your supplies. During your stay you must haul water, chop kindling for fire, and create your own entertainment. Solar energy runs the lights, fan, and CD player, and there is a propane refrigerator. A well-stocked pantry of nonperishables is complimentary, all necessary kitchen supplies are provided, and a barbecue stands outside. If you like the idea of waking to loon calls, hiking for blueberries to throw on your cornflakes, or canoeing to explore old gold mines and rock ridges, this is the place for you.

Tip *On the way in, stock up on groceries at a supermarket in Winnipeg or at a basic grocery store in Rennie.*

 8 cottages, 4 chalets, 1 log cabin Kitchens, microwaves. **Recreation:** bird-watching, fishing, hiking, horseback riding (nearby), mountain biking, rock climbing (nearby), running, wildlife viewing, beach, lake swimming, boating, canoeing, rowing, cross-country skiing, snowmobiling, snowshoeing. **Services:** bicycles, fishing equipment, canoes, pedal boats, and rowboats provided; boat and motor rentals; outdoor hot tub; sauna; boat launch; marina. Cable TV with movies, in-room fireplaces, some jetted tubs, private decks, some pets allowed (fee); no a/c C$75–C$1,160 MC, V.

 General Delivery, Rennie, MB R0E 1R0 *204/369–5336 or 877/467–0832* *204/369–5629* *www.invernessfalls.mb.ca.*

New Brunswick

INN AT WHALE COVE COTTAGES
Tranquil Outpost

Inside the rough, weathered smokehouses on Grand Manan Island, the herring hang like iridescent jewels. The island, about 90 minutes from Black's Harbour, is an old-world place where most people still find their livelihood on the sea. There are no movies, no malls, no McDonald's. Only 15 mi (24 km) long and 7 mi (11 km) wide, Grand Manan is home to about 3,000 people, more than 300 species of birds, myriad wildflowers, and whales—humpbacks, fin whales, minkes, and most of the world's remaining northern right whales.

In a clearing at the end of a shady lane and overlooking a cove frequented by whales, the Inn at Whale Cove Cottages is a cluster of weathered cedar-shingle buildings filled with treasures of their own. Built between 1816 and 1860, they are now furnished with Shaker antiques and old hand-braided rugs. The guest rooms are named for the "Cottage Girls" from New England, longtime guests who elevated the game of Scrabble to something like an Olympic sport.

A visit here is a good lesson in how to relax. The inn and the cottages don't have televisions so you won't be tempted to tune in to the world you left behind. It's likely you'll be content to gaze at the fire in the fireplace. A couple of deluxe apartments do have televisions, as well as whirlpool tubs. Book one of these, and you might just stay inside to take in the spectacular view from your windows. But step outdoors and you can watch birds from the lawn chairs overlooking the cove or hike the trail that passes through the property. If you're looking for quiet activity, go beachcombing, hiking, cycling, or sea kayaking, or take a whale- or bird-watching cruise. On cooler days you can play a board game or read one of the books (traditional classics to classic mysteries) from the inn's library. At night, sleep with your windows open and listen to the whales blow in the cove.

If you are staying in an inn room, you'll start each day with a hearty breakfast that always includes homemade oatmeal bread for toast and a hot entrée such as smoked salmon with scrambled eggs. If you are staying in a cottage or apartment, you can work your own magic in your fully equipped kitchen. There is no shortage of seafood in the island's grocery store, and a Saturday farmers' market brings you the freshest local ingredients. For a real treat, try the inn's gorgeous dinner menu. Entrées might include pork tenderloin with rhubarb sauce or seared scallops. Sunday through Saturday evening the menu includes a choice of salmon, scallops, lamb, beef, or pork and a vegetarian option.

Tip *If whales are your priority, come in August or September, when they are more apt to come into the cove at night. In those months they are also more easily seen from the hiking trails and whale-watching cruises.*

🐋 3 rooms, 4 cottages, 2 apartments ⟊ Full breakfast (inn rooms only), restaurant, grills, picnic area, some kitchens. **Recreation:** bird-watching, hiking, wildlife viewing, beach. Nearby: sea kayaking, 9-hole golf course, biking, library. ♿ Some in-room fireplaces, some jetted tubs, some pets allowed; no a/c in some rooms, no phones in some rooms, no TV in some rooms, no smoking ▨ Rooms C$120 per night, cottages C$800 per week (Sun.–Sun.) ▤ MC, V.

⌂ *26 Whale Cove Cottage Rd., Grand Manan, NB E5G 2B5* ☎ *506/662–3181* ⊕ *www.holidayjunction.com/whalecove/.*

INN ON THE COVE
Tranquil Outpost

Not far from downtown St. John, the Bay of Fundy rises and falls in the backyard of Inn on the Cove. When the highest tide in the world is in, waves wash or crash (depending on the weather) on the rocky beach. When the tide is out, you need the telescope in the Ocean Room just to see the water.

The Ocean Room's wall of windows overlooks terraced lawns and gardens, a sheep meadow, and the wooded point that tries to contain the moody sea. Outside, bald eagles soar, barn swallows swoop, and hummingbirds hover. Occasionally a white-tailed deer or even a moose strays from the forest into the meadow. In the bay, eider and black ducks bob with their ducklings, harbor seals swim, harbor porpoises dive, and none of them have any inkling that they are city dwellers. Observe them all from the Ocean Room, with its huge granite fireplace (which sometimes has a dog sleeping on the hearth), sofas, and dining tables. This is the heart of the inn, and you'll probably spend more time here than in the elegantly appointed living room next door.

Hike the coastal woodland trail that winds from the inn to Smuggler's Cove, passing through berry patches along the way. You might even recognize some rare plant specimens along the 40-minute hike. If you're up for some action, head next door to Irving Nature Park, a 600-acre peninsula with groomed trails, breathtaking vistas, and fascinating flora and fauna. It's easy to spend a full day here. Drive about a half hour down the Fundy Coast to go sea kayaking or whale-watching or to pursue any number of other water activities. Prefer to stay closer to home? A five-minute drive will take you to the heart of downtown St. John, where you can take in museums, galleries, crafts shops, live theater, and historic architecture.

You'll be well equipped to face the outdoors after putting away the breakfast perhaps prepared by innkeeper Ross Mavis—cod-salmon-crab cakes might be on the menu. Ross and his wife, Willa, or their staff, will gladly pack you a picnic lunch so you can enjoy a little lobster with a glass of wine on a table of black, jagged rock while the waves crash at the bottom of the cliff. At the end of the day, perhaps after a massage at the inn's spa, is dinner. Almost all of the ingredients come from fishmongers, butchers, and farmers in the Old City Market.

Inn on the Cove offers rooms in the original building and in a newer addition. The older rooms are elegantly furnished in antiques and have whirlpool tubs that overlook the gardens and bay from behind one-way glass. They are ideal retreats. Large, individually decorated rooms in the addition have up-to-the-minute conveniences like Internet connections and cable television, as well as air-jet tubs and balconies overlooking the water. A modern, two-bedroom apartment is great for families. For all of the rooms, though, it is the sight and the sound of the ocean that make them truly special. If you leave your balcony doors open at night, the bay will tell you stories older than words.

Tip *The inn's library contains many books on flora and fauna, which can help you better appreciate the area's ecology. There are also books on all kinds of general topics. If you finish the book you brought with you to the inn, leave it on the shelf and take one you haven't read.*

🛏 8 rooms, 1 apartment ⏐◉⏐ Full breakfast, 2 dining rooms, some kitchens. **Recreation:** biking, bird-watching, hiking, wildlife viewing, fishing, beach, kayaking, cross-country skiing (nearby), sleigh rides (nearby), library. **Services:** spa, hair salon, Internet access, laundry service. **Classes and programs:** yoga classes, health talks. ♿ Some cable TV, some in-room data ports, some jetted tubs, some private balconies, some pets allowed; no a/c in some rooms, no phones in some rooms, no smoking 📧 C$149–C$225 🛏 AE, DC, MC, V.

✉ *1371 Sand Cove Rd., Saint John, NB E2M 4Z9* ☎ *506/672–7799 or 877/257–8080* ⊕ *www.innonthecove.com.*

LITTLE SHEMOGUE COUNTRY INN
Romantic Retreat

The name Shemogue—pronounced shim-o-*gwee*—comes from the Mi'qmaq word *Chimaougoui,* which means "good feed for geese." It aptly describes the rich marshlands and waters of a little bay on the Northumberland Strait. If there were a Mi'qmaq word that meant "spectacular food and lodging for people," it would accurately describe Little Shemogue Country Inn, which overlooks Shemogue Harbour. The inn, about 25 mi from Shediac, is a genteel hideaway on New Brunswick's warm and mellow eastern coast.

On a backcountry road, the inn's discreet sign marks the beginning of a meticulously groomed lane that winds past shrubs, flowers, horses in a paddock, and usually a dog or two. Eventually the lane arrives at a big, brick-red farmhouse surrounded by flowers, lawns, and water. Inside, the inn is glossy-magazine stylish, but with personality—small-paned windows, pine floors, and country antiques. At first glance the furniture looks as if it's made from New Brunswick pine and ash, but it is actually 16th- and 17th-century German spruce and French oak, brought from Europe by Little Shemogue owners Klaus and Petra Sudbrack. A modern annex, across a footbridge from the inn proper, houses a sunny-yellow great room with two-story windows overlooking the ocean, and large, light, airy rooms that face the sea. The annex rooms contain European antiques as well as African pieces, some of them of hand-tooled leather.

The food served at the inn is elegant, eclectic, and authentic to the region. Petra, an interior designer, chef, and cookbook author, presides over an entirely fresh kitchen where nothing is ever canned or frozen. She grows her own herbs and salad greens and purchases supplies direct from oyster farmers, lobster trappers, market gardeners, and natural food stores. Dinner is always five courses and is served, by reservation only, in one of the four intimate dining rooms—unless it's a lobster boil; then everything moves outside to the picnic tables.

The 200-acre property has trails for all pursuits—biking, hiking, cross-country skiing, sleigh rides—and birds galore. The salt marsh is full of sandpipers; bald eagles, kingfishers, herons, and others fish in the estuary. On the private sandy beach, a small catamaran is available to any guest who knows how to sail it. Klaus has a racing catamaran of his own and often invites guests to join him. There are a couple of canoes for the less intrepid. Out on the water, you are likely to encounter workers on the oyster banks, and you might be offered a free sample. Nearby are world-class nature preserves and long sandy public beaches.

Nothing is left to chance at Little Shemogue Country Inn, especially the environment. Klaus changes the seawater in the hot tub every three days. All but the smallest laundry items are sent off property so as not to tax the water table. The Sudbracks respect every inch of the delicate ecosystem they inhabit. Long after they and their guests are gone, they want the little bay to remain a safe harbor, with good feed for geese.

Tip *Klaus might challenge you to identify some antique kitchen appliances in exchange for a free breakfast. It's a lot tougher than it sounds. Coffee helps with the answers.*

9 rooms Dining room. **Recreation:** biking, bird-watching, fishing, hiking, horseback riding (nearby), wildlife viewing, beach, canoeing, sailing, golf courses (nearby), ice-skating, sleigh rides, snowshoeing, library, piano. **Services:** canoes, catamaran, and bicycles provided; exercise equipment; outdoor hot tub; massage; dock; meeting room. **Classes and programs:** yoga classes. Satellite TV, some in-room fireplaces, some jetted tubs; no kids under 10, no smoking C$89–C$175 AE, MC, V.

2361 Route 955, Little Shemogue, NB E4M 3K4 506/538–2320 506/538–7494 *www.little-inn.nb.ca.*

ON THE POND
Romantic Retreat

Each morning before breakfast, On the Pond owner Donna Evans walks to the beaver pond in nearby Mactaquac Provincial Park. It's an easy walk, just about half an hour over groomed trails and a boardwalk, but rewarding just the same. You are invited to come along, and if you do you'll probably encounter geese, families of ducks, and, of course, beavers along the way. In fine weather, you'll return to breakfast on the terrace overlooking the marsh where great blue heron live. It isn't unusual for white-tailed deer, raccoons, or snowshoe hares to wander into the yard. Be sure to bring your binoculars so you can get an up-close look at all the wildlife.

A morning like this sets you up for just about any kind of day. Fishing, canoeing, biking, and birding are all on hand or close by. Mactaquac Provincial Park, with its championship golf course, nature trails, and beaches, is next door to the inn. In winter the hills of the golf course make exciting toboggan runs, and the water hazards are ideal skating ponds. Some of the trails are groomed for cross-country skiing, and a horse-drawn sleigh follows others. If the weather isn't cooperating, you can always exercise in the inn's well-equipped gym. Treat yourself to an hour in the spa at the end of an active day, or cut to the chase and spend the whole day enjoying mud, seaweed, and herbal wraps; hot-stone massages; and the hot tub, the whirlpool, and the sauna.

On the Pond overlooks a quiet spot along the St. John River, which backs up behind a dam near Fredericton. A European-style place built with generous proportions, exposed ceiling beams, stone and wood floors, and plump upholstered furniture, it is up to the rigors of heavy-duty relaxing. Guest rooms are decorated in a woodland theme that reflects the inn's setting. Each has a double as well as a queen-size bed made up with line-dried sheets that inspire dreams of fresh air. The dining room, furnished in antiques, overlooks the water. Dinner can be decadent if you like, but more often than not it is heart-healthy with all the flavors of decadence. Broiled salmon brushed with ginger, honey, Dijon mustard, and vermouth is a favorite. Dedicated to wellness, Donna caters to special diets and offers wellness weekends for stress management.

Tip *In early spring you may want to sleep with your window closed: the spring peepers (tiny but very vocal frogs) sometimes get carried away at night, and the songbird symphony can start as early as 4 AM.*

🛏 8 rooms 🍽 Dining room. **Recreation:** biking, bird-watching, fishing, hiking, wildlife viewing, canoeing, kayaking, badminton, boccie, volleyball, library, videocassette library. Nearby: beach, 18-hole golf course, ice-skating, cross-country and downhill skiing, sleigh rides. **Services:** canoes, kayaks, and bicycles provided; gym; outdoor hot tub; sauna; spa; dock; meeting room. **Classes and programs:** wellness weekends. ♿ In-room TV w/VCR, no smoking, no kids 💳 C$125–C$145 🗂 MC, V.

📫 *20 Hwy. 615, Mactaquac, NB E6L 1M2* ☎ *506/363–3420 or 800/ 984–2555* 📠 *506/363–3479* ⊕ *www.onthepond.com.*

Nova Scotia

HADDON HALL
Luxurious Resort

When you arrive at this hilltop estate, take a deep breath and slow down. Stroll across the manicured lawns to admire the well-kept gardens and century-old mansion—if you can take your eyes off the amazing and inescapable view of Mahone Bay. Grab a book from the library and sit poolside with a drink, but be warned: it may be hard to tuck into either, because that serene vista will keep calling you back.

Haddon Hall, an Edwardian summer home built in 1905, has a wide wraparound porch, stately pillars, arched windows, and a Victorian interior. At this cushy spot near the well-heeled town of Chester, about 40 mi from Halifax, large guest rooms are furnished with antiques, and handmade rugs are scattered on gleaming oak and pine floors. Everything here is geared for couples who want to unwind, from the in-room CD players and four-poster king-size beds to the fireplaces and marble baths. Gaze up at ceiling murals or skylights from the depths of your double whirlpool tub, and then don a terry robe and relax by the fire. If a room in the main house isn't your idea of privacy, ask for a suite in one of the three outer buildings. One even has a private deck with a "love swing chair" built for two. And while some rooms at Haddon Hall are billed as suitable for children, the gracious setting is not: there's no playground, the water in the pool is deep, and the dining room offers no kids' menu.

There's excellent birding and wildlife viewing to be had from the comfort of the inn's Adirondack chairs. If you prefer to get some exercise, spend your day at tennis, mountain biking, or golf, or sign up with one of the local charter boats that offer island picnics, shark fishing, and scuba diving. Relax on the deck for the inn's best views, and gaze at the yachts in the bay far below until they disappear into the sunset. Afterward, come inside and pick your spot in the lounge—a dark and rustic affair with a fire in the grate on chilly evenings. If you can pry yourself out of your duvet-laden bed in the early-morning quiet, you might see a family of deer nibbling on the roses. Take a peek from your front porch, and then steal back under the covers.

Tip *Haddon Hall prides itself on being a quiet, peaceful retreat. There's even a quiet curfew from 11 PM to 7 AM. Pack it in early to savor the tranquillity in the privacy of your own suite.*

◄ 4 rooms, 7 suites ⦿ Full breakfast, room service, bar, minibars, some refrigerators. **Recreation:** biking, bird-watching, hiking, mountain biking, running, wildlife viewing, pool, canoeing, tennis court, board games, videocassette library. **Services:** canoes, mountain bikes, and tennis equipment provided; dry-cleaning service; business services; concierge; Internet access; meeting rooms. ⚇ Cable TV, in-room fireplaces, in-room VCRs, jetted tubs, some private balconies, decks and terraces; no smoking ⊠ C$275–C$395 ▭ DC, MC, V.

⌂ *67 Haddon Hill Rd. (Box 640), Chester, NS B0J 1J0* ☎ *902/275–3577* 🖷 *902/275–5159* ⊕ *www.haddonhallinn.com* ⊗ *Closed late Oct.–early May.*

KELTIC LODGE
Tranquil Outpost

The drive out to this resort perched on the cliffs of the breathtaking Cabot Trail is, in a word, dramatic. You climb skyward around the mountains of the Cape Breton Highlands, then plunge to meet the waves, and do it all over again, and again. You might even feel winded when you finally arrive at your destination.

Keltic Lodge, built in 1940, is an old-style, full-service resort in the unspoiled wilderness of Cape Breton Highlands National Park. It has an air of history, yet it offers the comforts and conveniences of today. Where tennis courts, heated pools, and beaches used to make the grade, massages, in-room data ports, and cooking classes set the lodge apart in the 21st century. To immerse yourself in the resort's old-fashioned aura, ask for a room in the Tudor-style main lodge. Bedecked with Nova Scotia tartan and furnished with two twins or a queen-size bed, each room commands an excellent view. In the modern Inn at Keltic rooms are a bit on the smallish side, but they are furnished with antiques and draped in the same plaid as the rooms in the main lodge. Log cottages are handsomely furnished, with a living room in the middle and two private bedrooms on either end.

The Main Lodge is surrounded by groomed lawns that roll down to the jutting cliffs of Middlehead Peninsula. Benches are at the ready around the grounds for sitting and admiring the gardens and the never-ending view. Seemingly perched on the edge of the lodge's promontory, the pool overlooks the same scene, as do wilderness trails reserved exclusively for lodge guests. Stay on the lodge grounds or head out into the rest of Cape Breton Highlands National Park on well-maintained nature trails. Bring your bike or sturdy footwear to travel boardwalks aplenty, from which you can see centuries-old evergreen forests and the wildlife within. From the shores below the lodge, you can do some whale-watching and sea kayaking. Golfers will be happy to know that for decades Keltic has been synonymous with its next-door neighbor, the Highlands Links, the number one–rated public golf course in Canada.

Of an evening, make your way to the dining room, whose large picture windows afford still more views of the mountains and the Atlantic Ocean. The menu celebrates that very sea, offering only the freshest local seafood, from mussels to salmon to lobster. After dinner, don't turn in too early: there's live entertainment every night.

Tip *Consider coming to Keltic Lodge after the summer high season. The Cape Breton Highlands rival New England for striking foliage and harvest spirit.*

🛏 72 rooms, 11 cottages ❙⊚❙ Full breakfast, 2 restaurants, room service, bar, lounge, some microwaves, some refrigerators. **Recreation:** biking, bird-watching, fishing, hiking, running, wildlife viewing, beach, pool, sea kayaking, golf privileges, croquet, horseshoes, Ping-Pong, shuffleboard, board games, playground. **Services:** massage, guided fishing trips, dry-cleaning service, laundry service, shop, business services, meeting rooms, Internet access. **Classes and programs:** guided hikes, guided nature walks, arts and crafts classes, cooking classes. ♿ Cable TV, some in-room fireplaces, some private balconies and decks, some pets allowed; no a/c, no smoking 🖼 C$200–C$320 ▭ AE, D, DC, MC, V.

🏠 *Middlehead Peninsula, Ingonish Beach, NS B0C 1L0* ☎ *902/285–2880 or 800/565–0444* 🖨 *902/285–2859* ⊕ *www.signatureresorts.com/keltic* ☯ *Closed Nov.–mid-May.*

LISCOMBE LODGE
Family Hideout

Sprawling along the evergreen-fringed banks of the Liscomb River is a resort that's frequented by ospreys and eagles. A 2½-hour drive from the provincial capital at Halifax, Liscombe Lodge bills itself as the Nature Lover's Resort. Here, you have many ways to immerse yourself in the great outdoors.

The river is ideal for all kinds of boating, from canoeing to sailing, or you can sit back and admire the scenery from aboard a 12-passenger motor launch. Spend a morning beachcombing or rockhounding on the river's rock beaches, or while away an afternoon on a pedal boat. Off the water, children enjoy visiting with the lodge's bunny families. Nearby country roads are perfect for a bike ride. On-property, lace up your hiking boots and explore the seven trails that crisscross the land. Or ask the lodge to pack you a picnic lunch and set out for the two-hour hike along the Liscomb River Trail. The easy hike takes you to a swinging bridge over a waterfall, where you can pause to eat before heading back. Even if the weather turns gloomy you can get your exercise, in the fitness center and the indoor pool, and finish up in the sauna and whirlpool.

Hidden among the trees beside the river, the lodge's low-lying buildings evoke both an old-fashioned cottage colony and miniature ski resort. Try to spot avian guests from the lodge's veranda, or listen for the call of the loons from the deck of your chalet. Well-spaced among the conifers, the cottages and chalets are furnished in a modern, sparse style, but they are spacious and have a fireplace—and the only thing you see from your private deck is the river. Families favor the four-bedroom cottages with stone fireplaces. The main lodge, on the riverfront, contains guest rooms with private balconies.

The lodge whips up enormously hearty breakfasts featuring homemade fish cakes, brown breads, oatcakes, and smoked salmon. At dinner time you can watch the chef prepare the lodge specialty, planked salmon, in an open fire pit. There's more seafood, such as lobster and mussels, in the offing as well, accompanied by fresh local produce. In season, wild blueberries go into some truly delectable desserts.

Tip *In the shoulder seasons (May, June, and October), the lodge offers a two-night Family Adventure package at well-discounted rates for a family of four. The package includes breakfast, the use of small boats and fishing gear, a harbor cruise, and guest passes to Sherbrooke Village, a nearby 1860s living history museum.*

⇦ 30 rooms, 17 chalets, 6 cottages ⭤ Modified American plan, restaurant, room service, bar, some grills, some refrigerators. **Recreation:** biking, bird-watching, fishing, hiking, mountain biking, running, wildlife viewing, indoor pool, river swimming, canoeing, kayaking, rowing, sailing, sea kayaking, putting green, tennis court, basketball, billiards, horseshoes, Ping-Pong, shuffleboard, board games, piano, recreation room, videocassette library, playground. **Services:** tennis rackets and fishing gear provided; gym; hot tub; sauna; boat launch; dock; marina; babysitting; laundry facilities; laundry service; shop; meeting rooms; Internet access. ⬙ Cable TV with movies, some in-room fireplaces, some in-room VCRs, private balconies and decks, some pets allowed, no-smoking rooms, no-smoking floors; no a/c ▣ C$99–C$350 ▭ AE, D, DC, MC, V.

⌂ *2884 Hwy. 7 (R.R. 1), Liscomb Mills, NS B0J 2A0* ☎ *902/779–2307 or 800/665–6343* 📠 *902/779–2700* ⊕ *www.signatureresorts.com/liscombe* ☾ *Closed late Oct.–mid-May.*

MERSEY RIVER CHALETS
Family Hideout

Even the most hard-bitten city folk tend to loosen up at Mersey River Chalets. The 375-acre wilderness resort, cradled along the shores of the Mersey River in western Nova Scotia and 3 mi north of Kejimkujik National Park, epitomizes laid-back vacationing: doors are never locked, and everything, including sports equipment, is yours for the taking. Often, guests simply leave notes when they help themselves to treats like ice cream from the office. It's that honor system, without a fixed, all-inclusive price, that'll make you feel at home.

You'll no doubt feel tension melt away during your first few hours at Mersey River. Maybe it washes down the river on the gentle currents that bring such a sense of calm to the resort. The river is also the focus of activity here. More than 1 mi (2 km) of wooden boardwalks line the riverbank, and kayaks bob along the tree-lined shores. Kids of all ages can hardly be torn away from river-based activities like canoeing and swimming, and a tiny waterfall that gurgles over rocks keeps toddlers happy for hours. There's also a playground to keep the kids busy while Mom and Dad take to the trails through the forest.

Mersey River Chalets was designed not only for able-bodied people but for accessibility-challenged people as well. The riverside boardwalks and gravel paths are perfect for a rolling hike. Specially designed wharves provide wheelchair access to swimming, kayaking, and canoeing, and there's a wheelchair swing. Accommodations are engineered for wheelchair accessibility.

Furnished in a clean and modern motif, the chalets have two bedrooms and a combined living room/kitchen area with a woodstove. Plank floors and ceilings lend a touch of style, and colorful slipcovers add warmth. The larger chalets have decks with grills, and two pull-out sofas in the living room. To keep nature front and center, however, there are no phones or TVs. Sit down for a meal in the restaurant. With a huge granite fireplace as its focal point, the octagonal room offers casual dining. The menu changes with the seasons but always includes seafood. In summer, extend your day outdoors by eating on the patio beside the trees, with a distant view of the little waterfall.

More adventurous families might prefer to lodge in the tepee village, located where the river meets the shores of a nearby lake. Sioux-style tents are pitched on platforms, offering sleeping quarters and storage space for families of up to eight people. The beds where you unroll your sleeping bags are cushioned with high-density foam, and if you forget your sleeping bag there's plenty of bedding to spare at the office. There's a portable toilet near the tent village, and more substantial facilities with showers nearby. At night, kids can roast marshmallows during sing-alongs around the open-pit fire in the center of the village before nodding off under the canopy of stars and moon-lit trees.

Tip *Unlike most resorts in Nova Scotia, Mersey River Chalets is open year-round. In the off-season you can skate on the frozen river or cross-country ski on the snow-covered boardwalks, then retire to the comfort of your fire-warmed chalet.*

🛏7 chalets, 5 tepees, 4 rooms 🍴Restaurant (May–October), bar, some grills, kitchens. **Recreation:** bird-watching, fishing, hiking, running, wildlife viewing, river swimming, canoeing, kayaking, tennis court, cross-country skiing, snowshoeing, tobogganing, badminton, basketball, croquet, horseshoes, lawn bowling, volleyball, board games, playground. **Services:** kayaks, canoes, and tennis equipment provided; dock; guided fishing trips; babysitting; laundry service; airport shuttle; business services; meeting room; Internet access. **Classes and programs:** yoga classes. ♿ Some private decks, pets allowed; no a/c, no room phones, some room TVs, no smoking 💳C$110–C$205 ➡MC, V.

📬 *R.R. 2, Caledonia, NS B0T 1B0* ☎ *902/682–2443 or 877/667–2583* 📠 *902/682–2332* 🌐 *www.merseyriverchalets.com.*

TROUT POINT LODGE
Tranquil Outpost

From the 14-inch-thick spruce log-and-chiseled granite walls to the huge Adirondack chairs that sit sentry on its wraparound deck, Trout Point Lodge, about 25 mi from the Yarmouth ferry terminal, is a larger-than-life place. It's been here for only eight years, but already the lodge seems an organic part of the wilderness. And the wilderness here is abundant: the lodge's 200 acres border half a million acres of protected land in Tobeatic Wilderness Preserve and Kejimkujik National Park. Groves of evergreens and hardwoods cluster along winding rivers and placid lakes, providing homes for small mammals as well as bears and coyotes. Even the wildlife doesn't seem to mind the lodge. A turtle recently made her nest in front of the dining room, to the delight of guests who watched spellbound as she completed her task. Keep your eyes peeled as you walk around the expansive property: you are likely to see moose, beavers, otters, and bald eagles.

Designed and owned by Louisiana transplants, the lodge speaks to their French roots. They chose to build on Nova Scotia's French Acadian shore because the original Louisiana Cajuns came from this part of Canada. The Cajun and Creole cuisine is made with only the freshest ingredients from the lodge's own gardens and berry bushes; everything, including the bread, is made from scratch daily. Because this is Nova Scotia, seafood is served at every three-course lunch and four-course dinner. Everyone sits down at long wooden tables to partake of the grand feasts. (Tables for two are available if you book in advance.) In the dining room you can gaze through the windows at views of Tusket Lake or watch the embers dance in the room's book-ended fireplaces.

Once a month, Trout Point conducts cooking classes. Three-day programs in seafood and new Creole cuisine are offered from June through October. But don't worry that you'll become too much of a gourmand on your vacation: you can't help but be enticed by the boardwalk that weaves in and out of the surrounding forest. The lake and river are there for swimming, kayaking, and canoeing, and the woods are perfect for mountain biking. River rapids draw white-water rafters to Tobeatic Wilderness Preserve and Kejimkujik National Park.

With Tiffany-style lamps, Oriental rugs, handcrafted twig furniture, and four-poster beds, every guest room is an oasis. Like the food, the appointments are all handmade, right down to the rugs. Have a shiatsu massage before stretching out for a pre-dinner nap. After dinner on the patio, ease into a seat around the outdoor fire pit, or snuggle up in front of the Great Room's two fireplaces. In these quiet moments you can hear the coyotes calling to one another—or maybe it's just the people in the wood-fired hot tub down by the river.

Tip *Accompany the chefs as they collect fresh produce and organic herbs from the lodge's extensive gardens, wild mushrooms and berries from the forests, and fresh cheese from a nearby farm. Before you check out, pick up a copy of* The Trout Point Lodge Cookbook.

🛏 12 rooms 🍽 Full or modified American plan, restaurant. **Recreation:** biking, bird-watching, fishing, hiking, mountain biking, running, wildlife viewing, river swimming, canoeing, kayaking, board games, library, playground. **Services:** mountain bikes, canoes, kayaks, fishing rods, and tackle provided; outdoor hot tub; massage; guided fishing trips; ferry shuttle. **Classes and programs:** cooking classes. ♿ Some in-room fireplaces, private balconies, some pets allowed; no a/c, no room phones, no room TVs, no smoking 💳 C$177–C$354 💳 MC, V.

🏠 *P.O. Box 456, Kemptville, NS B0W 1Y0* ☎ *902/749–7629* 🌐 *www.troutpoint.com.*

Ontario

AROWHON PINES SUMMER RESORT
Tranquil Outpost

Tucked away in the wilds of Algonquin Provincial Park is a small, friendly hideaway treasured by devotees of peace, quiet, and glorious food. In this spacious sanctuary, a three-hour drive from Toronto, you can commune intimately with nature in your own way and at your own pace.

In a tradition honored by generations of visitors, Arowhon Pines is informal and free-spirited. Strict regimens and busy activities schedules simply do not apply. Think instead of lazy afternoons on the dock, splashing in the cool lake, walking as much (or as little) as you like, or snoozing, guilt-free, by the fire. Recreation is easily at hand; you can swim, sail, or windsurf, or steep in a hot tub.

The Kates family has perfected the art of unobtrusive hospitality, creating comfort without apparent fuss. In the pine-walled guest rooms, all with en suite baths, throw rugs, and antique pine or wicker furniture, there are no radios, TVs, or telephones. The thoughtful service includes a steady supply of linens and towels, white robes, and flowers freshly cut from the garden. Each cabin features a shared lounge with wood-burning fireplace. The two-bedroom cabins and private suites have their own fireplaces and decks.

There are plenty of low-key ways to enjoy yourself at Arowhon Pines. Room rates include the use of all recreation equipment, including canoes, sailboats, kayaks, tennis courts, and the sauna. You can paddle Little Joe Lake or hike trails through the forest, inspecting flowers, mushrooms, and ferns. Bird-watchers have a chance to search out some of the 250 species recorded in Algonquin Park. In the evenings and on rainy days, stop by the Tanglewood Lounge to read, play board games, or converse by the stone fireplace amid eclectic, old-fashioned furnishings.

The centerpiece of Arowhon is the Heritage Dining Room, whose food is among the best in Canada. In this hexagonal log building, the tables are arranged around a stone fireplace and windows on all six sides afford views of forest and water. Dishes are always prepared from scratch, using fresh, local foods and herbs from the lodge garden. For breakfast you can have hot porridge, homemade granola, ham, kippers, smoked cod, pancakes with maple syrup, or Welsh rarebit with Canadian pea-meal bacon. At noon there's usually a choice of soups, salads, several hot and cold dishes, and sweets. In good weather, this lunch buffet is sometimes replaced with a barbecue by the lake. Dinner begins with an enormous buffet of appetizers (try the arugula and mango salad) and a selection of hot and cold soups. Such entrées as grilled pickerel with orange and ginger, perfectly roasted Ontario lamb with homemade mint sauce, or roast beef and Yorkshire pudding are staples. No alcohol is sold in Algonquin Park, but you may bring your own wine.

Tip *Drive to Algonquin Park's Visitor Centre, 25 mi (40 km) east of Arowhon Pines on Hwy. 60, to learn about park history and enjoy the viewing deck. There you can sign up for the essential Algonquin experience: an evening wolf-howl. As expert guides mimic wolf calls, faraway packs send up their own eerie chorus.*

🛏 50 rooms in 13 cabins (available by the room or by the cabin) ¶◎¶ American plan, restaurant, grills, picnic area. **Recreation:** birdwatching, fishing, hiking, running, wildlife viewing, beach, lake swimming, canoeing, kayaking, sailing, 2 tennis courts, badminton, horseshoes, Ping-Pong, shuffleboard, volleyball, piano, recreation room. Nearby: horseback riding, mountain biking, golfing. **Services:** canoes, kayaks, and sailboats provided; sauna; dock. **Classes and programs:** movies, sing-alongs. ♨ Some in-room fireplaces, some private decks; no a/c, no room phones, no room TVs, no smoking ▱ C$170–C$362 ▭ MC, V.

✉ *Algonquin Park, Box 10001, Huntsville, ON P1H 2G5* ☎ *705/633–5661* 📠 *705/633–5795* ⊕ *www.arowhonpines.ca.*

THE DELTA GRANDVIEW RESORT
Family Hideout ~ Luxurious Resort

Overlooking lovely Fairy Lake near Huntsville, 140 mi from Toronto, the Delta Grandview Resort is buffered from the outside world by 850 acres (344 hectares) of groomed and wooded grounds. A fine old resort in the Muskoka tradition, the Grandview is keenly aware of its forest surroundings. A staff of naturalists conducts hikes and excursions on which you can learn about all things Muskoka, from Precambrian geology to wildflowers, animal tracks, and birdcalls. You can also join the naturalists for a visit to the Echo Valley Observatory, about 8 mi (12 km) from the resort, to peer at the infinity of stars that appear on clear nights.

Or go farther afield, to explore the untamed wonders of the Canadian Shield by canoe or kayak or even aboard a small aircraft. But you don't have to leave the resort to find something to do. Water-based sports, such as canoeing, kayaking, sailing, swimming, and fishing, are all read-ily available. Play on a Mark O'Meara–designed golf course. *Spirit of Muskoka* boat cruises on Fairy and Peninsula lakes are a highlight of any Grandview visit, and the Amba Spa is open daily for facials, mas-sages, and manicures.

Accommodations, from basic inn rooms to one- to three-bedroom pre-mium suites with private decks, all offer views of Fairy Lake, the rolling golf course, or the surrounding forest. Rooms have Colonial-style fur-nishings, colorful duvets, and wildlife art on the walls. The original hotel, which harks back to Muskoka's golden age, has been transformed into the Rosewood Inn Dining Room. Here, the culinary team serves rack of lamb, roast beef, grilled fish or steaks, and delicate pastas and risottos, all with an elegant touch. Another dining option, O'Meara's at the Club-house, is a more casual place that concentrates on seasonal vegetables, wild berries, and fish. Dine under the stars on the deck, or in the screened porch. At the Dockside Bar & Grill, summer cottage-style spe-cialties (burgers, wings, salads) are served on the lakeside patio. Be sure to try a Muskoka shake from the ice-cream bar.

123 rooms, 20 suites ⍟ 3 restaurants, pub, some kitchens. **Recre-ation:** biking, bird-watching, fishing, hiking, mountain biking, run-ning, wildlife viewing, beach, pool, indoor pool, lake swimming, tubing (water), waterskiing, windsurfing, boating, canoeing, kayaking, sailing, 9-hole golf course, 18-hole golf course, 2 tennis courts, cross-coun-try skiing, ice-skating, snowshoeing, tobogganing, basketball, volley-ball, playground. **Services:** canoes, kayaks, pedal boats, mountain bikes, cross-country ski equipment, snowshoes, and toboggans provided; health club; sauna; spa; boat launch; dock; marina; pro shop; babysit-ting; dry-cleaning service; laundry facilities; business services; car rental; concierge; Internet access, meeting rooms. **Classes and programs:** guided hikes, guided nature walks, natural history programs, children's programs (ages 4–12). In-room data ports, some in-room fireplaces, jetted tubs, some private balconies; no smoking C$227–C$470 AE, DC, MC, V.

939 Hwy. 60, Muskoka, ON P1H 1Z4 705/789–4417 or 877/814–7706 705/789–1674 *www.deltahotels.com.*

DOMAIN OF KILLIEN
Tranquil Outpost

Enjoying nature has been raised to a genteel art form at the Domain of Killien, an intimate retreat on a peaceful lake in the Haliburton High-lands, about a three-hour drive from Toronto. Built in 1927 with a pi-oneer-style squared-log facade, the main lodge harks back to a simpler time. Within, however, everything is thoughtfully and luxuriously up-dated for 21st-century visitors.

Choose accommodations in a handsome room in the lodge, or opt for one of seven lakeside chalets, which offer cheerful rooms with warm cedar walls, bentwood furniture, and extravagant linens. All have wood-burning fireplaces, down duvets, full Jacuzzi baths, stacks of fluffy towels, and views of the lake.

You're free to unwind in your own way at the Domain of Killien. The well-trained staff won't attempt to structure your time without your say-so—their aim is your complete relaxation. But if you're like most guests, you might opt for at least a few hours of sailing or canoeing on a sunlit afternoon, hiking in the sole company of forest songbirds, or fly-fishing for trout in bright, clean waters. Visitors regularly spot deer, beaver, and moose on their rambles. The Domain is surrounded by 5,000 private, unspoiled acres of emerald woodlands for you to explore. In winter, the quietness of the surroundings is never broken by roaring snowmobiles. Dogsledding is a popular alternative; there's nothing quite like riding behind an eager team of canines through the snowy forest. Sixteen miles (25 km) of private, groomed trails offer some of the best cross-country skiing in Ontario. You can also try snowshoeing or go skating under the stars on Delphis Lake.

There's food for mind and spirit at the Domain of Killien. For bodily nourishment, there's the superb dining room, renowned for great cuisine and an informed selection of vintage wines. If you plan to be out for a day's hiking, fishing, or paddling, you can order a chef-packed picnic lunch. Dinner menus change daily. The French chefs serve up Provençal-inspired dishes, using fresh, seasonal ingredients, including organic herbs and vegetables. You might start with chilled leek-and-potato soup, then choose from three entrées, possibly including a very Canadian offering like grilled rack of caribou glazed in maple syrup sauce. Fish is always featured, perhaps a fillet of sea bass infused with fennel and bathed in white wine and basil from the lodge garden. Another favorite is blinis (Russian pancakes) loaded with lodge-smoked Atlantic salmon in a cream-and-herb sauce.

Tip *A visit to Haliburton Forest and Wildlife Reserve (705/754–2198), about 25 mi (40 km) from the Domain of Killien, is worthwhile. The reserve promotes ecological awareness with astronomy programs, a wolf center, and the exciting Walk in the Clouds forest canopy tour (C$95 for adults).*

5 rooms, 7 chalets ❯❮ Modified American plan, restaurant. **Recreation:** biking, bird-watching, fishing, hiking, running, wildlife viewing (nearby), beach, lake swimming, canoeing, kayaking, sailing, cross-country skiing, dogsledding, ice-skating, snowshoeing. **Services:** fishing boats, fly rods, bicycles, canoes, kayaks, sailboats, and snowshoes provided; dogsled rentals; guided fishing trips; business services; Internet access. **Classes and programs:** cooking classes. ☖ Some in-room

fireplaces, some jetted tubs, some private decks; no room TVs
🖭 C$149–C$215 ▭ AE, DC, MC, V.

🖰 *Box 810, Haliburton, ON K0M 1S0* 🖷 *705/457–1100 or 800/390–*
0769 🖶 *705/457–3853* ⊕ *www.domainofkillien.com.*

THE IRWIN INN
Family Hideout ~ Luxurious Resort

It's dawn, and you're paddling through mist on a perfectly silent lake,
surrounded by ghostly islets and silver water. You could be anywhere
in time; the lake has changed little since Ojibwe canoes drifted through
a morning like this hundreds of years ago. Such is the magic of Stoney
Lake. It's the finest link in the chain of lakes called the Kawarthas, which
carve an intricate landscape northeast of Toronto, between the farm-
lands of Northumberland and the Haliburton Highlands. Two hours'
drive from Toronto, the lake is an ideal place to reacquaint yourself with
nature. On its shores the Irwin Inn is an ideal place to put everyday life
on hold for a while.

Made up of a rambling main lodge and cottages on 200 acres (81 hectares) of private grounds, the Irwin Inn has a number of traditional
summer-resort accommodations in different price ranges. In the main
lodge, most guest rooms have a queen-size bed plus a single bed. Country-style furnishings make the rooms warm and welcoming. The inn's
most desirable quarters are the two-level post-and-beam cottages at lakeside. These hideaways feature whirlpool baths, king-size beds, and
hardwood floors. Each has a stone fireplace, a bathroom on each level,
and a kitchen. Best of all, perhaps, each one has expansive views of
the lake from a cedar deck spacious enough to accommodate its own
private, heated pool.

Water activities are a given at the lakeside inn. Rambles along nature
paths can be made on foot or on horseback. The Irwin Inn has complete riding facilities, including an indoor arena, outdoor ring, and riding trails. Lessons in both English and Western riding styles are available,
and you may board your own horses at the inn's Milestone Stable.
Many of the inn's visitors prefer the Kawarthas in autumn, when nature holds court in a blaze of red and gold. Trail riding is truly inspir-
ing on cool fall days, especially when you can warm up by the fire
afterward. In winter, you can bundle up for a horse-drawn sleigh ride,
ice-skating, cross-country skiing, or snowmobiling.

The inn's dining room, often filled with the aroma of fresh-baked rolls
and biscuits made from treasured original recipes, has panoramic views
of the lake. Dinner selections include expertly grilled steak and poached
salmon. You may find yourself lingering at sunset, then walking to your
room under a sky of diamond-bright stars.

Tip *It's an easy drive to Petroglyphs Provincial Park, only 2 mi (3 km) northeast of Crowe's Landing at the village of Stoneyridge. View more than 900 ancient native-Canadian carvings of spirit figures on an expanse of rare white marble.*

🛏 9 rooms, 30 suites ⦿ Modified American plan, restaurant, picnic area, some kitchens. **Recreation:** biking, bird-watching, fishing, horseback riding, mountain biking, running, beach, pool, lake swimming, boating, canoeing, 9-hole golf course, golf privileges, tennis court, cross-country skiing, ice-skating, sleigh rides, snowmobiling, badminton, billiards, croquet, Ping-Pong, shuffleboard, volleyball. **Services:** pedal boats, canoes, and mountain bikes provided; motorboat rentals; massage; sauna; boat launch; horse boarding; Internet access. **Classes and programs:** horseback-riding lessons, children's programs (ages 3–12). ♿ Some in-room fireplaces, some jetted tubs, some private balconies and decks 💵 C$255–C$1,660 💳 AE, MC, V.

🏠 R.R. 2, Lakefield, ON K0L 2H0 ☎ 705/877–2240 or 800/461–6490 📠 705/877–2243 🌐 www.irwininn.com.

KILLARNEY MOUNTAIN LODGE & OUTFITTERS
Laid-Back Adventure

Perched on Georgian Bay's northern shore, Killarney Mountain Lodge has welcomed generations of visitors. They're lured here by a landscape that is the very essence of the untamed north: the Great Lakes Heritage Coast, where sheer cliffs plunge into the white-capped indigo waters of Lake Huron. In this wild corner of Ontario, 250 mi (400 km) north of Toronto, the rocky shores of the bay and islands are fringed with wind-gnarled, solitary pines.

The lodge is a gateway to the protected wilderness of Killarney Provincial Park, where paddling routes and hiking trails thread through the stunning, white quartzite Killarney Mountains. The lodge can outfit and supply you for extended journeys into the backcountry, or you can arrange to cruise the islands in a 50-foot (15-meter) sailboat. Take a guided two-hour hike on the nearby Chikanishing Trail or simply stroll along the shore, spotting birds and savoring the clear air. Georgian Bay's open waters, winds, and currents are a sea kayaker's dream.

The lodge was built in the 1950s for some Detroit truck manufacturers and their friends (who included Jimmy Hoffa, according to legend). Its pine-paneled rooms were made for ease and practicality rather than luxury. Killarney's present owners, Maury and Annabelle East, have kept the folksy '50s aura alive. Newer additions—suites, cabins, and chalets—are tucked away among the trees and along the shore, and a substantial marina fronts the property. The lodge has plain exteriors, log-walled common areas, crisp linens, country-style furniture, and canopied pathways that shelter you on your way to your chalet or cabin. This is classic, Canadian-style wilderness accommodation.

The woodsy, log-built dining room is finished with mounted hunting trophies and a stone fireplace, and the kitchen puts fresh ingredients into dishes cooked from scratch. Carnivores with appetites primed by a hard day's paddling can chow down on juicy barbecued ribs and steaks. Breakfast (don't miss the blueberry pancakes) and lunch are also served here.

Tip *Sign on for Killarney's three-day gastronomic adventure by sea kayak (C$675 per person). After a night at the lodge, you'll paddle among the pink granite islands of Georgian Bay, camping for two nights and feasting on menus prepared by the authors of the* Georgian Bay Gourmet cookbook.

🛏 24 rooms, 2 suites, 2 chalets, 6 cabins 🍽 Full or modified American plan, dining room, lounge, grills. **Recreation:** biking, bird-watching, fishing, hiking, mountain biking, wildlife viewing, beach, pool, lake swimming, windsurfing, boating, canoeing, kayaking, sailing, sea kayaking, tennis court, badminton, billiards, boccie, croquet, horseshoes, Ping-Pong, shuffleboard, volleyball, recreation room. **Services:** bicycle, canoe, kayak, and camping-equipment rentals; sauna; airstrip; boat launch; dock; guided fishing trips; marina; tackle shop; grocery shopping; shops; Internet access; meeting rooms; travel services. **Classes and programs:** guided hikes, guided nature walks, natural history programs, canoeing lessons, arts and crafts classes, photography classes, nature talks. ⚐ Some private decks; no a/c, no room phones, no room TVs, no smoking 🛏 C$115–C$177 ▤ AE, MC, V.

⬧ *Killarney Mountain Lodge, Killarney, ON P0M 2A0* ☎ *705/287–2242 or 800/461–1117* 🖷 *705/287–2691* ⊕ *www.killarney.com* ☼ *Closed mid-Oct.–mid-May.*

SMOOTHWATER OUTFITTERS & ECOLODGE
Laid-Back Adventure

People come from all over the world to nurture mind, body, and spirit at Smoothwater Ecolodge, 275 mi (440 km) north of Toronto in the legendary Temagami wilderness—12,000 square mi (30,000 square km) of old-growth forest, sparkling lakes, and unspoiled rivers. These waters were first traveled 6,000 years ago by the *Teme-Augama Anishinabe* (Deep Water People), and you can still find their haunting pictographs on the Precambrian rock of the islands and shorelines.

Smoothwater is a cross between a family-run B&B and an upscale wilderness camp. You'll dine at the main house and bed down in either the snug five-bedroom guest lodge or a shared bunkhouse. In the lodge rooms, you won't find plush carpeting or four-poster beds, but vibrant colors are thoughtfully chosen to combine well with original art, twig furniture, and bright quilts and duvets. The two bunkhouses sleep 10 each, in five bunk beds. These are basic, hostel-like accommodations where you'll need to bring your own sleeping bag and towels. You'll share two spacious washhouses, one for men and one for women. Wherever you stay, you're free to relax in the great room amid flowers, books, antiques, original art, and Temagami memorabilia. In the evenings you can watch long, fiery summer sunsets, then go out to stargaze.

Smoothwater's small size (total capacity 35) and its steadfast eco-consciousness create a sense of community that's solidified around the big dining-room table. Everyone sits together to savor fine regional cuisine, made entirely with organic products. The lodge garden provides essentials for such dishes as tomato, flower, and Jerusalem artichoke salad; or herbed vegetables, chicken, and roast lamb. Seasonal edibles, notably berries, are harvested from the wilderness, and meat, eggs, and dairy products come from local farmers. Everything from trapper's bread (baked with cranberries and sunflower seeds) to juniper-chokecherry sauce and maple-pecan pie is prepared with faithful attention to detail. The dining room isn't licensed to sell liquor, but you can bring your own wine to dinner.

There are dozens of ways to work up an appetite. Smoothwater's owners, Caryn Colman and Francis Boyes, specialize in both lodge-based programs and backcountry adventures. They can outfit trips on any scale, from hiking or winter skiing through rare, large stands of towering, 400-year-old pines to paddling on glassy lakes or churning white water.

But Smoothwater isn't just for backcountry enthusiasts. You can swim or canoe right at the lodge on James Lake, or walk nearby trails in search of birds and wildlife. Inner explorations, from Kripalu yoga and meditation to Jungian dream work, are guided by experts. Caryn, who holds a bachelor's degree in fine arts, leads watercolor workshops designed to liberate your creative spirit. You can also try your hand at making the kind of willow furniture that decorates your lodge room.

In winter, snowmobiles are not allowed to shatter the quiet at Smoothwater. Instead, you can ski or snowshoe along 31 mi (50 km) of well-maintained, signed, and mapped trails that traverse moose marshes, cedar groves, sugar maple copses, and pine forests. Afterward, head for the wood-fired sauna and a Finnish-style roll in the snow—or just plop down before the woodstove. Artists, historians, writers, and naturalists give evening talks about Temagami's natural and human history.

Tip *If you're a keen paddler, book a fly-in, canoe-out expedition to Lady Evelyn Smoothwater Provincial Park, a wilderness jewel that encloses Maple Mountain, Ontario's highest peak. Smoothwater Outfitters will* *arrange all the details, supplying guides, kayaks or canoes, meals, and all appropriate gear (C$85–C$150/day per person).*

5 rooms, 2 bunkhouses Modified American plan, dining room, picnic area. **Recreation:** bird-watching, fishing, hiking, mountain biking, running, wildlife viewing, lake swimming, canoeing, kayaking, cross-country skiing, dogsledding, ice-skating, snowshoeing, library. **Services:** canoes, kayaks, snowshoe, ski, and backcountry paddling equipment rentals; sauna; dock; guided fishing trips; Internet access; shop, meeting room. **Classes and programs:** natural history programs, canoeing and kayaking lessons, fitness classes, yoga classes, arts and crafts classes, photography classes, writing classes, history and science talks. Some pets allowed (fee); no a/c, no room phones, no room TVs, no smoking C$82 (lodge rooms); C$25 (bunkhouse per person, per night) MC, V.

Box 40, Temagami, ON P0H 2H0 ☎ *705/569–3539 or 888/569–4539* *705/569–2710* ⊕ *www.smoothwater.com.*

Prince Edward Island

DALVAY BY THE SEA
Tranquil Outpost

This gracious summer retreat has been a popular destination since it was built by a onetime president of Standard Oil Company in 1895. Constructed of PEI sandstone, the stately Victorian has the same earthy color as the famously reddish beaches and farmers' fields that surround it. Step inside and you'll see that rusty hue everywhere—the huge interior fireplaces were also constructed with sandstone blocks. The wood-paneled guest rooms are outfitted with wicker and pine furniture, successfully balancing country rusticity with modern comfort. There are also three-bedroom pine cottages with woodstoves and lofts, a private and family-friendly alternative to rooms at the inn.

Dalvay stands at the east end of Prince Edward Island National Park, just a few miles outside of Charlottetown, and operates as a private concession. Once you arrive, you may find no reason to leave the manicured property. With one of the island's only private beaches, it also has one of PEI's three freshwater lakes. Canoeing, rowing, and swimming are popular on lake and sea, but the shore also invites quieter pursuits like beachcombing and sand-castle building. If you look beyond the inn, you'll find a handful of national park beaches with boardwalks, hiking trails, and nature centers just minutes away. Have the kitchen arrange a picnic for your family and spend the day playing on the sand dunes. Or venture out for a long walk and watch fishing boats haul in their catches. Maybe you'll sight a piping plover, the endangered bird that nests in the dunes a few months of the year.

The flat island is perfect for sightseeing by bike. Along with bikes (including mountain bikes and hybrids), Dalvay rents baby trailers so you can take the little ones with you. Close to the inn is an excellent bike trail: the Confederation Trail, PEI's branch of the Trans-Canada Trail, is a product of a rails-to-trails project. When the cross-country railway lines were torn up, nature enthusiasts and politicians alike saw the potential in converting the rail beds into finely graveled hiking and biking trails. On PEI, 222 mi (357 km) of trail wends from one tip of the island to the other.

Back at Dalvay, grab a cool drink and relax in one of the Adirondack chairs out on the lawn. If it's too chilly outdoors, settle into a wing chair in front of one of the inn's three downstairs fireplaces. After an early supper for the kids (the 5:30–7 PM seating is geared toward families), tuck the youngsters under the quilts in their four-poster beds and sneak off for your own dinner. Take your pick of dining rooms: the new one, built in the 1990s, is a wood-paneled and maple-floored affair that curves around the main house and has views of Dalvay Lake. The original dining room, built in the 1890s, is more intimate, with seating for just 25. Whichever you choose, both offer scrumptious formal meals featuring island seafood (oysters, mussels, and lobster) and a gamut of fresh vegetables from the garden.

Tip *If you're passing through in July and August and want a sneak peek at Dalvay, stop by for afternoon tea, served from 2 to 4 PM. The fancy sandwiches include smoked salmon, shrimp, asparagus, and traditional English cucumber and watercress. To top it off, there's sticky date pudding, a wonderful Australian creation with vanilla ice cream and toffee sauce.*

➥ 26 rooms, 8 cottages ⦿ Modified American plan, restaurant, bar, lobby lounge, some refrigerators. **Recreation:** biking, fishing, hiking, mountain biking, running, wildlife viewing, beach, snorkeling, canoeing, rowing, driving range, 1 tennis court, basketball, croquet, horseshoes, lawn bowling, board games, library, piano, playground. **Services:** tennis rackets, rowboats, and canoes provided; mountain-bike rentals; babysitting; dry-cleaning service; laundry facilities; laundry service; shop; airport shuttle; business services; concierge; Internet access; meeting rooms. ⟳ No a/c, no room phones, no room TVs, no smoking 🚭 C$250–C$475 ▤ AE, DC, MC, V.

🏠 *16 Cottage Crescent (Box 8), York, PEI C0A 1P0* ☎ *902/672–2048* 📠 *902/672–2741* 🌐 *www.dalvaybythesea.com* ⊘ *Closed mid-Oct.–early June.*

INN AT BAY FORTUNE
Romantic Retreat

PEI may have a national reputation for potatoes, but its seafood—especially Malpeque oysters and Island Blue mussels—have earned the island international recognition. Out-of-the-way Inn at Bay Fortune, a destination for food lovers, takes cuisine so seriously that it even produced a TV cooking show *(The Inn Chef)*. Here, 50 mi (80 km) from Charlottetown, the fruits of the garden and of the sea are used in the most innovative ways, in pairings such as cauliflower and oysters in a brûlée or mussels and sweet potatoes in a chowder. The phenomenal dishes are flavored with herbs and vegetables straight from the expansive gardens. Before planning the day's meals, the chef consults with staff gardeners, and the happy result is that he can use the freshest produce in his creative feasts.

Two full-time gardeners care for the inn's gardens, some of which were designed at the same time as the house. The lush plantings attract birds by the dozen, making bird watching a quiet and wonderful pursuit for a summer's day. The herb garden contains more than 100 varieties of edible herbs, as well as an interesting sideline of medicinal plants. Take the inn's garden tour and you'll inhale the aromas of oregano, basil, and cilantro and admire row after row of leafy greens. You're likely to see the same produce on your plate at dinner.

The main house of the Inn at Bay Fortune was built in 1910 by Elmer Harris, who spent many years writing plays for Broadway and screenplays for Hollywood. He liked to return here every summer to relax and unwind. As you take in the view from the two towers attached to the main house (the suites in the towers are always booked up first), it's not hard to imagine why Harris was drawn here. The scenery still unfolds in vibrant contrasts, the reds and greens of the fields against the watery blues beyond. If you venture farther afield, you can explore the landscape up close. Wander beaches and twisty dirt roads, try flyfishing in the river, or take a break by the water's edge and gaze up at PEI's big sky.

After taking in all that fresh air and enjoying a fine dinner, you'll be ready to retire to your suite. Furnished with quilts and antique furniture, it's a place to daydream about what life was like back in Harris's day. Light a fire, sit back in a love seat or rocker, and enjoy the good life.

Tip *Make a reservation for the Chef's Table, offered nightly. You'll dine in a special glassed-in room in the kitchen, with a ringside view of course after course being prepared just for you.*

🛏 18 rooms 🍽 Full breakfast, restaurant, room service, lobby lounge. **Recreation:** biking, bird-watching, fishing, hiking, running, beach (nearby), river swimming, boccie, croquet, lawn bowling, Ping-Pong, board games, library. **Services:** mountain-bike rentals, babysitting, drycleaning services, laundry service, business services, concierge, Internet access, meeting rooms. **Classes and programs:** garden tours, cooking classes. ♿ Some in-room fireplaces, some private balconies and decks; no a/c, no room TVs, no smoking 💳 C$150–C$335 💵 AE, MC, V.

📮 *Mid-May–late Oct: R.R. 4, Souris, PEI C0A 2B0* 📮 *Late Oct.–mid-May: 135 State St., Wethersfield, CT 06109* ☎ *Mid-May–late Oct: 902/687–3745* ☎ *Late Oct.–mid-May: 860/563–6090* 📠 *Mid-May–late Oct: 902/687–3540* 📠 *Late Oct.–mid-May: 860/529–1929* 🌐 *www.innatbayfortune.com* ⊘ *Closed late Oct.–mid-May.*

Québec

AUX BERGES DE L'AURORE
Romantic Retreat

Every week Michel Martin gets about a gallon (nearly 4 liters) of goat cream from the farm next door. In summer, he churns some of it into ice cream, which he flavors with vanilla ground from pods he smuggled home from a trip to Madagascar. On sultry July afternoons he plops a couple of scoops of this into a chilled bowl and spoons on some strawberries (picked from the patch in his backyard and dunked for a few seconds in a sauce flavored with black pepper and tarragon). As a dessert or a snack, it's simple and perfect—two adjectives that apply equally well to Aux Berges de l'Aurore, the tiny inn that Michel and his companion, Daniel Pépin (along with cats Charlemagne and Constance), operate next door to the Mont Mégantic provincial park. The park is deep in Québec's Eastern Townships, 2½ hours from Montréal and Québec City.

The inn is a mid-19th-century farmhouse with a red tin roof, wide-plank floors, and a gingerbread veranda. Antique furniture, richly patterned wallpaper, and fresh cut flowers decorate its five modestly sized guest rooms. In the dining room, Michel—an IBM sales executive turned chef—uses local cheeses, his own herbs, fruit, and produce, and such game meats as venison and caribou, but given 24 hours' notice, he can whip up a vegetarian feast. Desserts include ice cream and Martin's feathery maple mousse.

Most of the inn's natural attractions are obvious in broad daylight: 10 acres of flower, herb, and vegetable gardens; miles of rolling countryside; the Appalachian mountains marching along the Maine border just 10 mi (16 km) to the south; and the soaring, 1,300-foot (390-meter) green wall of Mont Mégantic, just ½ mi (1 km) to the west. The area's most famous attractions, however, are visible only at night. Both professional and amateur stargazers flock to the region, drawn by its high elevation, clear air, and location far from big-city light pollution. The university observatory on the highest of Mont Mégantic's three summits is usually for pros only, but amateurs can set up telescopes on the summit, and the programs, lectures, and exhibits at the park-operated ASTROLab Interpretive Center at the foot of the mountain are open to everyone. Even seen with the naked eye, the show can be breathtaking.

Daytime activities include hiking, skiing, and snowshoeing on the park's 30 mi (48 km) of cross-country trails. (The less energetic can drive to the summit or use the park's shuttle service.) The park also offers guided nature hikes. Cyclists can roam the region's network of quiet backcountry paved and dirt roads to explore nearby villages. Scotstown still celebrates its Highland heritage, and Piopolis, on the shores of Lac Mégantic, was founded in 1871 by French-Canadian volunteers who had helped Pope Pius IX in his war against Garibaldi's Italian insurgents. Or you could just doze under a tree on Michel and Daniel's lovingly-cared-for 100-acre spread.

Tip *Stargazers who want to watch the annual Perseids meteorite showers that usually occur in early to mid-August should book months—if not years—in advance. The event is not suitable for children.*

⇌ 5 rooms, suite ⦿ Full breakfast, modified American plan available, restaurant, bar, lobby lounge. **Recreation:** Nearby: biking, bird-watching, fishing, hiking, wildlife viewing, lake swimming, canoeing, sailing, cross-country skiing, sledding, snowmobiling, snowshoeing. **Services:** Internet access. ⧖ Some a/c, no room phones, no room TVs, no smoking ▭ C$50–C$68 ▭ MC, V.

⌂ *139 Rte. du Parc Notre-Dame-des-Bois, QC J0B 2E0* ☎ *819/888–2715* 🖷 *819/888–2715* ⊕ *www.auberge-aurore.qc.ca* ⊘ *Closed Nov.–Apr.*

AUBERGE KAN-À-MOUCHE
Tranquil Outpost

Times have sure changed since the 1940s and '50s, when Carmelle Daury ran this little cluster of log-and-stone cabins as a wilderness retreat for the business and political elite, both foreign and domestic. In those macho days, the principal pastimes were fishing, hunting, drinking, and boasting. If those failed to satisfy, Carmelle would close the "house" she ran in Montréal and fly her "girls" north on a floatplane to entertain the guests. Carmelle also kept a freezer full of fish for those who got too distracted to catch their own. Guests back then included the notorious Maurice Duplessis (Québec's Huey Long–like premier), various members of the Rothschild clan, Jack Kennedy, and, on at least one occasion, according to locals, Marilyn Monroe.

Since Carmelle's heyday, the atmosphere at Auberge Kan-à-Mouche has mellowed. Most of the people who stay here are couples, many of them from Europe, with a sprinkling of Québec showbiz *vedettes* (stars). Although the place is still a magnet for anglers (Kan-à-Mouche means "fly-rod"), most folks come simply to enjoy the surroundings and maybe to do a little canoeing and cycling in summer or cross-country skiing and snowshoeing in winter. The interpretive trail that circles the lake, a 90-minute stroll, includes a stand of sugar maples.

The couple who manage the place—Gilles Desjardins and Leonora Ferretti—certainly don't fly in plane loads of girls anymore. In fact, the noisiest craft on the lake these days are the electric-powered boats the auberge rents to anglers and nature lovers. The place is hidden behind a ring of forested hills and separated from the main regional highway by ½ mi (1 km) of chassis-jarring gravel road. A family of beavers has built a lodge at the southern end of the spring-fed lake, but other than that you pretty much have the water to yourself for swimming, fishing, and boating.

The buildings haven't changed much. The most elaborate is the Abenakis, where people like Jack, Marilyn, and the Rothschilds would have relaxed by the stone fireplace in the stately two-story living room. Take note, however: the lodge's four, log-walled bedrooms—each with a tiny sink that dates from the '40s—share just two bathrooms, which makes the Abenakis more suitable for families than couples. Bathrooms with showers have been added to most of the other rooms, which are housed in small, one- and two-bedroom cottages along the shore or in a motel-like structure facing the lake. The rooms have exposed-log walls and details such as clothes hooks made from twigs.

The main lodge, with the dining room and the bar, is so close to the lake that lazy anglers who don't like to be too far from a cold beer can easily make their casts from its back deck. Chef François Lesoin learned his métier in Strasbourg, and his table d'hôte meals reflect his classical training. He relies heavily on local ingredients, particularly game meats and such local fish as trout, salmon, and doré (John Dory).

Tip *The inn is about two hours northeast of Montréal in the Lanaudière region, which is much overlooked by leaf-peepers despite its having some of Québec's most glorious fall colors.*

↩ 22 rooms ❑ Modified American plan, café, snack bar, restaurant, lobby lounge, bar, picnic area, minibars. **Recreation:** biking, birdwatching, fishing, hiking, mountain biking, beach, lake swimming, boating, canoeing, cross-county skiing, ice-skating, snowmobiling, snowshoeing, tubing (snow). Nearby: horseback riding, 18-hole golf course, dogsledding. **Services:** canoes, pedal boats, and mountain bikes provided; powerboat rentals; dock; guided fishing trips. **Classes and programs:** guided hikes, guided nature walks, trapping and First Nations culture talks. ♿ Some in-room fireplaces, some private balconies, no-smoking rooms ▭ C$156 ▭ AE, DC, MC, V.

🏠 *7639 Chemin Brassard, Saint-Michel-des-Saints, QC J0K 3B0* ☎ *450/ 833–6662* 📠 *450/833–2682* ⊕ *www.kanamouche.com.*

AUBERGE DU LAC TAUREAU
Family Hideout

The truly remarkable thing about Lac Taureau is not its its size (430 mi [690 km] of shoreline), or even its Caribbean-quality sandy beaches (chuck in a few palm trees and bits of it would look like St. Kitts). No, the truly remarkable thing about Lac Taureau is that it's not a lake at all but a natural-looking reservoir created by a network of flood-control dams. In winter, when the sluice gates are opened, those wide bays and long, narrow inlets drain away and the lake shrinks to a mere puddle.

The Auberge du Lac Taureau isn't quite what it seems to be, either. It looks like a huge log cabin, but it's not really—or not one that Abraham Lincoln or Daniel Boone would recognize. It's actually a post-and-beam building with log walls. That might seem like a quibble, but it means that the walls bear no weight and can accommodate the huge windows that flood the place with light. You'd be hard pressed to find a brighter, airier log cabin.

In spite of its location, 100 mi (160 km) from Montréal, the Auberge is not always the quietest place to enjoy nature. It's a family resort with plenty of organized activities for kids and adults of all ages—from sailing lessons and beach volleyball to campfires and sing-alongs. In winter the skaters on the artificial pond right in front of the Bistro Bar and the hotel's own sled-dog teams' yipping across the snowy flats on the lake bed can keep the decibels up. The property is huge, however, and the sandy beach is a mile (2 km) long, so it's always possible to find a quiet place simply to doze on a hammock and listen to the birds (or pause on your snowshoes and listen to your sinuses crackle in the frigid air).

A full buffet breakfast is served every morning in the log-beamed dining room with its big stone fireplace and sweeping views of the lake. Every evening chef Marc-André Ferland serves up table d'hôte dinners that focus on such regional specialties as smoked sturgeon, venison, grain-fed veal, and local fruit, cheeses, and produce.

Housed in three buildings, the resort's 100 rooms reflect local tastes as well, with pine furniture and original artwork. Worthy of special note are the authentic First Nations longhouse and wigwam, in a clearing at the northern end of the beach, that are used for special programs. Local Attikamekw craftsmen built both of the structures using traditional methods, which involve stitching together birch bark and alder poles with spruce roots. The Auberge organizes First Nations nights with songs, stories, and sometimes a traditional meal of stewed venison and bannock (fry bread). The native-built structures are also a reminder that this is an active wilderness. Loggers, hunters, and trappers—many of them First Nations people—make their living by harvesting its riches.

Tip *Dogsledding is not just a winter sport at the Auberge du Lac Tau-reau. You can try this exciting sport in spring and fall, too, using special wheeled "sleds." Summer is usually too hot for the dogs to run, and they spend their days resting in the shade. Smart dogs.*

⊷ 100 rooms ¶◯¶ Modified American plan, café, snack bar, restaurant, lobby lounge, bar, picnic area, minibars. **Recreation:** biking, bird-watching, fishing, hiking, horseback riding (nearby), mountain biking, beach, indoor pool, lake swimming, snorkeling, windsurfing, boating, canoeing, sailing, 18-hole golf course (nearby), 2 tennis courts, cross-county skiing, dogsledding, ice-skating, snowmobiling, snowshoeing, archery, billiards, horseshoes, Ping-Pong, shuffleboard, volleyball (nearby), recreation room, playground. **Services:** canoes, kayaks, pedal boats, snowshoes, and cross-country skis provided; ice skates, mountain bike, sailboat, pontoon boat, and flipper and mask rentals; hot tub; sauna; spa; dock; guided fishing trips; babysitting; laundry service; shop; Internet access; meeting rooms. **Classes and programs:** guided hikes, guided nature walks, natural history programs, sailing lessons, fitness classes, children's programs (ages 6–18), talks on trapping and First Nations culture, concerts, dances, movies, sightseeing tours, sing-alongs. ⟆ Cable TV, some in-room fireplaces, in-room safes, some private balconies and patios, no-smoking floors ▨ C$132 ▭ AE, DC, MC, V.

⌂ *1200 Chemin Baie du Milieu, Saint-Michel-des-Saints, QC J0K 3B0* ☏ *450/833–1919 or 877/822–2623* 🖷 *450/833–1870* ⊕ *www.lactaureau.com.*

GÎTE DU MONT-ALBERT
Laid-Back Adventure

The Chic-Choc Mountains get their name from a Mi'qmaq First Nations word that roughly translates as "great granite wall we can't get our canoes past." Indeed, the Chic-Chocs' sheer impenetrability preserved the interior of the Gaspé Peninsula from development well into the the 20th century. As a result bears, deer, and moose still roam the valleys and lower slopes of the Chic Chocs, and the world's southernmost herd of caribou graze on lichens on the tundra-like high plateaus. Québec's government has set aside more than 300 square mi (800 square km) of this wilderness—encompassing 25 peaks of more than 3,200 feet (975 meters)—as a national park.

Right in the heart of all this, in a cuplike valley almost 600 km (372 mi) east of Québec City, is the Gîte du Mont-Albert, a mountain lodge with most of the comforts of a resort hotel. There has been a *gîte* (guest-house) on the site since 1950, but all that remains of the original complex are a couple of cottages and the baronial dining room decorated in hunting-lodge style, with a big moose head mounted over its stone fireplace. The new hotel—built in the same steep-roofed style as its predecessor, with rows of dormer windows—opened in 1995. Its rooms and cottages overlook the rocky slopes of Mont Albert. The two- and three-bedroom cottages have wood burning stoves, full kitchens, and wood-paneled walls. Right next to the Gîte is the park's interpretive center, with lecture halls, natural history exhibits, a lunch room, a bistro, and a shop that sells a limited selection of camping and hiking supplies and equipment.

The bar's three-story-high front window offers even more dramatic views of the mountains. But it would be a waste just to admire the scenery from behind glass. Radiating from the Gîte's front door are more than 80 mi (130 km) of hiking and cross-country ski trails that lead to mountain lakes, caribou-grazing lands, and some of Québec's highest peaks. Hikers and skiers with the right equipment and training can make long multiday treks using the park's network of backwoods shelters and campsites, but there are also plenty of day hikes that range in difficulty from easy to extreme. Even the gentlest include a rewarding view and the possibility of an encounter with a moose or a caribou.

Camping under the stars certainly has its charms, but there's much to be said for returning to the Gîte each night for a sauna and a massage before a dinner of such local specialties as smoked salmon and braised farm-raised caribou. An after-dinner drink and perhaps a little boasting by the fireplace in the bar make a fitting end to the day.

Tip *Most of the programs offered at the park's interpretive center are primarily in French, so dig out your old phrase book and brush up your vocabulary. To get you started: A moose is "un orignal," a deer is "un cerf," and a caribou is (what else?) "un caribou."*

⤴60 rooms, 25 cottages ⍻Cafeteria, coffee shop, restaurant, bar, grocery store, grills, picnic area, some kitchens. **Recreation:** bird-watching, fishing, hiking, wildlife viewing, pool, cross-country skiing, ice climbing, snowshoeing, telemark skiing, playground. Nearby: lake and river swimming, canoeing, rowing. **Services:** boot, backpack, raincoat, canoe, rowboat, and backcountry-skiing equipment rentals; sauna; spa; laundry facilities; laundry service. **Classes and programs:** guided hikes, guided nature walks, natural history programs, nature talks. ⟁No-smoking rooms; no a/c, no room TVs ▣C$105–C$265 ▤AE, D, MC, V.

⌂ *2001 Rte. du Parc, Sainte-Anne-des-Monts, QC G4V 2E4* ☎*418/763–2288 or 866/727–2427* 🖷*418/763–7803* ⊕*www.sepaq.com/en/index.cfm (click on List of Parks and look under Gaspéesie)* ☉*Closed Nov.–Dec. 24.*

ÎLE-AUX-LIÈVRES
Rustic Escape

If there's one French word visitors to Île-aux-Lièvres should learn, it's *marée* (tide). The daily shifting of the seas sets the rhythm of life on this thin, wooded strip of land in the middle of the St. Lawrence Estuary, about two hours from Québec City. Tides determine when you arrive and when you leave, where you can hike and where you can't. It can be frustrating—delaying arrivals and hurrying departures—but there's something restful about surrendering to the waxing and waning of lunar gravity. Spending a few days in one of the island's five chalets is well worth the hassle of figuring out a tide table.

Each chalet sits in its own little clearing facing south over a strip of rocky shoreline. Each has two bedrooms upstairs and a living room, bathroom, and full kitchen downstairs. A deck with a gas barbecue completes the amenities. There are no televisions and, apart from the radiophone in the caretaker's cottage, no communication link to the mainland. You have to bring in all of your food supplies from the mainland, but Rivière-du-Loup (5 mi [8 km] away) has everything the discriminating vacationer needs, including such local delicacies as fresh shrimp, naturally fed veal, smoked fish, cheese, and fruit (especially strawberries and raspberries).

During the day you can watch the seabirds wheeling over Île-au-Pot just 100 yards (90 meters) away and the beluga whales bobbing for lunch in the main channel. Île-aux-Lièvres (Hare Island) is tiny—just a little over 7 mi (11 km) long and never more than ½ mi (1 km) wide—but it has more than 25 mi (40 km) of walking trails. One runs along a ridge on the island's northern edge, 130 feet (40 meters) above a virtually deserted, 7-mi (11-km) beach. From its heights you can see the mountains of the Charlevoix coast just 6 mi (10 km) across some of the chilliest salt water south of Labrador.

The island's only permanent residents are the hares that give the island its name, several partridge families, and the seals who bask on the rocks at the island's eastern tip. The only machines are a couple of small maintenance tractors and the generator that runs a few hours a day to charge the batteries that power the cottages' lights and refrigerators (the stoves use propane gas). Even bicycles are forbidden, so there's little to break the silence but the sound of the wind and the waves and the cries of the birds.

The island is one of eight owned by the Société Duvetnor, a not-for-profit corporation founded by biologists at Québec City's Université Laval. Most are seabird sanctuaries and closed to the public; the money generated by Île-aux-Lièvres helps finance the société's work. The group has also converted a 19th-century lighthouse on the nearby Île-au-Phare into a three-bedroom inn with a shared bathroom that's ideal for overnight getaways.

Tip *The Société Duvetnor launch—which leaves from Rivière-du-Loup at high tide only—has limited baggage space, so shop carefully and store your perishables in coolers for the trip.*

🛏 4 cabins, 6 rooms, 18 campsites ¶◎¶ Dining hall, picnic area, kitchens. **Recreation:** bird-watching, hiking, wildlife viewing, beach. **Services:** dock, Classes and programs: guided nature walks, natural history programs. ♿ No room phones, no room TVs, no smoking 🖼 C$125–C$180 ➡ MC, V.

🗺 *200 rue Hayward (Box 305), Rivière-du-Loup, QC G5R 3R9* ☎ *418/ 867–1660* 🖨 *418/867–3639* ⊕ *www.duvetnor.com* ☽ *Closed Oct. 3–May 20.*

LA POURVOIRIE DU CAP AU LESTE
Tranquil Outpost

Pourvoiries, which can range from humble cabins in the woods to lodges with every amenity, have traditionally focused on hunting and fishing. But the Pourvoirie du Cap au Leste has pretty much abandoned those pastimes for gentler wildlife activities. You can still go ice-fishing in winter and trout fishing in summer, but when it comes to moose or deer, a Nikon rather than a Winchester has become the shooting tool of choice.

As far as comfort goes, the Cap au Leste falls somewhere in the middle: its rough wood walls and bare floors might not be grand enough for an invasion of plutocrats, but its 36 large, airy rooms are furnished with an eclectic selection of antiques and all rooms have big, private bathrooms. The rooms are scattered throughout five squared-log lodges, each in its own patch of woods and each with its own fireplace-equipped living room, where guests gather in the evenings to chat, play cards, or stage impromptu sing-alongs.

The Cap au Leste's main lodge, with a dining room, deck, and informal bar-lounge, sits 200 mi (322 km) from Québec City atop a 350-foot cliff on the north shore of eastern North America's only mainland fjord. The Saguenay, Québec's deepest river, flows through the gorge, draining Lac Saint-Jean into the St. Lawrence Estuary. The dining room has more to offer than views, however. A young, local cook smokes his own trout and salmon on-site and grows many of his own organic vegetables. Local cheeses, organically grown meat and poultry, local berries, and wild mushrooms figure largely in his cooking.

The 6 mi (10 km) of hiking trails that weave through Cap au Leste's 700 forested acres (283 hectares) will help you work up an appetite. One trail switchbacks down the steep cliff to an old lighthouse at the edge of the fjord and snakes back up by a different route, affording ever-changing panoramic views of the fjord's southern cliffs. It's particularly magnificent in mid-September, when the leaves change and both shores are a blaze of red and gold. The Cap au Leste property butts up against Québec's Parc Nationale du Saguenay (a provincial park, despite the name), and its trails link up with a trail the Québec government is building along the top ridge of the northern escarpment.

Tip *The Lac Saint-Jean–Saguenay district claims to be the blueberry capital of North America. In late summer you can buy all kinds of blueberry products — jams, jellies, liqueurs. One of the most famous and unusual delicacies is the sheets of chocolate-coated blueberries made by a community of Trappist monks at the northern end of Lac Saint-Jean.*

🛏 34 rooms 🍽 Modified American plan, bar, lounge, grills, picnic area. **Recreation:** bird-watching, fishing, hiking, wildlife viewing, cross-country skiing, snowmobiling, snowshoeing, tubing (snow), playground. Nearby: horseback riding, mountain biking, windsurfing, boating, canoeing, sea kayaking, dogsledding, sleigh rides, board games. **Services:** guided fishing trips, helipad, meeting room. **Classes and programs:** guided hikes, guided nature walks, sing-alongs. ♿ Some private balconies, no-smoking rooms; no a/c, no room phones, no room TVs 💳 C$77–C$192 💳 AE, DC, MC, V.

🏨 *551 Chemin du Cap au Leste, Sainte-Rose-du-Nord, QC G0V 1T0* ☎ *418/675-2000* 🖷 *418/675-1232* ⊕ *www.capauleste.com.*

Saskatchewan

CYPRESS PARK RESORT INN
Tranquil Outpost

The highest point of land between the Rockies and Labrador, Cypress Hills Interprovincial Park is a 45,492-acre preserve in the southwestern corner of Saskatchewan, about four hours west of Regina. Stay at Cypress Park Resort Inn, the sole lodging in the park, and you are surrounded by a forest of lodgepole pines. Fescue grasslands with rare wildflowers break up the forest west of the inn, revealing spectacular views of countryside etched by prehistoric glaciers. Hiking or mountain biking along the 17½ mi (28 km) of multi-use trails winding around the resort and the park provides excellent bird and wildlife viewing. You can spot moose, mule deer, coyote, and elk as well as more than 200 avian species, such as red-winged blackbirds, hawks, Oregon juncos, red-shafted and yellow-shafted flickers, and turkey vultures. Seven hundred species of plants and orchids have been identified in the area.

The inn lies within walking distance (or a short drive) of the park's Loch Leven. Rent a boat, canoe, or pedal boat and drink in the sweet scent from the pines surrounding the loch. Cast your fishing line into the loch for a chance to catch cutthroat and brook trout, annually stocked in the waters. Or just wiggle your toes in the sand along the two beaches and soak up the view. At night, grab a patch of hillside and gaze at the stars. The view is so spectacular that each year the Royal Astronomy Society of Canada hosts its Summer Star Party here. Three hundred astronomers set up their equipment at the highest campground in the park and spend the weekend stargazing.

Autumn and winter at the inn are by far the best seasons for relaxation and solitude. The lodgepole pine needles turn yellow in fall and, along with the other native trees and grasses, produce a vivid display of color. In winter, cloudless skies arch over expanses of pure white snow along the cross-country ski trails and a designated snowmobile area. After ice fishing, skating, tobogganing, or snowshoeing in the park, head back to Ivan's, the resort's restaurant, for a hot chocolate and a window seat to watch the birds scuffle for seeds.

The inn offers three different types of no-frills accommodations. The main building, which resembles a mountain lodge, houses the hotel rooms, restaurant, lounge, indoor swimming pool, and conference facilities. Inside, the main building is unfussy, with large windows strategically placed to take in the incredible views of trees and wildlife. The guest rooms provide only the bare necessities—two double beds or one queen bed, a television, and a telephone. Condo accommodations, set away from the main building, have a bit more in the way of creature comforts, with a fireplace, private deck, TV, and telephone in addition to a full kitchen or kitchenette and a large living area. Again, the furniture and decor are minimal, but the views more than compensate. Self-contained one- and two-bedroom cabins are wood-shingled units set among the tall pines. They have a kitchen and kitchenettes, washroom, and shower but no TV or telephone. Within walking distance of the resort is a host of additional seasonal services, including a sauna, boathouse, golf pro shop, tackle shop, grocery shopping, and laundry services.

Tip *Expect to book two years in advance if you want to stay at the inn during July or August. The shoulder seasons from May to June and September to October are the ideal time to really enjoy nature and to feel like you have the park all to yourself.*

🛏 32 rooms, 20 condos, 18 cabins ⑩ Café, restaurant, lounge, grills, picnic area, some kitchens, some kitchenettes, some microwaves. **Recreation:** bird-watching, wildlife viewing, indoor pool, cross-country skiing, snowshoeing, tobogganing, volleyball. Nearby: fishing, hiking, horseback riding, mountain biking, running, beach, pool, lake swimming, canoeing, driving range, putting green, tennis court, ice-skating, snowmobiling, miniature golf, softball, library, videocassette library, playground. **Services:** toboggans and volleyballs provided, cross-country ski and snowshoe rentals, hot tub, Internet access, business services, meeting rooms. **Classes and programs:** guided hikes, guided nature walks, natural history programs, annual trail-run competition, arts and crafts classes, barbershop singing workshops, concerts, dances, movies. ♿ Some in-room fireplaces, some private decks, some pets allowed, no-smoking rooms; no a/c, no phones in some rooms, no TV in some rooms 🏷 C$65–C$160 plus park entry fee of C$7 (one day), C$17 (three days), or C$25 (one week) 💳 MC, V.

🏠 *Box 1480, Maple Creek, SK S0N 1N0* ☎ *306/662–4477* 🖨 *306/662–3238* ⊕ *www.cypressresortinn.com.*

LAND OF THE LOON RESORT
Family Hideout

Tucked into northern Saskatchewan's boreal forest, Land of the Loon Resort is a world away from . . . well, the world. The closest large city,

Saskatoon, is a 2½-hour drive from the resort. Here, where nature is the star attraction, you are likely to shed stress like the tamarack trees shed their needles in autumn. On Anglin Lake, the mournful call of the loons, the rustle of moose in the brush, and the cry of the bald eagle will clear your head of the noise of modern life. Deer have been known to wander through the resort grounds, and in the winter, you might spot wolf tracks on the snow-covered lake.

The resort nestles amid trees only a few feet from the shore of Jacobsen's Bay. With ample spacing between the buildings to protect your privacy, all of the lodgings are made from white spruce logs. Each has a view of the surrounding poplar and birch trees or of the bay. The cabins and chalets are basic, but they are homey with kitchens, full bathrooms, balconies or decks, and wood-burning fireplaces. Studio rooms are on the second floor of the main building, close to the on-site store and gift shop, and offer a double bed and sleeper sofa, kitchenette, bathroom, fireplace, and small deck.

The owners of the resort love to share their extensive knowledge of the area and its attractions. There are excellent daily boat tours of Anglin Lake, which is actually a chain of six lakes that cover 3,791 acres along the southeastern corner of Prince Albert National Park. With octogenarian Jack Greening at the helm, you get an educational and entertaining look at the lake and its history. Jack explains how these ancient birds have escaped extinction for thousands of centuries, despite having only one or two babies each year. Among North American lakes of its size, Anglin Lake has the highest population of nesting loons. If you listen and watch closely, you can hear their distinctive call and see their incredible diving and flying skills.

If you wish to explore the lake on your own, rent a canoe, kayak, or windrider from the resort. Early morning—when the lake is still and the only sounds are from songbirds—is the best time to cast your line in the waters to see if the walleye, northern pike, or perch are biting. Across the lake, Prince Albert National Park is home to abundant wildlife (the park has a no-hunting rule). Nearly 100 mi (166 km) of backcountry trails thread through prime bird-watching (close to 200 species populate the area in summer), cycling, hiking, snowshoeing, and cross-country skiing terrain. Within the park are more than 350 archaeological sites and 12 federal heritage buildings.

After all that exploring, you can savor nature's bounty in the resort's Snail's Pace dining room, where full menus are available for breakfast, lunch, and supper. Dine amid yellow log walls, a stone fireplace, loon-theme stained-glass windows, and a turn-of-the-20th-century baby grand piano. From a window seat, or from the deck outside, you have a spectacular view of the lake and the national park. Local ingredients are used in the meals whenever possible, wheat is ground on-site for baking, and wild berries are incorporated into many of the sauces. Try the northern Saskatchewan fish from Lac Laronge, panfried with butter and spices, or the hand-trimmed lamb chops. Wild rice, grown locally, is a popular side dish. After your meal, browse through the Raven Room, the resort's art gallery, which features local and national Canadian art.

Tip *Take an evening tour of Anglin Lake if you are interested in watching beavers as they leave their lakeside lodges.*

4 studio rooms, 3 cottages, 5 chalets ⦿ Modified American plan, dining room, ice-cream parlor, grocery store, grills, picnic area, some kitchens, some kitchenettes, microwaves. **Recreation:** biking, bird-watching, fishing, hiking, mountain biking, wildlife viewing, beach, lake swimming, boating, canoeing, kayaking, rowing, cross-country skiing, dogsledding, ice-skating, snowmobiling, snowshoeing, billiards, boccie, board games, library, piano, recreation room. Nearby: basketball, volleyball, playground, horseback riding, driving range, 4 golf courses, sleigh rides, horseshoes. **Services:** kayak, canoe, windrider, motorboat, cross-country ski, and snowshoe rentals; sauna; boat launch; dock; marina; guided fishing trips; grocery shopping; laundry facilities; laundry service; airport shuttle; business services; Internet access; meeting rooms; travel services. **Classes and programs:** guided hikes; guided nature walks; natural history programs; off-road tours; canoe and kayak competitions; dogsledding competitions; cycling, hiking, and canoeing lessons; children's programs; quilting, woodcarving, and wildflower classes; nature talks; annual bluegrass concert; dances; sightseeing tours. ♿ In-room fireplaces, some private balconies or decks, some pets allowed (fee); no room phones, no room TVs ⌸ C$75–C$185 ⊟ MC, V.

Box 4, Christopher Lake, SK S0J 0N0 ☎ *306/982–4478* 🖷 *306/982–4489* ⊕ *www.landoftheloonresort.com.*

Directories

Directory of Escape Types

Directory of Activities and Programs

BEACH

BIKING

NATURAL HISTORY PROGRAMS

PHOTO SAFARIS

PHOTOGRAPHY CLASSES

ROCK CLIMBING

SAILING

SCUBA DIVING

SEA KAYAKING

SNORKELING

Alphabetical Directory